Bicycle Justice and Urban Transformation

T0361118

As bicycle commuting grows in the United States, the profile of the white, middle-class cyclist has emerged. This stereotype evolves just as investments in cycling play an increasingly important role in neighborhood transformations. However, despite stereotypes, the cycling public is actually quite diverse, with the greatest share falling into the lowest income categories.

Bicycle Justice and Urban Transformation demonstrates that for those with privilege, bicycling can be liberatory, a lifestyle choice, whereas for those surviving at the margins, cycling is not a choice, but an often oppressive necessity. Ignoring these "invisible" cyclists skews bicycle improvements towards those with choices. This book argues that it is vital to contextualize bicycling within a broader social justice framework if investments are to serve all street users equitably. "Bicycle justice" is an inclusionary social movement based on furthering material equity and the recognition that qualitative differences matter.

This book illustrates equitable bicycle advocacy, policy and planning. In synthesizing the projects of critical cultural studies, transportation justice and planning, the book reveals the relevance of social justice to public and community-driven investments in cycling. This book will interest professionals, advocates, academics and students in the fields of transportation planning, urban planning, community development, urban geography, sociology and policy.

Aaron Golub is Associate Professor in the Nohad A. Toulan School of Urban Studies and Planning at Portland State University, Oregon, USA.

Melody L. Hoffmann is a mass communication instructor at Anoka Ramsey Community College near Minneapolis, Minnesota, USA.

Adonia E. Lugo is an urban anthropologist and co-founder of the Bicicultures network, USA.

Gerardo F. Sandoval is Associate Professor at the Department of Planning, Public Policy and Management and the Co-Director of the Center for Latino/a and Latin American Studies at the University of Oregon, USA.

Routledge Equity, Justice and the Sustainable City series

Series editors: Julian Agyeman, Zarina Patel, AbdouMaliq Simone and Stephen Zavestoski

This series positions equity and justice as central elements of the transition toward sustainable cities. The series introduces critical perspectives and new approaches to the practice and theory of urban planning and policy that ask how the world's cities can become "greener" while becoming more fair, equitable and just.

Routledge Equity, Justice and the Sustainable City series addresses sustainable city trends in the global North and South and investigates them for their potential to ensure a transition to urban sustainability that is equitable and just for all. These trends include municipal climate action plans; resource scarcity as tipping points into a vortex of urban dysfunction; inclusive urbanization; "complete streets" as a tool for realizing more "livable cities"; the use of information and analytics toward the creation of "smart cities".

The series welcomes submissions for high-level cutting edge research books that push thinking about sustainability, cities, justice and equity in new directions by challenging current conceptualizations and developing new ones. The series offers theoretical, methodological and empirical advances that can be used by professionals and as supplementary reading in courses in urban geography, urban sociology, urban policy, environment and sustainability, development studies, planning and a wide range of academic disciplines.

Planning Sustainable Cities and Regions
Towards more equitable development
Karen Chapple

The Urban Struggle for Economic, Environmental and Social Justice
Deepening their roots
Malo Hutson

Bicycle Justice and Urban Transformation
Biking for all?
Edited by Aaron Golub, Melody L. Hoffmann, Adonia E. Lugo and Gerardo F. Sandoval

For more information and to view forthcoming titles in this series, please visit the Routledge website: www.routledge.com/series/EJSC

Bicycle Justice and Urban Transformation

Biking for all?

Edited by Aaron Golub, Melody L. Hoffmann, Adonia E. Lugo and Gerardo F. Sandoval

LONDON AND NEW YORK

First published 2016
by Routledge

2 Park Square, Milton Park, Abingdon, Oxfordshire OX14 4RN
711 Third Avenue, New York, NY 10017

Routledge is an imprint of the Taylor & Francis Group, an informa business

First issued in paperback 2017

British Library Cataloguing-in-Publication Data
A catalogue record for this book is available from the British Library

Library of Congress Cataloging-in-Publication Data
A catalog record for this book has been requested

ISBN: 978-1-138-95024-5 (hbk)
ISBN: 978-0-8153-5920-3 (pbk)

Typeset in Goudy
by Keystroke, Station Road, Codsall, Wolverhampton

This book is dedicated to the millions of people for whom the simple act of pedaling a bicycle in the street is a risk due to traffic engineering failures (past and present), street crime and violence, or the threat of racial profiling and police brutality. We can surely do better.

"Bicycle justice has become a major concern in the US. This group of authors provides an impressive array of case studies on bicycle justice and the overlooked or invisible riders creating bicycle advocacy and planning. These bike advocates promote more transportation choices for everyone while the transportation justice advocates demand that bicycling and all forms of transportation be understood as a civil rights issue."

Glenn S. Johnson, Associate Dean for Research and Graduate Studies, Texas Southern University, Barbara Jordan Mickey Leland School of Public Affairs, Houston, Texas, USA

"This book may indeed help start a movement for inclusive, equitable bicycle justice. Grounded in clear thinking and strong examples, this unique collection offers a probing assessment of both the tendency to stereotype "deserving" bicyclists, marginalizing others, and the patently inequitable distribution of public investments in bicycle infrastructure."

June M. Thomas, Centennial Professor, Taubman College of Architecture and Urban Planning, The University of Michigan, USA

Contents

Figures

Tables

Contributors

Caroline Appleton is a PhD candidate in Public Policy at the Georgia Institute of Technology, USA.

Alexandra M. Armenta is a Program Manager at the Center of Excellence in Women's Health at the University of Arizona, USA. Ms. Armenta has spent the majority of her professional career working in program evaluation and data management on various projects focusing on reducing health disparities among underserved populations. She completed her Bachelor of Arts degree at the University of Arizona with a major in Political Science and a minor in Mexican American Studies.

Mariam Asad is a PhD student in the Digital Media program at the Georgia Institute of Technology, USA. Her work focuses on activism, design and social justice. Through her research, she explores how technology design can offer opportunities for civic participation through both policy- and grassroots/community-based initiatives.

Pasqualina Azzarello is a painter, public muralist and educator. She is the co-founder of the Youth Bike Summit and served as its director for its first five years. Whether working through academic, nonprofit or grassroots channels, she is committed to working with others to create spaces which are inclusive, generative and transformative for all involved.

Melyssa Banks is currently an undergraduate student studying Environmental Studies and Urban Studies at Queens College, City University of New York, USA. Her research interests include environmental justice, sustainability and conservation.

Simon Batterbury is Associate Professor of Environmental Studies, University of Melbourne, Australia. In 2015 he was a visiting research fellow at the Brussels Centre for Urban Studies at Vrije Universiteit Brussel, researching bike workshops in Brussels, Berlin and in France. His work is situated in political ecology in developing countries, but he has participated in citizen bike advocacy since 1993.

Joanna Bernstein is a planner, organizer and self-identified "street anthropologist" living and working in Pittsburgh, PA, USA. She has a Masters in Community and Regional Planning from the University of Oregon in Eugene, USA, where she began her self-directed immersion into the Latino immigrant community. She prides her work upon the informal approach that she takes to working and connecting with undocumented Latino immigrants, the homeless and other more shadowed populations that tend to be more bike-dependent.

Xiaodeng Chen is studying Urban Sustainability in CUNY-Brooklyn, USA, and is a Youth Board Member of the Brooklyn-based legal-aid co-operative, Atlas:DIY (Developing Immigrant Youth). He has volunteered in Mexico and Peru working with children of English-study camps and orphanages where he was inspired to study alternative urban developmental models.

Ryan J. Dann is a PhD student in the School of Urban Studies and Planning at Portland State University, USA. His research involves understanding newcomers' travel behaviors, and interactions between transportation, neighborhood change and equity.

Nedra Deadwyler is founder and operator of Civil Bikes, a bike-based business. Civil Bikes educates and promotes alternative, active transportation using historical bike tours and bicycling education classes. Nedra Deadwyler is a Master of Social Work from New York University, USA. She currently works with Georgia Bikes, a statewide bicycle/active transportation advocacy organization as the Safety Education Programs Manager and received the Gail and Jim Spann Educator of the Year award at the 2016 National Bike Summit, League of American Bicyclists.

Mario Giampieri is the Program Officer for Conservation Innovation at the Wildlife Conservation Society in New York City and a Research Assistant in the CARSI Lab at Hunter College, USA. Mario co-founded the Biking Public Project in 2012 while working as a food delivery cyclist. He received a Bachelor of Arts in Environmental Studies and Metropolitan Studies from New York University and believes in building better cities by listening to people and nature.

Tara Goddard is a PhD candidate in the Nohad A. Toulan School of Urban Studies and Planning at Portland State University, USA, where her dissertation research explores drivers' attitudes and behaviors towards bicyclists. She holds a Masters in Civil Engineering from the University of California, Davis. Ms. Goddard's research interests include all things bicycle and pedestrian safety-related, but in particular, the intersections of transportation and social psychology and their influence on differential experiences and safety outcomes on the road, especially for women and people of color.

Aaron Golub is Associate Professor in the Nohad A. Toulan School of Urban Studies and Planning at Portland State University, USA. His teaching and research interests include the social and environmental impacts of transportation, planning for alternative transportation modes and the history of urban transportation in the United States. Golub received his doctorate in Civil Engineering from the University of California at Berkeley in 2003.

James Hannig is a Transportation Planner at AECOM in Milwaukee, Wisconsin, USA. Hannig received a Bachelor of Science degree in Civil Engineering from Marquette University in 2007 and a Masters degree in urban planning from the University of Wisconsin-Milwaukee in 2015.

Cameron Herrington is a Master of Urban Studies student at Portland State University. His research and community-based practice centers on housing, community-controlled development and urban social movements.

Helen Ho currently works for the NYC Mayor's Office. Ho has her Masters in Urban Planning from Hunter College, USA. She founded and organized the first Tour de Queens for Transportation Alternatives and co-founded the Youth Bike Summit for Recycle-A-Bicycle. Her pet project is called the Biking Public Project which aims to expand local cycling advocacy discussions by reaching out to food delivery cyclists in New York City. She is also on the Equity Advisory Council at the League of American Bicyclists.

Melody L. Hoffmann is a mass communication instructor at Anoka Ramsey Community College near Minneapolis, Minnesota, USA. She also serves on Minneapolis Bicycle Coalition's Diversity and Equity Committee.

Gail Jennings has an MA in Linguistics from the University of Stellenbosch, South Africa, in which she examined the role of metaphor and myth in constructing the narrative of the private vehicle lifestyle. She has worked as a researcher for 25 years and in 2008 founded the transport policy journal MOBILITY. Jennings has published and presented widely on utility cycling, has planned the walking and cycling network for three Bus Rapid Transit (BRT) systems in South Africa, and undertaken a feasibility study for the implementation of a public bicycle system in Cape Town. She currently publishes the Cape Town Bicycle Map, and is working towards her PhD at the Centre for Transport Studies, University of Cape Town, contemplating the shifting ideas and ideologies about utility cycling in South Africa.

Kevin J. Krizek is Professor and Director of the Program in Environmental Design at the University of Colorado-Boulder, USA. He also serves as the visiting professor of "Cycling in Changing Urban Regions" at Radboud University in the Netherlands. Krizek was a 2013 fellow of the Leopold Leadership Program and was awarded a 2014 U.S.-Italy Fulbright Scholarship focusing on sustainable travel. From 2006–2012 he chaired TRB's Committee on Telecommunications and Travel, is a former member of Land Development and Travel Behavior and Values, and currently serves on the Bicycle Transport committee. Krizek's research and teaching interests focus on how cities are transforming themselves to advance transport needs for the next century, with cycling being an important part of such transformation.

Dorothy Le is the Director of Capacity Building for the Neighborhood Plaza Partnership (NPP) in New York City, USA. Prior to joining NPP in 2015, she was a Senior Transportation Planner at Rutgers University and Planning and Policy Director for Los Angeles County Bicycle Coalition. She holds a Masters in City and Regional Planning from the Bloustein School at Rutgers University and an undergraduate degree in Environmental Science from UCLA. In addition to Biking Public Project she is involved in a number of transportation, health and justice related work.

Christopher A. Le Dantec is an Assistant Professor in the Digital Media Program in the School of Literature, Media, and Communication at the Georgia Institute of Technology, USA. His research is focused on integrating theoretical, empirical and design-based investigations of mobile and social technologies in support of community and civic engagement. With an interest in digital disparities, he examines alternate constraints on mobile computing in urban life, information technology and social institutions, and the use of participatory design for articulating social issues and constructing publics.

Do J. Lee is an Environmental Psychology PhD candidate at The Graduate Center of the City University of New York, USA. He and the Biking Public Project are currently working on a participatory action research project with NYC food delivery cyclists. His work, teaching and research focus upon a critical exploration of sustainability by examining the processes, contexts and social justice dimensions of bicycling.

Donna Lewandowski is an independent planning consultant located in Tucson, Arizona, USA, with extensive local government experience in bicycle and pedestrian planning, alternate modes of transportation and the development of the Safe Routes to School program in Pima County. She derives the greatest joy in her professional life from helping others overcome their fears of riding a bicycle for transportation, fitness and fun. Ms. Lewandowski holds an undergraduate degree in Psychology with a minor in Criminal Justice, and earned her Masters degree in Urban Planning with a concentration on Environmental and Healthy Cities from the University of Arizona in 2007.

Amy Lubitow is an Assistant Professor of Sociology at Portland State University, USA. She conducts research and teaches courses related to environmental sociology, sustainability and transportation justice.

Kara Luckey is an urban planner and PhD Candidate in Planning and Design at the University of Colorado, Denver, USA. Her research centers broadly on the intersection between transportation planning, housing policy and social justice, with particular expertise in the role of urban infrastructure in community and economic development. She holds a BS in Civil Engineering from The Cooper Union for the Advancement of Science and Art and has seven years of experience as a transportation planning practitioner.

Adonia E. Lugo is an urban anthropologist and co-founder of the Bicicultures network, USA, who has studied the social worlds of bicycling since 2008. She received her PhD from the University of California, Irvine, USA, in 2013 and works to diversify the human infrastructure of sustainable transportation.

Karel Martens is an Associate Professor and Chanin Fellow at the Faculty of Architecture and Town Planning of the Technion – Israel Institute of Technology, Israel, and an Associate Professor at the Institute for Management Research of Radboud University, the Netherlands. His research interests include transport and justice, transport and land use interaction, parking policy, and democratization of governance. He is currently finishing a book titled *Transport Justice: Designing Fair Transportation Systems*, to be published by Routledge in 2016. Karel obtained his PhD in Policy Sciences from Radboud University in 2000.

Allison Mattheis is an Assistant Professor in the division of Applied and Advanced Studies at California State University, Los Angeles, USA. She is a former middle school science teacher and holds a PhD in Educational Policy and Leadership from the University of Minnesota, USA. Her research and teaching interests include community advocacy and engagement in public decision-making, teaching and leadership for social justice, and critical ethnographic exploration of formal and informal learning environments.

Daryl Meador is a filmmaker, cyclist and cultural geographer. She received her MA in Media Studies from the New School for Public Engagement, USA, in 2015. Her recent MA thesis and film, *Heroica Matamoros*, explores cycling, affectivity and filmmaking in the Mexican border city Matamoros, Tamaulipas.

Alfredo Mirandé, a native of Mexico City, is Professor of Sociology and Ethnic Studies at the University of California, Riverside, USA and has a PhD in Sociology from the University of Nebraska and a Juris Doctorate (JD) from Stanford University. Mirandé's teaching and research interests are in Chicano Sociology, Gender and Masculinity, Constitutional Law, Civil Rights and Race and Law. He is the author of nine books, including *Rascuache Lawyer* published by the University of Arizona Press, and a practicing attorney.

Martha Moore-Monroy, MA, is the REACH Program Director at the UA Center of Excellence in Women's Health and Rural Program Manager at the Arizona State Office of Rural Health, USA. In addition, Ms. Moore-Monroy is a lecturer at the Mel and Enid Zuckerman College of Public Health, and an adjunct faculty member at Prescott College. The primary focus of her professional career has been population health, women's health, community health worker interventions and the development of coalitions dedicated to the elimination of health disparities facing underserved populations. Ms. Moore-Monroy is the Southwest Regional Director for the National REACH Coalition Board of Directors, founding member of the Arizona REACH Network (Arizona

Health Disparities Network) and a member of the National Peers for Progress Initiative.

Daniel Piatkowski is an Assistant Professor of Community and Regional Planning at the University of Nebraska–Lincoln. Dr. Piatkowski received his PhD in Design and Planning from the University of Colorado Denver in 2013. His teaching and research centers on the impacts of land use and transportation on population health, environmental sustainability and social equity.

Jane Pirone is an Associate Professor at Parsons School of Design, New York, USA, where she is currently serving as Dean of the School of Design Strategies. Jane's research explores the use of design and collaborative practice to affect positive and equitable social change. She was a co-organizer of the Youth Bike Summit from 2013–2015.

Robert Rosenberger is an Assistant Professor of Philosophy at the Georgia Institute of Technology, USA, in the School of Public Policy. His research is in the philosophy of technology, with studies on topics such as Mars imaging, phantom phone vibrations, computer-simulated frog dissection, smartphone-induced driver distraction and the critique of anti-homeless public-space design.

Gerardo F. Sandoval is Associate Professor in the Department of Planning, Public Policy and Management and the Co-Director of the Center for Latino/a and Latin American Studies at the University of Oregon, USA. He earned his PhD in City and Regional Planning from the University of California at Berkeley.

Inès Vandermeersch works in an inner city community center in Brussels, Belgium, that develops projects with local residents. She is also a trained bike mechanic and one of the key organizers of Cycloperativa, a bike workshop in Annessens, a less affluent inner city neighbourhood of Brussels. She has recently completed a Masters of Social Action thesis on the contribution of bike workshops to the social economy in Brussels.

Kari Watkins is an Assistant Professor in Civil and Environmental Engineering at Georgia Tech, USA, where she became a faculty member in 2011 after completing her PhD at the University of Washington. Her teaching and research interests include multi-modal transportation planning, the use of technology in transportation, traveler information and complete streets design. Dr. Watkins' dissertation involved co-creating the award-winning OneBusAway program to provide transit information tools and assess their impacts on riders.

Ada M. Wilkinson-Lee is an Assistant Professor in the Department of Mexican American Studies at the University of Arizona, USA. Her research interests include Latino health and how cultural and societal factors affect the developmental processes of individuals, families and communities. Dr. Wilkinson-Lee received her Masters degree in Mexican American Studies with an emphasis in Latino Health from the University of Arizona in 2001 and her doctorate in Family Studies and Human Development from the University of Arizona in 2008.

Raymond L. Williams holds the title of Distinguished Professor in the Department of Hispanic Studies at the University of California, Riverside, USA. He has published 16 single-authored books on modern Latin American literature and articles that range from Carlos Fuentes and urban environment to García Márquez and new technology. A bicycle activist, he commutes daily on two wheels and has completed 75 organized cycling events of 200 miles and longer.

Acknowledgements

The editors wish to thank the authors for their contributions to this volume and for their inspiring work and commitment to this grand vision of bicycle justice. We also thank Stephen Zavestoski and Julian Agyeman for giving us the opportunity to take their initial concept for this book and pedal off with it. Finally, we thank Margaret Farrelly at Routledge for her assistance during the book's preparation.

1 Introduction

Creating an inclusionary bicycle justice movement

Aaron Golub, Melody L. Hoffmann,
Adonia E. Lugo and Gerardo F. Sandoval

Introduction

For much of the past century, the bicycle was not taken seriously as a means of mass mobility – overshadowed by the car almost as soon as the bicycle became affordable due to mass production in the early 1900s. After smaller waves of interest over the past century, a recent and seemingly sustainable bicycling boom in the U.S. and in many cities worldwide has caught the attention of transportation planners, policymakers, and the public as more people turn to the bicycle for mobility and exercise. Even though rates of cycling in the U.S. remain relatively low, especially when compared to other Western countries, there has been a noticeable increase in people using a bicycle for transportation. Growth in the number of bicycle commuters in the U.S. is now far outpacing the growth of other modes; between 2000 and 2012 when the total number of workers grew by 9 percent, bicycling to work grew by 61 percent while driving to work grew by 10 percent (Pisarski, 2013). In some cities, the growth was much greater; between 2000 and 2009, cycling to work more than doubled in Chicago and Portland, while cities like San Francisco and Minneapolis saw similar increases during the 1990s (Pucher et al., 2011).

A panoply of factors contribute to this growth in ridership, including improvements in cycling infrastructure in many cities, recognition of the health benefits of active travel, a cultural turn toward reduced environmental impact and petroleum dependence, and significant demographic and economic shifts which challenge traditional patterns of car ownership and licensure especially among younger age groups. A new profile of urban cycling has emerged, one associated with the middle-class whiteness that was once more at home in suburbs and SUVs, but is now venturing, mostly by choice, back into the city riding buses, trains, and bicycles. But this mediated profile of the upwardly mobile bicyclist is misleading. The greatest share of bicycle commuters in the U.S. fall into the lowest U.S. Census income bracket, Latinos have the highest rates of bicycle commuting, and African Americans doubled their rate of bicycling between 2001 and 2009 compared to only a 22 percent increase for whites (McKenzie, 2014; League of American Bicyclists and the Sierra Club, 2013). There are thus striking contrasts between the widely touted cycling renaissance as a signifier of being hip and the bicycle's more realistic utilitarian character as a low-cost transport mode for a broader range of riders and needs.

Bicycle advocates promote the bicycle as a form of freedom or emancipation from the doldrums and dilemmas of a car-dominated life—a choice made among various transportation alternatives often linked to larger displays of lifestyle or politics. But for many people in the U.S., the bicycle is not an emancipatory tool—it is not a statement about style or politics – but an outcome of oppression, leaving the bicycle as the only reasonable travel option due to inadequate public transportation, complex travel needs, or low wages and high transportation costs. Furthermore, street harassment and crime, sexual solicitations, and police violence are likely experiences that marginalized communities suffer from when they need or choose to ride a bicycle (Minnesota Healthy Kids Coalition, 2015; see also Coates, 2015). Common infrastructure tools used to lure new bicyclists such as off-street trails and protected bicycle lanes cannot address these common threats and vulnerabilities many experience in the public realm everywhere and every day. Thus, bicycling has varying potentials to be both an emancipatory and oppressive practice. Coming to understand how individuals, communities, and experts locate bicycling between these extremes, and how this shapes their own practices, sheds light on what "bicycle justice" could mean and how community advocates can strive to achieve it. That is the goal of this book.

Indeed, many communities are defining "bicycle justice" for themselves and in recent years a diverse range of people and projects have broken new paths toward making bicycling inclusive and accessible to all. The case studies collected in this book call attention to overlooked riders and what their invisibility means for bicycle advocacy, planning, and policy. Their lived struggles connect bicycling with larger issues of inequality in health, wealth, voice, and security. The dismissal of these struggles as irrelevant to bicycle advocacy and planning has allowed this affordable and flexible technology to become a symbol of urban gentrification, whiteness, privilege, and choice. This introduction continues with a framing of the overall issues and tensions at play in the process of broadening the voices and beneficiaries of bicycle advocacy and planning. We then describe the challenges of developing inclusionary and emancipatory bicycle justice and argue that it is vital to contextualize bicycling within a broader justice framework if public investment in the practice is to serve all street users equitably. We then present an overview of the chapters, and conclude by delineating themes and highlighting problems and solutions.

Transportation and the dimensions of injustice

Contemporary issues of bike planning and street design need to be understood in a context of uneven urban development which excludes and oppresses along class and racial lines. Transportation planning, policies, and investments shape and are shaped by these uneven and exclusionary processes and impact the geographies of opportunity for many communities and individuals. These transportation impacts are often racialized, with people of color routinely bearing the brunt of the exclusion. For example, freeways, integrated into other processes of "urban renewal," created concrete physical barriers in communities of color, facilitating the suburbanization of whites while destroying thriving neighborhoods and displacing entire communities (Gibson, 2007; Mohl, 1993). East Los Angeles was reshaped by the construction of multiple freeways and was "encircled, cut up, and glutted by freeways" (Avila, 1998, p. 18). Despite bicycle advocacy's inherent opposition to the automobile "system" and all of its injustices, inefficiencies, and externalities, many transportation justice advocates still connect bicycle planning with whiteness and privilege and thus see it as a continuation of this history of injustices, rather than a break with it (Maus, 2011–2012).

The pragmatic actions illustrated by some of the case studies in this book emerged in the context of and in response to these unjust urban processes. In fact, the U.S. Civil Rights movement emerged in part around transportation inequalities and injustices. In the early 1950s, African Americans in Baton Rouge, Louisiana, staged the nation's first successful bus boycott to protest their unequal treatment to whites on busses. From Rosa Parks to the Freedom Riders in the 1960s, to modern transportation justice movements such as the Bus Riders Union in Los Angeles or the national Transportation Equity Network, justice activists have demanded that transportation systems end their practices of discrimination against low-income and minority communities (Bullard et al., 2004; Grengs, 2002; Transportation Equity Network, 2015). The Bus Riders Union relied on the 1964 Civil Rights Act to prove that the Los Angeles County transit authority was actively discriminating against bus riders, overwhelmingly people of color and low-income, through the disparities they experienced in quality of service and subsidy levels compared to whiter patrons of rail systems in the region (Grengs, 2002). This case made it clear that transportation systems, including the outcomes of plans and investments and the planning processes themselves, are important civil rights issues.

While transportation justice movements were successful in elevating transportation as a civil rights issue, including bicycling in this framework has been complicated by images of bicycling as a lifestyle choice, by the delineation of bicycle advocacy as a white and middle-class space, and by the entanglement of bicycle investments in processes of real-estate upgrading associated with displacement and gentrification. An inclusionary and socially just bicycle justice practice will have to overcome these hurdles which we distill into two key challenges: (1) the othering of certain riders within organized bicycling, and (2) disparities in the benefits of bicycle investments.

The othering of certain riders within organized bicycling

In the U.S., bicycling takes place both where it is welcomed by attitudes and infrastructure and where it is not. Many bicyclists have cycled with or without the bicycle lanes, signals, and markings that advocates and planners view as crucial to luring drivers out of their cars (League of American Bicyclists and the

Sierra Club, 2013). Largely invisible or maligned in popular imagery, professional practice, and the mainstream cycling movement, these actually existing cyclists are generally poorly understood by the dominant trifecta of advocacy, engineering, and policy (Koeppel, 2005; Fuller and Beltran, 2010; Zavestoski and Agyeman, 2015b). It is also troubling that the pro-bicycling cultural and demographic shift occurring in U.S. inner cities is structurally linked with the gentrification and displacement of inner-city residents who are low-income and people of color, the exact population that is dependent on cycling as an affordable mode of transport. Through bicycle justice, we focus specifically on these othered riders and challenge the bicycle advocacy and planning norms which focus on white and middle-class commuters.

Understanding the socio-cultural elements of bicycling today can be a challenge amidst the various efforts to associate cycling with predominantly white, middle-class urbanism and lifestyles. Scholars have tracked the promotion of bicycle gentrification in Los Angeles and Minneapolis (Hoffmann and Lugo, 2014), Portland (Lubitow and Miller, 2013), and Memphis (Smiley et al., 2014), and the San Francisco Bay Area (Stehlin, 2015). "Bicycle gentrification" refers to the process through which bicycle infrastructure contributes to or accompanies a neighborhood's property value increases and resulting displacement effects, and the trend where key figures use bicycle infrastructure strategically to rebrand areas of the city in preparation for real-estate investment or redevelopment. Additionally, there has been a proliferation of bicycle iconography in U.S. advertisements and consumer goods and controversy about urban bicycling in the news media (Furness, 2010). These images, whether evoked positively or negatively, work to establish a hegemonic understanding of who bikes and who does not. Dominant images include the scofflaw bicycle messenger, the lycra-clad racer, or the bicycle commuter dressed in professional attire. The promotion or condemnation of these subcultural stereotypes as bicycling mascots skews public perceptions of who is actually using bicycles for transportation.

The gap between bicycling as image and as practice can be explained in part by the racial and socioeconomic homogeneity of professional bicycle advocates and planners. Promoting bicycling is a networked practice that includes the act of advocating and participating in transportation planning process and also participation in conferences, email lists, consuming and creating bike-related media, and coordinating advocacy activities across many cities. The result is what we here call *organized bicycling* in order to differentiate it from the basic physical activity of riding a bicycle. Organized bicycling could be a catalyst for social inclusion of diverse community needs, but in the past its push to "normalize" bicycling has tended to "other" bicycle users who do not participate in organized bicycling's self-selecting and exclusive social spaces. Currently, most of its efforts simply do not account for the economic and discriminatory challenges still faced by many in the U.S., including individuals for whom bicycle transportation is a survival strategy and not an enthusiastic choice. Within organized bicycling, there has been discussion about socially marginal "invisible riders" for some time (Koeppel, 2005). What we suggest here is that continuing to mark some bicyclists as a separate category of users does not disrupt exclusion. Instead, we draw attention to organized bicycling's process of othering that consequently produces outside riders. By confronting this problematic categorization, we hope this can be a site for change in bicycle advocacy work.

The production of outsider bicycle users in organized bicycling can be seen in data collection. Bicycle advocates who want to increase investments in bicycling rely on quantitative methods that do not capture existing diversity among bicycle users. For example, bicycle counts, a popular model for tracking the rate of bicycling in U.S. urban spaces, uniformly do not record a bicyclist's race, ethnicity, or income. The count methodology assumes that a street user's gender can be ascertained visually but avoids guessing other statuses. Aside from this small concession to monitoring the gender gap in bicycling, the methodology posits that all bicycling bodies are equal. This flattens diversity among bicycle users, turning their bodies into a data point that experts use to lobby for changes derived from their own qualitative experiences of bicycling. It is not a method for gathering data on lived experiences of bicycling which are often mediated by class, gender, and racial inequities. Furthermore, counts are often made only in main, radial, commute corridors into and out of central activity centers and not in peripheral areas or on key connections to major low and medium skilled job centers such as airports, suburban shopping malls, or light industrial sites. This further biases planning and investments toward already privileged commuters (often traveling in corridors already served by the best public transit services). In these ways, othered bicycle users become invisible to official processes, even as organized bicycle enthusiasts struggle to gain recognition for bicycles in mainstream planning practice.

The homogeneity of today's organized bicycle enthusiasts stems from a more formal history of racial exclusion within bicycle advocacy. For example, the League of American Bicyclists is an influential national bicycle organization with one of the largest memberships among U.S. bicycle organizations today. It also has a sordid history of excluding people of color (Furness, 2010). In 1894, at the peak of the bicycling boom when it was known as the League of American Wheelmen, the organization instituted a ban on "colored" members. The League did not formally remove this language until 1999. In the same public statement striking the color bar from their bylaws, the League also posthumously awarded Marshall "Major" Taylor a League membership. Taylor is the most famous African-American cyclist in history, due in part to his relentless pursuit of breaking colorlines in professional sports at the turn of the 19th century (Ritchie, 2009). Major Taylor Cycling Clubs, currently active across the U.S., are named in his honor. Even within studies of the bike movement, this lesser-known racialized history is usually only footnoted for completeness, or ignored altogether. It has not been treated as a formative feature of bicycle culture and advocacy.

We argue that racialized exclusion within organized bicycling does matter, because planning processes are shaped by powerful forces such as racism, sexism, classism, and white supremacy (Pulido, 2000). Planning scholar Bent Flyvbjerg

(2001) argued that it is normal rather than exceptional for planners and advocates to draw on their own perspectives in developing their recommendations. So, while it is not unusual for bicycle expertise to overemphasize white, middle-class norms if its practitioners are white and middle class, we question whether this homogeneous group of experts can produce solutions that will improve biking for all.

Bicycling is not a homogeneous practice; it takes on novel meanings in different social and geographic situations (Horton et al., 2007). Researchers have identified the assemblage character of bicycling, where the particular combinations of individuals, physical environments, and machines produce different effects (Hoffmann, 2016; Lugo, 2013; McCullough, 2013; Vivanco, 2013; Furness, 2010). Despite this critical attention to the potential for diversity in bicycling, bicycle research tends to record little deviation from organized bicycling's in-group norms. It is likely that this is because researchers who study bicycling are usually also bicycle enthusiasts, working from a personal experience of vulnerability while riding a bicycle. Like many bike advocates, they feel threatened and want to do something about it; many may know people who were killed while riding. The effects of this embodied vulnerability on research design and findings deserves further study, but it is clear that it gives bicycle activism an emotional urgency that both bonds like-minded cyclists together and tends to villainize car dependence. Add to this mix the conviction that everyone must transition to low-resource "sustainable" lifestyles to prevent ecological disaster (Horton, 2006) and the result is advocates who can come across as self-righteous crusaders rather than collaborators in equitable social change.

The recent "bike equity" turn in organized bicycling shows that advocates are aware of this negative image (League of American Bicyclists and the Sierra Club, 2013). However, their moves to correct it tend to tokenize bicyclists who are people of color rather than investigate the roots of othering in organized bicycling. Trying to make themselves respectable in the eyes of their own white, middle-class culture still takes precedence over integrating more diverse perspectives deeper within advocacy strategy.

The project of trying to change the dominant culture (as symbolized by the car) lies at the heart of bike activism, which explains in part why it has been difficult for participants in organized bicycling to examine how they produce a dominant culture within bicycling itself. The current era of bicycle advocacy efforts operating under the banner of ecological security and street safety began in the 1970s in culturally influential places such as New York City and San Francisco (Furness, 2010). Their direct action approach to calling the public's attention to the need for a more humane streetscape culminated with the almost spontaneous invention of Critical Mass bike rides in San Francisco in 1992. Critical Mass rides are now found around the world and have been a catalyst for bike movements in numerous cities (Furness, 2010; Carlsson et al., 2012). Another significant innovation of this direct action approach to bicycle promotion is the bicycle recycling and repair model for popular education. The earn-a-bike program for children was developed at Transportation Alternatives in

New York and became Recycle-A-Bicycle, while the repair education model was developed at Bikes Not Bombs in Boston. Today bicycle repair cooperatives are bike movement hubs in cities around the world, and as community centers they attract a more diverse group than do mainstream bicycle advocacy organizations.

However, organized bicycling has largely turned away from supporting and participating in direct action approaches such as Critical Mass, and while advocacy organizations may coordinate with local community bicycle education centers, lessons learned in those diverse spaces rarely trickle upwards into bicycle advocacy work. Instead, advocates look to national organizations and intercity professional networks to select new trends for promotion to elected officials and planning agencies. Prominent bicycle organizations focus on building legislative and political support for infrastructure and contracted systems such as bike share. Starting in the 1980s, the policy and funding advocacy efforts focused on accessing public funds for highways in order to pay for bicycle projects (Mapes, 2009; Wray, 2008). This pushed advocates to pay more attention to building top-down political will and working behind the scenes to secure legislative wins, de-emphasizing the importance of integrating the broader cycling public. Although active transportation consulting firms such as Alta Planning + Design and Toole Design Group have been able to expand through increased public spending on bicycling, it is unclear whether othered riders have benefited from the political legitimization of organized bicycling.

Sharing in the benefits of bicycle investments

As several case studies in this volume illustrate, moving beyond race, class, and gender tokenism in bicycle advocacy and planning is a central struggle for social justice activists participating in "bicycle equity." Instead of working to further their own urbanist preferences, bike advocates could consider how their work broadens, or not, the beneficiaries of investments in bicycle infrastructure across boundaries of race, class, gender, language, or national origin.

Professional bicycle networks train advocates to value innovations coming from Northern European countries such as Denmark, Sweden, and the Netherlands. That built environment interventions will lead to a more civil street culture is assumed as fact in bicycle advocacy, though this cause and effect relationship has been questioned (Oosterhuis, 2014). The possibility that Northern Europe's prized public spaces and transportation investments reflect a much broader social and political commitment to equality and dignity does not come up in the pitch for U.S. bike infrastructure. Instead, the benefits for efficiency and optimization are highlighted as advocates push for molding U.S. streets in a European image. This design-determinism does not connect to the civil and human rights projects of correcting the social exclusion existing in the urban U.S. today. It is unlikely that street designs from Copenhagen can themselves remedy the effects of the freeway program on urban Black communities or reduce the insecurity of Black bodies in public spaces (Coates, 2015).

The rise of cycling and related planning runs counter to now 100 years of transportation planning paradigms that prioritize the automobile, which themselves are intertwined with broader social changes, including the rise of the mass consumption society (Norton, 2008; Golub, 2015). On U.S. streets, bicycles have long been grudgingly allowed a marginal existence, with the general understanding that people in cars "deserve" more road space. Understandably, as the only "first class" mode, access to cars has been an important project for the transportation justice movement, the drawbacks and injustices of the automobile system notwithstanding (Gilroy, 2001; Bratman and Jadhav, 2014). The car is a central element of the mass consumption society and an important symbol of our mass belief that we are all middle class in the U.S.; for white people with economic security to promote bicycling throws a harsh light onto the struggle by many to even enter the mainstream of our consumer society. Advocates ignore the fact that significant segments of the population were met with discrimination in employment, wages, housing, and access to credit and education – fair access to road space was at the bottom of their list of concerns (Massey and Denton, 1993). Advocates who succeed in funneling resources toward bicycling should be aware that challenging transportation hierarchy reveals their own privilege much more quickly than it extends it to others. (Similar dynamics also play out internationally as members of the middle class in developing world cities reject the status quo drive for automobility in their quest for lifestyles of health and sustainability— see e.g. Anantharaman (2015).)

Formal transportation planning processes aided these processes of social exclusion and segregation in three ways: (1) unequal access to participation in the planning process, (2) unequal exposure to localized environmental burdens, and (3) unequal distribution of mobility benefits from transportation investments (Denmark, 1998; Golub, 2015; Golub et al., 2013). The confinement of minorities to central cities and the common placement of freeway facilities proximate to those communities mean that urban minorities are often disproportionately exposed to resulting environmental burdens and safety risks (Bullard et al., 2004; Golub, 2015; Hilton, 2006). In this light, transportation justice is about overcoming these barriers to broader social integration and focuses more on creating mass mobility through improved public transportation and access to automobiles, jobs, and housing than a concern over the rights to the bicycle more specifically. Additionally, transportation justice conceives of its target populations not as user groups defined by transport mode, but as racialized and classed groups defined by historical disempowerment. Even though these racialized and classed groups have encountered similar disenfranchisement in bicycle infrastructure planning, transportation justice largely ignores bicycle issues. We argue that transportation justice needs to encapsulate bicycle advocacy due to the exclusionary nature of organized bicycling as well as the real material potential of the bicycle for mobility.

The current neoliberal era is characterized by a pattern of reinvestment in inner-cities as cheap property values attract developers while long-standing communities are priced out (Smith, 2002). Automobiles remain the dominant and prioritized form of transportation in these cities, but the lure of built environment interventions such as bicycle infrastructure allows car ownership to be a choice, not a necessity, for the re-urbanizing upwardly mobile. While there are real needs for alternatives to the automobile, the processes of recent urban market-based upgrading and rebranding have recast new investments in public transportation or cycling as tools to attract investment rather than to create broader solutions (Golub, 2015; Grengs, 2004). This places the emergence of planning for cycling in a messy conundrum: it joins a set of development processes which are more about attracting growth and less about serving mobility needs for existing residents. As stated earlier, white, upwardly mobile people are not the majority of bicyclists in the U.S. today, and they will likely not be in the future due to other demographic shifts. They are, however, a desirable group to attract to gentrified urban cores, which is why real-estate marketers, city boosters, policymakers, and bicycle advocates continue to focus on their preferences.

Inclusionary, equitable bicycle justice

In a broad sense, bicycle justice is achieved through projects located closer to the emancipatory pole of an imagined continuum from oppression to emancipation. By this we mean to acknowledge directly that for some people bicycling and land use strategies embedded in related advocacy work can actually be oppressive; cycling is slow, dirty, unsafe, and relegated to a marginal status on most streets, in most cities. Whether they feel positively about bicycling or not, the choice to ride for some indicates their economic and social vulnerability rather than their travel preferences. An emancipation framework, by contrast, works toward including all bicyclists, especially those currently othered as "invisible cyclists," within organized bicycling and its design goals. This would transform cycling into a public good, rather than an object of consumer or lifestyle aspiration.

Emancipatory bicycle justice considers how power influences the development of transportation policies and programs along dimensions of race, class, gender, and language. Iris Marion Young (2011) argues that equity means making institutional amends to historically marginalized groups by broadening access to decision-making power. Hence, emancipatory bicycle justice is not only a distributional paradigm but one based on representation and empowerment.

The editors of this book define bicycle justice as an inclusionary social movement and practice based on furthering material equity and recognizing that a diverse range of qualitative experiences should influence public investment in transportation. Bicycle justice transforms oppressive, exclusionary transportation planning practices into inclusive equity initiatives. It creates emancipatory outcomes that support safe and affordable access to resources such as social services, education, employment, urban amenities, housing, and connections to other modes of transportation such as buses and light rail.

The resilience of organized bicycling as a movement where white, middle-class norms are taken for granted has limited the field's ability to address the emancipation/oppression dichotomy. This volume builds on the work started in

Incomplete Streets: Processes, Practices, and Possibilities (Zavestoski and Agyeman, 2015a), which focused on exclusion within the emerging transportation planning innovation, Complete Streets. There are many innovative, creative, and new ways to encourage people to ride bikes that are different from mainstream bike advocacy. But today, those who seek to make bicycling a truly equitable form of mobility continue to encounter racism (Sulaiman, 2015a, Sulaiman, 2015b).

The chapters of this book conceptualize and illustrate equitable bicycle advocacy, policy, and planning and suggest how to operationalize bicycle justice. In synthesizing the projects of critical cultural studies, transportation justice, and planning as applied practice, this book reveals the relevance of civil rights and social justice concerns to public interventions intended to increase cycling. Bike movement and transportation justice perspectives on bicycling continue to diverge in important ways. For bike advocates, giving people more transportation options provides avenues away from car-dependent lifestyles that have been destructive to population and environmental health, especially for communities of color. For transportation justice advocates, giving people more transportation options includes continuing the fight for access to a driver's licenses and cars because they are still seen as the best avenue to mobility in the U.S. and abroad.

In mediating both of these approaches, this book documents how people have used bicycling in service to social justice, and what structural constraints stand in the way of using the bicycle to meet community needs. There is more to the question of equitable access than street design, as illustrated through projects that interpret bicycling through more nuanced cultural lenses. Bicycle justice is an ongoing critical and transformative project intended to shed light on community realities where it will take more than infrastructure investments to make bicycling into the positive transportation and health solution a growing chorus of experts would like it to be.

Chapter overview

This book contains 17 contributed chapters covering a variety of practices, methodologies, and vantage points. Contributing authors were challenged to focus on addressing these key questions:

1   What are the structural, political, and economic forces that shape bicycling transportation systems and who currently benefits from these systems?
2   How have marginalized bicyclists organized, operated, and formed community outside of mainstream bicycle advocacy and related sites typically centered in whiteness?
3   How can these existing alternative perspectives inform a justice-focused planning practice in order to address a wider range of bicycling needs than previously considered in the mainstream dialogue?

The editors of this book have situated much of the bicycle equity discussion in the U.S. but the chapters in this book extend beyond the U.S. and include analyses of bicycle advocacy in Mexico, Belgium, and South Africa. Themes of visibility, voice, and borderlands repeat as they become important theoretical underpinnings to help readers understand that bicycle justice can be as diverse as its intended community.

Conceptualizing and theorizing bicycle justice

The book's first chapters deconstruct the politics of current bicycle practice and conceptualize a rights-based framework for bicycle justice. Aaron Golub begins this section in Chapter 2 by exploring the conflicts between the broader transportation justice movement and the bicycle movement. He asks: why are the two movements so separate, and why is bicycle transportation not a key issue for the transportation justice movement? He dissects the emerging bicycle movement as a socio-technical system and contrasts it with the transportation justice framework, developing a list of tensions and synergies which may keep the two movements separate for some time. To be complete, we challenge the reader to consider how the chapter does not question the normative framework of the transportation justice movement. Doing so would confront the uneasy reality that perhaps that framework, in its fight for broader participation in the main-stream economy, is also limited in its potential and that bicycling, in some ways rejecting mainstream consumptive society with its own history of oppression, may actually offer emancipatory potential.

How does bicycle infrastructure spur gentrification? This is a question that rightfully plagues urban planners, bicycle advocates, and community members. Perhaps this question has played out most publicly in Portland, Oregon—home to a large but homogeneous bicycle advocacy community. In Chapter 3, Cameron Herrington and Ryan Dann address this question by tracking the movement of white people into communities of color and the correlation of that process with new bicycle infrastructure and increased bicycle use. The authors found that an area's increase in whiteness and educational attainment predicted large increases in bicycle use at the neighborhood level, suggesting that the celebration of Portland's bicycle success is, in at least some neighborhoods, a celebration of displacement and gentrification.

Shifting from this U.S.-rooted rights perspective, in Chapter 4, Gail Jennings notes a shift in South Africa's mainstream bicycle advocacy that addresses the concerns laid out in this Introduction. Jennings argues that the bicycle advocates who now promote social justice are the same "privileged minority" that formerly argued for the bicycle's green, low-cost, and sustainable possibilities. Her chapter chronicles an emerging tension: as the modernizing and socially integrating republic emerges from decades of apartheid, its dream of motorized mobility for everyone conflicts drastically with the push to encourage more sustainable modes. This is similar to the questions raised in the U.S. case in Chapter 2, to which her chapter offers few easy answers.

In Chapter 5, Christopher Le Dantec, Caroline Appleton, Mariam Asad, Robert Rosenberger, and Kari Watkins, using an example of a project where crowdsourced bicycle user data relying on self selection and lacking in minority participants, argue that with better procedures, such data could be used to advocate for the needs of a great diversity of bicyclists. The authors argue that the democratic potentials of new forms of technology are not exempt from the barriers to participation present in existing models.

In a less practice-oriented piece, Chapter 6 authors Karel Martens, Daniel Piatkowski, Kevin J. Krizek, and Kara Luckey ask the basic distributive justice question: when are publicly produced cycling interventions, at the expense of other investments, warranted on the basis of justice? Using liberal-egalitarian theoretical perspectives, most specifically the capabilities approach, they derive conditions which should be met for cycling interventions to be warranted on the grounds of justice (even as they may be promoted for other reasons). This approach differs from the focus on social processes of power and exclusion used in the other chapters in this book, and as such offers an interesting twist to consider for bicycle justice policy design.

Othered bicycling and community knowledge

In this section, authors speak to how race and class status can directly impact perceptions of bicycling and related amenities such as bicycle lanes and bicycle sharing systems. These chapters point to the tendency for the middle-class bicyclist to be held up as the preferred, desirable, and morally superior user of bicycle amenities. When bicyclists are categorized in this way, it others and marginalizes bicyclists that fall outside of the preferred user category.

In Chapter 7, Tara Goddard uses social psychological theories to argue that a person's implicit biases may impact and predict their behavior towards "vulnerable road users." For example, Goddard suggests that the reasons why Blacks and Latinos are disproportionately killed in traffic crashes may relate to people's implicit biases toward these populations, mixed with people's understandings of the social-cultural context and physical environment.

In New York City, Latino and Asian immigrant food delivery cyclists are often criminalized for behaving in ways similar to those of their white, male bike messenger counterparts. In Chapter 8, Do Lee, Helen Ho, Melyssa Banks, Mario Giampieri, Xiaodeng Chen, and Dorothy Le complicate the "invisibility" of these workers by arguing that the term "invisible cyclist" is synonymous with being a "bad" bicyclist and thus highly visible to disciplinary surveillance. Through their work with these invisible/visible delivery bicyclists, the authors highlight participatory action research as potential means to foster public knowledge, created by the cyclists, as a "means to provide counter-narratives and a basis for more equitable policies and restructurings of the street landscape in the pursuit of bike justice."

In Chapter 9, Alfredo Mirandé and Raymond Williams apply the Mexican concept of rascuachismo to the cycling scene. They discuss the idea of the bicycle as an object that enables rascuache, youth, the poor, and subordinated persons to transcend geographical, psychological, social, economic, cultural, and spiritual borders. They also take a critical view of legal and public policy attempts to regulate the urban landscape. The authors argue that significant policy changes are needed with respect to justice and sustainability in urban transportation to avoid the criminalization of rascuache bicyclists.

Joanna Bernstein explores in Chapter 10 how typical outreach tactics to encourage bicycling will fail to entice "unauthorized immigrants." Bernstein illustrates that biking as a deportable human being produces an experience of fear while biking that has not been included in street safety discussions. Bernstein tells the stories of three undocumented Guatemalans living in Pittsburgh who bike because it is their best transportation option. Though biking is not what they would choose, their livelihood in this country depends on it. At the same time, biking exposes them to more risk than they would otherwise encounter if they were to walk or take public transportation to their destination. Sharing the poignantly intimate stories of Diego, Jeremias, and Jose, Bernstein hopes to start a much needed dialogue within the bike community, as well as between bike- and immigration-oriented agencies and organizations, surrounding the differential experiences of undocumented cyclists and the social, legal, and physical risks that they disproportionately face as a result of having no choice but to bike. This chapter lays out culturally specific outreach methods that advocates can utilize to build trusting relationships with unauthorized Latino cyclists and other marginalized communities.

In Chapter 11, Daryl Meador describes the work of the Doble Rueda bicycle collective in a Mexican border town that is plagued by violence and state corruption. Residents of Matamoros participate in Doble Rueda group rides as a demonstration of their presence and vitality, as a form of safe mobility at night, and as a communal mode of transportation to traverse the city. The authors argue that the collective's desire to make Matamoros a more humane city, through cycling, may set an example for bicycling communities in conflict zones and violence-ravaged cities across the world.

In Chapter 12, Nedra Deadwyler introduces Civil Bikes, a bicycle tour company which works to challenge people's perceptions of bicycling in the City of Atlanta while exploring and preserving the city's unique history of segregation and the Civil Rights movement. Civil Bikes uses a racial-, income-, gender-, and age-inclusive outlook, offers programs that are woman-centered and empowering and participates in regional advocacy for transportation solutions which address the needs of citizens across a range of neighborhoods. This work powerfully connects past processes of racial exclusion and civil rights activism with current processes of neighborhood change from gentrification and displacement.

Opening organized bicycling

How can grassroots knowledge impact institutional agenda-setting and address inequity in mainstream bicycle advocacy? We can do this by integrating the lived experiences highlighted in the previous section into bicycling professions. Adonia Lugo establishes this section in Chapter 13 with a discussion about exclusion and inclusion in bicycle advocacy. Lugo uses the history of U.S. bike advocacy to explain how organized bicycling continues to be racialized, and argues that diversifying bicycle advocacy, policy, and planning will have inclusionary effects on public investment in alignment with the federal government's commitment to environmental justice.

Community bicycle workshops are explored in Chapter 14 as another possible form of bicycle advocacy outside of mainstream efforts. Simon Batterbury and Inès Vandermeersch argue that a bicycle workshop in Brussels, Belgium, challenges the invisibility of bicyclists and creates new spaces of socialization and cultural exchange in a city rich with immigrant communities. Bike repair spaces offer an avenue for building demand for bicycling, alongside more "supply-side" interventions such as infrastructure projects.

Although bicycle share, in its third generation, is a booming form of U.S. bicycle investment, it has also been associated with neighborhood turnover and the upwardly mobile, white bicyclist community that already receives the greatest share of bicycle infrastructure and amenities. In Chapter 15, James Hannig looks at two Midwest U.S. bicycle share programs to investigate how underserved populations perceive this amenity. Through his interviews with bicycle share operators, users, and critics, Hannig concludes that for bicycle share to resonate with underserved populations, equitable practices need to be explored and implemented to the greatest extent possible, particularly through community inclusion and engagement.

The importance of representative bicycle advocacy work is operationalized in Chapter 16 through the community work of the Pima County REACH Coalition, who led the ten-year-long development of a bicycle program in a dense, low-income, Latino neighborhood on the Southside of Tucson, Arizona. Authors Martha Moore-Monroy, Ada Wilkinson-Lee, Donna Lewandowski, and Alexandra Armenta discuss how a community-led approach to improve the access to cycling resources and infrastructural improvements for Latinos built on the community's assets. The success of this project was primarily due to the coalition's strong commitment to community-led participatory action and attention to making the program and approach replicable.

One sector of organized bicycling bucks the tendency toward racial homogeneity: organizations that serve youth. Youth participants in organized bicycling tend to represent U.S. diversity, with many young people staying involved with urban community bike organizations after graduating from earn-a-bike programs. The Youth Bike Summit is a growing U.S.-based meeting space for youth leaders and their bicycle organizations to discuss their advocacy and educational work. In Chapter 17, Pasqualina Azzarello, Jane Pirone, and Allison Mattheis discuss how the Youth Bike Summit has become a "generative space for collective youth voice" and perhaps the most advanced model of what a bike justice movement could look like.

In Chapter 18, Amy Lubitow argues that community engagement is needed to address neighborhood concerns over gentrification and bicycle infrastructure. Lubitow suggests that, although community engagement around urban infrastructure decisions may have limited utility in stemming rapid gentrification, community-led economic development projects can dramatically alter the experiences and perceptions of local residents. A community-led bike shop in Humboldt Park (a Puerto Rican neighborhood in Chicago) has allowed local residents to become empowered both economically and politically in ways that impact broader decision-making processes in Chicago. Lubitow highlights the importance of the community leading its own bicycle development projects rather than being folded into existing projects brought in by outside interests.

Moving forward: toward a just bicycle practice

The voices documented in these chapters show that organized bicycling does not have to go far to find new solutions. The editors of this book have been impressed by both the limits of the mainstream bicycle advocacy system and the triumphs of subaltern, othered, and alternative bicycle advocates in engaging and recruiting a diversity of bicyclists on the road, in urban planning, and in advocacy work. Our concerns, and those of the authors of this book, include the status quo of bicycle advocacy and connected urban planning that continues to prioritize those with societal, cultural, racial, class, and gender privilege. Our concerns also include infrastructure-based displacement, barriers to community and grassroots involvement in advocacy work, the isolation of people of color-focused bicycle advocacy, and the need for marginalized bicyclists to create their own spaces to promote bicycling. Just bicycle practices highlighted in this book emphasized five themes; we address each of these briefly here. In reality, many actions will cut across these domains, addressing multiple concerns.

1 Recognition of and planning for the diversity of cyclists and cycling travel patterns and uses

Mainstream planning and engineering approaches emphasize and count those cyclists who are privileged. But the majority of cyclists in cities are low-income, bike-dependent, and remain invisible. They are undercounted by the institutional regulatory and legal frameworks of transportation biking policy. Biking justice recognizes the importance of informality and the transcendence of geography as demonstrated by Rascuache cyclists (Chapter 9) and the Doble Rueda bicycle collective rides in Matamoros (Chapter 11).

The media, advocates, and the public should better understand and portray the reality of who is really cycling, as this recognition is a first step toward forming a more inclusive bike movement. Better understanding of the diversity of biking populations should shed light on the disconnect between current strategies and the actual needs of these populations. For example, biking justice problematizes the gentrification debate as demonstrated in Chapter 3. Biking infrastructure should not be a tool for displacement and the consequent changing of a neighborhood's economic class or ethnic makeup.

2 Creating inclusive participation and grassroots advocacy

Deep democracy and participation looks and feels differently in different communities. Communities differ in how they congregate, communicate, and participate in public life and this is an important fact that bicycle planning (or all planning) processes must appreciate. Grassroots activism, as a response to top-down biking infrastructure, is a helpful response to pushing for more community-based biking justice projects. This means that a more robust bicycle planning process should be adaptive to community practices and needs, to the differing abilities to participate (whether because of time constraints, a lack of "technical" knowledge, or other modes of exclusion), and more open to diverse voices and kinds of knowledge. Youths, "non-experts," elders, and locals all have specific and important knowledge about community conditions and needs which should be part of a truly just planning process. This broader participation can lead to better outcomes, stronger and more sustainable and community-relevant solutions, in more effective ways, as illustrated in Chapter 18.

3 Making investments in existing communities

There is evidence that cycling infrastructure is used to "brand" and "spruce up" neighborhoods in an effort to ready them for investment or development. Many existing communities are in need of different improvements and have been requesting them for years, sometimes decades. Planners and advocates must ask, therefore: for whom are we making this improvement? Is it for some expected or desired newcomer, or for a community in need of safety improvements but unlikely to draw in new investments or growth? Who was involved in the decision making? Are the investments part of a rebranding effort? This will lead to a better understanding of the broader needs of a community which may not include bicycling infrastructure at this point in time. These questions should be asked for infrastructure, but also for services such as bike share. Whose transportation needs are bike-sharing systems designed to serve? Are these bike-share systems implementing strategies to become more accessible to low-income residents?

4 Responding to the diverse meanings and experiences of "safety" and "security" for different communities

For many communities, public spaces are places of danger due to racial profiling, police intimidation, or other street violence. The lack of bicycle lanes may not be the main barrier to cycling—and solutions to the needs of cyclists in these communities may come in the form of advocating for safer public spaces. This can be manifested in various ways depending on the type of marginalization various groups are experiencing. For example, some groups are marginalized via racialization as Goddard suggests in Chapter 7 and this affects traffic safety for Black and Latino cyclists. Other groups are marginalized via their legal status. In Chapter 10, Bernstein argues that bike justice advocates should be working with immigrant rights groups to create safer public spaces for undocumented cyclists who place themselves at greater risk every time they ride their bikes. Advocates and planners need to recognize and respond to these diverse understandings of public spaces, and how solutions to safety, such as increased surveillance or policing, can make matters worse for many potential cyclists.

5 Integrating cycling into broader community development processes

Meaningful bicycle justice investments need to tackle community concerns that go beyond transportation infrastructure. Community concerns need to be tackled simultaneously with biking issues, such as poverty, violence, community health, housing affordability, and safety. In many important ways, communities already understand their own needs related to bike issues, and biking justice advocates just need to learn to listen. Taking an assets-based approach, such as the participatory outreach done by the REACH Coalition in Chapter 16, highlights the importance of integrating broader community development processes into biking justice practice. Biking justice advocates can focus on how bike projects further community benefits and further establish a mechanism for encouraging community ownership of the bicycle justice process. Chapter 18 highlights a community-led economic development bike project that actually led to community benefits.

These chapters taken as a whole highlight new directions for biking justice theory and practice. The authors connect the discourse and practice of civil rights and social justice to public interventions intended to increase cycling. We hope this book can be used as a critical guide for advocates in building a more equitable bicycle movement. There is a long-standing social justice project in the U.S. bike movement as well as in urban planning practice, but these approaches remain in tension. We hope that bicycle practice can be a useful site for advocacy planning, but we also propose that in some cases, it may not be about the bicycle, or infrastructure, or investments of any sort, but more about creating a just process, wherein multiple voices and concerns can finally be heard.

References

Anantharaman, M. (2015) *Elite and ethical: The defensive distinctions of new middle class bicycling in Bangalore, India.* Working Paper.

Avila, E. (1998) The Folklore of the Freeway: Space, Culture, and Identity in Postwar Los Angeles. *Aztlan: A Journal of Chicano Studies*, 23(1), pp.15–31.

Bratman, E. & Jadhav, A. (2014) How Low-Income Commuters View Cycling. *Citylab Blog*. [Online] Available from www.citylab.com/commute/2014/07/how-low-income-commuters-view-cycling/374390/ [Accessed November 3, 2015].

Bullard, R., Johnson, G. & Torres, A. (eds) (2004) *Highway Robbery: Transportation Racism and New Routes to Equity*. Cambridge, MA: South End Press.

Carlsson, C., Elliott, L. & Camarena, A. (eds) (2012) *Shift Happens! Critical Mass at 20*. San Francisco, CA: Full Enjoyment Books.

Coates, T. (2015) *Between the World and Me*. New York: Spiegel & Grau.

Denmark, D. (1998) The Outsiders: Planning and Transport Disadvantage. *Journal of Planning Education and Research*, 17(3), pp.231–245.

Flyvbjerg, B. (2001) *Making Social Science Matter: Why Social Inquiry Fails and How It Can Succeed Again.* Sampson, S. (trans.). New York: Cambridge University Press.

Fuller, O. & Beltran, E. (2010) The Invisible Cyclists of Los Angeles. *Progressive Planning Magazine, Planners Network.* [Online] Available from www.plannersnetwork.org/2010/07/the-invisible-cyclists-of-los-angeles/ [Accessed November 3, 2015].

Furness, Z. (2010) *One Less Car: Bicycling and the Politics of Automobility.* Philadelphia, PA: Temple University Press.

Gibson, K. (2007) Bleeding Albina: A History of Community Disinvestment, 1940–2000. *Transforming Anthropology*, 15(1), pp.3–25.

Gilroy, P. (2001) Driving While Black. In D. Miller (ed.) *Car Cultures*. New York: Berg.

Golub, A. (2015) Moving Beyond Fordism: "Complete Streets" and the Changing Political Economy of Urban Transportation. In S. Zavestoski & J. Agyeman (eds) *Incomplete Streets: Processes, Practices, and Possibilities.* Abingdon: Routledge, pp.36–53.

Golub, A., Marcantonio, R.A. & Sanchez, T.W. (2013) Race, Space, and Struggles for Mobility: Transportation Impacts on African Americans in Oakland and the East Bay. *Urban Geography*, 34(5), pp.1–30.

Grengs, J. (2002) Community-Based Planning as a Source of Political Change. The Transit Equity Movement of the Los Angeles' Bus Riders Union. *Journal of the American Planning Association*, 68(2), pp.165–178.

Grengs, J. (2004) The Abandoned Social Goals of Public Transit in the Neoliberal City of the USA. *City*, 9(1), pp.51–66.

Hilton, J. (2006) *Race and Ethnicity in Fatal Motor Vehicle Traffic Crashes 1999–2004.* Washington, DC: US Department of Transportation, National Highway Traffic Safety Administration.

Hoffmann, M. (2016) *Bike Lanes are White Lanes: Bicycle Advocacy and Urban Planning.* Lincoln, NE: University of Nebraska Press.

Hoffmann, M. & Lugo, A. (2014) Who Is 'World Class'? Transportation Justice and Bicycle Policy. *Urbanities*, 4(1), pp.45–61.

Horton, D. (2006) Environmentalism and the Bicycle. *Environmental Politics*, 15, pp.41–58.

Horton, D., Rosen, P. & Cox, P. (eds) (2007) *Cycling and Society.* Burlington, VT: Ashgate Publishing Company.

Koeppel, D. (2005) Invisible Riders. *Bicycling Magazine*. December.

League of American Bicyclists and the Sierra Club (2013) *The New Majority: Pedaling Towards Equity.* League of American Bicyclists and the Sierra Club.

Lubitow, A. & Miller, T.R. (2013) Contesting Sustainability: Bikes, Race, and Politics in Portlandia. *Environmental Justice*, 6(4), pp.121–126.

Lugo, A. (2013) *Body-City-Machines: Human Infrastructure for Bicycling in Los Angeles.* Ph.D. dissertation, University of California, Irvine.

McCullough, S. (2013) *Mechanical Intuitions: The Origins and Growth of Mountain Biking.* Ph.D. dissertation, University of California, Davis.

McKenzie, B. (2014) *Modes Less Traveled: Bicycling and Walking to Work in the United States 2008–2012.* American Community Survey Reports. Washington, D.C.: U.S. Census Bureau.

Mapes, J. (2009) *Pedaling Revolution: How Cyclists are Changing American Cities.* Corvallis, OR: Oregon State University Press.

Massey, D.S. & Denton, N.A. (1993) *American Apartheid: Segregation and the Making of the Underclass.* Cambridge, MA: Harvard University Press.

Maus, J. (2011–2012) 'The Williams Ave Project' Blog Series. *Bike Portland.* [Online] Available from http://bikeportland.org/tag/williams-avenue-bikeway-project/ [Accessed November 3, 2015].

Minnesota Healthy Kids Coalition (2015) *Active Transportation: From Our Own Perspectives And Voices.* [Online] Available from http://media.wix.com/ugd/783cdd_40f03a3ca55a4c738d14ebf9ca0bbb58.pdf [Accessed November 10, 2015].

Mohl, R.A. (1993) Race and Space in the Modern City: Interstate-95 and the Black Community in Miami. *In* A. Hirsch & R. Mohl (eds) *Urban Policy in Twentieth-Century America.* New Brunswick, NJ: Rutgers University Press, pp.100–158.

Norton, P.D. (2008) *Fighting Traffic.* Cambridge, MA: MIT Press.

Oosterhuis, H. (2014) Bicycle Research between Bicycle Policies and Bicycle Culture. *Mobility in History,* 5, pp.20–36.

Pisarski, A. (2013) *Commuting in America 2013: The National Report on Commuting Patterns and Trends.* [Online] Available from http://traveltrends.transportation.org/Pages/default.aspx [Accessed November 10, 2015].

Pucher, J., Buehler, R. & Seinen, M. (2011) Bicycling Renaissance in North America? An Update and Re-Appraisal of Cycling Trends and Policies. *Transportation Research Part A: Policy and Practice,* 45(6), pp.451–475.

Pulido, L. (2000) Rethinking Environmental Racism: White Privilege and Urban Development in Southern California. *Annals of the Association of American Geographers,* 90(1), pp.12–40.

Ritchie, A. (2009) *Major Taylor: The Fastest Bicycle Rider in the World.* San Francisco, CA: Van der Plas/Cycle Publishing.

Smiley, K.T., Rushing, W. & Scott, M. (2014) Behind a Bicycling Boom: Governance, Cultural Change, and Place Character in Memphis, Tennessee. *Urban Studies.* [Online] Available from http://usj.sagepub.com/content/early/2014/10/24/0042098014556590.abstract [Accessed November 30, 2015].

Smith, N. (2002) New Globalism, New Urbanism: Gentrification as Global Urban Strategy. *Antipode,* 34(3), pp.427–450.

Stehlin, J. (2015) Cycles of Investment: Bicycle Infrastructure, Gentrification, and the Restructuring of the San Francisco Bay Area. *Environment and Planning A,* 47(1), pp.121–137.

Sulaiman, S. (2015a) Filed Under: Ugly Things You Find on the Interwebs. *StreetsBlog LA.* [Online] Available from http://la.streetsblog.org/2015/01/14/filed-under-ugly-things-you-find-on-the-interwebs/ [Accessed September 10, 2015].

Sulaiman, S. (2015b) Are You Supposed to be Here?: Officer Harasses Black Cyclists during MLK Day Parade. *StreetsBlog LA.* [Online] Available from http://la.streetsblog.org/2015/01/20/are-you-supposed-to-be-here-officer-harasses-black-cyclists-during-mlk-day-parade/ [Accessed September 10, 2015].

Transportation Equity Network (TEN) (2015) Homepage. [Online] Available from www.transportationequity.org/ [Accessed November 20, 2015].

Vivanco, L. (2013) *Reconsidering the Bicycle: An Anthropological Perspective on a New (Old) Thing.* New York: Routledge.

Wray, J.H. (2008) *Pedal Power: The Quiet Rise of the Bicycle in American Public Life.* Boulder, CO: Paradigm.

Young, I.M. (2011) *Justice and the Politics of Difference.* Princeton, NJ: Princeton Press.

Zavestoski, S. & Agyeman, J. (eds) (2015a) *Incomplete Streets: Processes, Practices, and Possibilities.* Abingdon: Routledge.

Zavestoski, S. & Agyeman, J. (2015b) *Invisible Cyclist Blog.* [Online] Available from http://invisiblecyclist.com/ [Accessed November 3, 2015].

2 Is the right to bicycle a civil right?

Synergies and tensions between the transportation justice movement and planning for bicycling

Aaron Golub

Introduction

This chapter was inspired by a long-standing debate among transportation justice and equity advocates about the importance of investments in bicycle transportation as a goal of the transportation justice movement. Bicycle investments are notably absent in transportation equity analyses for regional plans (e.g. Metropolitan Transportation Commission, 2013), and from broader transportation justice discussions (for instance the word "bicycle" does not appear in the index of the overview of transportation justice practice published by the American Planning Association (Sanchez and Brenman, 2007)). The transportation justice movement, with its lineage in the civil rights and environmental justice movements, focuses on improving the transportation planning process to address the burdens and inequities that many low-income and minority communities have suffered at the hands of transportation planning over the past century. In contrast, there is a movement for "bicycle space": the struggle for fair and safe access to road space for bicycling supported by policy and financing for bicycling investments (Henderson, 2013). We ask here: why are the two movements so separate? This chapter will explore the emerging bicycle movement and contrast it with the transportation justice framework and attempt to understand where they synergize and where they conflict, and why.

As this entire volume highlights an emerging social practice of bicycle justice, clearly there are many who see the two movements as fruitfully coinciding, and that bicycling is important to the human right to safety in public spaces and streets. Still, we can hardly say the two movements have joined in any significant way, and we still see strange hesitations and missteps by the bicycle advocacy community when it comes to issues of race and class (see Lugo, Chapter 13, this volume and Lubitow and Miller (2013)).

This chapter synthesizes analyses from urban sociology and geography with the history of transportation planning, policy and finance. It begins by reviewing some of the basic rights frameworks at play in the two movements we are comparing. We then explore, through a social justice lens, the bicycle movement by dissecting it as a larger socio-technical system. Different parts of that system are examined for their potential impact on the relationship with the transportation justice movement. We then return to discuss the chapter's basic research questions.

Delineating the bicycle movement and transportation justice movements

Before continuing, we take a moment to more clearly define the two movements this chapter is exploring. We use the term "bicycle movement" which refers to the social movement to gain access to road space, policies and investments to support the use of bicycles for transportation. In many ways it is a justice frame viewing access to road space as a justice issue, much like the broader right of the city movement—in effect addressing the long-standing inequities that have resulted from prioritizing the movement of automobiles in streets (Henderson, 2013; Furness, 2010). The bicycle movement has taken and continues to take many forms, beginning with the invention and mass production of the bicycle in the late 1800s. This movement pushed for the improvement of roads and the rationalization of street operations to favor through-movement, ironically setting the stage for street re-engineering prioritizing automobile travel to the detriment of most other road users (Furness, 2010). Surges in interest in cycling arose again after the oil crises of the early and late 1970s, but momentum stalled as gas prices fell and people returned to their older habits. (For a variety of reasons, similar bicycle movements arising at the same time in Europe maintained their momentum through the 1980s, explaining some of the difference in provisions for cycling there.)

The current incarnation of the movement has strong ties to urban anarchist traditions as seen in the Critical Mass movement beginning in the early 1990s, dovetailing with more mainstream bicycle advocacy focused on local streets and paths improvements and city, state and federal planning and policies to gain favor for bicycling. The bicycle movement is very diverse as we show in this volume, though there are some common characteristics of the mainstream advocacy apparatus which we will discuss later.

The transportation justice movement focuses on addressing the failures of transportation planning along three main dimensions: (1) unequal distribution of mobility benefits from transportation investments, (2) unequal exposure to localized environmental burdens from transportation infrastructure, and (3) unequal access to participation in the planning process (Golub et al., 2013; Sanchez and Brenman, 2007). Like many other aspects of urban infrastructure and services, transportation is unequally distributed—often significantly so along class and racial dimensions. A lack of transportation services can mean a lack of opportunities for work, school, recreation and social interaction and can have a profound impact on the well-being of individuals, households and communities (Blumenberg and Waller, 2003; Ihlanfeldt and Sjoquist, 1998; Sanchez and Brenman, 2007). Furthermore, transportation infrastructure shapes the local environment physically by altering its sounds, smells, shadows and views and it can divide neighborhoods and cut people off from former neighbors. Thus, transportation justice is an environmental justice issue to many advocates. Finally, the transportation planning process is an important arena for demo-cratic involvement in political life at a variety of jurisdictional scales. Racial discrimination prevented minorities from effective participation in the urban development process and access to decision making continues to be key goal of the transportation justice movement (Grengs, 2004; Golub et al., 2013).

The struggle for transportation justice has a long and significant place in the history of the United States. While it was a well-known transportation struggle—the anti-segregation bus boycotts in Montgomery, Alabama, in 1955—which sparked the modern civil rights movement, it was the Supreme Court decision to uphold segregated seating in rail cars, back in 1896, which legalized segregation in the first place (Bullard et al., 2004). As the fight for civil rights inspired new social struggles such as the environmental justice movement, transpor-tation remained a significant point of contention and struggle. Erasing the physical scars of these various injustices will take decades and major shifts in investment priorities. This is why transportation justice advocates look closely at the burdens and benefits of big regional plans, policies and projects and may overlook smaller scale issues like bicycle access to street space (Sanchez and Brenman, 2007).

Transportation justice rests on a strong legal framework. The adoption of the Civil Rights Act of 1964 ended "separate but equal" and prohibited discriminatory practices across a range of domains such as education, hous-ing, employment and transportation. Title VI of the Act explicitly mentions a concern for the distribution of benefits from government programs and policies, reading:

> No person in the United States shall, on the ground of race, color, or national origin, be excluded from participation in, be denied the benefits of, or be subjected to discrimination under any program or activity receiving Federal financial assistance.

Guidance for implementing Title VI along with the Environmental Justice Executive Order 123898 in the practice of transportation planning was provided by subsequent regulations and rulings by Department of Transportation (DOT) agencies over the ensuing five decades (Sanchez and Brenman, 2007). These guidelines address the three main concerns listed above: the improved parti-cipation of groups traditionally marginalized in the transportation planning process, the distribution of burdens from exposure to the externalities of transpor-tation systems and the distribution of the costs and benefits of transportation investments and policies among various communities (DOT, 2012; Federal Highway Administration (FHWA) and Federal Transit Administration (FTA) of the United States, 1999).

Dissecting the bicycle movement

In this section we explore more deeply the dimensions of the bicycle system and the movements behind it. We can begin by understanding just what basic rights govern mobility by bicycle. To start, the right to mobility is considered a basic human right and is preserved in the U.S. constitution and in the U.N. Universal Declaration of Human Rights. Bicyclists have substantial rights, in theory, in terms of use of public rights of way. Bicycles are considered road vehicles in most state traffic codes and thus have access to most roadways, except for some limited access facilities like interstate highways and bridges. As vehicles they have access to the main travel lanes, though in many traffic codes, cyclists are required to ride as far to the right as reasonable (Mionske, 2007) and in some states are required to use a bicycle lane or path if one is provided along the roadway. While the responsibilities of cyclists and drivers in the roadway can often be a source of confusion and lead to tensions, we won't address those kinds of issues in this chapter. In a similar vein, we won't address explicitly the "vehicular cycling" (VC) subset of the bicycle movement, which views access to the main roadway lanes as the paramount issue for the movement. VC proponents feel that confinement to special bicycle lanes and paths are dangerous and keep cycling "second class" (Furness, 2010). This question of status does enter later, however, when the issue of cycling being a second class mode is addressed.

The socio-technical system of the bicycle movement

Moving beyond a broad and idealized notion of rights as they pertain to cycling, to better understand the social justice implications of investments in cycling, we must look at the bicycle movement within its social and political contexts. While bicycle improvements are often seen as an engineering or infrastructure investment problem, it is the social systems onto which these interventions are placed which are essential considerations for how the bicycle movement and transportation justice intersect. Bicycling, bicycle planning and the bicycle movement are embedded in a socio-technical system involving a complex constellation of individuals, groups, norms, institutions and processes as it is developed and implemented in the real world (Geels, 2005). While the analysis of socio-technical systems is a well-established field, for simplicity, we will focus on four areas of the socio-technical system making up the bicycle system we feel are most important to its justice impacts: (1) Practices, (2) Social Norms, (3) Infrastructures, and (4) Personal Resources. We will discuss each of these in the following sections.

The bicycle movement—practices

There are a lot of issues at play when considering the various practices of the bicycle movement and related actors which coincide to produce the bicycle system. With limited space, we must simplify here. The practices of the bike movement happen at various scales from the very local such as the specific streets impacted by a bicycle project, to city-wide traffic engineering issues, to regional-scale transportation plans, regional bike plans, bike wayfinding or connectivity projects or other larger-scale interventions. At the state level there are bicycle plans, questions of accommodation for bicycles in state managed facilities such as state highways, and state traffic codes related to bicycling. Federal policies also impact bicycles as they affect the federal funding for bicycle infrastructure.

Though each of these dimensions of planning practice differ significantly, there are some broadly uniform characteristics which describe the general practice of bicycle planning. A key paradigm of the practice is the emphasis on peak hour commute trips as the ideal travel patterns bicycle investments should support. Radial trips into and out of a central district, and especially those during the peak hour, are typically seen as the most important trips for which to plan in transportation planning. While this is related to capacity issues—these trips place the greatest stress on the transportation system—it also related to a bias in valuing the time and convenience of professional workers in central business districts (CBDs). This is reflected in how cyclists and bicycle trips are counted (using census or similar data based on questions about mode choice to work and making bicycle counts on key links heading into and out of CBDs) and the kinds of facilities which are often promoted (improving radial-type trips into CBDs).

The result of emphasis on commuting travel is that other types of bicycle travel are seen as less important to the transportation planning process: "shadow travel" or "invisible cyclists" (Zavestoski and Agyeman, 2015; Fuller and Beltran, 2010). Trips of less value consist of "reverse commuting" from inner city neighborhoods out to suburban job centers, or increasingly "circumferential" trips from suburb to suburb, and often at off peak times reflecting shift type work. These could also include travel for work purposes such as delivery or services like landscaping or skilled trades (see Lee, et al., Chapter 8, this volume).

These issues mirror citizenship issues, as it is minority and low-income travelers who are more likely to be "invisible cyclists" (Fuller and Beltran, 2010). In many ways the ability to secure rights and have them recognized and protected is a reflection of one's citizenship status, regardless of one's legal citizenship status. Citizenship in this light varies from group to group: some groups experience "shadow" citizenship status where they are presumed by many to be less than full citizens, regardless of actual legal citizenship status. Minority groups, especially blacks and Hispanics are often subject to questions about their citizenship and the legitimacy of claims they may make on society. While questions over the citizenship of minority groups continue to appear and reappear and continue to be posed today, it is specifically discrimination along dimensions of race and national origin which are protected by civil rights legislation like the Civil Rights Act. That is, the treatment as shadow citizens in transportation planning and investments is prohibited by civil rights legislation (Sanchez and Brenman, 2007).

Related to the legitimacy of certain kinds of travel and travelers over others, it can be shown that bicycle advocates are often over represented by and respond to white and middle-class commuters and residences (see Lugo, Chapter 13, this volume). These are the exact communities which are more versed in the transportation planning process and know how to connect to planners, elected officials and others involved in transportation planning and policy. They can show up to the right meetings at the right time and be heard.

A final issue connected to the process of bicycle planning is evidence that bicycle infrastructure accompanies processes of rapid neighborhood change—displacement or gentrification of existing working class and communities of color in inner neighborhoods or inner suburbs of metro areas (Zavestoski and Agyeman 2014; Stein, 2011; Lubitow and Miller, 2013; Hoffmann and Lugo, 2014). While it is not easy to show that investments in bicycle infrastructure cause these changes, they are often part of the suite of physical changes promoted and implemented as part of neighborhood "upgrading" which accompanies shifts in residential and commercial characteristics. Even if causation is impossible to show, the perceived connection to these processes do paint the bicycle planning process in a particular way.

The bicycle movement—social norms

An important component of all socio-technical systems are broadly shared norms which shape the behavior of individuals, groups and institutions involved in the system. The social norms surrounding the bicycle movement are not uncontroversial when considered from a social justice framework. The social norms intertwined with the early bicycle movement emphasized how cycling would benefit the supposed racial superiority of whites, and racial segregation was part of the early bicycle movement's organization (Furness, 2010). While this is not characteristic of the current movement, the continued white and middle-class leadership and planning emphasis on the needs of white and middle-class bicyclists show that the issue of diversity is still an issue in the bike movement.

Another strong normative issue relevant here is that bicycling is still a "second class" mode in the national psyche. For most adults in the United States—nearly all—a bicycle is a toy and bicycling is a recreation or hobby and not a serious solution to the nation's transportation needs. On the other end of the spectrum are things with high social meaning (see Martens et al., Chapter 6, this volume); access to education, health care and food are of large social concern and society attempts to regulate the provision of these items to ensure some minimal distribution of them among most of society. Transportation broadly enjoys a high social meaning: at all levels of government, transportation is heavily regulated and billions of dollars in fees and taxes are collected and then redistributed through investments in public infrastructure and services. The transportation system and the services it provides are essential to the workings of society and cuts across a range of issues related to the economy, employment, environment and health. Thus, transportation is the object of great struggle on the part of many organized groups, not limited to the transportation justice movement described earlier.

But, the question remains: is the subset of transportation focused on bicycling of sufficient social significance to warrant a broader social effort to promote bicycle use for everyone? Bicycle advocates clearly think so, and there is no doubt that bicycling's social significance has grown over the past two decades; bicycling has been growing in popularity and in some large cities has doubled or tripled over the past decades (Pucher et al., 2011). In a handful of corridors in some cities, bicycles are used in as many as 25 percent of trips. Federal transportation legislation and finance packages have increased their funding for bicycling over the past two decades starting with Intermodal Surface Transportation Efficiency Act (ISTEA) in 1991. Bicycling is now funded through several programs including the congestion mitigation and air quality (CMAQ) and Transportation Enhancements (TE) grant programs amounting to around 2 percent of the total funding through federal transportation programs since that time (Golub, 2014).

Bicycling is slowly improving its image in this national psyche, and intertwined with this transformation is the fact that cycling rates have increased for minorities and low-income communities across the country (League of American Bicyclists and the Sierra Club, 2013). Therefore, regardless of the social norms surrounding the "second class" status of the bicycle and the whiteness of the advocacy apparatus, the real material benefits cycling offers are being seen by many as something to consider seriously. Newer bicycle groups have shown much greater diversification and in fact many bike shops, community bike centers and community rides are focusing strongly on the bicycling needs of communities of color and low-income communities. (It is these developments that we are highlighting in this book and expect to grow in the future.)

Still, for bicycle advocates, the social equity and broader racial and class concerns of bicycling have only recently become a big concern of the movement. There are a growing number of reports and studies about how to improve racial and class representation within the bike movement (League of American Bicyclists and the Sierra Club, 2013; Clifton et al., 2012). Clearly there is a concern that bicycling has not reached a sufficient social meaning to be included within a broader transportation justice framework, which holds back the development of a justice-focused turn in the mainstream bike movement (Lugo, 2015).

The bicycle movement—infrastructures

Since improvements to street infrastructure are often the most prominent and expensive fruits of bicycle advocacy, infrastructure is an important aspect of the socio-technical system of the bicycle movement. This infrastructure includes restriping of roads with bike lanes, separate paths, bridges over key barriers, bike storage systems and public bike sharing, and traffic engineering improvements like signals and signage which make cycling faster and safer. Improvements in bike infrastructure have been shown to foster increases in ridership over time along with co-benefits for other road users such as pedestrian and transit users. These benefits have made cycling infrastructure an important part of transportation plans and investment programs in many metropolitan areas around the country.

Furthermore, as was mentioned earlier, federal financial support for bicycle infrastructure greatly expanded through the modernization of the transportation funding system with ISTEA. This makes bicycle planning an important potential source of funding for transportation improvements affecting cyclists as well as pedestrians and transit users.

One twist to the issue of bicycle infrastructure, however, is its association with displacement and gentrification processes mentioned earlier. This pattern of using bicycle investments as amenities for neighborhood "upgrades," which then interact with real estate speculation and rebranding, is an important reality to consider for its justice implications (Hoffman and Lugo, 2014; Lubitow and Miller, 2013; Stein, 2011; Stehlin, 2015; Zavestoski and Agyeman, 2014).

A final point to consider is that the public spaces and rights-of-way, where bicycle infrastructure is located, are places of vulnerability in many communities. The continued targeting of, and the resulting vulnerabilities experienced by, differently racialized bodies in public is a key concern of a growing movement to recognize and confront the continued human rights abuses suffered by communities of color (e.g. the Black Lives Matter movement, see also Coates (2015)). Broad assumptions about the perceived uses and benefits of changes to public infrastructure must be understood by planners through these lenses. The question then becomes: as a travel mode, how does bicycling compare to other modes for its ability to address or reduce this public vulnerability? The answer is not clear.

The bicycle movement—personal resources

A final dimension of the bicycle socio-technical system pertains to the personal resources needed to both ride a bicycle and to engage in bicycle advocacy. Bicycles clearly offer a cheap and efficient transportation mode for many people. When households can forgo the high cost of car ownership and trade off one or more vehicles for public transit and bicycling, the cost savings can be significant; studies show transportation spending can go from over 30 percent of the household budget to less than 10 percent if car ownership can be reduced (Public Policy Institute of California (PPIC), 2004). Those savings can ease household budgets and allow more spending on other productive uses such as education, food or housing.

The physical demands of cycling, however, would preclude the mode from being a truly mass mode; a good share of the population is likely unable or uninterested in bicycling because of its physical demands and other problems like sweat or potential injury. Another key personal issue around cycling, as stated earlier, is the vulnerability experienced by many communities in public spaces due to crime and police profiling, though this extends well into other mobility systems such as public transit and driving as well.

A final aspect of personal resources as they relate to the bicycle system is the time and knowledge needed to participate effectively in planning processes.

The ability to show up at public meetings and engage continuously in a planning process is important and essential to improve the planning process. This is, however, a challenge for many households who are balancing multiple jobs, job shifts in off-hours and who also may not be linguistically connected with the social and information networks involved in the planning process. That is, many are simply unaware of how to get involved in planning or where to learn more about it. While, ideally, processes are able to involve a broader cross-section of the community, this is still a challenge in most places. It is precisely because of these barriers, married with the fact that professional bicycle advocates often play an intermediary role as representatives of public opinion in the planning process, that some bike advocates have grown concerned by a lack of transportation justice principles in the bike movement.

Conclusions

Here we will wrap up with some conclusions reflecting on the reality of the bike movement socio-technical system and concerns within the transportation justice movement. We find both important synergies and conflicts between the two movements and highlight concerns which would need to be addressed to create a more socially just bicycle movement.

Synergies between the bicycle movement and transportation justice

It is clear there are some real synergies between bicycles and the transportation justice movement. The fact that bicycle infrastructure is part of the public right of way and is now receiving an increasing amount of financial resources should make it the target of equity analyses by transportation justice advocates, regardless of how advocates view the mode itself. Bike infrastructure equity should be a concern because it is drawing public resources away from other modes. Indeed, the distribution of finances among modes is a concern shown by civil rights law and transportation advocates, especially as it pertains to the tensions between spending programs for bus and rail (Golub et al., 2013, Grengs, 2004). There is no reason then that advocates would not become interested in bicycle programs for their distributive effects as well—exploring where the investments are made and who is benefiting from them.

Bicycles have the potential to assist low-income households with their travel—it offers cheap and, in a few corridors, faster transportation which could help with complex travel patterns involving multiple family members, children and complex work shifts at various times of the day. The bicycle doesn't have a fixed time-table and with regular maintenance, can be quite low-cost and dependable. This basic reality of the utility of the bicycle, like any other travel mode, should make it a concern of the transportation justice movement; for some people, bicycling can undoubtedly improve their mobility.

The broader social status of the bicycle is also rising and therefore we would assume the transportation justice movement would want to target this mode as an issue of distributional rights. Compounding this value is the fact that many minority and low-income travelers are actually using the bicycle, regardless of whether the transportation justice community views bicycling as an elitist pastime; the potential benefits of cycling must be recognized. "Invisible cyclists" and community-based cycling programs are a first sign that the demands of transportation justice advocates and those of the bicycle movement may begin to synergize. As a more diverse cycling community becomes aware of the distributional issues around bicycle planning, it may enter the radar screen as an objective of transportation justice advocacy (Hoffman and Lugo, 2014).

Conflicts between the bicycle movement and transportation justice

There are many serious conflicts between the bicycle movement and the transportation justice movement. The fundamental reality that bicycling is considered a second class mode may lead many in the transportation justice community to ignore it as an object of aspiration; equal access to first class mobility has always been the primary goal of transportation justice advocates dating back to Plessy vs. Ferguson (see Gilroy (2001)). As the bicycle rises above the status of a child's toy in more minds, this may change.

As bicycling requires one to put oneself in public rights-of-way and in further exposure to the dangers of street violence and police brutality, it is not surprising that bicycling may remain outside of the transportation justice frame. Bodily safety is a primary concern of many communities and should be understood by transportation planners as an important outcome from planning, though it is clearly related to forces outside of the hands of transportation planners.

Another significant conflict is the association of bicycle investments and infrastructure with rapid social and demographic change in neighborhoods resulting in displacement of existing communities. This association may prevent many transportation justice advocates from connecting strongly with the bicycle as the very communities being displaced are those traditionally involved in the transportation justice movement.

Finally, the white and middle-class optics of the bike movement may prevent many from seeing how it can connect with a wider public and the civil rights concerns of the transportation justice movement. This disconnect could create shadow advocates who can bring forth missing voices and perspectives (as highlighted in this book) into both the mainstream transportation justice and bicycle movements.

If current patterns and trends continue, our cities and transportation systems will embrace the bicycle only more and more, and transportation justice advocates may need to focus more squarely on the bicycle, for better or for worse. This book is an effort to bridge some of those gaps, jumpstart this conversation and highlight where justice concerns have indeed been addressed through efforts by both cities and communities and where more work is needed.

References

Blumenberg, E. & Waller, M. (2003) The Long Journey to Work: A Federal Transportation Policy for Working Families. *The Brookings Institution Transportation Reform Series* (July), pp. 1–20.

Bullard, R. D., Johnson, G. S. & Torres, A. O. (Eds.) (2004) *Highway robbery: transportation racism and new routes to equity*. Boston, MA: South End Press.

Clifton, K., Bronstein, S. & Morrissey, S. (2012) *The path to Complete Streets in underserved communities: Lessons from U.S. case studies*. Portland, OR: Portland State University.

Coates, T. N. (2015) *Between the world and me*. Text Publishing. New York, NY: Spiegel & Grau.

Department of Transportation of the United States (DOT) (2012) *Order 5610.2(a) Department of Transportation Actions to Address Environmental Justice in Minority Populations and Low-Income Populations*. [Online] Available from www.fhwa.dot.gov/environment/environmental_justice/ej_at_dot/order_56102a/index.cfm [Accessed March 3, 2013].

Federal Highway Administration and Federal Transit Administration of the United States (FHWA and FTA) (1999) *Memorandum on Implementing Title VI Requirements in Metropolitan and Statewide Planning*. [Online] Available from www.fhwa.dot.gov/environment/ejustice/ej-10-7.htm [Accessed June 1, 2010].

Fuller, O. & Beltran, E. (2010) The Invisible Cyclists of Los Angeles. *Progressive Planning Magazine, Planners Network*. [Online] Available from www.plannersnetwork.org/2010/07/the-invisible-cyclists-of-los-angeles/ [Accessed November 3, 2015].

Furness, Z. (2010) *One less car: Bicycling and the politics of automobility*. Philadelphia, PA: Temple University Press.

Geels, F. W. (2005) *Technological transitions and system innovations: a co-evolutionary and socio-technical analysis*. Northampton, MA: Edward Elgar Publishing.

Gilroy, P. (2001) Driving while black. In D. Miller, ed. *Car cultures*. New York: Berg.

Golub, A. (2014) Moving beyond Fordism: "Complete Streets" and the changing political economy of urban transportation. In S. Zavestoski & J. Agyeman, eds. *(In)Complete streets: processes, practices and possibilities*. Abingdon: Routledge, pp. 36–53.

Golub, A., Marcantonio, R. A. & Sanchez, T. W. (2013) Race, space, and struggles for mobility: transportation impacts on African Americans in Oakland and the East Bay. *Urban Geography*, 34(5), pp. 1–30.

Grengs, J. (2004) The abandoned social goals of public transit in the neoliberal city of the USA. *City*, 9(1), pp. 51–66.

Henderson, J. (2013) *Street fight: the politics of mobility in San Francisco*. Amherst, MA: University of Massachusetts Press.

Hoffman, M. L. & Lugo, A. (2014) Who is 'world class'? Transportation justice and bicycle policy. *Urbanities*, 4(1), pp. 45–61.

Ihlanfeldt, K. R. & Sjoquist, D.L. (1998) The spatial mismatch hypothesis: a review of recent studies and their implications for welfare reform. *Housing Policy Debate*, 9(4), pp. 849–892.

League of American Bicyclists and the Sierra Club (2013) *The New Majority: Pedaling Towards Equity*. [Online] Available from http://bikeleague.org/sites/default/files/equity_report.pdf [Accessed November 3, 2015].

Lubitow, A. & Miller, T. (2013) Contesting sustainability: bikes, race, and politics in Portlandia. *Environmental Justice*, 6(4), pp. 121–126.

Lugo, A. (2015) "Unsolicited Advice for Vision Zero" Blog Post in Urbanadonia.com. Sept 30, 2015.

Metropolitan Transportation Commission (MTC) (2013) *Plan Bay Area: Equity Analysis Report.* [Online] Available from http://onebayarea.org/pdf/final_supplemental_reports/FINAL_PBA_Equity_Analysis_Report.pdf [Accessed November 3, 2015].

Mionske, B. (2007) *Bicycling & The Law: Your Rights as a Cyclist.* Boulder, CO: Velopress.

Public Policy Institute of California (PPIC) (2004) *How Much Do Low-Income Californians Pay for Transportation?* Research Brief 91.

Pucher, J., Buehler, R. & Seinen, M. (2011) Bicycling renaissance in North America? An update and re-appraisal of cycling trends and policies. *Transportation Research Part A: Policy and Practice,* 45(6), pp. 451–475.

Sanchez, T. & Brenman, M. (2007) *The Right to Transportation. Moving to Equality.* Chicago, IL: APA Planners Press.

Stehlin, J. (2015) Cycles of investment: bicycle infrastructure, gentrification, and the restructuring of the San Francisco Bay Area. *Environment and Planning A,* 47(1), pp. 121–137.

Stein, S. (2011) Bike lanes and gentrification New York City's shades of green. *Progressive Planning: The Magazine of Planners Network,* Summer, 2011. [Online] Available from www.plannersnetwork.org/wp-content/uploads/2011/07/PNmag_Summer_Stein.pdf [Accessed November 3, 2015].

Zavestoski, S. & Agyeman, J. (Eds.) (2014) *Incomplete Streets: Processes, Practices, and Possibilities.* Abingdon: Routledge.

Zavestoski, S. & Agyeman, J. (2015) *Invisible Cyclist Blog.* [Online] Available from http://invisiblecyclist.com/ [Accessed November 3, 2015].

3 Is Portland's bicycle success story a celebration of gentrification?

A theoretical and statistical analysis of bicycle use and demographic change

Cameron Herrington and Ryan J. Dann

Introduction

Between 2000 and 2010, bicycle ridership more than tripled in Portland, Oregon. This rapid growth in pedal-powered commuting has positioned Portland as the leader in bicycle ridership among the nation's 70 largest cities. As of 2014, over 6 percent of the city's workforce commuted by bike. From *Portlandia* to *The New York Times*, references to Portland conjure images of bicycles. But the celebration of Portland's bicycle ascendancy has overshadowed another, more disturbing transition. During this period of rapid growth in bicycle use, people of color have been pushed out of close-in neighborhoods by the thousands, while white, well-educated newcomers have moved in. In Portland, growth in bicycle ridership has corresponded temporally and spatially with gentrification.

After suffering for decades from various manifestations of institutional racism—redlining, disinvestment, political marginalization, and forced displacement via numerous "urban renewal" projects (Gibson, 2007)—the Albina district in North/Northeast Portland has undergone dramatic gentrification over the past 20 years. Thousands of African Americans have been displaced by skyrocketing housing costs as private investment and new public infrastructure, including bicycle facilities, have remade the neighborhood. Portland's ambitious bicycle investments and its willful neglect of Albina's longtime African American residents collided in 2011, when the planning process for a bike lane cutting through the heart of Albina sparked a racially charged controversy about gentrification and the future of the neighborhood.

Through theoretical and statistical analysis, this chapter explores the connections between increased bicycle ridership and demographic change in Portland, asking: Has bicycling increased more in Portland's gentrifying neighborhoods than in nongentrifying neighborhoods? Is bicycle ridership a characteristic of white gentrifiers? Why, during a bike lane planning process, did gentrification emerge as the major issue of public debate? In exploring these questions, we raise concerns about urban planning and public participation in the "postpolitical" era. We explore connections among the neoliberal growth model, gentrification, and sustainability planning, and examine how debates about race and gentrification come to be displaced to the realm of seemingly benign infrastructure planning processes.

This study finds that, between 2000 and 2010, increases in whiteness and educational attainment predicted large increases in bicycle use at the neighborhood level—suggesting that the celebration of Portland's bicycle success is, in many neighborhoods, a celebration of gentrification. This finding exposes a largely unrecognized tension between two goals recently established by the Portland City Council: dramatically increasing bicycle ridership, and preventing the displacement of low-income people of color from their neighborhoods. Our analysis raises the prospect that Portland's celebrated national leadership in bicycle ridership has been achieved, at least in part, through gentrification, and that these two goals are contradictory under current conditions of neoliberal urban development.

The North Williams Avenue controversy

In 2011, planning for additional bicycle lane capacity on North Williams Avenue erupted in controversy. Williams is a one-way arterial that runs north through the heart of the city's historic African American district, Albina. This district saw its black population drop precipitously during the 2000s (Scott, 2012), while bicycle ridership and the white population grew dramatically. North Williams Avenue now serves as the major bicycle commuting route between downtown Portland and gentrified Albina.

At public meetings held by the Portland Bureau of Transportation (PBOT) to discuss plans for reconfiguring Williams Avenue, leaders of the black community raised concerns about the prioritization of infrastructure for bicyclists, who they perceived to be primarily white newcomers to the neighborhood, in contrast to decades of neglect and disinvestment when the neighborhood had been largely black. The implication was that City spending and priorities were aligned with the lifestyles of gentrifiers, and would result in bicycle facilities that would attract still more gentrifiers.

Jerrell Waddell, a member of the project's original Stakeholder Advisory Committee who represented one of Albina's remaining African American churches, contended that the PBOT planning process was skewed to privilege the interests of newcomers to the neighborhood. These new residents brought with them a new preferred transportation mode that required special investments from the City. Speaking at a June 7, 2011, meeting, Waddell said, "This room is made up of predominantly a particular population who wants to see bicycles come in" (Maus, 2011c).

Black residents protested that they had not been included in initial phases of the planning process, and argued that white cyclists were largely ignorant of and insensitive to the neighborhood's bleak history of disinvestment, displacement, and disempowerment (Maus, 2011b). For long-time residents of Albina, this history stood in stark contrast to PBOT's enthusiastic responsiveness to the infrastructure demands of the growing population of cyclists. It was a cruel irony, they pointed out, that the African American community had long advocated for safety improvements on Williams Avenue (Lubitow and Miller, 2013): "We wanted safe streets back then," one resident said, "but now that the bicyclists want to have safe streets . . . it's all about the bicyclists getting safe streets" (Maus, 2011b).

The conflict that surfaced at public meetings in 2011 prompted PBOT to extend and revamp the public participation process (Lubitow and Miller, 2013). A more diverse advisory committee was convened, and in August 2012 PBOT issued a consensus plan for the reconfiguration of the street (City of Portland Bureau of Transportation, 2012). Following construction in 2014, a new, wider bicycle lane is now in use (City of Portland Bureau of Transportation, 2013). Despite this resolution, the underlying issues that triggered the controversy remain firmly entrenched; the process of gentrification marches forward (Scott, 2012), and the Albina district continues to be remade—through housing, businesses (Sullivan and Shaw, 2011), and public infrastructure—to meet the consumption demands of new residents (Beauregard, 1986).

"We want to be involved in the change . . ."

Even as they decried the North Williams project's *a priori* privileging of (white) bicycle interests over other community concerns, critical residents made clear that they were not opposed to either bicycling nor the reconfiguration of Williams Avenue, *per se*. "I'm trying to paint the picture that we're not against bicyclists, we're not against change," Sharon Maxwell Hendricks said. "But we as a community of color, we want to be involved in the change, we want to be participators in the change" (Maus, 2011c). In a commentary posted at BikePortland. org, long-time Williams Avenue resident Donna Maxey wrote, "The hurt and anger are not at the cyclist—[they are] at the losses we suffered and the historical hubris exhibited by the power structure" (Maus, 2011a). Seemingly caught off guard by the emergence of these issues, then-Mayor Sam Adams stated, "This [project] began as the reconsideration of a public space and quickly evolved into a community-wide discussion about the history of a neighborhood and its historical treatment by government, changing demographics and the nature of decision-making" (City of Portland Bureau of Transportation, 2012).

Bicycling, then, served as the impetus for the surfacing of longstanding and well-founded resentments related to much larger forces. The North Williams Traffic Safety Operations Project and its public-involvement component took on the weight of decades of injustice suffered by Portland's African American community at the hands of the City, the real estate industry, and the white power structure (Gibson, 2007). At a July 20, 2011, community meeting, Maxey articulated the connection between the specific issue of the street configuration and the history of the neighborhood:

What is causing the anger and resentment is that it's only an issue of safety now that whites are the ones who are riding bicycles and walking on the streets. Because we have been in this community for years and it has not been an issue and now it's an issue. So that's the resentment you're hearing . . . years of people being told, you don't count, you don't matter . . . but now that there's a group of people who's coming in that look like the people who are the power brokers—now it's important.

(Maus, 2011b)

Maxey's statement aligns with Beauregard's understanding of the central socio-political dynamic of gentrification: existing residents are rendered "economically and politically powerless relative to the gentrifiers" (Beauregard, 1986, p.50).

To be sure, gentrification is a chaotic, complex process (Beauregard, 1986) that exists at the nexus of historical forces, policy decisions at various scales of governance, public and private investment, the real estate and housing markets, migration patterns, and transformations in the broader political-economy. Most of these political, economic, and social forces operate at scales far larger than that of a single neighborhood. And few ever crystallize in concrete decision-making or planning processes over which residents might have any real expectation of exerting power. Instead, gentrification entails a reshaping based on top-down plans and an influx of "cataclysmic capital" (Jacobs, 1961) from outside of the neighborhood. Existing residents have little influence over this wealth and power (DeFilippis, 2004), nor over expert-driven planning decisions that privilege "the power brokers" that Maxey refers to.

Consequently, while black residents of Albina remained largely powerless to alter the dynamics of gentrification that were reshaping their neighborhood, the Williams Avenue planning process provided a forum for the discussion of longstanding racial injustices. The emergence of these issues in the context of a street reconfiguration project fits well with Piven and Cloward's assertion that people seek out "strategic opportunities for defiance" (Piven and Cloward, 1977). Residents openly defied the City's attempts to constrain the discussion to the narrow issue of the street configuration by bringing race and gentrification to the forefront, and bringing the planning process to a standstill.

People generally take political action in the context of their daily practices, and in response to institutions that shape their immediate experiences of injustice, which are in turn manifestations of larger structural issues. Workers, therefore, "experience the factory, the speeding rhythm of the assembly line, the foreman, the spies and the guards, the owner and the paycheck. They do not experience monopoly capitalism" (Piven and Cloward, 1977, p.20). African American residents of Albina, by analogy, do not experience neoliberal urban development. Rather, in this case, they experienced and organized in response to a bicycle lane that catered to incoming white residents.

Postpolitical Portland: neoliberalism and gentrification

The politics of urban development in Portland—and most elsewhere, for that matter—fit Swyngedouw's conception of the "postpolitical condition" (Swyngedouw, 2007). In the postpolitical era, democracy is reduced to techno-cratic decision-making on particularized questions of policy implementation. Postpolitical dynamics discourage and foreclose debate on larger ideological and structural questions, and instead facilitate decision-making within a narrow range of possible outcomes, any of which would support the same general ideo-logical direction. Political contestation has been eclipsed by apolitical consensus. Mechanisms for public participation in policymaking channel residents' advo-cacy and organizing efforts into giving feedback on relatively benign questions of policy implementation, while marginalizing voices that question the underlying premises of the decisions being made. In this section we discuss the postpolitical ideology of neoliberal urban development, and examine how it affected the North Williams bike lane planning process.

In short, neoliberalism entails the subordination of governance to market forces (Purcell, 2003; Hackworth, 2007). Policy is therefore a means of facilitat-ing private profit-making, rather than a tool to prevent or mitigate unjust market outcomes (Squires, 1994)—such as the displacement of low-income people of color from gentrifying neighborhoods. Neoliberal urbanism can be considered a "postpolitical" concept in the sense that it cannot be questioned in the context of mainstream political and planning discourse without jeopardizing the legi-timacy of the questioner. We argue that the North Williams controversy was shaped by the postpolitical constraints of this ideology: because the neoliberal development model inherently entails gentrification (Hackworth, 2007; Harvey, 2012), and because that model (discussed in terms of "job creation" or "neighbor-hood prosperity" (Portland Development Commission, n.d.)) is beyond reproach within mainstream political discourse, discussions of race and gentrification were displaced in this case to the venue of a bike lane planning process.

Though they are generally posited as inevitable, if unfortunate side effects of place-based economic development, gentrification and displacement can more accurately be understood as an explicit economic development strategy—one that is inherent in the neoliberal model (Hackworth, 2007). Attracting higher-income residents to a targeted location is not a mere byproduct of urban redevelopment. Rather, it is simultaneously the *raison d'être* for redevelopment, and the means by which it generates profit and higher property taxes for the private sector and the municipality, respectively. This "economic growth through gentrification" increases speculative property values and spurs the establishment of higher-rent businesses that cater to the consumption demands of the new, higher-income population (Beauregard, 1986).

Because the purpose and effect of neoliberal redevelopment are to drive up costs (of property, housing, retail space, goods and services, etc.), it inherently entails the immediate displacement of existing lower-income residents, dispro-portionately people of color, and the long-term displacement of affordable housing opportunities. That is, unless there is a concerted public sector strategy to counteract the displacement effects of increased property values by strictly regulating the housing market (as through rent control) and decommodifying a substantial amount of property (through land trusts, cooperatives, and other non-speculative, community-controlled forms of ownership) (Marcuse, 2012). Such action at any meaningful scale is, of course, both ideologically dissonant and empirically nonexistent in the context of a neoliberal development model. Increasing property values and curtailing the redistributionary and regulatory functions of the local state are, after all, the concurrent goals of the neoliberal city (Smith, 1987; Hackworth, 2007). This is particularly true in Portland's designated Urban Renewal Areas, including the N/NE neighborhoods bisected by North Williams Avenue, where taxes generated by rising property values are siphoned off by the Portland Development Commission to pay for new infrastructure and subsidize sweetheart deals for developers.

"A critical assumption" undergirding the neoliberal model, according to Squires, is that "the city constitutes a unitary interest and all citizens benefit from policies that enhance aggregate private economic growth" (Squires, 1994, p.94). This "unitary interest" is a fundamental characteristic of Swyngedouw's "post-political condition," because a unitary interest precludes politics. In a similar vein, Mele argues that neoliberal urban development is generally portrayed as "consensual" and "socially-neutral" (Mele, 2012, p.599). The demographic changes experienced in Albina, however, clearly demonstrate that neoliberal development produces winners and losers. Over the course of the 1990s—a decade in which "the City of Portland put concerted effort into the revitalization of Albina"—the number of homes in the neighborhood owned by blacks decreased by 36 percent, while those owned by whites increased by 43 percent (Gibson, 2007, p.20).

It is a symptom of the postpolitical, neoliberal era that meaningful local state action opposed to gentrification is so difficult to imagine. Criticism from out-side of the neoliberal consensus—such as from those who stand to be displaced by redevelopment—is marginalized as radical and unrealistic. "The consensual times we are currently living in," Swyngedouw concludes, "have thus elimi-nated a genuine political space for disagreement" (Swyngedouw, 2007, p.25). Gentrification and racial justice are never part of a political debate over the city's neoliberal development model, for such a debate is never held. Rather, these issues emerge only in narrowly bounded spaces set aside for planning *the imple-mentation of* discrete pieces of the model—such as bicycle lanes. In such forums, however, questions of ideology and politics are often dismissed as counterproduc-tive and irrelevant to the concrete topic at hand. "I'm worried I might offend people with this statement," one attendee of the North Williams bike lane meet-ings said, "but I honestly don't understand how a safety campaign on Williams is an issue of gentrification or racism" (Maus, 2011b).

Even in self-consciously progressive Portland, the postpolitical consensus around neoliberal development forecloses consideration of alternative develop-ment strategies. Gentrification is part-and-parcel of this unquestioned subservience of policy to market forces. Economic growth via gentrification is in, and mitigating its inherent, predictable displacement effects is out. Community participation is limited to advisory roles on decisions about relatively minor details that are inscribed within the larger, incontrovertible agenda. The planning process for the North Williams project, therefore, served as a rare forum in which the structurally determined issue of gentrification could be publicly contested. That this interjection of politics into a consensus-based planning effort was successful in temporarily derailing the process and raising the profile of structural critiques is noteworthy in and of itself.

The unanswered question raised by the North Williams controversy

We have made the case that the North Williams controversy reflects a displacement of structural critiques to the realm of a narrow, postpolitical public-involvement process. This assertion notwithstanding, we do not mean to imply that the connection drawn by black residents between bicycling and gentrification is erroneous. On the contrary, we believe that their perception raises an important empirical question that was overshadowed by the unexpected politicization of the North Williams project. Critics of the North Williams planning effort viewed bicycle ridership as a proxy for and manifestation of gentrification. With the immediate issue of the street reconfiguration now resolved, we believe it is time to return to that original question. Is there an empirical connection between gentrification and bicycle ridership?

In asking this question, we do not presume to be able to identify any causal relationship between bicycle infrastructure and gentrification. We do not, in other words, ask whether bicycle lanes *cause* gentrification, or *vice versa*. Rather, we ask if increased bicycle ridership and gentrification have occurred concurrently in Portland. Questions of causality must be explored through further research, using other methods. In any case, the issue of causality is peripheral to our purpose. We are not so much concerned with understanding which comes first, the chicken or the egg, but rather whether the chicken and egg are even from the same species: Are bicycling and gentrification part of the same process? Is the perceived link between them corroborated by statistically observable phenomena? And, what are the implications of such a link for Portland's simultaneous goals of increasing bicycle ridership while also preventing displacement?

Demographic characteristics of Portland's cyclists

As context for our statistical analysis of the link between gentrification and bicycle ridership in Portland, we first provide an overview of the city's recent growth in bicycle use, and the demographic makeup of its cyclists. Between 2000 and 2010, Portland's growth in bicycle ridership far surpassed that of all major U.S. cities. In 2000, Portland had the nation's fifth-largest share of bicycle

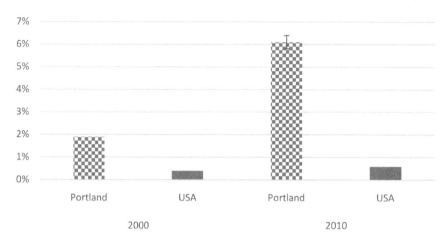

Figure 3.1 Change in bicycle commute mode share in Portland vs. USA, 2000 and 2010

Source: 2000 U.S. Census Decennial Census and 2010 American Community Survey.

commuters (1.8 percent), but by 2010 had jumped to number one (6.0 percent) (League of American Bicyclists, 2012) (Figure 3.1). In absolute terms, ridership more than tripled, from roughly 5,000 bike commuters to over 17,000.

Race and bicycle ridership

The growth in Portland's bicycle ridership is predominantly driven by white people, which is contrary to national trends. Nationally, non-white bicycle use is growing faster than white bicycle use (The League of American Bicyclists and The Sierra Club, 2013); the opposite is true for Portland. The bicycle commute rate for whites in Portland increased by 243 percent between 2000 and 2010 (from 2.1 percent to 7.2 percent); nationwide the increase was 100 percent (from 0.3 percent to 0.6 percent) (U.S. Census Bureau, 2010). Meanwhile, bicycle commuting for blacks in Portland increased at roughly half the rate of whites, by 127 percent (from 1.1 percent to 2.5 percent), compared to a nationwide decrease for blacks from 0.3 percent to 0.2 percent. Portland's workforce population was 77 percent white in 2010, yet 89 percent of bicycle commuters were white. In the same year, 4.5 percent of Portland's workforce was black, though just 1.9 percent of bicycle commuters were black (see Figure 3.2).

Highly educated Portlanders love bikes

Between 2000 and 2010, the percentage increase of whites with bachelor's degrees in Portland was almost twice that of whites at the national level. The percentage increase in bachelor's degree attainment for black Portlanders

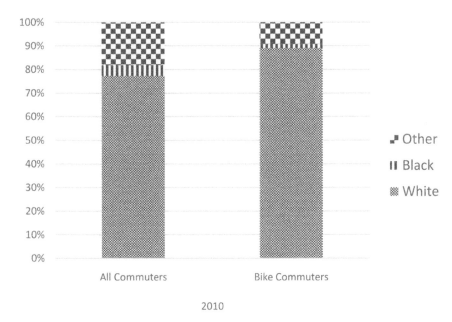

Figure 3.2 Racial composition of Portland's bicycle commuters

Source: 2000 U.S. Census Decennial Census and 2010 American Community Survey.

during the same period, however, was lower than that of blacks at the national level (see Figure 3.3). Regardless of race, 65 percent of Portland's bicycle commuters in 2010 had attained at least a bachelor's degree, compared to 43 percent of the city's overall population (see Figure 3.4). Nationally, 28 percent of bicyclists had bachelor's degrees, which was roughly equivalent to the general population.

Neighborhood change and bicycle ridership: pedal-powered gentrification

Bicycle ridership has long been known to have a spatial component: it is more prevalent in areas with higher urban densities, which allow shorter trip distances (Baltes, 1996). A combination of greater street connectivity, abundant destinations, and more bicycle infrastructure makes for an environment that is more suitable for bicycling (Rietveld and Daniel, 2004). Not surprisingly, whereas bicycle use exploded during the 2000–2010 period in Portland's central neighborhoods, it remained largely unchanged, or even decreased, in outlying areas (see Figure 3.5).

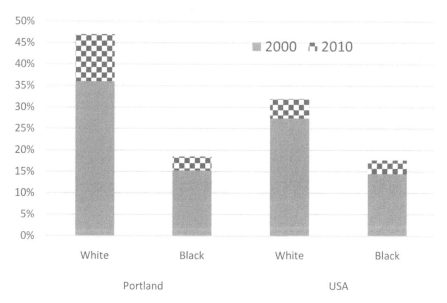

Figure 3.3 Bachelor's degree attainment by race, Portland vs. USA, 2000 and 2010

Source: 2000 U.S. Census Decennial Census and 2010 American Community Survey.

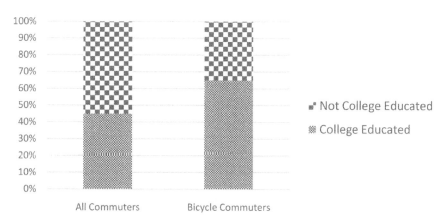

Figure 3.4 Bachelor's degree attainment by commute mode in Portland, 2010

Source: 2010 American Community Survey.

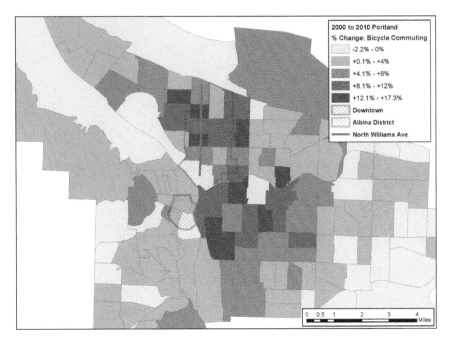

Figure 3.5 Portland percentage change in bicycle community, 2000–2010

Source: 2000 U.S. Census Decennial Census and 2010 American Community Survey.

This basic spatial trend masks the role that demographic change has played in Portland's bicycle success story. Ridership growth has not been distributed solely as a function of population density, but rather in correlation with the changing demographics of the city's inner neighborhoods. The statistical analysis that follows examines this link between bicycle ridership and gentrification.

Methodology and data

Our analysis uses commute mode-share data from the U.S. Census Bureau's 2000 Census and 2010 American Community Survey (ACS). The Census and ACS measure bicycle ridership by asking respondents, 16 years and older, about their primary method of transportation for trips to work. Individuals who are under 16, retired, and/or unemployed are not included in this measure. Additionally, trips that are non-work related, which make up over 70 percent of all trips (FHWA, 2011), are not reported. Despite these limitations, the ACS continues to be the most robust dataset for measuring bicycle ridership in the U.S., and provides a consistent measure of commute mode-share across our study period.

We analyzed the 2000–2010 timeframe in order to align our findings with a widely discussed (in Portland) 2013 study of gentrification commissioned by the

Portland Bureau of Planning and Sustainability (BPS) (Bates, 2013). This decade witnessed both the mass displacement of African Americans from the Albina neighborhoods in N/NE Portland (Gibson, 2007), and a dramatic increase in bicycle ridership citywide. The unit of analysis for our study is the census tract. Because census tract boundaries in Portland changed between 2000 and 2010, we made slight boundary adjustments to maintain a consistent area of analysis.

Our definition and measures of gentrification rely upon the 2013 BPS study, conducted by Dr. Lisa Bates, which tracks gentrification from 2000–2010 and predicts the susceptibility of Portland's neighborhoods to gentrification and displacement in the coming years. Bates follows a method originally developed by Lance Freeman in 2005 (Bates, 2013, p.26).

"While there are intense debates in academic circles about how to describe gentrification as a process," Bates writes, "the common characteristics for defining the effects are: housing market changes, economic status changes, and demographic changes in a neighborhood that alter its character" (Bates, 2013, p.9). Based on this understanding, Bates measures gentrification using four indicators. "In short," Bates writes, "these demographic change indicators likely capture both the in-migration of 'gentrifiers' and the out-migration of longtime residents" (Bates, 2013, p.28):

1   change in the percentage of white population;
2   change in the percentage of residents with bachelor's degrees;
3   change in median family income;
4   change in the percentage of households that own their homes.

In examining the period between 2000 and 2010, Bates defines census tracts that have undergone significant "gentrification-related demographic change" as those that meet one of two criteria:

1   The census tract has experienced above-city-average change in at least three of the four indicators; or
2   The census tract has experienced above-city-average change in indicators 1 and 2 only (whiteness and educational attainment).

This definition places a *de facto* weight on the racial and educational attainment attributes of gentrification, while deemphasizing the income and homeownership attributes. This decision is well-supported by the gentrification literature, which recognizes that some iterations and stages of gentrification do not entail immediate gains in income or homeownership. An influx of well-educated whites, though they may for the time-being be renters of moderate means, nonetheless represents a significant shift in the character of a neighborhood, compromises the ability of lower-income households to maintain their residence, and paves the way for later stages of gentrification.

Location of gentrification and bicycle ridership

In order to narrow our analysis and focus on the parts of the city that have experienced gentrification and displacement most acutely, we analyze only those census tracts that exhibit a level of demographic change in the top *quartile* of all census tracts, rather than the top half (as per Bates' study). We retain Bates' standard of requiring three out of four indicators to be in the top quartile, or for change in whiteness and change in educational attainment to be in the top quartile. Figure 3.6 highlights the census tracts that were most dramatically gentrified between 2000 and 2010, according to the four above-described indicators. Figure 3.7 highlights census tracts that were in the top quartile for growth in bicycle ridership.

Intersection of gentrification and bicycling

Figure 3.8 shows the overlap areas of Figures 3.6 and 3.7, highlighting the census tracts in Portland that experienced the greatest degree of gentrification and were *also* within the top quartile for growth in bicycle ridership, 2000–2010. Six of the ten census tracts that met both criteria are in the historic Albina district in N/NE Portland. North Williams Avenue serves as a primary bicycle commute route connecting downtown Portland with seven of the ten tracts.

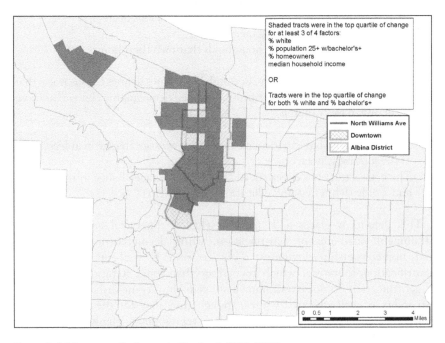

Figure 3.6 Most gentrified areas in Portland, 2000–2010

Source: City of Portland Bureau of Planning and Sustainability.

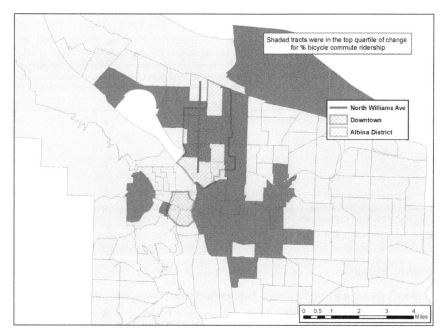

Figure 3.7 Top quartile of growth in bicycle commuting in Portland, 2000–2010

Source: 2000 U.S. Census Decennial Census and 2010 American Community Survey.

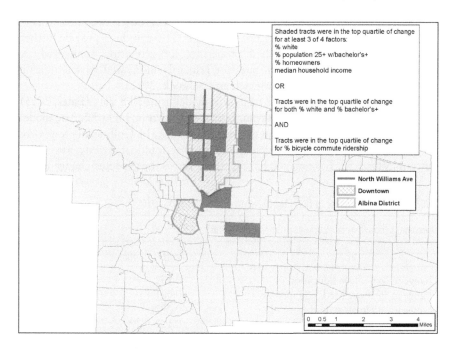

Figure 3.8 Figure 3.6 and Figure 3.7 data overlapped

Source: City of Portland Bureau of Planning and Sustainability, 2000 U.S. Census Decennial Census and 2010 American Community Survey.

Table 3.1 Correlation between City of Portland Bureau of Planning and Sustainability gentrification indicators and change in bicycle ridership at Census tract level, 2000–2010

% Change in BPS Measure in Census Tract	*% Change in Bicycle Ridership in Census Tract*	
	Corr.	*Sig.*
Whiteness	0.5	**
Education	0.42	**
Homeownership	0.05	
Median Income	0.17	*
BPS Index	0.35	**

Source: City of Portland Bureau of Planning and Sustainability, 2000 U.S. Census Decennial Census and 2010 American Community Survey.

Note: * p<0.05, ** p<0.01.

Statistical analysis

Table 3.1 shows statistical correlations we find when testing the change in bicycle ridership against the BPS gentrification index as a whole, and against each of the four BPS gentrification indicators separately. Overall, we find a moderate association between the change in bicycle ridership and the BPS index, at the census tract scale. Looking at the four indicators separately, strong relationships are found between the change in bicycle ridership and the changes in whiteness and education. Associations between bicycle use and the other two indicators—income and homeownership—are not significant. These findings provide further evidence of Portland's established propensity for attracting young, white, college-educated newcomers who are not primarily motivated by maximizing their economic opportunities (Jurjevich and Schrock, 2012).

The results of a multiple linear regression model using BPS data (Bates, 2013) and Census data (U.S. Census Bureau, 2010) are shown in Table 3.2. The model provides an acceptable fit to the dataset, with an R^2 of 0.314. Collinearity tests were carried out for all variables, which indicated that multicollinearity was not a concern (VIF<1.36, Tolerance<0.83). Table 3.2 shows the expected change in the

Table 3.2 Determinants of bicycle ridership growth, 2000–2010

Outcome: Change in bicycle use, multiple regression			
	Coeff.	*Sig.*	*t*
Change in % College Education	0.157	**	[3.45]
Change in % above Med. HH income	0.001		[0.03]
Change in % Homeownership	−0.072		[−1.37]
Change in % White	0.192	**	[5.14]

Source: City of Portland Bureau of Planning and Sustainability and 2010 American Community Survey.

Note: ** p<0.01.

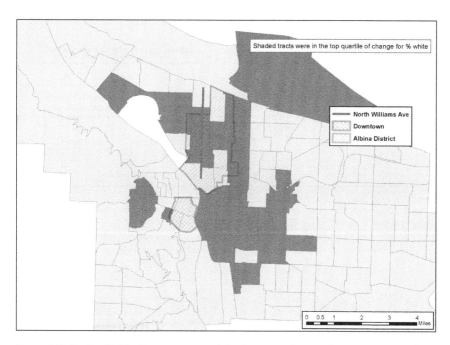

Figure 3.9 Portland U.S. Census tracts with highest quartile growth in percentage of white population

Source: 2000 U.S. Census Decennial Census and 2010 American Community Survey.

dependent variable (percentage of bicycle riders) for a one-percent change in each independent variable when the other covariates are held constant. Two coefficients were statistically significant at the $p<0.01$ level: change in whiteness and change in educational attainment. The other two independent variables (change in median household income and change in homeownership) did not have a significant effect on the change in bicycle use. The model suggests that census tracts that experience an increase in whiteness and/or educational attainment will also experience an increase in bicycle ridership. Of these two factors, an increase in the percentage of white residents will result in the greatest increase in bicycling (0.19 percent increase in bicycle ridership for every 1 percent increase in white population). Figures 3.9 and 3.10 show the Portland census tracts with the highest quartile growth in percentage of white population and educational attainment, respectively.

Conclusions, implications, and solutions

Conclusions

The North Williams Avenue bicycle lane controversy simultaneously represents: (1) discontent with gentrification and displacement—which are products of

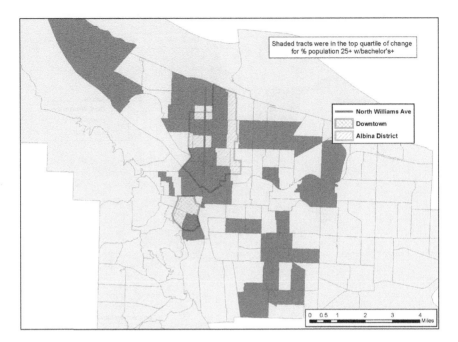

Figure 3.10 Portland U.S. Census tracts with the highest quartile growth in percentage of educational attainment

Source: 2000 U.S. Census Decennial Census and 2010 American Community Survey.

historical injustices and the contemporary neoliberal model of urban development; and (2) the perception that increased bicycle ridership is a manifestation of gentrification in Portland. The emergence of debates over race and gentrification in the context of the North Williams planning process also exposes the postpolitical nature of Portland's embrace of neoliberal development, which has foreclosed opportunities for challenging the neoliberal model itself, and thus displaced political contestation to the realm of, in this instance, a bicycle infrastructure project.

Taking seriously the contention of many African American residents that the reconfiguration of North Williams Avenue was carried out to meet the demands of new white residents, we conducted two statistical tests in order to investigate the link between bicycle ridership and gentrification. With Portland's census tracts as the units of analysis, we found a significant statistical correlation between high levels of gentrification (top quartile of the BPS index) and high levels of increased bicycle ridership (top quartile of bicycle commute growth). Among the four gentrification indicators (race, educational attainment, income, homeownership), two were significantly and strongly correlated with increased bicycle ridership at the census tract level: increased percentage of white residents, and increased percentage of residents with bachelor's degrees.

Based on these results, we conclude that gentrification and bicycle ridership go hand-in-hand in Portland. From 2000–2010, neighborhoods experiencing the most dramatic gentrification and displacement also experienced the largest increases in bicycle ridership. Citywide growth in bicycle ridership depended heavily on an influx of college-educated whites into gentrifying neighborhoods.

Under current patterns of urban development and demographic change, Portland's established goals of preventing displacement (The City of Portland, 2012) while also reaching 25 percent bicycle ridership (City of Portland Bureau of Transportation, 2010) seem to be incompatible.

Policy and research implications

We have demonstrated that bicycle ridership and displacement are correlated in Portland. However, the root cause of contemporary displacement lies in the market-based provision of housing, not in the distribution of bicycle infrastructure (though further research into the effects of bicycle infrastructure on surrounding property values would be of interest, along the lines of El-Geneidy and Wasfi (forthcoming)). It is the city's orientation toward promoting growth, rather than ensuring housing stability, that allows seemingly benign neighborhood improvements such as bicycle infrastructure to serve as signifiers of gentrification, in so much as they align with the lifestyle preferences of incoming residents, while lower-income residents are pushed out. It is telling, though not surprising, that Portland has a long-range master plan for bicycle infrastructure, yet does not have a serious plan for preventing displacement.

To seriously combat displacement, then, would require a concerted, co-ordinated policy response centered on intervention in the property and housing markets. This has not happened in Portland, as the neoliberal model of urban growth and governance embraced by this city entails the abandonment of the local state's redistributionary and regulatory functions (Hackworth, 2007). Recently, however, a broad-based coalition of 30 Portland advocacy organizations has joined forces to push back against the City's market-oriented development model.[1] Known as Anti-Displacement PDX, this coalition includes organizations representing specific racial, ethnic, and cultural populations (Urban League of Portland, Portland African American Leadership Forum, Asian Pacific American Network of Oregon, Coalition of Communities of Color), neighborhood-based groups (Living Cully, N/NE Neighbors for Housing Affordability), issue-specific organizations (Upstream Public Health, Community Cycling Center, Housing Land Advocates, Community Alliance of Tenants), and non-profit affordable housing providers (ROSE Community Development, PCRI, Proud Ground Community Land Trust).

Anti-Displacement PDX has advanced a platform of 11 anti-displacement measures, and pushed for their inclusion in Portland's new Comprehensive Plan—a 20-year plan governing growth, development, and infrastructure investment (Manning, 2015). In July 2015, Portland's Planning and Sustainability Commission adopted its recommended draft of the Plan, including all 11 measures proposed by Anti-Displacement PDX (Bell, 2015). Portland City Council was scheduled to begin hearings on the Plan in fall 2015, with a final vote expected in early 2016.

Many of the measures the coalition supports would directly challenge Portland's neoliberal trajectory by requiring the City to intervene in the real estate and housing markets, with the dual goals of preventing displacement of current residents and expanding access to affordable housing citywide. One of the central pillars of Anti-Displacement PDX's agenda is an impact analysis that would be carried out by the City to anticipate how future plans, investments, and development would affect housing affordability and displacement (Law, 2015). Other proposed measures include stronger protections for renters, land-banking to remove property from the market and set it aside for affordable housing, and mechanisms to recapture windfall property values created by public investments and infrastructure (potentially including bicycle facilities).

Closing remarks

Having examined the link between bicycling and gentrification in Portland, we believe the demographic and spatial makeup of the city's bicycle ridership gains need to be better understood by policymakers, bicycle activists, and scholars. Our analysis leads us to conclude that the celebration of Portland's bicycle success is, simultaneously, a celebration of gentrification. If Portland continues to be the U.S. model for "green" transportation, other cities may also face the dynamics brought to light by our analysis.

Just as bicycles and bicyclists do not *cause* gentrification and displacement, but are rather part of the particular way that those forces manifest themselves in Portland (and likely other cities), gentrification and displacement will not be solved in the realm of bicycle infrastructure and policy. Gentrification is a structural phenomenon, requiring structural solutions—such as those put forward by Anti-Displacement PDX. Bicycle advocates and others who are concerned with equitable access to high-opportunity, bike-able, accessible neighborhoods, would do well to ally with those groups in their cities that are advancing agendas to fundamentally shift the neoliberal orientation of local government, especially in relation to the property and housing markets.

Note

1 Co-author Cameron Herrington is an employee of one of these 30 organizations.

References

Baltes, M. (1996). Factors Influencing Nondiscretionary Work Trips by Bicycle Determined from 1990 U.S. Census Metropolitan Statistical Area Data. *Transportation Research Record: Journal of the Transportation Research Board*, 1538, pp.96–101.

Bates, L. (2013). *Gentrification and Displacement Study: Implementing an Equitable Inclusive Development Strategy in the Context of Gentrification*. Portland, OR: City of Portland

Bureau of Planning and Sustainability. [online]. Available from: www.portlandoregon.gov/bps/article/454027 [Accessed September 19, 2015].

Beauregard, R.A. (1986). The Chaos and Complexity of Gentrification. In N. Smith & W. Peter, eds. *Gentrification of the City*. Boston, MA: Allen & Unwin, pp. 35–55.

Bell, J. (2015). City Will Consider Adopting Affordable Housing, Anti-Displacement Language into Comprehensive Plan. *Portland Business Journal*. [online]. Available from: www.bizjournals.com/portland/blog/real-estate-daily/2015/07/city-will-consider-adopting-affordable-housing.html [Accessed September 19, 2015].

City of Portland Bureau of Transportation. (2010). *Portland Bicycle Plan for 2030*. Portland, OR. [online]. Available from: www.portlandoregon.gov/transportation/article/289122 [Accessed September 19, 2015].

City of Portland Bureau of Transportation. (2012). *North Williams Traffic Operations Safety Project*. Portland, OR. [online]. Available from: www.portlandoregon.gov/transportation/article/417219 [Accessed September 19, 2015].

City of Portland Bureau of Transportation. (2013). *N Williams Traffic Safety Project Map*. Portland, OR. [online]. Available from: www.portlandoregon.gov/transportation/article/498535 [Accessed September 19, 2015].

DeFilippis, J. (2004). *Unmaking Goliath: Community Control in the Face of Global Capital*. New York, NY: Routledge.

El-Geneidy, A. & Wasfi, R. (Forthcoming). Do People Value Bicycle Sharing? A Multilevel Longitudinal Analysis Capturing the Impact of Bicycle Sharing on Residential Sales in Montreal, Canada. *Transport Policy*.

FHWA. (2011). *Summary of Travel Trends: 2009 National Household Travel Survey*. Washington, DC: U.S. Department of Transportation & Federal Highway Administration.

Gibson, K.J. (2007). Bleeding Albina: A History of Community Disinvestment, 1940–2000. *Journal of the Association of Black Anthropologists*, 15(1), pp. 3–25.

Hackworth, J.R. (2007). *The Neoliberal City: Governance, Ideology, and Development in American Urbanism*. Ithaca, NY: Cornell University Press.

Harvey, D. (2012). *Rebel Cities*. New York, NY: Verso.

Jacobs, J. (1961). *The Death and Life of Great American Cities*. New York, NY: Random House.

Jurjevich, J. & Schrock, G. (2012). *Is Portland Really the Place Where Young People Go to Retire? Migration Patterns of Portland's Young and College Educated, 1980–2010*. [online]. Available from: http://mkn.research.pdx.edu/wpcontent/uploads/2012/09/JurjevichSchrockMigrationReport1.pdf [Accessed September 19, 2015].

Law, S. (2015). 11-point Plan Strives to Slow Gentrification. *Portland Tribune*. [online]. Available from: http://portlandtribune.com/pt/9-news/263964-136208-11-point-plan-strives-to-slow-gentrification [Accessed September 19, 2015].

League of American Bicyclists (2012). *Bicycle Commute Data from 1990 to 2011 for the 70 Largest U.S. Cities, Including Percentage of Bicycle Commuters and Percent Change*. Washington, DC. [online]. Available from: www.bikeleague.org/sites/default/files/70 largest cities.xls [Accessed September 19, 2015].

Lubitow, A. & Miller, T.R. (2013). Contesting Sustainability: Bikes, Race, and Politics in Portlandia. *Environmental Justice*, 6(4), pp. 121–126.

Manning, R. (2015). Portland City Leaders Support Anti-Displacment Proposals. *Oregon Public Broadcasting*. [online]. Available from: www.opb.org/news/article/portland-city-commissioners-support-anti-displacment-proposals/ [Accessed September 19, 2015].

Marcuse, P. (2012). A Critical Approach to Solving the Housing Problem. In *Cities for People, Not for Profit*. New York, NY: Routledge, pp. 215–230.

Maus, J. (2011a). *A Williams Ave Resident Addresses History, Traffic Safety Issues*. [online]. Available from: http://bikeportland.org/2011/07/26/a-williams-ave-resident-addresses-history-traffic-safety-issues-56815 [Accessed September 19, 2015].

Maus, J. (2011b). *Meeting On Williams Project Turns into Discussion of Race, Gentrification*. [online]. Available from: http://bikeportland.org/2011/07/21/racism-rears-its-head-on-williams-project-56633 [Accessed September 19, 2015].

Maus, J. (2011c). *North Williams Project Delayed to Address Community Concerns – Updated*. [online]. Available from: http://bikeportland.org/2011/06/07/williams-bikeway-project-delayed-to-address-community-concerns-54361 [Accessed September 19, 2015].

Mele, C. (2012). Neoliberalism, Race and the Redefining of Urban Redevelopment. *International Journal of Urban Regional Research*, 37(2), pp. 598–617.

Piven, F.F. & Cloward, R.A. (1977). *Poor People's Movements*. New York, NY: Pantheon Books.

Portland Development Commission. *Neighborhood Prosperity Initiative & Main Street Network*. [online]. Available from: www.pdc.us/for-businesses/business-district-programs-support/neighborhood-prosperity.aspx [Accessed November 30, 2015].

Purcell, M. (2003). Citizenship and the Right to the Global City: Reimagining the Capitalist World Order. *International Journal of Urban and Regional Research*, 27(3), pp. 564–590.

Rietveld, P. & Daniel, V. (2004). Determinants of Bicycle Use: Do Municipal Policies Matter? *Transportation Research Part A: Policy and Practice*, 38(7), pp. 531–550.

Scott, A. (2012). By the Grace of God. *Portland Monthly*. [online]. Available from: www.pdxmonthly.com/articles/2012/2/17/african-american-churches-north-portland-march-2012 [Accessed September 19, 2015].

Smith, N. (1987). Gentrification and the Rent Gap. *Annals of the Association of American Geographers*, 77(3), pp. 462–465.

Squites, G.D. (1994). *Capital and Communities in Black and White: The Intersections of Race, Class, and Uneven Development*. Albany, NY: SUNY Press.

Sullivan, D.M. & Shaw, S.C. (2011). Retail Gentrification and Race: The Case of Alberta Street in Portland, Oregon. *Urban Affairs Review*, 47(3), pp. 413–432.

Swyngedouw, E. (2007). Impossible 'Sustainability' and the Postpolitical Condition. In R. Krueger & D. Gibbs, eds. *The Sustainable Development Paradox: Urban Political Economy in the United States and Europe*. New York, NY: The Guilford Press, pp. 13–40.

The City of Portland. (2012). *The Portland Plan*. Portland, OR: The City of Portland. [online]. Available from: www.portlandonline.com/portlandplan/ [Accessed September 19, 2015].

The League of American Bicyclists & The Sierra Club. (2013). *The New Majority: Pedaling Towards Equity*. Washington, DC. [online]. Available from: www.bikeleague.org/sites/default/files/equity_report.pdf [Accessed September 19, 2015].

U.S. Census Bureau. (2000). *2000 Census Summary File 1*. Washington, DC. [online]. Available from: http://factfinder2.census.gov [Accessed September 19, 2015].

U.S. Census Bureau. (2010). *American Community Survey, 2010 American Community Survey 1-Year Estimates*. Washington, DC. [online]. Available from: http://factfinder2.census.gov [Accessed September 19, 2015].

4 Freedom of movement/ freedom of choice

An enquiry into utility cycling and social justice in post-apartheid Cape Town, 1994–2015

Gail Jennings

Introduction

Since at least the 1970s in Cape Town, South Africa, recreational cyclists have been advocating for bicycle lanes and associated facilities, in an attempt to persuade more people to ride as a mode of transport; their arguments have largely focused on the environmental, lifestyle, health, and fuel-saving benefits of bicycle mobility. That bicycle transport might contribute toward a social justice outcome is a more recent narrative, emerging since the development of a user-oriented transport policy after the first democratic elections in 1994.

In this chapter, social justice or equity – as a broad concept – refers to an equitable or progressive distribution of the benefits and impacts of a particular transport intervention, or its potential to redress a legacy of inequity (Litman, 2014; Martens and Golub, 2011). South Africa's Bill of Rights (Chapter 2 of the Constitution) implicitly guarantees access and mobility: for example, access to housing, health [care], food, water, and education. Subsequent policy commits the state to redress spatial inequities, attend to transport users' needs, alleviate poverty, and 'democratise' decision-making.

This chapter has two key aims: to broadly determine in what way utility cycling is able to contribute toward social justice; and to understand how effective an explicit social justice narrative is in achieving this outcome. In an attempt to answer these questions, the chapter examines the public and policy discourse around social justice and utility cycling, as well as the practice of bicycle planning, implementation, and bicycle use. The chapter draws on a variety of sources, including public policy, media releases, official speeches, city reports, and social media. What seems to emerge is that for utility cycling to achieve full integration into the mobility system, a more nuanced understanding is required of the narratives that either encourage or discourage political commitment and increase bicycle use. The post-apartheid narrative may see 'motorisation for all' as an extension of the broader transformation narrative, and until bicycle mobility resonates unambivalently with that transformation narrative, its use may remain a symbol of the state's failure to triumphantly emerge into the modern world.

Background

Utility cycling (cycling as a mode of transport) in South Africa exists within a spatial context where the means of mobility has historically been deployed as an instrument of control (Czeglédy, 2004). As von Schnitzler has described it, 'apartheid was . . . made functional via its infrastructures insofar as [it] was at one level simply a grand scheme to channel and police mobility' (2015).

In his budget debate of April 2013, South Africa's then deputy Minister of Transport (and Deputy General-Secretary of the SA Communist Party) Jeremy Cronin eloquently summarised the transport inequities that continue to entrench disadvantage and poverty:

> Why after 18 years of democracy do we still encounter so many challenges with public transport in our country? Throughout the 20th century, segregationist urban settlement controls increasingly reproduced the structural reality: the black working class was settled in remote, peri-urban reserves, dormitory townships, far enough away from the commanding heights of power and wealth to be contained and controlled, close enough to be migrated daily to work in factories, shops, and white suburban homes. This has resulted in a persisting, racialised urban geography. Black workers and the urban poor continue to be hugely disadvantaged by their geographical marginalisation in dormitory townships. The average public transport trip in London is 8 km, in Cape Town the average bus trip is 20 km.

In Cape Town, the average travel time to work (across all motorised travel modes) is 90 minutes, with public transport users averaging 110 minutes (Hitge and Vanderschuren, 2015). The debilitating consequences of urban sprawl include the reduced viability of public transport systems, which are infrequent during off-peak. As Cronin describes it: 'The bus fleets can only make one over-crowded trip in the morning and one in the evening peak periods.'

Transport fares account for a disproportionate percentage of the income of the poor (Bruun et al., 2016); according to a StatsSA report (Nicolson, 2015), 37 per cent of people in the country do not have enough money to purchase both food and non-food items, thus sacrifice food to pay for necessities such as transport. Non-motorised transport users, overwhelmingly low-income, bear an inequitable burden of road traffic deaths. In Cape Town, walking accounts for between 40–57 per cent of road fatalities (Jobanputra, 2013; Behrens, 2006); cycling is a minor mode, somewhere between 0.5–1 per cent of all trips (Bruun et al., 2016), yet accounts for 3 per cent of fatalities.

Bicycle transport and associated facilities were not the immediate focus of post-1994 planners and politicians; like much of the developing world, in a country eager to leapfrog its history as a marginalised global player and re-envision itself as a modern state, private cars and modern buses have come to symbolise private as well as national economic achievement and social status (Buliung et al., 2015). Even South Africa's Public Transport Strategy (NDoT, 2007a) in noting the extent of transport disadvantage in the country, used private cars as the benchmark: '[there are] 38 million citizens live in households with NO access to a car [original capitalisation]; and 40 million citizens do not have a driver's licence'.

When delivering his address at the National Council of Provinces in 2009, Minister of Transport Sibusiso Ndebele[1] voiced the country's hegemonic under-standing of our transport future: 'We cannot be a developed country unless our transport system is developed.' Thus in setting out to redress the spatial and transport-disadvantage legacies of apartheid, the political focus was on the transformative and 'big bang' possibilities of high-tech, high-visibility mega-projects such as bus rapid transit (BRT) (Jennings, 2015b). These projects promised to deliver greater transport justice or equity, and it is upon these systems that South Africa seems to have pinned its transport hopes and dreams (Lucas, 2011). South Africa's Public Transport Strategy, affirming that transport is indeed able to act as a 'catalyst . . . in correcting spatial distortions', described BRT as 'the mobility wave of the future and . . . the only viable option that can ensure sustainable, *equitable* and uncongested mobility in livable cities . . .' (NDoT, 2007a).

Bicycle transport: a mode for the marginalised

There is certainly an argument that like BRT, bicycle transport is also able to ensure sustainable and uncongested mobility, and alleviate poverty. Bicycling is immediately available, flexible, low-cost (after the initial purchase), door-to-door and on-demand. Public transport transformation, on the other hand, has long lead times to implementation, and requires significant investment; it is likely that current poor-quality services will remain in Cape Town for a considerable period of time.

There is consensus within the limited peer-reviewed research that cycling has considerable potential, particularly among low-income users (Behrens et al., 2015). And policy positions have broadly recognised this transformative potential of the bicycle, for improving local access, reducing travel costs, and contributing toward poverty alleviation and sustainable livelihoods (Jennings, 2015a; Labuschagne and Ribbens, 2014).

Although in the White Paper on National Transport Policy (1996) no specific mention of NMT[2], or bicycle transport, was made, one of its formal outcomes was the Public Transport Action Plan (NDoTb, 2007); this Plan regards NMT primarily as a feeder mode to public transport, and sees bicycles – as taxis and rental schemes for tourists – as offering *job-creation* opportunities. The Action Plan proposes mechanisms by which to distribute free bicycles to potential low-income users, as '*access* to bicycles is key factor in increasing the number of people that cycle to *access* public transport.'

The Draft National NMT Policy (NDoT, 2008) is more explicit in its goals to redress inequities: the foreword, by the then Minister of Transport, Jeff Radebe, states that 'this NMT Policy is one of the Department of Transport's interventions towards *reversing challenges of accessibility* and *mobility* . . . and eventually putting NMT where it belongs, i.e. as a recognised mode of transport'.

Using somewhat ambivalent language, the policy describes cycling as 'a necessary mode of transport for the poor who can afford nothing else besides the other alternative, which is to walk' (NDoT, 2008); these cyclists are categorised as 'captive users', '*forced* to use NMT due to its affordability . . . and disadvantaged by distance' (PGWC, 2009).

Among the NMT Policy statements are a desire to 'meet the mobility needs and improve the quality of life of *marginalised* peoples, to use NMT to *bridge the economic and social gaps between* . . . *first and second economies*', and a commitment to 'ensure that cycling as transport plays a role in *economic development* and *poverty alleviation*.' NMT is described positively in the policy: healthy, non-polluting, versatile, *affordable*, *accessible* and *reliable*; NMT modes '*encourage local movement* and *hence support local community facilities*' and deliver '*significant potential economic and environmental benefits to society*.' At provincial government level, the Draft NMT in the Western Cape Strategy (PGWC, 2009) aims to 'redress past imbalances', particularly the 'situation of *inequity* in urban development and transport provision.'

The City of Cape Town (CCT)'s draft NMT Policy and Strategy (CCT, 2005) raises the concern that '*access* for all citizens . . . is becoming more problematic and is fundamentally a result of *inequity* on various levels.' Its vision is to contribute toward improved access by '*increas[ing] cycling and encourage[ing] walking by creating a safe and pleasant bicycle and pedestrian network of paths* . . .'. A secondary objective is to 'effect *social and economic empowerment* through improved *low-cost mobility*'.

The policy discourse has accurately captured the motives for utility cycling in Cape Town. While the print and social media make the claim that an increasing number of private-vehicle owners now travel by bicycle, most surveyed bicycle commuters live in the disadvantaged, peripheral areas where private car ownership is low and reliance on public transport is high (Boulle, 2013; NDoT, 2007a; Bechstein, 2010; Engelbrecht and Grobler, 2010; CCT, 2009). These cyclists ride to save money on minibus-taxi fare and experience travel flexibility and independence (Lucas, 2011): '*I save a lot of money – R500 per month. I've used a [minibus]-taxi before, now I'm saving all that*' (28-year-old, interviewed by Engelbrecht and Grobler, 2010).

Two friends in their twenties describe the way in which bicycles offer the flexibility and independence not created by public transport: [we] '*don't like taxis because they always make us late. With a bicycle you don't have to ask anyone,*' notes the younger of the two. '*You just go*' (Engelbrecht and Grobler, 2010).

There is also evidence of the use of bicycles to make a living, particularly in order to deliver or sell goods or to increase mobility. In 2013, the press widely reported the story of Sizwe Nzima of Khayelitsha, a low-income area on the outskirts of Cape Town. Nzima started social enterprise Iyeza Express to deliver chronic medication by bicycle from the local clinic to the patients' homes; in that same year he was included in Forbes Africa's 30 Young Entrepreneurs Under 30.[3] Home-based carers at clinics in Cape Town have declared being able to visit at least twice as many patients by bicycle as on foot,[4] and non-governmental organisation Qhubeka reports its bicycle beneficiaries experiencing reduced fatigue (particularly school-going learners), reduced travel time, and travel cost savings.[5] These stories remain a rarity, however, with little by way of legislative, regulatory, or entrepreneurial assistance. National Government's own country-wide programme to distribute affordable bicycles, Shova Kalula, attained between 6–8 per cent of its planned targets between 2008 and 2010. 'At this

Figure 4.1 Qhubeka's marketing campaign: the campaign includes a focus on the social justice possibilities of bicycle transport – reducing travel time, travel costs and fatigue

Source: © Qhubeka.

rate,' writes one of the programme directors, 'the programme is unlikely ever to achieve its goal of . . . mainstreaming bicycles in the transport system' (Mashiri et al., 2013).

Bicycle transport: 'faster than a car'

> It is inappropriate to claim that [bicycle lanes in wealthy areas] are an anti-poor measure . . . The first victims of climate change will not be the [wealthy . . .] but millions of the poorest. . . .[6]

A substantial mode shift from private vehicle to utility cycling has the potential to mitigate climate change and reduce the number of road deaths caused by vehicles, both of which have an inequitable impact on the poor (Vasconcellos, 2012; CCT, 2014b). There is eventually a social justice outcome when policies and programmes promote bicycle use among the privileged.

South Africa's National NMT Policy (NDoT, 2008) acknowledges that bicycle transport could attract the car-owner, describing the bicycle as a 'silent', 'economical' [fuel-saving], 'discreet' vehicle that is, 'above all . . . faster than a *car* over short distances' (NDoT, 2008). The Western Cape's NMT Strategy categorises these cyclists as somewhat fickle 'choice' users, who:

> choose to use NMT, primarily cycling, as a form of transport because of the many benefits associated with NMT use, even though they may have access to a motorised mode. These discretionary users require a high quality of services and infrastructure, and may revert to motorised travel if quality is not adequate.
> (PGWC, 2009)

It is these 'choice' users who are the target audience for the 'green transport' narrative: the bicycle as a low-carbon, sustainable, non-polluting, healthy, climate-mitigating, fuel-saving, parking and congestion-reducing vehicle relatively routinely features in the policy and public discourse (e.g. NDoT, 2008; CCT, 2005, 2013b, 2014b: Mashiri et al., 2013; Glaser et al., 2013). In the scope of work issued by the City of Cape Town for a Cycling Strategy (2015), the request was for an exploration of the core benefits of cycling, listed as congestion reduction, emissions reduction, and health benefits.

When interviewed, bicycle commuters who do have access to personal motorised transport reveal a set of reasons for riding[7] in common with the resistance or revolutionary culture of the United States (Furness, 2010; Mapes, 2009). These cyclists are more likely to ride as a way of reducing their individual carbon footprint, to 'show motorists that we have the right to be in the road', and to evangelise about urban quality, social justice, and car-dependencies.

'Paperwork rather than progress'

Neither the social justice nor the 'green lifestyle' policy discourse has been particularly successful in delivering a 'bicycle-friendly' Cape Town to either choice or captive users: despite the benefits for those individuals who choose to

Figure 4.2 The third print edition of the Cape Town Green Map features City of Cape Town Executive Mayor, Alderman Patricia de Lille, on the cover.

Figure 4.3 An article featuring cyclists in Cape Town, in *Highlife* South Africa magazine. The introduction to the article, pictured above, reads as follows: 'There was a time when only entrants in the Cape Argus, the world's largest individually timed cycle race – dared navigate the streets of Cape Town by bicycle. But these days there's a new tribe of cyclists on the streets'

Source: © Highlife South Africa magazine, edition March 2014, photographed by www.knittogether. co.za.

ride, utility cycling remains marginal, difficult, and dangerous on the whole. The visionary infrastructure of South Africa's Public Transport plan has not materialised on a comprehensive scale.

There is little sustained attention paid to encouraging utility cycling, with a largely fragmented and inconsistent application of bicycle infrastructure and erratic integration with public transport (Labuschagne and Ribbens, 2014; Jennings, 2015b), which reduces the potential for easy intermodality. Bicycle lanes are rarely enforced,[8] the road safety record remains poor, and helmets are mandatory. Utility bicycles are relatively expensive to purchase, and by-laws pertaining to mobile trading are a barrier to micro-enterprise (Boulle, 2013). Bicycle promotion activities are the domain of volunteer and non-governmental organisations. The available travel survey data in Cape Town supports neither a claim that bicycle mode share is increasing, nor that bicycle travel is becoming safer (Jennings, 2015b).

Appeals for car-competitive bicycle facilities gathered momentum in the 1970s, when the 'oil crisis' led to campaigns by civil society for 'the provision of cycle paths ... In an age of soaring costs of fuel, vehicle licences, car prices, insurance . . . the pedal cycle has become an increasing attractive proposition'.[9] The call was met by political support: the national minister overseeing the fuel strategy was photographed on the cover of the leading Sunday newspaper, claiming that bicycles are 'a healthy way to beat the fuel crisis'.[10] In 1977, two recreational riders organised the first 'Big Ride-In' to draw attention to the need for cycle infrastructure, led by the then mayor of Cape Town John Tyers. Thirty-five years later, one of the founders conceded that 'the Ride-In was a "dismal failure" as the pace of cycle lane construction has been extraordinarily slow'.[11]

Since 2010, Cape Town has implemented approximately 25km of purpose-designed and built bicycle lanes,[12] complementing what the City describes as an NMT network of some 435km (CCT, 2013a). This tally includes a number of reallocated sidewalks that cyclists are permitted to share with pedestrians and street furniture, and 100km or so of lanes either painted on the roadway or marked within the shoulder.[13] Recent road upgrades on key connecting bicycle routes have not included bicycle facilities, with limited road space, and a concern that the level of service for private vehicles will be reduced, cited as the reasons.[14]

Mashiri et al. suggest that, essentially, there is less to the policy support for utility cycling than meets the eye; a 'politically correct' inclusion without genuine conviction. 'Paperwork rather than progress characterises the government's stance on making cycling safe' (Mashiri et al., 2013).

Asking users what they need: nothing about us without us

If the outcome of local and national policy has failed to date to significantly shift either the pace of implementation of high-quality facilities, or the promotion and rate of bicycle use, has the planning process at least 'democratised' decision-making? 'Process' or 'opportunity' equity (Levinson, 2010) concerns the extent to which someone has fair access to a planning process that affects them. However, policy-makers and planners notoriously ignore NMT users and their needs (Mitullah and Opiyo, 2012; Pendakur, 2005; Kane, 2006) and unless determined steps are taken to invite the participation of the marginalised, only the needs of the most vocal lobby groups, frequently motorists or choice cyclists, are likely to be heard (Barter and Raad, 2000).

South Africa's White Paper on National Transport Policy (NDoT, 1996) does propose measures to '*democratise decision-making*' within the transport sector, and the National Land Transport Act (NLTA) (NDot, 2009) mandates the increased use of public transport that, among others, 'encourages, promotes and facilitates public consultation and participation in the planning, regulation and implementation of public transport.'

Engagement and consultation with Interested and Affected Parties is a critical step within each local authority's Integrated Transport Plan (ITP) (CCT, 2013b). However, invitations to engagement around NMT matters[15] reflect an almost entirely 'choice user' database. During public engagement processes associated with high-profile bicycle interventions – such as the dedicated facilities linking the suburbs to the CBD, the 2010 FIFA World Cup 'fan walk', the Phase 1 BRT routes, and Woodstock's Albert Road – stakeholders largely comprise organisa-tions that reflect a choice or sports and recreational ridership, though some have adopted the sincere rhetoric of social justice, equity, poverty alleviation, or community connection/social inclusion in their vision statements.[16]

Public participation meetings are usually advertised in the local and neigh-bourhood press and radio, social media and email, on the CCT's website, as well as with mail drops and posters. When a particularly popular scenic coastal bicycle route (Cape Town's Muizenberg/Kalk Bay main road) was to be upgraded between 2007 and 2010, intercept interviews with commuter cyclists, however, pointed to perhaps 10 per cent of them living within the public participation 'catchment' area; most live some 12–20km beyond the middle-class neighbourhood, and traverse this route from nearby low-income areas on their way to work. When questioned, they were not aware of public participation opportunities, nor had they registered as interested and affected parties. One Kalk Bay harbour worker interviewed, who had been cycling on and off the route for eight years, said that once the upgrade was finished it was going to be 'OK' for motorists, although it was still going to be difficult for cyclists. '*Sometimes you just have to put up with things.*'[17]

The absence of the voice of the marginalised cyclist has not gone unnoticed by the local authority, with the CCT repeatedly issuing a call for represent-atives or representative bodies at bicycle forum meetings from low-income user groups.[18] Yet such organisations have proven difficult to find. Where popular transport-related activism does exist, the call is largely for improved, more affordable public transport – as it has been since at least the 1940s (Lodge, 1983).

In 2013, the CCT used its review of the ITP (CCT, 2013b) as an opportunity to consult transport users though an intercept survey, including car-drivers, public transport users, and people captive to NMT or unable to travel at all. The key issues experienced by the latter two were the poor safety and security on public transport, its high costs and long waiting times, and walking distances to public transport: users expressed an urgent need for better, affordable, accessible public transport.

Transport commuter and passenger associations continue to exist in low-income areas throughout the country; some with high-profile constitutional court victories to their name. Each is focused on public transport (bus or rail) – the most recently founded organisation, Public Transport Voice in Cape Town, has an explicitly rights-based agenda, promoting '*the rights to equality and public transport, with the firm belief that these will enable the poor and working classes to an equal opportunity in life.*'[19]

A desire for better motorised transport is keenly felt even among bicycle users. In 2007, I conducted a series of interviews with health-care workers who paid home visits on bicycles donated by an international non-governmental organisa-tion. All understood that bicycles were faster and more efficient than walking, and cheaper, healthier, and more flexible than public transport. Yet most pre-ferred public transport, and one group asked that donors provide a dedicated minibus-taxi rather than another tranche of bicycles. Said one of the carers in her mid-twenties: 'I have to muster all my courage to ride.'

Bicycle facilities *versus* public transport provision found fertile ground in Western Cape party politics in 2011, where the political opposition[20] (the African National Congress in alliance with the Congress of South African Trade Unions and the South African Communist Party) condemned new bicycle facilities associated with MyCiTi phase 1 network as an additional transport option for the already 'choice' user, when the funding should have been spent elsewhere:

> The public policy outcomes funded by the public purse must . . . respond firstly to people who have no alternative transport. So, if ever there is a contest . . . then the workers needs should be prioritised, and his mode of public transport prioritised. . . . prioritise the urgent needs of the majority, before we give additional options to the over-privileged. The bicycle routes are important, but they must be second to the train routes, given the realities of our communities.[21]

Freedom needs twenty-first century transport

It should come as no surprise that political mobilisation as well as public policy has centred on public transport and its opportunities for redressing spatial inequity, given public transport's poor quality and reach, and that it carries almost 50 per cent of commuters nationally, and close to 40 per cent in Cape Town (Bruun et al., 2016).

While the language of bicycle activists highlights the freedom a bicycle brings,[22] the political elite have suggested otherwise: it's a restrictive or limiting mode. In 2009, Minister of Transport Sibusiso Ndebele proposed that: '*Everywhere in our country must be reachable by car. Having a car is freedom.*'[23] In 2010, mayor of Johannesburg Amos Masondo, and past-president of International Local Governments for Sustainability (ICLEI), declared that bicycle commuting [for him] is an example of 'going to the extreme.'[24]

The low-esteem in which bicycle transport is held by certain of the political elite is also reflected by the urban poor, precisely the mobility constrained for whom bicycle transport is proposed a solution (Labuschagne and Ribbens, 2014; Pendakur, 2005; Rwebangira, 2001; Servaas, 2000; Mashiri et al., 2013).

Interviews with cyclists in two low-income areas in Cape Town bear this out. A 29-year-old Malawian citizen who has lived in Cape Town for 11 years travels 10km every day. He rents a one-roomed shack, and has been riding for eight years. 'They (locals) don't ride bicycles,' he says. 'They feel sorry for us (foreigners): it's like we are suffering and that we don't have money to pay for a taxi.' His 26-year-old neighbour says that bicycles are an 'old-fashioned way' and they 'lower your individual status'.[25]

In their interviews with 'everyday cyclists', Engelbrecht and Grobler (2010) encountered a young, educated bicycle salesperson in central Cape Town, who vividly described his dilemma:

> To come with a bicycle [in Cape Town] . . . here is a no, no . . . It's a matter of status. You know, I speak for black people – they would say: "Why don't you have a car?" . . . A friend of mine was like "Wow, shit, you can't be riding a bicycle." And she put that on Facebook. . . . We need to break the stigma that when you ride a bicycle you're poor. Because people have that mentality of thinking, you have to drive a Mercedes or whatever.

Yet alongside the dual narratives of low-cost mobility for the poor, and low-carbon transport for the wealthier, is a rhetoric of bicycles as 'world-class' – contesting the hegemonic narrative of a strictly motorised modernity. Perhaps this follows the lead of Western Europe and the United States, where cycling has exploded in popularity over the past two decades (Pucher et al., 2011). This latter narrative punctuates the history of utility cycling in Cape Town and the country as a whole; an unexpected catalyst to the gradual increase in bicycling's visibility.

In March 2006, Cape Town hosted an international bicycle planning conference, Velo Mondial, which closed with Cape Town being awarded 'Gold Status' for its bicycle planning. The tourism and global branding potential of 'bicycle-friendliness' was invoked in support of the city's business case for a public bicycle system, and in preparation for its (successful) World Design Capital 2014 bid – bicycles are seen as an indicator of 'world-class', 'global competitiveness' (CCT, 2014b; Hoffman and Lugo, 2014; Jennings, 2014; PGWC, 2013).

The big push for bicycle infrastructure came when South Africa won the bid to host the 2010 FIFA World Cup and set about allaying critics' fears of how they would move between matches and venues – bicycle parking was installed in Cape Town's central city, and as part of Cape Town's 'vision to provide a world-class sustainable transport system for all'[26] a 5km 'fan walk' was built between Cape Town Station and the Cape Town Stadium, comprising wide, segregated bicycle and pedestrian facilities as well as bicycle signalisation.

In July 2010, Minister of Transport Sibusiso Ndebele praised that legacy of the World Cup: *'the tournament has brought South Africa's transport system into the 21st century.'* And while that '21st-century' transport system meant the beginnings of BRT, it also introduced an attendant focus on NMT infrastructure on feeder routes. When Cape Town's most ambitious, dedicated bicycle route was revealed in 2011, it travelled parallel and as a feeder to MyCiTi's phase 1 corridor, and was launched by yet another Cape Town mayor on a bicycle, Dan Plato. Recognising that these routes would be used largely by 'choice' cyclists, the City invited riders to *'abandon their cars'* for the celebratory community ride.[27] The next phase of MyCiTi is in planning stage – this time serving low-income communities in the south-east of Cape Town; the associated NMT facilities are likely to be shared sidewalks rather than exclusive lanes, because of concerns with road space and the demands BRT infrastructure places on the available road reserve.[28]

Concluding thoughts

This chapter set out to consider the interface between utility cycling and social justice. Can bicycle transportation deliver social justice in post-apartheid Cape Town? Can a social justice narrative best deliver better bicycle transportation?

Activism among the mobility-disadvantaged centres on the provision of motorised rather than non-motorised modes and facilities. Those who passionately call for cycling-led social justice and social integration, steering the discourse from 'green transport' to one in which the bicycle is a vehicle to 'ride the [social, spatial, or racial] divide', are largely the privileged, the 'choice' cyclists with accessible alternatives. This is a risky though well-meaning strategy, in a country with a history of constrained and constraining mobility, where the choices of the majority were for centuries limited by the privileged few.

Where social justice means redressing transport disadvantage, meeting the expressed needs of the majority – who wait in long queues, in darkness, in rain, for trains or buses that might never come – then the transformation of public transport is a priority. It is true that utility cycling is affordable, extends access to facilities necessary to participate fully in urban life and the local economy, and is unrestricted by schedules, waiting times, and off-peak infrequency. Yet little has changed spatially since the end of apartheid (Turok et al., 2011); travel distances remain extensive, more often than not too far for a comfortable ride.

But social justice also means access to decision-making and planning processes: despite an apparent disinterest in bicycle activism and public engagement, many thousands of low-income commuters *do* ride: it would be a mistake to assume that the less vocal bicycle commuters do not desire high-quality, exclusive bicycle networks, or to regard the 'captive-choice' division as impermeable and that all low-income cyclists would shift to public transport were it to be provided.

There certainly is evidence that bicycle mobility can contribute to social justice: as has been argued, bicycles have delivered cost savings, increased access and mobility, and opportunities for sustainable livelihoods in Cape Town. Nor are the broad environmental, lifestyle, health and fuel-saving benefits of bicycle mobility in doubt. But it should be recognised that the post-apartheid narrative may see 'motorisation for all' freedom of movement – as an extension of the broader transformation narrative, and that utility cycling is a second best option, entrenching the inequities of the past. Until bicycle mobility resonates unambivalently with the transformation narrative, its use may remain a symbol of the state's failure to triumphantly emerge into the modern world.

In South Africa, bicycle mobility has risen to the top of the agenda when the world is looking in our direction – the 2010 FIFA World Cup, the Conference of the Parties (COP) 17, the World Design Capital – and where cycling has been shown to be what the 'modern' world is doing. In the most recent example, the international ICLEI EcoMobility festival was held in Johannesburg in October 2015. The current Minister of Transport, Dipuo Peters, delivered the opening address: '*Cycling should become a way of life, our municipalities must become sustainable*'.[29]

There is danger in a narrative that is 'us' and 'them': a mobility agenda proposed by the privileged for the 'benefit' of the poor, no matter how real that benefit may be. Ultimately, a narrative that envisions bicycles not as a mode for the marginalised, or a greener trip than the car, but as one of many modern, 'world-class' urban options for all, might be the one that changes the pace of paperwork to progress – after all, 'no one wants to be associated with poverty' (Mashiri et al., 2013).

Acknowledgements

With gratitude to Assoc/Prof. Mark Zuidgeest (UCT) for his insightful comments on the numerous drafts; to James Irlam (UCT) for his reading of this chapter at short notice; and to Brett Petzer for pointing me in the direction of references I would have not found otherwise.

Notes

1 Cape Town, 7 July 2009.
2 In South Africa, walking, cycling, skateboarding, and animal-drawn transport is referred to as non-motorised transport (NMT), and is usually planned as a single mode.
3 See, for example, http://200ysa.mg.co.za/2013/sizwe-nzima/ [accessed 21 September 2015].
4 Interviews conducted by the author in 2009 for MOBILITY magazine.
5 Qhubeka.org.
6 Universities of Cape Town and Western Cape public health professors Leslie London, Louis Reynolds, and David Sanders, *Cape Times*, 14 April 2011.
7 Interviews conducted by the author in March 2010.
8 See: Anel Lewis, 15 December 2014, 'Motorists override Cape cycling lane', IOL; and Kieran Legg, 6 July 2015, 'Cape Town cycling lanes "a failure",' IOL.
9 *The Argus*, 28 May 1976.
10 *Sunday Times*, 25 February 1979.
11 Interview by the author with the founder of the Ride-In, March 2010.
12 See CCT media releases 'New cycle lanes to link southern suburbs with Cape Town central business district', 12 June 2014, and 'IRT bike paths designed for cyclists, by cyclists', 11 March 2010.
13 These calculations are approximate, sourced from the 2014 Cape Town Bicycle Map (www.capetownbicyclemap), as Cape Town largely reports infrastructure facilities by combined NMT mode.
14 For example, Camps Bay, Kalk Bay, Ou Kaapse Weg, and Kommetjie main roads: interviews with CCT officials by the author between March and October 2015.
15 For example, stakeholder invitation list to comment on NMT facility guidelines (September 2014); invitation to ITP engagement with NMT sector (26 September 2013); invitation to 'Cycling Safety Discussion: an opportunity for engagement between government and cycle organisations to make our city more cycling friends' (8 November 2012).
16 CycleLinks (wdccapetown2014.com) for, e.g., aims to 'connect communities . . . enabling commuters to connect on levels beyond social barriers and social stereotypes'; Bicycle Cape Town (bicyclecapetown.org) . . . advocate[s] to 'transform the city together'; the Bicycling Empowerment Network (benbikes.org.za) aims to 'address poverty alleviation and facilitate the accessing of opportunities through delivery of bicycles, imparting of skills and creation of employment'; and the Freedom Ride

(freedomride.co.za) 'celebrates the power of the bicycle to connect our communities and our cities.' Pedal Power Association (pedalpower.org.za), another regular contributor to engagement opportunities, is the largest cycling association in the country, most closely associated with racing and events management.

17 Interviews conducted by the author in March 2010.
18 Personal communication and attendance at Cycle Forum at which one such request was made, 7 February 2014.
19 Public Transit Voice, https://publictransportvoice.wordpress.com/.
20 Although the ANC is currently (2015) the ruling party in national government, it is the opposition party in the Western Cape as well as the City of Cape Town.
21 Tony Ehrenreich, Secretary General of COSATU Western Cape, 3 February 2011.
22 E.g. the Freedom Ride, www.freedomride.co.za.
23 Address at the National Council of Provinces in Cape Town, unscripted. Transcribed to the best of the author's ability.
24 So Many Questions, Chris Barron asks Amos Masondo, *Sunday Times*, September 2010.
25 Interviews conducted for the author by Peter Luhanga, March 2010, Dunoon, Cape Town.
26 CCT media release, 27 January 2009, 'Bicycle commuters to get more space to ride'.
27 CCT media release, 11 May 2011, 'Celebrating Cape Town's cycle paths'.
28 Email communication with CCT MyCiTi planners, 2 November 2015.
29 EcoMobility, 5 October 2015.

References

Barter, P. & Raad, T. (2000) *Taking steps: a community action guide to people-centred, equitable and sustainable urban transport*. Kuala Lumpur, Malaysia: Sustainable Transport Action Network for Asia and the Pacific (The SUSTRAN Network).

Bechstein, E. (2010) Cycling as a supplementary mode to public transport: A case study of low income commuters in South Africa. *29th Southern African Transport Conference, Pretoria*.

Behrens, R. (2006) What the national household travel survey reveals about NMT in South Africa. *25th Southern African Transport Conference, Pretoria*.

Behrens, R., Muchaka, P., Salazar Ferro, P., Schalekamp, H., & Zuidgeest, M. (2015) Mobility and access in Sub-Saharan African cities: The state of knowledge and research environments. *Volvo Research and Educational Foundations (VREF) Workshop Proceedings*.

Boulle, M. (2013) *The role of bicycles and bicycle empowerment centres in improving the mobility and livelihoods of the poor, and assisting with low-carbon development in Cape Town*. Masters dissertation, University of Cape Town.

Bruun, E., del Mistro, R., Venter, Y., & Mfinanga, D. (2016) The state of public transport in three sub-Sahran African cities. In: Behrens, R. et al. (eds.), *Paratransit in African Cities*. London: Earthscan, Ch. 2, pp. 26–58.

Buliung, R. N., Shimi, A. C., & Mitra, R. (2015) Automobility and NMT in the global south. In: Watts, A. (ed.), *The Urban Political Economy and Ecology of Automobility: Driving Cities, Driving Inequality, Driving Politics*. Abingdon: Routledge, Ch. 8.

City of Cape Town (CCT) (2005) NMT Policy and Strategy Volume 1: Status Quo Assessment.

—— (CCT) (2009) 2009 General Household Survey: Analysis for Cape Town. Strategic Development Information and GIS Department.

—— (CCT) (2013a). Development of a City-Wide Integrated Public Transport Network Household Survey Report.

—— (CCT) (2013b) Integrated Transport Plan 2013–2018.

—— (CCT) (2014a) Economic Growth Strategy.

—— (CCT) (2014b) Low-Carbon Central City Strategy.

—— (CCT) (2015) Scope of Work, Cycling Strategy, Reference No 343C/2014/15.

Czeglédy, A. (2004) Getting around town: Transportation and the built environment in post-apartheid South Africa. *City and Society*, 16(20), 63–92.

Engelbrecht, S., & Grobler, N. (2010) Bicycle portraits: Everyday South Africans and their bicycles. [Online] Available from: www.dayonepublications.com/Bicycle_Portraits/Index.html [Accessed 18 July 2014].

Furness, Z. (2010) *One Less Car: Bicycling and the Politics of Automobility*. Philadelphia, PA: Temple University Press.

Glaser, R., Cohen, B., & Mason-Jones, K. (2013) *Low Carbon Frameworks: Overview of Legal and Policy Instruments and Institutional Arrangements Relating to Transport, Land Use and Spatial Planning in South Africa*. WWF.

Hitge, G. & Vanderschuren, M. (2015) Comparison of travel time between private car and public transport in Cape Town. *Journal of the South African Institute of Civil Engineering*, 57(3), pp. 35–43.

Hoffman, M. & Lugo, A. (2014) Who is 'world class'? Transportation justice and bicycle policy. *Urbanities*, 4(1), pp. 45–61.

Jennings, G. (2014) Finding our balance: Considering the opportunities for public bicycle systems in Cape Town, South Africa. *Research in Transportation Business & Management*, 14, pp. 6–14.

Jennings, G. (2015a) A bicycling renaissance in South Africa? Policies, programmes and trends in Cape Town. *34th Southern African Transport Conference, Pretoria*.

Jennings, G. (2015b) Public transport interventions and transport justice in South Africa: a literature and policy review. *34th Southern African Transport Conference, Pretoria*.

Jobanputra, R. (2013) *Vehicle-pedestrian and infrastructure interaction in developing countries*. Thesis, Doctor of Philosophy in Civil Engineering, University of Cape Town.

Kane, L. (2006) Instilling pro-poor values into transport assessment. *Conference on Transport, Gender and Development, Port Elizabeth, South Africa*.

Labuschagne, K. & Ribbens, H. (2014) Walk the talk on the mainstreaming of NMT in South Africa. *33rd Southern African Transport Conference, Pretoria*.

Levinson, D. (2010) Equity effects of road pricing: A review. *Transport Reviews*, 30(1), pp. 33–57.

Litman, T. (2014) Evaluating transportation equity. *World Transport Policy & Practice*, 8(2), pp. 50–65.

Lodge, T. (1983) *Black politics in South Africa since 1945*. London; New York: Longman.

Lucas, K. (2011) Making the connections between transport disadvantage and the social exclusion of low-income populations in the Tshwane Region of South Africa. *Journal of Transport Geography*, 19(6), pp. 1320–1334.

Mapes, J. (2009) *Pedaling revolution: How cyclists are changing American cities*. Corvallis, OR: Oregon State University Press.

Martens, K. & Golub, A. (2011) Accessibility measures from an equity perspective. *Bijdrage aan het Colloquium Vervoersplanologisch Speruwerk* 24 & 25 November 2011, Antwerpen.

Mashiri, M., Maphakela, W., Chakwizira, J., & Mpondo, B. (2013) Building sustainable platform for low-cost mobility in South Africa. *32nd Southern African Transport Conference, Pretoria*.

Mitullah, W. V. & Opiyo, R. (2012) Mainstreaming NMT in policy and planning in Nairobi: Institutional issues and challenges. *31st Southern African Transport Conference, Pretoria.*

National Department of Transport (NDoT) (1996) National Transport Policy.

—— (NDoT) (2007a) Public Transport Strategy.

—— (NDoT) (2007b) White Paper, Public Transport Action Plan.

—— (NDoT) (2008) NMT Policy.

—— (NDoT) (2009) National Land Transport Act.

Nicolson, G. (2015) 'South Africa: Where 12 million live in extreme poverty' *Daily Maverick*, 3 February.

Pendakur, V. S. (2005) 'Non motorised transport in African cities: Lessons from experience in Kenya and Tanzania', *SSATP Working Paper No. 80.*

Provincial Government Western Cape (PGWC) (2009) NMT in the Western Cape Draft Strategy.

—— (PGWC) (2013) Western Cape Green Economy Strategy Framework.

Pucher, J., Buehler, R., & Seinen, M. (2011) Bicycling renaissance in North America? An update and re-appraisal of cycling trends and policies. *Transportation Research Part A: Policy and Practice*, 45, pp. 451–475.

Rwebangira, T. (2001) Cycling in African cities: Status & prospects. *World Transport Policy & Practice*, 7(2), pp. 7–10.

Servaas, M. (2000) *The Significance of NMT for Developing Countries*, I-ce, Interface for Cycling Expertise, Utrecht, the Netherlands.

Turok, I., Robinson, S., Boulle, J., & Harrison, K. (2011) *Cape Town Competitiveness Study: Final Synthesis Report for City of Cape Town*. City of Cape Town.

Vasconcellos, E. (2012) Equity evaluation of urban transport in urban transport. In: Dimitriou, H. & Gakenheimer, R. (eds.), *The Developing World: A Handbook of Policy and Practice*. London: Edward Elgar, Ch. 12.

Von Schnitzler, A. (2015) *Infrastructure, Apartheid Techno-politics, and Temporalities of 'Transition'* [DRAFT], University of the Witwatersrand.

5 Advocating through data

Community visibilities in crowdsourced cycling data

Christopher A. Le Dantec, Caroline Appleton,
Mariam Asad, Robert Rosenberger and
Kari Watkins

Introduction

In the U.S., there has been intense recent interest in bringing computing to bear on the challenges of democratic participation. Part of this interest was captured in the 2010 report from the President's Council of Advisors on Science and Technology where it focused on leveraging social media to create a truly *digital democracy* (President's Council of Advisors on Science and Technology, 2010). By digital democracy, we refer to a "collection of attempts to practice democracy without the limits of time, space and other physical conditions using [computing] as an addition [to], not a replacement for traditional 'analogue' political practices" (Hacker & van Dijk, 2000, p.1). A critical component of this vision is that the tools built to establish and enable digital democracy do so by empowering citizens to both *produce* and *consume* relevant data, thus providing new avenues for concerned citizens with diverse perspectives to more directly participate in shaping their futures. Increased participation, moreover, is a critical social justice goal, explicitly called out by the Department of Transportation of the United States (DOT) as a guiding principle to "ensure the full and fair participation by all potentially affected communities in the transportation decision making process" (DOT, 2012).

To begin to understand how new forms of data can be used in efforts to govern and inform public works, we examine a project focused on developing new cycling infrastructure as part of the Atlanta Regional Commission's Livable Center Initiative (Atlanta Regional Commission, 2013). Our involvement in the project comes by way of the project's stated goal to increase participation in the planning process by engaging in alternate forms of public consultation. To address that goal, the assistant director of Atlanta's transportation planning office contacted Dr. Kari Watkins, head of the Urban Transportation Information Lab, to develop a smartphone application that enabled cyclists to record their rides. Dr. Watkins then enlisted the help of Dr. Christopher Le Dantec, head of the Participatory Publics Lab, and this larger team then set about building an app that would both broaden participation in the planning process and provide a new kind of data to inform the development of infrastructure plans.

The questions that became of immediate interest to us centered on the conditions of cycling data production and ways in which the data facilitated alternate forms of participation and new modes of representation. Who participated? What did the data reveal about the city? How should the data be interpreted? What impact did digitally mediated participation have on the broader goals of inclusion?

The civic and the social

Excitement about the potential of digital and data-based democratic participation has been percolating in the U.S. for decades: looking to the late 1960s, we find hopeful examples of how computing and real-time data might instigate, support, and improve public action (Sackman, 1968); more recent literature provides sanguine examples of how computing can transform democratic engagement (e.g. Becker, 2001; Snellen, 2001); finally, contemporary scholarship has begun to examine the implications of current social media platforms on public policy and city planning (e.g. Evans-Cowley, 2010; Bond et al., 2012). Together these perspectives raise important questions about who controls and has access to data, the ways in which these data might be used to improve the common good, and the balance between the values of equity, liberty, community, efficiency, and security that participatory public policy aspires to achieve (Stone, 2002; Sarpard, 2003).

Participation in activism and planning

In addition to examining computing's impact on communities, computing researchers and scholars have begun to look at alternative ways of using computing to support different forms of activism. Some of this work supports and prompts reflection on how existing computing capacities, or those we might design, might be marshalled to enable concerned citizens to organize around and resist present social conditions (e.g. Asad et al., 2014; DiSalvo et al., 2010). Each of these projects—and many more that are beyond the scope of this discussion—center on modes of activism and ways in which new forms of computing can support participation, public discourse, and modes of re-envisioning the city.

This turn toward computing to augment community engagement in policy complements recent scholarship in public policy as it provides a means for communities—or issue-based publics (Le Dantec & DiSalvo, 2013)—to act on policy at the point of formation. Traditionally, governmental action—whether distributive, redistributive, regulatory, or constituent—takes policy in its final form as a given and evaluates politics solely along the lines of coercion (Lowi, 1972). Within this frame, there is no place for publics to co-produce policies with policy makers. Rather, there is only acceptance or resistance when operating with the causal assumption that "policies determine politics" and not the other way around (ibid., p.299).

To enable alternate forms of productive resistance within policy development there has been a recent shift toward bottom-up participatory policy analysis aimed at "expand[ing] the range of actors/stakeholders involved in the making and execution of public policy in a discursive or deliberative mode" (DeLeon & Varda, 2009, p.59). Where prior models of policy development used privilege to create and control a "hierarchy of policy knowledge" (Smith & Larimer, 2009, p.116), the push of participatory models re-democratizes and legitimizes "public policy [by working] in expressive rather than instrumental terms" (ibid., p.117). This requires taking seriously the heterogeneity within and between policy makers, personnel implementing the policy, and community stakeholders (Yanow, 2003, p.238).

The push toward participatory engagement in both public policy and computing research suggests that digital democracy does not just intervene in a politics that was "already always existing in preestablished interest groups or classes . . . [but instead, comes] into being when somebody draws attention to the inequality in social order" (McCarthy & Wright, 2015, p.41). That is, the politics of resistance and struggle develop out of making sensible the social conditions via participation from, and interaction between, policy makers, public officials, and concerned stakeholders (Rancière, 2006). The confluence of participatory planning practices and digital democracy challenges the way we develop public policy. Put simply, tools like Cycle Atlanta help create a change in the public's values through their non-coercive mode of participation; they create a foundation for shifting policy through stronger policy tools that rely on a shared set of values (e.g. creating a new tax base or new enforcement regimes). Therefore, data tracking tools like Cycle Atlanta, and the larger category of applications that fall under the umbrella of digital democracy, are integral to understanding when, where, and how to transition into the more tangible forms of policy action.

New forms of civic action

As we use computing to create and mediate new forms of civic engagement, we must attend to how the affordances of those systems support (or discourage) different kinds of democratic participation. To create a basis for such an evaluation, van Dijk (2000) synthesized models of democracy, models of communication, and models of social interaction into a rich theoretical foundation for understanding digital democracy. This foundation provides a point of departure for understanding the different communication and interaction affordances present in digital democracy, and how those affordances enable or impede the *means* and the *ends* of different kinds of democratic work. Through this model, we can examine the intersection of democratic practices (e.g. forming opinions or taking action) with the ways we communicate and the affordances of particular technologies. This in turn advances a more nuanced evaluation of how digital democracy may in fact perpetuate or exacerbate the exclusion of historically marginalized communities, which is essential given the racial inequality of the Atlanta, Georgia, landscape (Paget-Seekins, 2013).

Background, System Design, and Deployment

The urban planning project under which our work took place was a regionally supported effort to study both the current use of and possible improvements to cycling infrastructure in Atlanta, Georgia. Within the broader scope of regional development, the project was one of several that fell under the umbrella of a livable-centers initiative that aimed to create sustainable communities.

Local commitments and expectations

The regional initiative began in 2011 and identified five core transportation corridors crucial to providing robust bicycle infrastructure for access to centers of health care, housing, employment, retail, and cultural arts. A component of the project was the creation of an on-going collaboration between the Georgia Institute of Technology (the authors' home institution) and the City of Atlanta's transportation planning office. Through the collaboration, we developed and deployed a smartphone application (for Android and iOS) that facilitated the collection of cycling route data to better understand current cycling practices in and around the city.

Along with the data collection, a secondary goal of the project was to create new avenues for public participation in the development of plans for new cycling infrastructure. One of the on-going challenges in urban planning is the tension between, on the one hand, the need for broad and substantial participation by affected citizens to improve both plans and acceptance of those plans (Burby, 2003; Insua et al., 2008), and, on the other hand, the constraints imposed on direct participation as people have jobs and obligations that make attending public meetings over sustained periods of time onerous (Galston, 2004; Skocpol & Fiorina, 1999). We saw this project as an opportunity to explore alternate forms of public participation, where the cycling community could present arguments and support for particular infrastructure choices *in absentia* by providing bicycle trip data through our smartphone app. The app we deployed focused on collecting three kinds of information: trip data describing individual rides a user completed, note data indicating specific places of concern in Atlanta, and demographic data describing the rider.

Recording a trip

The core functionality of the Cycle Atlanta app was recording trips taken by cyclists. To record a trip, the user taps the "Start" button on the main screen and begins their ride (see Figure 5.1). At the end of their ride, they tap "Save" and are then stepped through prompts describing more about the trip (see Figure 5.2). Once completed, the app saves the trip details and uploads it to our database.

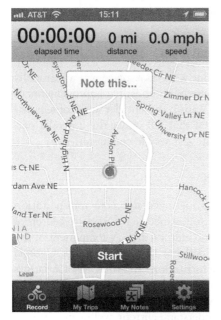
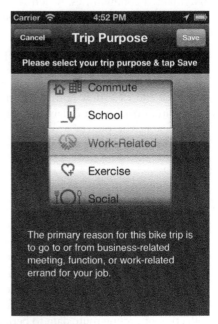

Figure 5.1, 5.2, 5.3 Screenshots from the Cycle Atlanta iPhone app

Source: Christopher Le Dantec.

Recording a note

Users may record specific locations in the city that might be of interest to planners as either acute issues the city should address or assets already present in the environment; we call these locations "notes" (see Figure 5.1). To create a note, the user taps the "Note this . . ." button on the app's main screen and then follows prompts to indicate note type, optionally provide a photo, and finally enter free-form text describing the note. Once finished, the app saves the data about the note and uploads them to our database.

Demographic data

In addition to the general questions on age, gender, ethnicity, and house-hold income, we asked users for zip codes for home, work, and school to help contextualize likely centers of activity between which they might be traveling. We also asked users to indicate how frequently they cycle, what kind of rider they consider themselves to be, and how long they have been riding a bicycle (see Figure 5.3). The rider type categories—strong and fearless, enthused and confident, comfortable but cautious, interested but concerned—were based on prior work done in Portland, Oregon, and help contextualize the choices riders make with respect to route choice as well as assess potential high-impact improvements (Misra et al., 2015; Dill & McNeil, 2012).

Case study: mapping community visibilities

We released the smartphone app at a public event in October 2012. The partnership with our university served as an example of digital- and data-driven governance, and extolled the app as a progressive move to broaden participation in the planning process. The public event fit within a larger rhetorical move being made by Atlanta to directly engage with citizens in innovative approaches for public participation. This rhetorical framing is important as it created a clear explanation for why someone should use the app—to record data to inform and guide planning decisions.

From autumn 2012 until the time of writing in late summer 2015, 1,576 cyclists had contributed just over 30,000 rides to the dataset. These data provide insight into the particulars of different rider habits, demographic and rider characteris-tics of a largely commute-focused rider population, and a means of examining changing ride patterns over time as new cycling infrastructure opened following the app's release. Given these attributes, one plausible path for understanding how the app operated in the world runs through the ways in which planners and the public reasoned about design alternatives using the submitted data. Indeed, in previous work, we have taken on just those questions, looking at how these data circulate in public design meetings (Le Dantec et al., 2015), the implica-tions for crowdsourced data collection practices on transportation planning and analysis (Misra et al., 2014), and the differences in route preference between transportation versus fitness cycling by comparing our data to data collected through the more popular fitness-oriented app Strava (Watkins et al., 2016).

Mapping the data; mapping the knowledge

When taken in aggregate, the Cycle Atlanta data carve out a network within Atlanta experienced by the subset of cyclists who have voluntarily recorded a trip. By mapping these data, we can begin to see how this particular subset of the cycling public navigates the city. Figure 5.4 shows an aggregate map of rides recorded since the launch of the Cycle Atlanta app—each line on the map is a recorded ride. The rides have been color coded against a self-selected rider-type profile that helps indicate the differences in how cyclists of varying abilities navigate the city: the map could just as easily be indexed against gender, income, ethnicity, or trip purpose. By segmenting the data in these categories, we can begin to see how different groups chose alternative routes, such as females going out of their way to use more protected trails and cycle tracks, or older riders avoiding hills. Even in a dataset that is highly self-selected, careful data analysis can tease out important differences in route choice that help planners better understand decision factors for underrepresented groups in a more accountable effort to build equitable infrastructure.

The map provides a direct way of visualizing who participated in data production. We also know something about why they participated: the cyclists who used our app were doing so under the expectation of influencing the decisions planners make about cycling infrastructure. This self-interest becomes more apparent when we look beyond the aggregate façade of the map and find that with few exceptions, the heavily trafficked routes indicated in the map are not the result of a plurality of riders but are instead the work of a small number of dedicated individuals who have diligently recorded their rides over an extended period of time. The net result is that a very small minority of habitual app users render themselves more visible than the casual app users who make up the vast majority of our user base.

The challenge then is to develop both social and technical innovations recognizing that data "do not exist in isolation but are created by social actors" (Räsänen & Nyce, 2013, p.659). If new models of digital democracy are to work, then the kinds of participation they involve need to reflect the labor and agency of those participating, which is to say that data are introduced into the process from ways of knowing about the city rather than being the atomic components that lead to knowledge (Tuomi, 1999).

When we consider different modes of use in how cyclists recorded their rides—either through casual use which presented a broad sampling of routes, or through habitual use where a very small number of routes were recorded repeatedly—we have two very different kinds of participation and representations of ways of knowing. Casual users are more representative of the overall app-user population—in confidence level (tending toward less confident in traffic), as well as demographic profile (tending toward less white and male dominated). This is

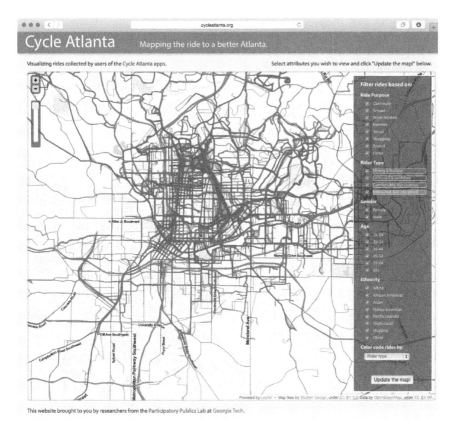

Figure 5.4 Map of rides submitted through the Cycle Atlanta app

Source: Christopher Le Dantec.

important for planners because the least confident rider population is where the largest latent demand for cycling exists (Dill & McNeil, 2012). As shown by measures such as the Level of Traffic Stress (Mekuria et al., 2012), less confident riders (adults with less experience, children, and those who are risk-averse) decide to cycle only when there are roadways with dedicated infrastructure available. Bicycle transportation planning practices already accept that the absence of dedicated facilities are a deterrent to these types of cyclists, but the more crucial point is that it only takes one segment of high traffic stress to break the network between origin and destination and cause a mode shift from bicycle to automobile (ibid.). These routes are rendered invisible due to the nature of the app, yet are some of the most important for creating a more complete bicycle infrastructure network.

Yet, ignoring the deep knowledge of the habitual app users creates a confounding challenge for planners in examining the data. Privileging the less confident rider potentially masks important knowledge about how to navigate Atlanta. It cannot be assumed that more confident riders are always choosing routes that less confident riders would avoid—less confident riders avoid roads for a complex set of reasons, including the amount and speed of vehicular traffic, the geography they need to traverse, the availability of dedicated facilities (Dill & Carr, 2003; Buehler & Pucher, 2012), as well as social issues such as drawing unwanted attention from police—an issue of particular concern for minority populations (Warren et al., 2006).

Taking the position that data produced by cyclists *leads to* knowledge that will help guide the development of new infrastructure creates choices about what data to excise and under what conditions. On the other hand, if we start from the position that the data result *from* a way of knowing about the city then we have a different orientation to those same trade-offs. The depth of knowledge conveyed by very active users becomes more important to preserve, not just as knowledge about cycling on certain roads, but as knowledge about the kinds of civic participation that produce desired outcomes. This is important to keep in mind— digital democracy is not just about working toward some imagined institutional efficiency, but about advocating for access to resources that support particular constituencies (Hacker & van Dijk, 2000; van Dijk, 2000).

Reading between the lines

With over 1,500 contributing users, the app cast a wide net for cyclists to contribute to the planning process. When compared to the tens of people who participated in in-person discussion about proposed street designs, participation and representation through the app was at a different order of magnitude. The challenge of building computational and institutional process around new forms of digital participation, however, is not limited to examining the pure number of riders who used the app. We need to consider who is and is not present if we are to make progress toward the goal of broadening public involvement. This public involvement in planning processes cannot be counted simply through absolute numbers, but must reflect the diversity of the city.

Despite the fact that the demographic makeup of our app users—mostly male (75.9 percent), mostly white (80.2 percent), mostly wealthy (58.4 percent reporting annual income greater than $60k), and mostly young (55 percent younger than 35)—are reflected in other forms of cycling census data from several external sources (Poznanski, 2013), the app user demographics need to be situated within the context of a city whose population is majority African American (53.5 percent) and where only 40.8 percent of its residents report an annual income greater than $60k. This helps illustrate one of the most essential paradoxes of public policy: defining the democratic value of equity in policy design is not a given and what is equitable for one or more groups is not objective, but is in relation to the subjective experiences and histories of a variety of stakeholders.

To demonstrate the subjectivity of equity, we can return to our map in Figure 5.4. As is often the case with maps, a visualization that purports to illustrate one thing in fact renders legible alternative narratives and experiences. In this instance, while the map in Figure 5.4 suggests different ways of knowing about Atlanta based on how riders of different ability and confidence navigate the city, the map also paints a clear picture of how whole communities are not represented in the data. The result is that planners still need to make decisions in the absence of data. Importantly, it is often the communities absent from the data that stand to be impacted most. Certainly, mediating participation in the project through smartphones, and through particular uses of smartphones, created barriers and selection bias—both of which we recognized from the outset. Yet, even as we knew the social and material limits of data collected via smartphones, as the data accumulated, alternate narratives about those who were not included became more difficult and risked rendering out of existence those not present in the data.

The issue of data-based participation, then, is directly connected to the challenges posed to collective action. When advocacy for public resources—transportation infrastructure or otherwise—occurs in public, there are clear places and ways to respond to such advocacy; they are communicative acts that bridge social bonds with professional practice (Innes, 2007; Evans-Cowley, 2010). However, when those arguments occur through data, the visibility of the argument changes along with the accessibility of supporting or refuting its claims. On one hand, the aggregated route data made cyclists in Atlanta much more visible as a population; on the other hand, taking those data at face value excludes whole neighborhoods and individuals who do not identify as cyclists, conflating data aggregation with consensus.

This tension in data-based participation matters on three counts. First, there is a mismatch between the individual act of submitting data to guide policy and the aggregate analysis to which planners and transportation researchers routinely subject data (Meyer & Miller, 2001). We saw the byproduct of this mismatch where data production practices differed such that a very small number of active cyclists accounted for a disproportionate component of the data. The trade-offs with respect to data-as-knowledge or knowledge-through-data mentioned above would then lead to privileging very different ways of representing cycling patterns and cyclist-based knowledge about the city.

Second, as Gilbert rightly points out, "the problem of democracy is never simply that of making collective decisions, but is also, indissolubly, the problem of bringing 'the collective' into being at all" (Gilbert, 2013, p.24). The app did not obviate the problem of bringing "the collective" of cyclists into being, even while it enabled many more people to participate. The affordances of the app as a data collection tool turned what was historically a public engagement—soliciting public input into proposed plans—into a private exchange, one partitioned from other individuals with shared concerns and goals. This shift to individual exchange is an often glossed-over consequence of the push to digital democracy where the civic milieu is reimagined as a service exchange between consumer and producer and not as a collective enterprise of consultation, contestation, and compromise.

Finally, the mode of participation matters because of the ways exclusion makes it easy to dismiss non-use as an issue of access rather than the enactment of social norms around computing or the purposeful contestation of a specific civic process. Demonstrating this point, invisibility of some of Atlanta's neighborhoods in the data makes it tempting to attribute the dearth of cycling routes as evidence that those low-income communities are not engaging with the tools of digital democracy. However, access to enabling technologies is not the key factor. Recent Pew reports describe how smartphone ownership and use among African American and Hispanic communities outpaces ownership trends among white communities, though consistent access to data plans does remain an issue for low-income minority families (The Pew Research Center, 2015). Despite this, in certain uses of social media, for example participation on Twitter, minority populations are over represented within the population of internet users which suggests a willing and wired population (Duggan, 2015). This divergence denotes that factors beyond access and use are behind the paucity of cycling data in those particular neighborhoods. It is more readily the case that individuals in these areas do not self-identify as a "cyclist"—they ride their bike out of necessity and do not have strong social connections to the cycling community where app recruitment and use was occurring—or that making themselves more visible brings unwanted attention.

Instead of reducing participation to issues of access, it is important to examine how those neighborhoods are isolated from the rest of Atlanta along economic, social, ethnic, and political axes. Such a reading of the cycling data aligns with recent scholarship demonstrating how and why Atlanta is a city with very poor income mobility (Leonhardt, 2013; Chetty & Hendren, 2015; Chetty et al., 2015), where a confluence of factors including the city's racial history, rapid economic expansion, balkanized approach to urban planning, and low urban density focus and ossify social and economic inequity (Priester et al., 2013). Connected to these factors are concerns about urban redevelopment: some planners observed during our fieldwork that residents in these communities often see the arrival of bike paths as a sign of impending gentrification. Cycling, while an everyday practice for many, is becoming a signifier of an upwardly mobile class whose introduction into low-income neighborhoods often means the displacement and further marginalization of indigenous residents (Glick, 2008). Within the microcosm of cycling infrastructure, we have an agonistic interaction where the politically powerful and the publicly favorable (wealthy, white, recreational bicyclists) along with a rapidly growing class of semi-powerful and semi-favored (upwardly mobile middle class who exercise transportation mode choice) are encroaching on the politically disempowered and publicly unfavorable (impoverished communities of color, obligatory bicycle commuters) (Schneider & Ingram, 1990).

Data-based public participation

In behavioral approaches to policy, digital democracy tools are providing the *capacity* to participate with a lower barrier to entry and an *incentive* to participate with respect to both the reason for the policy artifact's existence (e.g. because planners wanted input) and the app's feature of providing a louder "voice" to those who record their same route diligently. However, the same artifact in its general form can take on differing meanings across adjacent geographies (Yanow, 2003). For example, bicyclists in one neighborhood may see the app as a form of empowerment, while bicyclists in another may be absent from the process due to a lack of social connections, a lack of interest, or even a fear that it is just another tool of gentrification.

The combination of data, and the agency and intent exercised through the act of their collection exist in a world where issue advocacy still normally occurs in public fora—through council meetings, neighborhood association meetings, or a range of locally developed processes that are in place to both solicit specific feedback regarding governance and urban planning and as an opportunity for broad public communication about policy details (Innes, 2007). Indeed, the purpose of digital democracy is to augment those in-person processes with computing tools that increase the opportunities of more meaningfully contributing to decision making and governance (Hacker & van Dijk, 2000). However, by shifting civic engagement from a synchronous experience of advocacy via discourse in public fora, to an asynchronous experience where advocacy occurs via collected data, we dramatically change the conditions of public participation and introduce new forms of argumentation into the milieu.

Returning to van Dijk's enumeration of how different computing systems amplify and impede different democratic ends (van Dijk, 2000), the affordances of the smartphones and the particular design choices made in the cycling app we released created an environment with inherent limitations on how the public participated. By focusing exclusively on mobile interactions, the system privileged data collection and impeded the kind of feedback needed for productive discourse within the cycling community, as well as discourse between the cycling community and the city government. One way local groups countered the privileging of data collection was through proxy measures of participation like neighborhood-specific "Tweet and Greet," where cyclists were invited to a group ride along a well-travelled bike route in an underserved community. In these events, participants would share their diverse experiences of cycling in the city both for other cyclists to follow via social media and as a way to publicly support allocating resources for the community in which the ride took place. The alternative that these kinds of events offer is to shift the computing component away from pure data collection and instead leverage public social interactions to create cross-neighborhood ties and amplify local community voices.

The larger picture here is that addressing the challenges of broadening public involvement through data-based civic participation means engaging with the epistemic questions bound up in data as a form of participation. Whether collected through the geolocative capabilities of smartphones or through events documented and broadcast on social media, we need to be able to account for data production (Klaebe et al., 2009; Räsänen & Nyce, 2013), attending to how the data often convey authority divorced from the agency motivating that production. In our case, the presence of recorded routes produced by cyclists was an authoritative claim about where and when cyclists moved through the environment, but the data did not provide insight into why they chose particular routes, if those routes were preferred, or if they were simply least-worst options given the available alternatives.

Furthermore, when viewed through the lens of city planning, transportation mode choice is often reduced to issues of infrastructure: are there adequate bike lanes and ancillary facilities to promote cycling? We would point out, however, that the choice to ride is far more complicated, not just in terms of everyday mundane constraints (e.g. picking up kids or stopping by the store), but by experiences of race and how different modes of transportation expose individuals to systemic bias (Warren et al., 2006). Consequently, programs that develop such data-based modes of participation need to support participation that goes beyond simple data collection and instead cultivates public analysis and interpretation of the data to guide policy makers and governance.

Building up new practices of civic participation could be accomplished by attending to two theoretical and practical areas. First, addressing the challenge of linking individual acts of data production through personal devices to forms of collective action, thereby supporting the formation of publics around a shared set of issues. Second, examining the practices that emerge around app use and participation in digital modes of civic participation so that expectations for impact and relevancy are met with appropriate feedback mechanisms to help sustain participation over time. Meaningful public participation is ultimately an expression of agency, of expertise, of tacit knowledge, and of individual and community interwoven identities.

Attending to these facets of public participation become ever more important as notions of the smart city expand out through instrumenting infrastructure toward instrumenting and objectifying citizens. Building out an agenda of data-based civic participation necessarily means enabling and recognizing the subjectivities of data and resisting programs of normativity that ignore the individual, the neighborhood, the community. The Cycle Atlanta project begins to outline these concerns with some urgency where a tension arises between the subjectivity of data collected by cyclists and the normativity of the cycling community as a kind of political identity. Imperfect as the project's implementation is, it does give shape to new practices of civic participation enabled by linking individual acts of data production to forms of collective action.

References

Asad, M., Fox, S., & Le Dantec, C.A. (2014) Speculative Activist Technologies. In Kindling, Maxi & Greifeneder, Elke (eds.) *iConference 2014 Proceedings: Breaking Down Walls. iSchools.*

Atlanta Regional Commission (2013) *2013 Livable Centers Initiative Implementation Report.*

Becker, T. (2001) Rating the Impact of New Technologies on Democracy. *Communications of the ACM.* 44(1) pp.39–43.

Bond, R.M., Fariss, C.J., Jones, J.J., Kramer, A.D., Marlow, C., Settle, J.E., & Fowler, J.H. (2012) A 61-Million-Person Experiment in Social Influence and Political Mobilization. *Nature*. 489(7415) pp.295–298.

Buehler, R. & Pucher, J. (2012) Cycling to Work in 90 Large American Cities: New Evidence on the Role of Bike Paths and Lanes. *Transportation*. 39(2) pp.409–432.

Burby, R.J. (2003) Making Plans that Matter: Citizen Involvement and Government Action. *Journal of the American Planning Association*. 69(1) pp.33–49.

Chetty, R. & Hendren, N. (2015). The Impacts of Neighborhoods on Intergenerational Mobility: Childhood Exposure Effects and County-Level Estimates. Harvard University Working Paper.

Chetty, R., Hendren, N., & Katz, L.F. (2015) The Effects of Exposure to Better Neighborhoods on Children: New Evidence from the Moving to Opportunity Experiment. Harvard University Working Paper.

Deleon, P. & Varda, D.M. (2009) Toward a Theory of Collaborative Policy Networks: Identifying Structural Tendencies. *Policy Studies Journal*. 37(1) pp.59–74.

Department of Transportation of the United States (DOT) (2012) Department of Transportation Environmental Justice Strategy [Online] Available from www.fhwa.dot.gov/environment/environmental_justice/ej_at_dot/dot_ej_strategy/index.cfm [Accessed November 30, 2015].

Dill, J. & Carr, T. (2003) Bicycle Commuting and Facilities in Major US Cities: If You Build Them, Commuters Will Use Them. *Transportation Research Record: Journal of the Transportation Research Board*. 1828 pp.116–123.

Dill, J. & McNeil, N. (2012) *Four Types of Cyclists? Testing a Typology to Better Understand Behavior and Potential*. Portland State University.

Disalvo, C.F., Light, A., Hirsch, T., & Le Dantec, C.A. (2010) HCI, Communities and Politics. In *CHI '10 Extended Abstracts on Human Factors in Computing Systems*. New York: ACM.

Duggan, M. (2015) Mobile Messaging and Social Media 2015. Pew Research Center. [Online] Available from: www.pewinternet.org/2015/08/19/mobile-messaging-and-social-media-2015/ [Accessed November 30, 2015].

Evans-Cowley, J. (2010) Planning in the Age of Facebook: The Role of Social Networking in Planning Processes. *GeoJournal*. 75(5) pp.407–420.

Galston, W.A. (2004) Civic Education and Political Participation. *Phi Kappa Phi Forum*.

Gilbert, J. (2013) *Common Ground*. London, UK: Pluto Press.

Glick, J. (2008) Gentrification and the Racialized Geography of Home Equity. *Urban Affairs Review*. 44(2) pp.280–295.

Hacker, K.L. & van Dijk, J. (eds.) (2000) *Digital Democracy: Issues of Theory and Practice*. London, UK: Sage Publications, Inc.

Innes, J.E. (2007) Information in Communicative Planning. *Journal of the American Planning Association*. 64(1) pp.52–63.

Insua, D.R., Kersten, G.E., Rios, J., & Grima, C. (2008) Towards Decision Support for Participatory Democracy. *Information Systems and e-Business Management*. 6(2) pp.161–191.

Klaebe, H., Adkins, B., Foth, M., & Hearn, G. (2009) Embedding an Ecology Notion in the Social Production of Urban Space. In Foth, M. (ed.) *Handbook of Research on Urban Informatics*. New York: Information Science Reference, pp.179–194.

Le Dantec, C.A. & Disalvo, C.F. (2013) Infrastructuring and the Formation of Publics in Participatory Design. *Social Studies of Science*. 43(2) pp.241–264.

Le Dantec, C.A., Asad, M., Misra, A., & Watkins, K.E. (2015) Planning with Crowdsourced Data: Rhetoric and Representation in Transportation Planning. In *CSCW '15: Proceedings of the 18th ACM Conference on Computer Supported Cooperative Work & Social Computing*. New York: ACM.

Leonhardt, D. (2013) In Climbing Income Ladder, Location Matters. *The New York Times*.

Lowi, T. (1972) Four Systems of Policy, Politics, and Choice. *Public Administration Review*. 32(4) pp.298–310.

McCarthy, J. & Wright, P. (2015) *Taking [A]part*. Cambridge, MA: MIT Press.

Mekuria, M.C., Furth, P.G., & Nixon, H. (2012) *Low-Stress Bicycling and Network Connectivity*. Mineta Transportation Institute.

Meyer, M.D. & Miller, E.J. (2001) *Urban Transportation Planning: A Decision-Oriented Approach*. 2nd ed., McGraw-Hill Higher Education.

Misra, A., Gooze, A., Watkins, K., Asad, M., & Le Dantec, C.A. (2014) Crowdsourcing and Its Application to Transportation Data Collection and Management. *Transportation Research Record: Journal of the Transportation Research Board*. 2414(-1) pp.1–8.

Misra, A., Watkins, K.E., & Le Dantec, C.A. (2015) Socio-demographic Influence on Cyclists' Self Classification by Rider Type. Transportation Research Board 2015 Annual Meeting.

Paget-Seekins, L. (2013) Atlanta: Scarcity and Abundance. In Institute for Mobility Research (ed.) *Megacity Mobility Culture: How Cities Move on in a Diverse World*. Berlin, DE: Springer-Verlag, pp.149–160.

Poznanski, A.J. (2013) Analyzing Demographic and Geographic Characteristics of "Cycle Atlanta" Smartphone Application Users. Georgia Institute of Technology.

President's Council of Advisors on Science and Technology. (2010) Designing a Digital Future: Federally Funded Research and Development in Networking and Information Technology.

Priester, R., Kenworthy, J., & Wulfhorst, G. (2013) The Diversity of Megacities Worldwide: Challenges for the Future of Mobility. In Institute for Urban Mobility Research (ed.) *Megacity Mobility Culture: How Cities Move on in a Diverse World*. Berlin, DE: Springer-Verlag, pp.23–54.

Rancière, J. (2006) *The Politics of Aesthetics: The Distribution of the Sensible*. London, UK: Continuum International Press.

Räsänen, M. & Nyce, J.M. (2013) The Raw is Cooked: Data in Intelligence Practice. *Science, Technology & Human Values*. 38(5) pp.655–677.

Sackman, H. (1968) A Public Philosophy for Real Time Information Systems. In *AFIPS '68 (Fall, part II): Proceedings of the December 9–11, 1968, fall joint computer conference*. New York: ACM.

Sarpard, K. (2003) From Counting to Cash: How MIS Impacts the Homeless. *The International Journal of Applied Management and Technology*. 1(1) pp.17–27.

Schneider, A. & Ingram, H. (1990) Behavioral Assumptions of Policy Tools. *The Journal of Politics*. 52(2) pp.510–529.

Skocpol, T. & Fiorina, M.P. (1999) *Civic Engagement in American Democracy*. Washington D.C.: Brookings Institution Press.

Smith, K. & Larimer, C. (2009) *Public Policy Theory Primer*. Philadelphia, PA: Westview Press.

Snellen, I. (2001) ICTs, Bureaucracies, and the Future of Democracy. *Communications of the ACM*. 44(1) pp.45–48.

Stone, D. (2002) *Policy Paradox: The Art of Political Decision Making*. New York: W.W. Norton & Co.

The Pew Research Center. (2015) *The Smartphone Difference*. [Online] Available from: www.pewinternet.org/2015/04/01/us-smartphone-use-in-2015/. [Accessed November 30, 2015].

Tuomi, I. (1999) Data is More than Knowledge: Implications of the Reversed Knowledge Hierarchy for Knowledge Management and Organizational Memory. *Journal of Management Information Systems*. 16(3) pp.107–121.

van Dijk, J. (2000) Models of Democracy and Concepts of Communication. In Hacker, K. L. & van Dijk, J. (eds.) *Digital Democracy: Issues of Theory and Practice*. London, UK: Sage Publications Ltd., pp.30–53.

Warren, P., Tomaskovic-Devey, D., Smith, W., Zingraff, M., & Mason, M. (2006) Driving while Black: Bias Processes and Racial Disparity in Police Stops. *Criminology*. 44(3) pp.709–737.

Watkins, K., Ammanamanchi, R., Lamondia, J., & Le Dantec, C.A. (2016) Comparison of Smartphone-based Cyclists GPS Data Sources. Transportation Research Board 2016 Annual Meeting.

Yanow, D. (2003) Accessing Local Knowledge. In Hajer, M. & Wagenaar, H. (eds.) *Deliberative Policy Analysis: Understanding Governance in the Network Society*. Cambridge, UK: Cambridge University Press, pp.228–246.

6 Advancing discussions of cycling interventions based on social justice

Karel Martens, Daniel Piatkowski,
Kevin J. Krizek and Kara Luckey

Introduction

In many transport planning initiatives globally, cities are aiming to spur more bicycle use; they are doing so, because cycling is touted as an egalitarian mode of transport, alongside its broader ecological and health benefits. This argument is particularly evident in advocacy efforts, which often place cycling just behind walking in terms of its ability to enhance transport accessibility for all. Most justifications for such are relatively straightforward. Bicycling requires nominal investment from the user (a bike) and modest physical ability. Assuming a minimum degree of protection from the dangers of auto traffic is provided for and there are ample destinations to bike to, such a view posits that cycling can become a tool of access and empowerment for marginalized communities.

Upon further inspection, however, some assumptions underlying these arguments have been left unexamined. Therefore, the degree to which bicycling (and bicycling infrastructure) should be promoted to advance social justice is unclear. This chapter addresses this question by specifying conditions under which publicly produced cycling interventions, at the expense of the wider community, are warranted on the basis of justice. We first consider three prominent liberal-egalitarian theories of justice to understand their relevance in exploring fairness and equity associated with cycling interventions. Note that these theories propose principles of fairness for public actions, i.e. they provide the moral basis for public policy. This contrasts with the social justice lenses used in most of the other chapters in this book, which criticize the underlying social *processes* of oppression and exclusion that may result in a particular—fair or unfair—'cycling landscape.' Using liberal-egalitarian theoretical perspectives—and Amartya Sen's and Martha Nussbaum's capability approach, in particular—we specify two conditions which must be met for cycling interventions to be warranted on the grounds of justice. We first argue that interventions should enhance accessibility levels for those with substandard accessibility levels (e.g. persons without access to private vehicles or who are unable to drive, such as children or the elderly). Second, we suggest that cycling interventions are only warranted on the basis of justice if they are effective and efficient in promoting accessibility.

   Cycling's effectiveness in this framework largely depends on two foundations: (1) an individual's ability and propensity to cycle, and (2) the degree to which land use patterns enable bicycling to advance accessibility in a meaningful way. We apply our framework to the US and to the Netherlands to further clarify how these tenets play out. While interventions to promote cycling can indeed serve as a tool of empowerment among marginalized communities, they can also serve to reinforce injustice and perpetuate systems of privilege if the fundamental assumptions upon which they are justified are not critically examined.

Theoretical perspectives

Considering justice in any context, regardless of the theoretical framework employed, requires one to address 'distributive justice.' Distributive justice concerns the extent to which an individual or community should forgo resources or make other sacrifices in order to enable another individual or community to have their 'fair share.' Applying the question of distributive justice to cycling involves asking what one individual should give up so that another can cycle. There are many things that one individual can (and perhaps should) give up so that others can cycle: speed, and thus, time (when 'I' have to drive slower so that 'you' can cycle more safely), space (when 'I' give up a traffic lane or car parking facilities to free up space for a bicycle lane so that 'you' can cycle safely and comfortably), or money (when 'my' tax contributions are allocated to infrastructure that provides 'you' with bicycle facilities). Considering justice in the context of cycling thus requires thinking about how these sacrifices are realized differently across different populations and geographies, and how the importance of one person's being able to cycle weighs against the sacrifices it requires from another. We next consider three leading theories of social justice to help understand distributive justice in the context of cycling.

Rawls' theory of justice

The most influential theory of justice in recent times is John Rawls' (1971) 'justice as fairness' theory. Rawls proposes a 'difference principle' for the distribution of income and wealth, which demands selecting the economic arrangement that generates the highest possible level of income and wealth for the least-advantaged group. While transportation researchers have extensively drawn on Rawls' difference principle (e.g. Khisty, 1996; Langmyhr, 1997; Viegas, 2001; Tyler 2006), its application is often based on a misunderstanding of his theory since the principles of justice he offers do not relate to *every* distributive decision within a society, only to the 'primary good' of income and wealth (Rawls, 1971). Thus, while Rawls' theory provides powerful lessons for thinking about justice in the context of basic institutions, it is not appropriate for guiding the distribution of specific goods, including those related to transport (see Martens, 2016). We therefore do not rely upon this theory in the discussion that follows, although it is important to mention because of the role it often plays in debates around transport justice.

Walzer's spheres of justice

Like Rawls, Michael Walzer (1983) takes a distributive approach to understanding justice. However, Walzer argues that the distributive question is not relevant to *all* goods. Rather, distributive questions are only relevant to real, tangible, goods that are produced, exchanged and distributed in society. He claims that some goods have a distinct social meaning which sets them apart from 'regular' goods. For instance, in most modern societies, health and education have distinct social meanings that are quite different than the meaning ascribed to regular goods like pencils or napkins. In Walzer's perspective, regular goods can be exchanged in the market place based on people's ability and willingness to pay while accepting a given income distribution. In contrast, he argues that goods to which a particular society ascribes a distinct social meaning (e.g. health and education) should be removed from the sphere of free exchange and distributed within their own distributive sphere based on their distinct social meaning.

Extending Walzer's argument to cycling requires one to assess cycling from two perspectives. First, is the social meaning of cycling distinct enough to warrant its distribution outside of the sphere of free exchange? Second, if cycling has a distinct social meaning, has this meaning become dominant in society (i.e. has the particular social meaning become uncontested and broadly shared)? Strong feelings among a segment of the population are in themselves not enough for a social good to be positioned outside the domain of free exchange. Many people are passionate about cycling, as evidenced by the proliferation of bicycle advocacy groups around the world. Coffee or wine also shares such traits. However, in most societies, cycling (like coffee and wine) has not acquired a dominant social meaning.

Yet, social meanings are the result of a process of social construction and can change over time, building on latent or subversive meanings apparent in society (Lessig, 1995; see also Martens et al., 2012). Bicycle advocacy groups (and others) can aim to change the social meaning of cycling or of bicycles, as we see occurring today. Still, such efforts are not enough to create a separate sphere around cycling until it obtains a truly distinct social meaning that becomes dominant and broadly shared. Indeed, it is unlikely that a change in the social meaning of cycling will be sufficient to set it apart from other goods. The 'deeper' meaning of cycling does not derive merely from the joy of cycling, the benefits to choose from a range of transportation means, or its low costs. Rather, cycling's deeper meaning stems from the fact that it promotes abstract goods that *do* have a distinct social meaning, like accessibility, health and, perhaps, environmental quality. The relevance of cycling from the perspective of justice thus relates to the fact that these latter goods have a distinct social meaning. The proper distribution of the possibilities to cycle should thus be derived from the distribution of these abstract goods. There are clear avenues by which cycling can contribute to the social goods of accessibility and health. Only if cycling succeeds in doing so, promoting it may be justified on the basis of distributive justice.

Sen's and Nussbaum's human capability approach

We have shown that while both Rawls' and Walzer's frameworks help to elucidate the theoretical issues at play, neither definitively addresses issues of distributive justice as they relate to cycling. The question remains: What should one individual forgo so that another can cycle? We therefore turn to Sen's and Nussbaum's capability approach.

The core claim of the capability approach is that fairness requires interpersonal comparisons that do not focus on resources or welfare, but on people's capabilities. Capabilities are defined as the possibility to achieve basic societal functionings like 'being well nourished' or 'being literate' (Robeyns, 2013). The set of capabilities experienced by a person determine "what people are actually able to do and be" (Nussbaum, 2003, p. 33). According to the capability approach, 'progress' should be defined as the expansion of capabilities, or an expansion of the set of 'functionings' an individual has the freedom to choose from.

In a discussion of the 'standard of living' concept, Sen (1983) explains the notion of capability using the bicycle as an example:

> Take a bicycle. It is, of course, a commodity. It has several characteristics, and let us concentrate on one particular characteristic, *viz.*, transportation. Having a bike gives a person the ability to move about in a certain way that he may not be able to do without the bike. So the transportation *characteristic* of the bike gives the person the *capability* of moving in a certain way. That capability may give the person utility or happiness if he seeks such movement or finds it pleasurable. So there is, as it were, a *sequence* from a commodity (in this case a bike), to characteristics (in this case, transportation), to capability to function (in this case, the ability to move), to utility (in this case, pleasure from moving). It can be argued that it is the third category—that of capability to function—that comes closest to the notion of standard of living. The commodity ownership or availability itself is not the right focus since it does not tell us what the person can, in fact, do. I may not be able to use the bike if—say—I happen to be handicapped. Having the bike—or something else with that characteristic—may provide the basis for a contribution to the standard of living, but it is not in itself a constituent part of that standard. On the other hand, while utility reflects the use of the bike, it does not concentrate on the use itself, but on the mental reaction to that use.
>
> (p. 160)

Sen thus argues that the debate on justice should focus on capabilities rather than resources or utilities. This is in line with what was suggested above: the social importance of cycling does not lie in the bicycle itself (the resource), nor in the fact that it may make a person happy to cycle (the utility of cycling). The importance of cycling lies in the expansion of a person's *capabilities*. In order to be justified on the basis of justice, cycling must therefore expand the things a person is 'able to do and be.' It should enlarge the set of functionings from which a person can choose. Both accessibility and health represent a particular type of capability. Accessibility refers to the capability of a person to physically access particular destinations and thus delineates a potential to engage in particular activities (Martens and Golub, 2012). The larger a person's accessibility level, the larger the set of possible functionings, and thus the larger a person's capabilities. (A comparable argument could be developed for health, a benefit of cycling, although it will require a somewhat more extensive argument, which we leave to another occasion.)

A framework to consider how cycling advances justice

Both Walzer's 'social meanings' and Sen's and Nussbaum's capability approaches provide a basis to understand the distributive question as it relates to cycling (i.e. what should one individual have to forgo so that another can cycle?). The answer lies in cycling's ability to enhance a person's capability to access destinations through the socially important good of accessibility. We posit that cycling is only warranted on the basis of distributive justice (that is, it is justifiable to ask one individual to make a sacrifice so that another can cycle) if two conditions are met.

First, if a person's accessibility (i.e. their level of capability) is below a socially accepted 'standard of living,' it is justifiable for those with accessibility or income levels (well) above the standard to make a sacrifice. Translated to practice, this criterion implies that pro-cycling interventions are acceptable based on justice only if they enhance the levels of accessibility of persons 'disadvantaged' in terms of the sub-standard accessibility levels, for instance those who lack access to a private vehicle due to financial circumstances or those who are not able to drive, but can cycle, independently (e.g. some children, elderly, disabled persons).

Second, interventions to promote cycling must be effective and efficient means to enhance the accessibility of persons with a poor standard of living. This condition suggests that for a cycling intervention to be warranted on the basis of justice, it must not only benefit disadvantaged persons (the first condition), but must *also* effectively and efficiently promote the socially valued good (accessibility) among those persons. The effectiveness of cycling interventions depends on a number of factors, most notably land use patterns and the propensity of people to use the bicycle. Cycling may substantially enhance persons' accessibility in dense (urban) environments, with a mix of land uses, but is likely much less beneficial in low density environments or those with few destinations. Furthermore, interventions that promote cycling can only be effective if persons hold attitudes towards cycling that render them with a high propensity to actually cycle. This propensity is, of course, subject to change and influence and should not necessarily be taken as a given. However, it does suggest that in order to be justified, cycling interventions may have to go beyond the provision of cycling lanes and parking facilities to include bicycle lessons and awareness campaigns (van der Kloof et al., 2014).

If we accept the argument that cycling interventions must meet these two criteria in order to be warranted on the basis of justice (i.e. they must: (1) benefit persons with sub-standard accessibility levels and (2) meaningfully enhance accessibility for those persons), then it follows that fairness requires radically distinct cycling policies across space and time.

In some cases, sacrifices by some to enhance the ease of cycling for others (or themselves) can be justified based on equity concerns. In other cases, such sacrifices would be unwarranted based on justice. For example, sacrifices would be in line with requirements of justice in the case of high-density neighborhoods with a mix of land uses, a relatively poor public transport system and a large share of households without cars. There, bicycling policies may substantially enhance accessibility for the car-less population, particularly if cycling is perceived as a feasible transport mode among the local population. Monetary sacrifices would be warranted from the wider community to finance such policies, for instance through a sales tax, while the local community could be required to make sacrifices in terms of reduced road space, reduced parking spaces or reduced traffic speeds. Alternately, these same sacrifices would go beyond requirements of justice if serving a population with already multiple transportation options and a high level of accessibility, as they would do little to augment accessibility.

Application to international contexts

As a low-cost, low-energy form of transport, bicycling has a long history of being tied to empowerment and opportunity. Indeed, bicycling investments are increasingly being justified based on their ability to advance social equity; however, their actual impact on enhancing accessibility (and thus capabilities, using Sen's terminology) for disadvantaged groups is often unclear. As we have described, bicycling's potential role in enhancing capabilities varies widely across space. In this section, we explore the recent history and current conditions of cycling in two radically different cycling cultures: the US and the Netherlands. We examine these two examples through the lens of the two criteria described above.

US application: transportation capability confused with cultural signifier

Prior to the advent of the automobile age in the early 20th century, bicycling in the US was widely heralded as a travel mode of empowerment and individual freedom. However, in the ensuing decades, large-scale changes to the built environment have significantly reduced the bicycle's utility as a means of transportation. Particularly after World War II, a combination of government housing and transportation policies dramatically changed the physical and demographic character of American cities. Federal housing policies at this time spurred the movement of white, middle-class Americans to single-family suburban development and the passage of the Interstate Highway Act in 1956 financed the building of the Interstate Highway System, leading to street design and land use development standards that prioritized the car. Jane Jacobs described the physical process of applying highway design standards to city streets as a gradual 'nibbling away' of the streetspace to accommodate only the automobile (Jacobs, 1961; see also Norton, 2011). As this process unfolded, the risks associated with bicycling increased, bicycle accessibility decreased and bicycle use all but ceased.

Despite its decline as a utilitarian mode of transport, the growing popularity of recreational bicycling helped foster bicycling infrastructure. And, commuter cycling rates are slowly—yet steadily—increasing nationally, with some cities and regions experiencing significant increases. High-quality, off-street facilities are in relatively high demand as a neighborhood amenity, but their success in enhancing accessibility, particularly for disadvantaged groups, strongly depends on the local land use and built environment conditions.

Cyclists in the US today generally fall into three categories: (1) low-income, mostly minority, individuals; (2) upper middle-class white males; and (3) recreational cyclists. While admittedly an oversimplification, it assists in exploring the implications of the framework outlined here.

Transportation planners and advocates use terms like 'captive riders' to describe the first group—individuals who, out of economic necessity, travel by ways other than driving. This wording underscores the disadvantaged position of these individuals, not only in terms of income, but also in terms of experienced accessibility levels. The latter two groups are often referred to as 'choice riders.' While investments and policies most often focus on choice riders, as their travel and mode choices are subject to influence, only the 'captive riders' group meets our first condition for socially just investment in cycling infrastructure.

Historically, low-income households lived in areas of central US cities in which employment and services were typically located within cycling distances and land use patterns were highly supportive of cycling. There, cycling could have substantially increased the accessibility levels of disadvantaged groups. However, the rapid suburbanization of employment since the 1960s has changed the landscape for low-skilled workers dramatically, resulting in a spatial mismatch between residential and job location. Much of the employment is now located well-beyond feasible cycling distance. Accordingly, cycling investments in these urban neighborhoods would not meet our second condition: they are neither an effective nor efficient means to improve the accessibility levels of low-income households. Though admittedly a small number do make these long work trips by bicycle, it is unlikely for this activity to grow into a broader solution (compared to driving or public transit). This analysis would ignore, however, the potential of the bicycle for non-commute travel, such as trips to school, shops, urban services and to family and friends. By focusing only on labor market participation and commuting trips, the potential empowering effect of cycling interventions are thus overlooked. For instance, cycling investments in poor urban neighborhoods may well be an efficient way to reduce the 'food deserts' that have emerged over the past decades (McKenzie, 2014).

The situation is not that different for the increasing population of low-income households residing in suburban areas. While these groups show higher levels of car ownership than their urban counterparts, not all households, nor all adults, have access to a car. Furthermore, some households may be 'forced' into car ownership, 'choosing' income poverty over transport poverty. Households may also own a car but be very selective in the use of the car to reduce operating and maintenance costs, implying that owning a car may not necessarily translate into car-based accessibility. These households thus also meet the first condition: they are disadvantaged in terms of their accessibility levels. At first sight, the bicycle may do little to improve accessibility levels. Suburban environments typically have low densities and separated land uses, resulting in large distances to services and employment.

In some suburban environments, however, cycling investments may well be an effective and efficient means to increase accessibility levels for disadvantaged persons; they may thus be warranted from a justice perspective for three reasons. First, some residential areas outside central cities may be located sufficiently close to suburban centers of employment and services. Second, most suburban neighborhoods have excess road space that could be converted at relatively low cost—i.e. efficiently—into safe bicycle lanes. Third, alternatives to cycling investments may be less effective and less efficient in increasing accessibility levels of these disadvantaged population groups. Public transport is often inefficient in suburban areas due to low densities and unsuitable street layouts (but see Mees, 2010). Subsidies on car ownership, in turn, are politically contentious and may do little to promote accessibility for all household members (i.e. if only one car is subsidized, and because youth are excluded from driving). Depending on the exact geography of the suburban landscape, investments in cycling facilities, in particular infrastructure that connects neighborhoods to nearby activity centers, may thus meet the second condition outlined above.

The second general group of cyclists—upper middle-class white males—is comprised of two populations often associated with the current bicycle movement: the millennial generation (those born in the last two decades of the 20th century) and the baby-boomer generation (those born between 1946 and 1964). Clearly, the reality is that only small subsets of these groups are responsible for this movement (Lachman and Brett, 2015; Keenan, 2010; Farber and Shingle, 2011). The cycling part of the baby-boomer generation tends to be white, highly educated and with higher incomes. While a growing number of Americans of all ages are seeking an alternative to auto-dependency in downtown neighborhoods, this population is able to realize this desire, frequently at the expense of incumbent low-income residents. This group can voluntarily forego car ownership, as they tend to work in close vicinity to their new residence and are able to gain access to destinations through walking, cycling, public transport and car sharing services. While they may be formally car-less, these households have the resources to obtain car-based accessibility whenever the need arises. They thus do not meet our first condition: they are not disadvantaged in terms of their levels of accessibility. In turn, investments in cycling facilities that have often paralleled the process of gentrification are not warranted from a justice perspective: there is hardly a reason why 'you' or 'I' should give up some of our income, through taxation, so that local authorities can supply 'them' with cycling infrastructure. Indeed, it seems more reasonable that cycling infrastructure, if desired by these population groups, would be self-financed, for instance through an additional form of taxation that appropriates a share of the often sharp increases in property values in gentrifying neighborhoods. When ranking the social justice impacts of cycling facilities financed through general forms of taxation, investments in gentrified neighborhoods should be clearly at the bottom of the priority list.

The situation is perhaps somewhat different for the millennial generation. One of the reasons for decreasing car ownership and use among this group in comparison to previous generations is the lower levels of income and income security. In comparison to the baby-boomers, car-free or 'car-light' lifestyles are thus only partly a matter of choice or environmental attitudes for the millennials (McDonald, 2015). At the same time, this population group is clearly much better off than the urban and suburban poor, certainly if their future perspective is taken into account. Furthermore, 'car-free' millennials often have the resources to *choose* a car-free lifestyle in an inner city location over a car-dependent lifestyle in the suburbs. Clearly this population is substantially less disadvantaged, both in terms of opportunities and in terms of their potential level of accessibility, than the urban and suburban poor. This suggests that the millennial generation does not fully meet our first condition—and that investments in cycling for this group should therefore be critically scrutinized.

The third group of cyclists—recreational cyclists—does not meet our two conditions. This is so because (a) they are often a privileged group, overlapping substantially with upper middle-class white male cyclists; and (b) interventions to exclusively promote recreational cycling often have marginal impact on accessing needed destinations, and therefore are likely to do little to enhance accessibility levels. Investments in cycling infrastructure for this group are thus not warranted based on their ability to advance justice. This does not rule out that such investments may be justified on other grounds, such as promoting health (which may in turn enhance capabilities for disadvantaged groups), but that would require a separate line of argument beyond the scope of this chapter.

Dutch application: ubiquitous bike planning in need of more

The Netherlands is well-known for its high levels of bicycle ridership and its high-quality cycling infrastructure. In this section, we briefly reflect on a number of bicycle policies that have brought cycling levels in the Netherlands to where they now are, exploiting the justice lens developed in the beginning of this chapter.

Modern bicycle policy in the Netherlands emerged in the 1970s, in part in response to the oil crisis of 1973, the increasing environmental awareness strengthened by the 'Limits to Growth' report, as well as the mounting critique about the lack of road safety, with 3,000 traffic deaths at its peak in 1971, many of whom were (young) cyclists. The Netherlands adopted a national policy in 1975, the first country to do so. The policy introduced a fund, which provided 50–80 percent subsidy to local authorities for the construction of urban and rural bicycle facilities. Local authorities used the funds to build separate bicycle lanes along main roads in cities and along secondary and tertiary roads out of town, to cater for commuting, school and shopping trips by bicycle. Within a decade, 227 million euros were provided as subsidies, distributed over virtually all Dutch municipalities (Rietveld, 2004).

Were these investments warranted from the perspective of justice? Largely speaking, yes. The bicycle paths served a population that depended on bicycling for accessibility and mobility. Car ownership was still at a relatively low level, so many lower-income workers relied on the bicycle to travel to work. Likewise, schools in the Netherlands rarely provided bus services. Because of the schooling system, children in the age between 12 and 18 typically also had to travel over substantial distances to school, ruling out walking as a feasible option. While both groups already travelled by bicycle, the high fatality rate among cyclists and rapidly increasing car ownership and use clearly posed a threat to their accessibility. By building safe and comfortable bicycle lanes, accessibility for these groups could be safeguarded. The investments thus clearly met the first requirement of justice: they benefited persons with (potentially) sub-standard accessibility levels.

The degree to which these investments were effective and efficient is more difficult to answer, as it would require a systematic comparison with possible alternative transportation interventions. Yet it could be argued that enhancing cycling safety was indeed an effective and efficient way to protect the independent mobility and thus independent accessibility of children below the driving age. School buses can never provide the same level of freedom, as they only serve the home-to-school trip at a particular time of the day. The only alternatives providing a comparable level of freedom to this group would have been costly improvements to the public transport system or subsidies on travel by taxis. During this period, public transport ridership was rapidly falling and, in response, service was reduced. Maintaining or improving the quality of service would have required substantial funds. Likewise, salaries were rapidly increasing in these years, while technologies to efficiently pool rides were still missing, making taxis a relatively expensive option (and, if only provided for trips to school or work, providing a much lower level of accessibility). We therefore conclude that both public transport and taxi services would probably have been much more expensive than the investments in bicycle paths to guarantee independent accessibility to the groups mentioned above.

Some advances were also made via changes in street design, notably traffic calming measures (Pharoah and Russell, 1991). Strictly speaking, traffic calming does not aim to promote cycling. The goal of traffic calming measures is to reduce the speed of motorized vehicles in order to increase traffic safety, primarily in residential streets. Traffic calming thus requires a sacrifice from 'me' in terms of speed, travel time and travel comfort, so that 'you' can enjoy a safer street space. The benefits thus flow from car (and bus and truck) drivers to pedestrians and cyclists as well as playing children. Following earlier policy initiatives, traffic calming returned to the Dutch policy agenda in the second half of the 1990s. In 1997, a covenant was signed by all involved authorities, outlining a two-stage strategy. In the first stage, running from 1998–2003, the focus was on completing easily implementable measures, including infrastructure, legislative, educational and enforcement measures. In the second stage, starting in 2004, traffic calming was to be integrated into a comprehensive transport policy and infrastructure measures were to be integrated in regular road maintenance and upgrading. Key components of these policies were the introduction of 30 km/h zones and street redesigns to physically reduce driving speeds. These measures serve pedestrians as well as cyclists, by reducing car speeds and creating a safer environment for cycling, and thus safeguarding accessibility by bicycle for both 'choice riders' and disadvantaged groups who may rely on cycling. Broadly speaking, traffic calming thus meets the justice principles outlined here: they benefited persons with sub-standard accessibility levels, such as children or car-less households. However, traffic calming measures were mostly introduced as streets or underlying infrastructure were in need of refurbishment. As such, traffic calming measures were prioritized based on maintenance requirements, as opposed to population needs. The national traffic calming strategy, while largely in line with the principles outlined here, thus could have done more to promote justice in the domain of accessibility.

In recent years, bicycle highways have been aggressively employed, particularly targeting (higher-income) commuters. In order to obtain national funding, authorities promoting bicycle highways are often required to show that these 'highways' lead to reductions in congestion on the road network and thus to substantial travel time savings. Bicycle highways are thus justified, at least in part, by their ability to replace car trips. Consequently, these investments focus first and foremost on choice riders, rather than on persons whose accessibility could be most improved. Moreover, bicycle highways typically serve destinations already well-connected to the bicycle network, while lower-wage employment locations on urban edges are often poorly connected to the bicycle network in many cities. In light of these particularities, investments in bicycle highways are hardly in line with our justice principles.

In contrast, our framework suggests that funding bicycle lessons for minority and immigrant residents so that they may benefit from the vast bicycle network in Dutch cities is well-warranted on the basis of justice. These population groups show low car-ownership levels and often reside in bicycle-accessible cities and neighborhoods. Assisting these residents to 'appropriate' the bicycle may thus substantially increase their levels of accessibility, in particular in medium-sized cities with relatively sparse public transport networks. Yet, in contrast to the substantial funds reserved for bicycle highways, these programs struggle to obtain funding from local authorities and often rely on volunteers to continue operation (van der Kloof, 2015). Clearly, enhanced investment in bicycle lessons is warranted on justice grounds.

This brief reflection on Dutch bicycle policies shows that, while historic investments in bicycle infrastructures are largely in line with the justice framework proposed here, more recent investments are less equitable. At the same time, the well-developed cycling network and dense urban fabric provides a fertile context for measures that do live up to our two conditions of justice. This includes continuing investments to enhance convenient and safe cycling for groups that depend on cycling for their accessibility (youth, car-less and often low-income households, car-less elderly) as well as 'soft measures' to promote bicycle uptake among groups that could substantially enhance their accessibility through cycling (ethnic minorities in cities).

Conclusion

In this chapter we argue that two conditions must be met for public interventions promoting cycling to be warranted based on arguments of social justice within a liberal-egalitarian framework. First, they must enhance accessibility of persons with sub-standard accessibility (e.g. those who are not allowed to or cannot afford to drive a car). Second, cycling interventions are warranted on justice grounds if they effectively and efficiently improve accessibility for underserved populations. Interventions are warranted whenever cycling interventions can substantially enhance accessibility for groups experiencing substandard accessibility levels, i.e. in lower-income areas with relatively low car-ownership levels and a mixture of destinations within cycling distance. Such interventions may also be warranted in communities in which private motorized transport is the domain of a small, wealthier group and where public transport provides poor levels of service, such as towns and cities in the developing world. It is warranted in neighborhoods with large numbers of children who depend on cycling for their independent mobility. Yet, it is less warranted in communities enjoying high levels of accessibility due to a well-developed public transport system or because of high levels of car ownership in conjunction with a functioning road system. Likewise, cycling might be less warranted in (suburban) areas in which most destinations are farther away than most persons are willing to cycle.

Our argument also implies that sacrificing road space now reserved for motorized transport is justified if car accessibility is high and reduced road space would not push car-based accessibility levels below a socially accepted standard of accessibility (defining the socially acceptable threshold is context-dependent and beyond the scope of this chapter). However, sacrificing bus lanes to enhance cycling is not likely warranted, given the sub-standard accessibility levels provided by existing public transport systems in most cities. The second condition furthermore suggests that whenever cycling is, or is expected to be, a transport mode used by only a small minority, interventions and policies aimed at enhancing accessibility levels of disadvantaged groups through modes other than cycling may be better-supported based on arguments of justice.

Our argument for the social good of accessibility can also be developed for other goods with a distinct social meaning, such as health or environmental quality. For instance, the enormous health costs of traffic accidents suggest that it is warranted to ask for sacrifices in terms of reduced driving speed, thereby enhancing the safety of cycling. Likewise, the enormous impacts of transport-related environmental externalities on the livelihoods of persons in developing countries seems to imply that sacrifices may be warranted to avoid a further decrease in the standard of living of people who are already deprived. These lines of reasoning, however, are more complex in nature than the one relating to accessibility, as they expand the line of reasoning into domains beyond transportation (health) and far beyond the borders of the metropolitan region (environment, both local and global).

We identify how efforts to promote cycling requires rethinking assumptions about cycling culture, neighborhood change and planning processes. Justifications for why certain efforts are advanced should be interrogated in robust planning processes. Simply promoting cycling across the board for reasons of health, environment or 'choice' often leads to misplaced priorities that do little to address the plight of population groups who are often neglected in transportation planning and could *best* benefit from more bicycle-friendly neighborhoods and cities.

References

Farber, N. & Shingle, D. (2011) *Aging in place: a state survey of livability policies and practices*. National Conference of State Legislatures and the AARP Public Policy Institute.

Jacobs, J. (1961) *The death and life of great American cities*. New York/Toronto: Random House.

Keenan, T. (2010) *Home and community preferences of the 45+ population*. Washington, DC: AARP.

Khisty, C.J. (1996) Operationalizing Concepts of Equity for Public Project Investments. Transportation Research Record: *Journal of the Transportation Research Board*, 1559. pp.94–99.

Lachman, L. & Brett, D. (2015) *Gen Y and Housing: what they want and where they want it*. Washington, DC: Urban Land Institute.

Langmyhr, T. (1997) Managing equity: the case of road pricing. *Transport Policy*, 4(1). pp.25–39.

Lessig, L. (1995) The regulation of social meaning. *The University of Chicago Law Review*, 62(3). pp.943–1045.

McDonald, N. (2015) Are millennials really the 'go nowhere' generation? *Journal of the American Planning Association*, 81(2). pp.90–103.

McKenzie, B.S. (2014) Access to supermarkets among poorer neighborhoods: a comparison of time and distance measures. *Urban Geography*, 35(1). pp.133–151.

Martens, K. (2016) *Transport justice: designing fair transportation systems*. New York/London: Routledge.

Martens, K. & Golub, A. (2012) A justice-theoretic exploration of accessibility measures. In: Geurs, K.T., Krizek, K.J., & Reggiani, A. (eds.), *Accessibility analysis and transport planning: challenges for Europe and North America* (NECTAR Series on Transportation and Communications Networks Research). Cheltenham: Edward Elgar, pp.195–210.

Martens, K., Golub, A., & Robinson, G. (2012) A justice-theoretic approach to the distribution of transportation benefits: implications for transportation planning practice in the United States. *Transportation Research Part A: Policy and Practice*, 46(4). pp.684–695.

Mees, P. (2010) *Transport for suburbia: beyond the automobile age*. London/Washington DC: Earthscan.

Norton, P. (2011) *Fighting traffic: the dawn of the motor age in the American city*. Cambridge, MA: MIT Press.

Nussbaum, M.C. (2003) Capabilities as fundamental entitlements: Sen and social justice. *Feminist Economics*, 9(2–3). pp.33–59.

Pharoah, T.M. & Russell, J.R.E. (1991) Traffic calming policy and performance: the Netherlands, Denmark and Germany. *Town Planning Review*, 62(1). pp.79–105.

Rawls, J. (1971) *A theory of justice*. Cambridge, MA: Harvard University Press.

Rietveld, P. (2004) *Urban Transport Policies: The Dutch Struggle with Market Failures and Policy Failures*. Tinbergen Institute Discussion Paper No. 04–126/3.

Robeyns, I. (2013) The capability approach (and social justice). In: Gaus, G. & D'Agostino, F. (eds.), *The Routledge companion to social and political philosophy*. New York/London: Routledge, pp.456–466.

Sen, A. (1983) Poor, relatively speaking. *Oxford Economic Papers*, 35(2). pp.153–169.

Tyler, N. (2006) Capabilities and radicalism: engineering accessibility in the 21st century. *Transportation Planning and Technology*, 29(5). pp.331–358.

van der Kloof, A. (2015) Lessons learned through training immigrant women in the Netherlands to cycle. In: Cox, P. (ed.) *Cycling cultures*. Chester: University of Chester Press, pp.78–105.

van der Kloof, A., Bastiaanssen, J., & Martens, K. (2014) Bicycle lessons, activity participation and empowerment. *Case Studies on Transport Policy*, 2(2). pp.89–95.

Viegas, J.M. (2001) Making road pricing acceptable and effective: searching for quality and equity in urban mobility. *Transport Policy*, 8(4). pp.289–294.

Walzer, M. (1983) *Spheres of justice: a defense of pluralism and equality*. New York: Basic Books.

7 Theorizing bicycle justice using social psychology

Examining the intersection of mode and race with the conceptual model of roadway interactions

Tara Goddard

Introduction

Planners and engineers have come a long way in understanding the inequitable ways that infrastructure investment can benefit certain communities while negatively impacting, even destroying, others (Martens et al., 2012). There has been increasing recognition that infrastructure planning and implementation, especially (but not exclusively) in the United States, often negatively affects people of color and immigrants; for example, via highway construction or transit-system decisions (Martens et al., 2012). These system-level decisions of *where* and *for whom* are often made far away from planning charrettes or engineering plans for individual projects. That does not mean, however, that decisions made at the design and engineering level are exempt from consideration of potentially inequitable impacts. When advancing the dual goals of increased bicycle ridership and bicyclist safety, planners, engineers, and advocates must acknowledge that people's interactions with infrastructure do not occur in an asocial vacuum, and roadway users do not interact with or experience the roadway environment in exactly the same ways. Understanding the underlying mechanisms for these differing experiences is vital to creating a bicycle transportation system that is not only effective and safe, but just.

This chapter links several established social psychological concepts and applies them to interactions between roadway users to provide guidance on accounting for race and racism in bicycle policy and planning. It introduces a conceptual model of roadway interactions as a framework for understanding the potential impacts and interactions of physical, individual, and sociocultural factors on the interactions of drivers and bicyclists. This model suggests that explicit or implicit racial biases, both at the individual and system level, might help explain the increased perceptions and realities of danger for bicyclists of color in particular.

After briefly presenting the racial imbalance in safety statistics, I examine the ways that current applied research and planning discussions ignore or erase race, even among some of the best examples of bicycle planning discourse and research.

In the next section, I introduce important social psychological concepts and theories relevant to roadway interactions, including those most relevant for understanding potential impacts of bias in roadway interactions. Next, I bring those concepts and theories together in the conceptual model, which provides graphical representation of the interrelationships of the social psychological concepts and theories. Finally, I conclude with a discussion of why engaged bicycle professionals should concern themselves with these social psychological factors of roadway interactions, and how these aspects of roadway interactions are poorly understood but of vital importance to a just bicycle future.

Defining the problem

Bicycle safety statistics

Vulnerable road users (pedestrians, bicyclists, motorcyclists) comprise nearly half (46 percent) of traffic fatalities worldwide and the majority of severe traffic injuries and fatalities in large cities, despite their relatively small mode share, while car occupants, the dominant mode, represent fewer than 10 percent of fatalities (Shinar, 2012). In the United States, bicyclists are 12 times more likely to be killed in a traffic crash than people in cars (Pucher and Dijkstra, 2003). These injuries and fatalities are not distributed equally amongst the bicycling population, however. Even controlling for urban exposure and socio-economic status, Black and Hispanic vulnerable road users are disproportionally represented in US traffic deaths; the fatality rate for Hispanic bicyclists is 23 percent higher than for White bicyclists, while Black bicyclists' fatality rate is 30 percent higher than for White bicyclists (League of American Bicyclists, 2013). When you consider that, in 2009, Black and Latino/Hispanic bicyclists took a combined 657 *million* trips, and these groups had the first and third highest rates of growth in bicycle trips, respectively, this inequitable danger represents a significant public health and safety impact.

Why is bicycling dangerous?

Bicycling is not an inherently dangerous activity. Drivers represent the greatest danger to bicyclists, particularly where traffic speeds are high (Siman-Tov et al., 2012). Bicyclists in an automobile-involved collision are over three times as likely to suffer a serious injury (Rivara et al., 1997) and significantly more likely to suffer a traumatic brain injury (Juhra et al., 2012) than bicyclists in non-automobile-involved crashes. Crashes between drivers and bicyclists are frequently attributed to a driver's failure to see a bicyclist, due to inattention or "Looked but failed to see (LBFTS)" (Wood et al., 2009), and there is ample evidence from psychology that "seeing" is not purely objective but is influenced by socially directed thoughts and beliefs (Mack and Rock, 1998).

Existing research into the crash causation of bicycling traffic deaths has focused primarily on instrumental factors (e.g. intersection type, vehicle speed) but little research has probed the role of attitudes or socio-cognitive mechanisms in inter-actions between roadway users (Musselwhite et al., 2010). It is a widely held, but incorrect, view that driving is mainly a perceptual-motor skill (Groeger, 2002), wherein people perceive everything in their environment and then merely need to respond accordingly by physically operating the vehicle. In reality, people do not attend to or process all information in their environment (Mack and Rock, 1998). Since much information processing is automatic, attitudes and biases can subconsciously affect how people attend to and process information (Ajzen and Fishbein, 2000). When humans interact, brain activity called "socio-cognitive processing" is automatically invoked, and research shows that interacting with bicyclists puts additional cognitive demands on drivers, in addition to the per-ceptual and motor skills involved in operating a vehicle (Walker, 2005). As humans have been shown to rely on social information in many other domains, particularly under time or cognitive constraints, it is likely that social judgments affect roadway interactions.

There is evidence that drivers do not treat all road users equally. The visible "humanness" of vulnerable road users, in particular, triggers automatic and involuntary (i.e. implicit) cognitions and processes (Walker, 2005). While the physical bodywork of a car essentially anonymizes drivers, bicyclists are visible in their variety of shapes, sizes, ages, gender, and "racialized bodies" (Urry, 2007, p. 48). Drivers have shown bias in yielding behavior by the race, apparent disabled status, or age of a crossing pedestrian (Goddard et al., 2015; Harrell, 1992; Rosenbloom and Nemrodov, 2006), while drivers in higher status cars were less likely to yield to a pedestrian (Piff et al., 2012). When interacting with bicyclists, drivers used greater passing distance when the bicyclist was unhelmeted or appeared female (Walker, 2007).

Although none of these studies tested drivers' attitudes or biases directly, it is clear that, all else being equal, drivers make conscious or subconscious decisions about how to behave around other roadway users based on visible features that have socially constructed importance. Furthermore, the bodywork of a car pro-vides anonymity to drivers that acts as a social shield from behind which discrimination can be enacted with low chance of social reprisal (Urry, 2007). Considering the complexity of the roadway environment, visible humanness of bicyclists and anonymity of drivers, ubiquity of implicit and explicit racial bias, and disproportionate ability of drivers to cause harm, it is important to understand the additive or multiplicative contributions of these factors to the experience and safety of bicyclists of color.

Previous work and the resounding silence on race

This book starts by problematizing the invisibility or denigration of certain types of bicyclists in the "dominant trifecta of advocacy, engineering, and policy" (see Introduction, this volume). Research, too, is guilty of excluding race from data collection, analysis, and theory. Even as the idea of "equity" has entered the ver-nacular of bicycle planners and advocates, equity is often conceived of from a modal standpoint, not a social or racial one. Whether because of the lasting impact of environmental determinism, discomfort with asking what are seen as "sensitive questions," privileging the expertise of a White, middle-class viewpoint (Vivanco, 2013), a lack of understanding about the potential impacts of social identity, or likely, a combination of these, race is often absent from many studies of bicycling planning and safety, which has the effect of erasing it entirely. In their critique of traditional travel behavior approaches, Skinner and Rosen call for a more inclusive and mutable approach that shifts the focus away "from the circumstances and choices of an archetypal individual towards an understanding of the varied conditions in which differently-placed people negotiate transport problems and choices" (Skinner and Rosen, 2007, p. 85). Yet even they, while explicitly mentioning age, gender, employment, and geography, subsume race under "and so on" (p. 85).

The 2012 book *City Cycling* (Pucher and Buehler, 2012), which covers a broad range of topics and is aimed at practitioners, is imminently readable and useful on a variety topics, but is virtually silent on race. There are chapters devoted to women and cycling, and children and cycling, respectively, but no chapter devoted to the experience of racial minorities or a discussion of intersectionality beyond those somewhat narrow gender and age discussions. It is unlikely that this reflects any conscious choice to exclude issues faced by bicyclists of color, nor a conscious dismissal that they matter. Rather, it may reflect what the introduction to this volume describes as a common practice of privileging certain experiences when experts "lobby for changes derived from their own qualitative experiences of bicycling" (see Introduction, this volume). Many of the dominant voices in bicycle planning and research are themselves bicyclists, and have firsthand knowledge of the vulnerability of being a bicyclist. But engineering, planning, and bicycle advocacy are all spaces historically and presently occupied largely by White men who do not face structural and individual discriminations based on their gender, race, or other social identities. Thus, they may not even conceive of the idea that drivers might enact racially biased behaviors on top of modally biased ones.

Even recent sociological works like the excellent *Cycling Cultures* (Cox, 2015) speak very little to the ways that social identity, especially race, intersect with bicycling as a mode. While the introductory chapter lays solid groundwork for considering the social nature and the potentially problematic "travelling body" of bicyclists (Cox, 2015, p. 7), most of the curated chapters use words like "minority" (p. 20), "sub-culture" (p. 29), "diversity" (p. 43), "marginalized" (p. 69), and "colonized" (p. 71) primarily to refer monolithically to bicycling as a mode and to problematize automobility and car culture. While addressing automobility is necessary for improving safety of all bicyclists, this co-opting of language often used to understand structural racism can itself erase the presence of other social identities, including race, that intersect and may dominate over someone's modal status. After all, a "cyclist" who otherwise has dominant group membership (i.e. White, male, cis-gendered, middle- or upper-class) can walk away from their bicycle and shed that "marginalized" modal identity, while a person of color or anyone who does not fit the default social status cannot shed their multiple stigmatized social group memberships.

In his seminal text *Mobilities*, the sociologist John Urry states that a "[mobility] turn is spreading in and through the social sciences, mobilizing analyses that have been historically static, fixed, and concerned with predominantly a-spatial 'social structures'" (Urry, 2007, p. 6). The corollary is also needed: to move away from a-social spatial approaches and incorporate tools from the social sciences. Planners, engineers, and anyone advocating for and promoting bicycle transportation must be willing to confront the potential impacts of racism in their work. A practical approach to bicycle planning and promotion must include "the social dimensions and tacit meanings people make" about their everyday travel (Vivanco, 2013, p. 10). While anthropology and sociology provide valuable processes for understanding the roadway at the historical and socio-structural and systemic level, social psychological theories, methods, and empirical evidence provide useful tools for understanding these interpersonal and intergroup behaviors in roadway interactions.

The social psychology of roadway interactions

There is a need for more theoretical analysis of the social psychological aspects of travel behavior in general (Van Acker et al., 2010). Transportation psychologists study the symbolic and affective factors of these interactions, but the literature on the social aspects of interactions between users of different modes is sparse. In the following sections, I describe some key social psychological theories and their potential to explain behavior between roadway users, particularly when mode type intersects with salient social identities like race. I then propose a theoretical model that seeks to capture the many dimensions of individual, environmental, and social contributions to roadway interactions. The model helps visualize how bicycle planning does not happen in an a-social or a-racial environment, and why people involved in promoting a just bicycle future need to understand how race and mode intersect.

Social psychology in the transportation context

Social psychology explores the ways that an individual's thoughts, feelings, and behaviors are influenced by the real or imagined presence of others (Allport, 1994). Put another way, social psychology is the study of the individual embedded in the social context (Baumeister, 2008). Social psychological research demonstrates that behavior has both reasoned and unreasoned components, while social psychological theories can help operationalize perceptions, attitudes, and preferences (Van Acker et al., 2010).

A primary focus of social psychology is the attitude construct, which describes organization of often-enduring beliefs, evaluations of, and behavior toward objects, groups, or events (Ajzen and Fishbein, 2000). How humans perceive the world and respond to stimuli is not purely objective, but rather is affected by our attitudes (Fazio, 1990). Although attitudes are recognized in transportation research and planning as important to reasoned behaviors like mode choice, their potential effects on interpersonal roadway behaviors is not well-studied. Even less well-understood or researched is the role that implicit attitudes may play, particularly in the complex, high-cognitive load environment of the roadway.

Explicit versus implicit attitudes

Implicit attitudes reflect a person's expectation or evaluation of a person or situation based on previous experiences, stereotypes, or other affective evaluation, and the impact of those previous experiences are not known to the individual to be influencing their attitude to the current object or experience, and are not accessible for self-reporting or conscious awareness (Greenwald and Banaji, 1995). Explicit attitudes, by contrast, can be consciously accessed and reported by an individual. Even if an individual chooses to give a socially acceptable answer that may be different than how they actually feel, they are, by definition, aware of their explicit attitudes.

Research on implicit racial attitudes is extensive (Nosek et al., 2007). In their 2013 book *Blind Spot: Hidden Biases of Good People*, Banaji and Greenwald share results from their decades of work on measuring implicit biases. As indicated by the title, many people truly want to believe they are egalitarian, but research shows that even people with explicit egalitarian beliefs display implicit racial biases and biased behavior (Banaji and Greenwald, 2013). A majority of Americans hold negative racial stereotypes (Nosek et al., 2007), which likely manifest in roadway behavior as they do in a multitude of other domains, including interpersonal interactions in the workplace, shopping, healthcare, and policing (Dovidio, 2001; Dovidio et al., 2002; Hebl et al., 2002; Kahn and Davies, 2011). Drivers, those with the most power to harm or discourage bicyclists, are likely to be affected consciously or subconsciously by their biases, and the characteristics of the roadway environment may facilitate the enactment of negative, and potentially fatal, racial biases.

These negative attitudes neither develop nor exist in a vacuum. Social psychological theories, methods, and empirical evidence provide useful tools for understanding these interpersonal and intergroup behaviors in roadway interactions. The concepts of social identity, stereotypes, social dominance, system justification, and culture can help explain how these negative attitudes arise and are enacted, and how they may contribute to negative roadway interactions.

Social identity

The primary tenet of Social Identity Theory is that social behavior is explainable through intergroup behavior, and one outcome of relating through group membership is that humans are motivated to view their own group (the "in-group") positively, while associating negative attributes with other groups (the "out-group") (Tajfel and Turner, 2004). Group membership increases identification with the in-group and perceived competition with the out-group. We see evidence of this in drivers' positive views of the rule-following behavior of other drivers, and the negative views of bicyclists' rule-following (Goddard et al., 2016), despite evidence that bicyclists may be even more law-abiding than drivers (Thompson, 2015).

The specific characteristics of the roadway environment may move interactions further toward this "intergroup" end of the spectrum: the physical separation of the car removes the necessity to observe face-to-face etiquette (Urry, 2007), while bicyclists' social identities (i.e. group memberships), may be highly visible. In a study probing drivers' view of other roadway users, participants described people in cars in "object-based" language (e.g. car, traffic, it) but described people walking or using bicycles in "human-based" language (e.g. bicyclist, pedestrian, person, they) (Walker, 2005). This visible humanness of vulnerable roadway users may make social identities salient (Steinbach et al., 2011). Travel mode affects people's perceptions of their environment, particularly when the situation is ambiguous or social cues are unclear (Gatersleben et al., 2013).

The misidentification of visual cues may lead to more socially construed, and potentially incorrect, evaluations of other roadway users. When asked to evaluate a simulated interaction of kids on a playground from the perspective of a passing pedestrian or driver, Gatersleben et al. found that respondents who viewed the scene from the perspective of a driver were the most likely to rate the interaction as negative or threatening, while respondents who viewed the video as though they were pedestrians evaluated the playground interaction as positive and judged the kids to be engaged in play (Gatersleben et al., 2013). This suggests a roadway-specific intersectionality, in which mode and social cognitions interact. We do not perceive ourselves, or each other, to be just one thing; rather, our multiple identities intersect and can be cumulative (Purdie-Vaughns and Eibach, 2008). To consider the intersectionality of mode and race, in particular, it is necessary to understand how stereotypes play a role in intergroup relations.

Stereotypes

Stereotypes are positive or negative evaluations of an entire group, and are a normal (if often problematic) way for humans to give order to our world. People attribute a set of characteristics (good or bad) to all members of a group solely based on group membership (Fiske et al., 2002). This concept is well-understood from a modal standpoint, where media or pop culture portrayal of bicyclists are often reductionist and othering (Basford et al., 2002). Unfortunately, stereotypes are usually more negative than positive (Banaji and Greenwald, 2013). Negative racial attitudes, even subconscious ones, can cause people to avoid contact with people of color, use less eye contact or fewer words in an interaction (and thus appear unwelcoming or hostile), and enact microaggressions, often without being aware of their behavior. This aversive behavior more often arises among people who do not want to believe that they hold any implicit racial bias, and fear being seen as racist, hence their "aversion" to being in a potentially uncomfortable situation and their guarded and shortened interactions (Dovidio et al., 2002). In the context of roadway interactions, the avoidance of eye contact or an aversion to interaction could lead to potentially miscommunicated intentions and unintended, unsafe behaviors.

Social dominance and system justification

Group membership happens at the system level as well as the individual level. Across all cultures, humans organize into "group-based social hierarchies" in which dominant groups have privileged access to resources (Pratto et al., 2006). Social Dominance Theory describes the discriminatory effects of this privilege at the institutional, individual, and intergroup levels. The more legitimate a system is perceived to be, the greater in-group favoritism and out-group discrimination that dominant users will display (Pratto et al., 2006). Our automobile system, although less than a century old, is inarguably the dominant mode. The automobile is considered the default mode in much of the Western world, as evidenced by mode share and even the term "alternative transportation" applied to bicycling and walking. One distinguishing characteristic of social dominance is that "the degree of lethality . . . is often orders of magnitude greater" by the dominant group toward the subordinate group (Pratto et al., 2006, p. 3). As discussed earlier, the roadway environment has a high degree of lethality: automobiles are a leading cause of preventable death (Pollack et al., 2012).

Considering the many subordinate groups in the automobile-dominant system, one might expect more resistance to the existing system. According to System Justification Theory (SJT), however, sometimes subordinate group members will justify the dominant system, even when it goes against their own interests (Jost et al., 2004). As negative is the automobile on the system level, at the individual household level it still represents a convenient, autonomous, status-conferring option (Handy et al., 2005). At the individual level, this suggests that drivers might view bicyclists as not just a momentary annoyance, but a threat to their social identity as a driver, and the system that both creates and requires that identity.

Social Dominance Theory and System Justification Theory can thus contribute to critical approaches to bike justice by understanding the multiplicative effects of both mode and race as delineating dominant and subordinate groups that compete for resources.

The conceptual model of roadway interactions

Synthesizing the social psychological theories above and applying them to the roadway environment, I propose a tripartite structure that considers the sociocultural context, the physical environment, and the individual (Figure 7.1). These three macro structures are found in the conceptual model of travel behavior advanced by Van Acker et al. (2010), but here they are conceptualized as adjacent and overlapping, rather than nested, structures. There are contributions

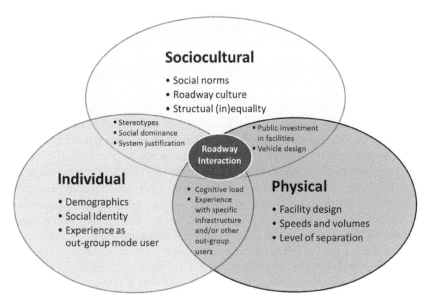

Figure 7.1 A conceptual model of roadway interactions

Source: Tara Goddard.

to roadway interactions that may be unique to one structure, and other factors where any two structures overlap. The central space of this diagram describes the context in which a roadway interaction occurs. The salience and relative strength of any one or several of the contributing factors predicts whether that roadway interaction is civil or negative, whether roadway users behave safely toward each other or not, whether the environment separates users or facilitates safe and courteous behavior, whether users are attentive to the task and physically and mentally capable of safe roadway interactions, whether an individual's beliefs about other road users or their own right to the system affects their behavior, and even what infrastructure is being constructed.

The expansion of the theoretical constructs in this conceptual model not already discussed above is outside the scope of this chapter. For a thorough examination of automobility and roadway culture, refer to Urry (2007) and Furness (2010). For discussion of the way that decisions about public investment in facilities are both physical and sociocultural, refer to *Incomplete Streets* (Zavestoski and Agyeman, 2014).

Discussion

Even if planners and engineers accept that racial biases may play a role in roadway behavior and the safety and experiences of bicyclists, it can be difficult to see what we can do about people's biases. Especially for those of us involved in questions of design and infrastructure, addressing intersectional modal and racial bias can feel like a problem over which we have no influence. However, because physical space is not the only factor structuring people's transportation choices (Lugo, 2013), those of us who advocate for, plan, design, and implement physical space for bicycle transportation are not exempt from trying to understand, and reduce, the impact of biased roadway behaviors. Interventions that address social identity, stereotypes, and attitudes are needed to broaden the possibilities for improved safety and roadway relations. Understanding the underlying psychology in roadway interactions is an important area for continued and expanded research, which can then be used to design interventions.

Infrastructure can be a form of a passive, population-based intervention that increases safety without individuals having to "opt in" (Teschke et al., 2012), but the majority of transportation studies evaluate behaviors related to infrastructure from an environmentally deterministic worldview, rather than considering the shaping role played by social norms and identity. For example, contact theory and its ability to reduce discomfort in interracial interactions (Singletary and Hebl, 2009) suggests that a prime area of research is potential interventions that increase understanding of other modes, particularly compensatory strategies that have shown promise in other domains. Compensatory strategies are concrete actions that people can take to counteract subconsciously held biases, by engaging in deliberate, rather than automatic, behaviors (Singletary and Hebl, 2009). For example, by being aware that yielding behavior may be dictated by racial bias, drivers can take extra care to see and stop for all pedestrians, regardless of their race. Personal experience may also affect how we treat other road users; for example, experience as a bicyclist may impact a driver's understanding and behavior around bicyclists (Goddard et al., 2016; Jacobsen, 2003). Perhaps most directly relevant to planners and engineers is better understanding of what infrastructure or designs can effectively pre-empt racial biases and facilitate safer, more equitable behavior that can directly create a more just environment for bicyclists of all social groups.

The psychology of driver–bicyclist interactions is understudied, and needed to understand the impact of encouragement programs and safety interventions in the short and long term. A greater understanding of roadway culture and the roadway as a system of dominant and subordinate groups may suggest how the non-dominant modes can be normalized and de-stigmatized. Efforts by bicycling advocates and planners, however, cannot continue to focus only on de-stigmatization of bicycling as a mode without recognizing the additional stigmas and discrimination faced by bicycling bodies that do not fit the default narrative about who is a bicyclist.

Conclusion

As planners, engineers, advocates, researchers, and engaged citizens, we must remember that travel behavior is comprised of social interactions, and like any other social interactions are subject to automatic processing, stereotyping, and bias. Roadways are highly congested (and thus contested), publicly funded space, and both space and funding are a finite and limited resource. This results in the perception and reality of roadway competition as a zero-sum game between roadway users (Aldred, 2012). It may be that this "realistic" competition is a stand-in for social competition; that is, the roadway is a battle ground for social domination, rather than just access to physical space. Of course, not all roadway interactions result in conflict and notions of incompatibility can shift. The goal of research in roadway interactions should be to understand when and why (or why not) conflict happens, and the roles that infrastructure, enforcement, and education play in avoiding or mitigating that conflict. As the case studies throughout this volume show, planning that engages with and is sensitive to local contexts can lead to environments with more equitable outcomes and greater possibility of avoiding conflict, including conflict caused by the social and literal collision of racism and mode-based bias.

Interactions between different types of roadway users, particularly between drivers and bicyclists, may be particularly influenced by social identity, social dominance and system justification, stereotype and stereotype threat, attentional and confirmation biases, fundamental attribution error, or other aspects of social psychology outside the scope of this chapter. Despite some empirical work in modal identity and intermodal interactions (Gatersleben et al., 2013; Murtagh et al., 2012; Salmon et al., 2014; Walker, 2005, to name a few), there is a need for a theoretical framework that ties together relevant theories from social psychology. The conceptual model of roadway interactions presented here is an attempt to create a theoretical model of roadway interactions that takes into account social psychological theories that address both interpersonal and intergroup relations, and which can be used to examine the intersectionality of race and mode.

I hope this discussion of important social psychological theories and the proposed model provide planners, engineers, and researchers with a better understanding that interactions on the roadway are not a-political or a-racial, and social cognitions may play a large role in both qualitative experiences and safety outcomes in the roadway. It is not enough to understand the structural and systemic racism that affects our transportation system; racial bias can have very real impacts at the interpersonal, individual-behavior scale on the roadway. The admirable goals of "safe and comfortable" bicycle infrastructure do not exist in an environmentally deterministic vacuum, but rather raise important questions about "comfortable in what way?" and "safe for who?"

References

Ajzen, I. & Fishbein, M. (2000) Attitudes and the Attitude-Behavior Relation: Reasoned and Automatic Processes. *European Review of Social Psychology*. 11 pp.1–33.

Aldred, R. (2012) Incompetent or Too Competent? Negotiating Everyday Cycling Identities in a Motor Dominated Society. *Mobilities*. 8 pp.252–271.

Allport, F.H. (1994) *Social Psychology*. London: Routledge/Thoemmes Press.

Banaji, M.R. & Greenwald, A.G. (2013) *Blindspot: Hidden Biases of Good People*. New York: Delacorte Press.

Basford, L., Reid, S., Lester, T., Thomson, J. & Tolmie, A. (2002) Driver's Perceptions of Cyclists. TRL Reports no. 549. Wokingham, UK: TRL.

Baumeister, R.F. (2008) *Social Psychology and Human Nature*. Belmont, CA: Thomson Higher Education.

Cox, P. (2015) *Cycling Cultures*. Chester, UK: University of Chester Press.

Dovidio, J.F. (2001) On the Nature of Contemporary Prejudice: The Third Wave. *Journal of Social Issues*. 57 pp.829–849.

Dovidio, J.F., Kawakami, K. & Gaertner, S.L. (2002) Implicit and Explicit Prejudice and Interracial Interaction. *Journal of Personality*. 82 pp.62–68.

Fazio, R.H. (1990) Multiple Processes by which Attitudes Guide Behavior: The Mode Model as an Integrative Framework. In Zanna, M.P. (ed.). *Advances in Experimental Social Psychology*. Academic Press, pp.75–109.

Fiske, S.T., Cuddy, A.J.C., Glick, P. & Xu, J. (2002) A Model of (Often Mixed) Stereotype Content: Competence and Warmth Respectively Follow from Perceived Status and Competition. *Journal of Personality and Social Psychology*. 82 pp.878–902.

Furness, Z. (2010) *One Less Car: Bicycling and the Politics of Automobility*. Philadelphia PA: Temple University Press.

Gatersleben, B., Murtagh, N. & White, E. (2013) Hoody, Goody or Buddy? How Travel Mode Affects Social Perceptions in Urban Neighbourhoods. *Transportation Research Part F: Traffic Psychology and Behaviour*. 21 pp.219–230.

Goddard, T., Kahn, K.B., & Adkins, A. (2015) Racial Bias in Driver Yielding Behavior at Crosswalks. *Transportation Research Part F: Traffic Psychology and Behaviour*. 33 pp.1–6.

Goddard, T., Dill, J. & Monsere, C. (2016) Driver Attitudes about Bicyclists: Negative Evaluations of Rule-Following and Predictability. *Transportation Research Record: Journal of the Transportation Research Board* [Submitted].

Greenwald, A.G. & Banaji, M.R. (1995) Implicit Social Cognition: Attitudes, Self-Esteem, and Stereotypes. *Psychological Review*. 102 pp.4–27.

Groeger, J.A. (2002) Trafficking in Cognition: Applying Cognitive Psychology to Driving. *Transportation Research Part F: Psychology and Behaviour*. 5 pp.235–248.

Handy, S., Weston, L. & Mokhtarian, P.L. (2005) Driving by Choice or Necessity? *Transportation Research Part A: Policy and Practice*. 39 pp.183–203.

Harrell, W.A. (1992) Driver Response to a Disabled Pedestrian Using a Dangerous Crosswalk. *Journal of Environmental Psychology*. 12 p.345.

Hebl, M.R., Foster, J.B., Mannix, L.M. & Dovidio, J.F. (2002) Formal and Interpersonal Discrimination: A Field Study of Bias Toward Homosexual Applicants. *Personality and Social Psychology Bulletin*. 28 pp.815–825.

Jacobsen, P. (2003) Safety in Numbers: More Walkers and Bicyclists, Safer Walking and Bicycling. *Injury Prevention*. 9 pp.205–209.

Jost, J.T., Banaji, M.R. & Nosek, B.A. (2004) A Decade of System Justification Theory: Accumulated Evidence of Conscious and Unconscious Bolstering of the Status Quo. *Political Psychology*. 25 pp.881–919.

Juhra, C., Wieskötter, B., Chu, K., Trost, L., Weiss, U., Messerschmidt, M., Malczyk, A., Heckwolf, M. & Raschke, M. (2012) Bicycle Accidents: Do We Only See the Tip of the Iceberg? A Prospective Multi-Centre Study in a Large German City Combining Medical and Police Data. *Injury*. 43 pp.2026–2034.

Kahn, K.B. & Davies, P.G. (2011) Differentially Dangerous? Phenotypic Racial Stereotypicality Increases Implicit Bias among Ingroup and Outgroup Members. *Group Processes Intergroup Relations*. 14 pp.569–580.

League of American Bicyclists (2013). The New Majority: Pedaling Towards Equity. Washington, D.C. [Online] Available at: www.bikeleague.org/sites/default/files/equity_report.pdf [Accessed August 9, 2015].

Lugo, A.E. (2013) CicLAvia and Human Infrastructure in Los Angeles: Ethnographic Experiments in Equitable Bike Planning *Journal of Transport Geography*. 30(2) pp.202–207.

Mack, A. & Rock, I. (1998) *Inattentional Blindness*. Cambridge, MA: MIT Press.

Martens, K., Golub, A. & Robinson, G. (2012) A Justice-Theoretic Approach to the Distribution of Transportation Benefits: Implications for Transportation Planning Practice in the United States. *Transportation Research Part A: Policy and Practice*. 46 pp.684–695.

Murtagh, N., Gatersleben, B. & Uzzell, D. (2012) Multiple Identities and Travel Mode Choice for Regular Journeys. *Transportation Research Part F: Traffic Psychology and Behaviour*. 15 pp.514–524.

Musselwhite, C., Avineri, E., Susilo, Y., Fulcher, E., Bhattachary, D. & Hunter, A. (2010) Understanding Public Attitudes to Road User Safety. UK Department for Transport. Road Safety Research Report no. 111. [Online] Available from: www.dft.gov.uk/pgr/roadsafety/research/rsrr/theme5/researchreport111/. [Accessed April 9, 2015].

Nosek, B.A., Smyth, F.L., Hansen, J.J., Devos, T., Lindner, N.M., Ranganath, K.A., Smith, C.T., Olson, K.R., Chugh, D., Greenwald, A.G. & Banaji, M.R. (2007) Pervasiveness and Correlates of Implicit Attitudes and Stereotypes. *European Review of Social Psychology*. 18 pp.36–88.

Piff, P.K., Stancato, D.M., Côté, S., Mendoze-Denton, R. & Keltner, D. (2012) Higher Social Class Predicts Increased Unethical Behavior. *PNAS*. 109 pp.4086–4091.

Pollack, K.M., Kercher, C., Frattaroli, S., Peek-Asa, C., Sleet, D. & Rivara, F.P. (2012) Toward Environments and Policies that Promote Injury-Free Active Living—It Wouldn't Hurt. *Health & Place*. 18 pp.106–114.

Pratto, F., Sidanius, J. & Levin, S. (2006) Social Dominance Theory and the Dynamics of Intergroup Relations: Taking Stock and Looking Forward. *European Review of Social Psychology*. 17 pp.271–320.

Pucher, J. & Dijkstra, L. (2003) Promoting Safe Walking and Cycling to Improve Public Health: Lessons From The Netherlands and Germany. *American Journal of Public Health*. 93 pp.1509–1516.

Pucher, J.R. & Buehler, R. (2012) *City Cycling*. Cambridge, MA: MIT Press.

Purdie-Vaughns, V. & Eibach, R.P. (2008) Intersectional Invisibility: The Distinctive Advantages and Disadvantages of Multiple Subordinate-Group Identities. *Sex Roles*. 59 pp.377–391.

Rivara, F.P., Thompson, D.C. & Thompson, R.S. (1997) Epidemiology of Bicycle Injuries and Risk Factors for Serious Injury. *Injury Prevention*. 3 pp.110–114.

Rosenbloom, T. & Nemrodov, D. (2006) Yielding Behavior of Israeli Drivers: Interaction of Age and Sex. *Perceptual and Motor Skills*. 103 pp.387–390.

Salmon, P.M., Lenne, M.G., Walker, G.H., Stanton, N.A. & Filtness, A. (2014) Exploring Schema-Driven Differences in Situation Awareness between Road Users: An On-Road Study of Driver, Cyclist and Motorcyclist Situation Awareness. *Ergonomics*. 57 pp.191–209.

Shinar, D. (2012) Safety and Mobility of Vulnerable Road Users: Pedestrians, Bicyclists, and Motorcyclists. *Accident Analysis & Prevention*. 44 pp.1–2.

Siman-Tov, M., Jaffe, D.H. & Peleg, K. (2012) Bicycle Injuries: A Matter of Mechanism and Age. *Accident Analysis & Prevention*. 44 pp.135–139.

Singletary, S.L. & Hebl, M.R. (2009) Compensatory Strategies for Reducing Interpersonal Discrimination: The Effectiveness of Acknowledgments, Increased Positivity, and Individuating Information. *Journal of Applied Psychology*. 94 pp.797–805.

Skinner, D. & Rosen, P. (2007). Hell is Other Cyclists: Rethinking Transport and Identity. In Horton, D., Rosen, P. & Cox, P. (eds.). *Cycling and Society*. London: Ashgate, pp.83–96.

Steinbach, R., Green, J., Datta, J. & Edwards, P. (2011) Cycling and the City: A Case Study of How Gendered, Ethnic and Class Identities Can Shape Healthy Transport Choices. *Social Science & Medicine*. 72 pp.1123–1130.

Tajfel, H. & Turner, J.C. (2004) The Social Identity Theory of Intergroup Behavior. In Jost, J.T. & Sidanius, J. (eds.). *Political Psychology: Key Readings*. New York: Psychology Press, pp.276–293.

Teschke, K., Harris, M.A., Reynolds, C.C., Winters, M., Babul, S., Chipman, M., Cusimano, M.D., Brubacher, J.R., Hunte, G., Friedman, S.M., Monro, M., Shen, H., Vernich, L. & Cripton, P.A. (2012) Route Infrastructure and the Risk of Injuries to Bicyclists: A Case-Crossover Study. *American Journal of Public Health*. 102 pp.2336–2343.

Thompson, S.R.R. (2015) Bicyclist Compliance at Signalized Intersections. M.A. thesis, Portland State University.

Urry, J. (2007) *Mobilities*. Malden, MA: Polity.

Van Acker, V., Van Wee, B. & Witlox, F. (2010) When Transport Geography Meets Social Psychology: Toward a Conceptual Model of Travel Behaviour. *Transport Reviews*. 30 pp.219–240.

Vivanco, L.A. (2013) *Reconsidering the Bicycle: An Anthropological Perspective on a New (Old) Thing*. New York: Routledge.

Walker, I. (2005) Road Users' Perceptions of Other Road Users: Do Different Transport Modes Invoke Qualitatively Different Concepts in Observers? *Advances in Transportation Research*. 6A pp.25–36.

Walker, I. (2007) Drivers Overtaking Bicyclists: Objective Data on the Effects of Riding Position, Helmet Use, Vehicle type and Apparent Gender. *Accident Analysis & Prevention*. 39.

Wood, J.M., Lacherez, P.F., Marszalek, R.P. & King, M.J. (2009) Drivers' and Cyclists' Experiences of Sharing the Road: Incidents, Attitudes and Perceptions of Visibility. *Accident Analysis & Prevention*. 41 pp.772–776.

Zavestoski, S. & Agyeman, J. (2014) *Incomplete Streets: Processes, Practices, and Possibilities*. New York: Routledge.

8   Delivering (in)justice

Food delivery cyclists in New York City

Do J. Lee, Helen Ho, Melyssa Banks,
Mario Giampieri, Xiaodeng Chen
and Dorothy Le

Introduction

New York City (NYC) affords its residents the luxury of ordering food to be delivered anytime, anywhere. However, that luxury comes at a steep price. Food delivery cyclists are usually low-income, male, and Asian and Latino immigrants. Despite being an integral part of the city, these cyclists are one of the most underrepresented, unheard, and exploited labor forces in NYC. Yet, many NYC residents who order delivery food castigate and fear the food delivery workers as "bad" cyclists who threaten public safety as seen in this quote from a *NY Post* article:

> **Szechuan Psychos.** Working for tips and of questionable immigration status, they serve in the mechanized infantry of General Tso's army. Rusted rides and dumpling physiques generally prevent these wonton warriors from building up much speed – but they prowl residential neighborhoods at night. You'll never see the one that gets you. Nor will you be able to sue him for all he's worth, unless you don't mind being paid in moo shu pork.
>
> (Smith, 2009)

We often choose to ignore the voices and experiences of immigrant food delivery workers who often voice counter-narratives to their public denigration:

> Alvarez recounts his life in America as a cautionary tale for immigrants, one he says is common in the restaurant industry. "I don't believe in the law, not even here," he says. "This is the country of freedom? Not for everybody."
>
> (Delivery City, 2011)

As we explore in this chapter, the production of "bad" food delivery cyclists illustrates the problematic tensions present in how cities in concert with bike planners and advocates move to conceptualize and enact bike justice in our streets.

NYC has been on a prosperous upward tick as the white flight trend has reversed itself. Increasingly, the city has become a desirable place to live for affluent whites with gentrification rapidly increasing and displacing low-income residents (Newman and Wyly, 2006). In this context and with the Internet, food delivery has been growing at a dizzying pace that may account for upwards of half of a restaurant's business in NYC (Marritz, 2015; Transportation Alternatives, 2015).

In 2007, then-Mayor Bloomberg appointed Janette Sadik-Khan as the city's Transportation Commissioner. She became known informally as the "Bike Commissioner" (Grynbaum, 2011). Thrilling bicycle advocates, Sadik-Khan worked to reorder street life to allow room for bicyclists who historically struggled for space. In her seven-year tenure, Sadik-Khan built 366 miles of bike lanes, initiated bike share, and has a legacy that continues onward (Flegenheiner, 2013). Bike movements usually represent and advocate for largely privileged white and affluent populations (Blue, 2013). Simultaneously, bicyclists feel marginalized within streets designed for drivers where cyclists are often harmed, stigmatized, and harassed. Bicyclists comprise the smallest share of users of the street although NYC bicycling has been rapidly growing (Pucher et al., 2010). To build bike lanes quickly, NYC officials sought the blessing of local communities and this resulted in bike advocates and their allies getting bike lanes in affluent and rapidly gentrifying neighborhoods. This rapid growth of NYC's bike infrastructure has neglected low-income cyclists who are often poorly served by mass transit (Applebaum et al., 2011).

In bike infrastructure conversations, immigrant food delivery cyclists are absent. Although food delivery cyclists may comprise upwards of 45 percent of the NYC bike riding population, they are not organized within bike advocacy (Tuckel and Milczarski, 2009). As Chapter 1 notes that bicycling on the margins can be experienced as oppressive, our analysis will demonstrate how food delivery cycling is produced systematically as "bad" cycling that results in the criminalization of immigrant working cyclists. This criminalization is reinforced by tip-based livelihoods that strongly incentivize delivery cyclists to break the car-based rules of the street in order to meet the time demands of delivery. We will discuss the potential of mutual implication to build solidarities across cyclists and to value the public knowledge generated by the marginalized (Torre, 2009). Public knowledge from marginalized cyclists such as food delivery workers can provide the foundation for counter-narratives and more equitable restructurings of the street and city landscapes in the pursuit of bike justice.

Throughout this chapter, we the authors share short vignettes in *italics* that highlight our connection to and our mutual implication with food delivery cycling. The following is one such example:

> *On my very first delivery to an upscale apartment building in the West Village, I called the customer when I got to the building, and she sounded confused: why had I expected her to come down to get her food? Unfortunately I hadn't brought a lock to secure my bike (I really didn't know what I was doing), and I began to panic.*

I asked the front desk attendant if I could leave my bike in the lobby. "Absolutely not, you can't bring that in here," he responded, looking at me like I was lost. Eventually I convinced him to let me leave the bike by the service elevator around the block, and took the service elevator up. Our exchange was brief: the door opened, I handed her a box of food, and the door closed.

—Mario

Methodology

We employed a theoretical analysis of food delivery cycling based upon three key themes: (1) visibly invisible cyclists; (2) crossing borders; and (3) mutual implication, which is how people are connected in the production of each other's lives. Our analysis is also informed by Scott's (1990) public and hidden transcripts. Public transcripts are what is being said openly between the dominant and the subordinate while hidden transcripts are the dialogues that happen out of the direct view by the powerful (Scott, 1990). Therefore, Scott (1990, p. 5) contends, "By assessing the discrepancy between the hidden transcript and the public transcript we may begin to judge the impact of domination on public discourse." In this way, our theoretical analysis is supported through a media analysis of food delivery cycling (Altheide, 1996). Our theoretical and media analyses examine the difference of what is being said about food delivery cyclists by the powerful and how delivery cyclists speak back to power.

We looked for themes in discourses about NYC food delivery cyclists in various media sources. This case study draws on a wide range of materials. We searched online using three search terms: "food delivery NYC," "food delivery cycling," and "food deliverymen" and identified 74 media stories that talked about food delivery cyclists. The media sources included: (1) newspapers such as *The New York Times*, *NY Post*, and *NY Daily News*; (2) online news media such as *The Atlantic*, *Gothamist*, *Voices of NY*, and *Huffington Post*; (3) online blogs, websites, or other media such as Transportation Alternatives, *My Upper West Side*, *Streetsblog*, and *WNYC*. Media stories were selected if they appeared between 2004 and 2015 as food delivery cycling grew exponentially in this period. We thematically coded media stories, which allowed us to analyze evidence that supports and provides specificity and nuance to our theoretical framework (Braun and Clarke, 2006).

Visibly invisible cyclists

While working as a food delivery cyclist in midtown Manhattan, I was riding the right way down the street when I noticed a well-dressed woman about to step into the street. I slowed down and veered to avoid her, as she didn't look for traffic in the right direction before attempting to cross. As I passed her, she yelled out, "Wrong way!" I was angry. They were jaywalking, and I was careful not to hit them, but they assumed I was in the wrong.

—Xiaodeng

Facing criticism of unequal investments of bicycling infrastructure, planners have begun to acknowledge "invisible" cyclists, such as low-income people of color often ignored in bike planning (Fuller and Beltran, 2010). The "invisibility" of these cyclists within transportation is constructed partly through biases in how cyclists are counted, using methods that often undercount food delivery cyclists (Kennedy, 2012; Stehlin, 2014). The "invisibility" has occurred despite evidence that non-whites and immigrants often cycle at equivalent or even higher rates than white cyclists (People for Bikes and Alliance for Walking & Biking, 2015; Smart, 2010). While bike planners and advocates may use the term "invisible" cyclists as a well-intentioned way of recognizing inequalities in bike investments, this term also highlights problematic processes and discourses among bicycling experts. The use of "invisible" by bike advocates and planners dehumanizes and distances these cyclists, marking them as outsiders to the white, affluent cycling being promoted while ignoring the structures and systems within bike advocacy and planning that marginalize these cyclists.

The invisibility label also obscures how so-called "invisible" cyclists are highly visible as "bad" cyclists. The mainstream media commonly paints a picture of food delivery cyclists as "out-of-control" and "one of the great hazards" to pedestrians (Rakowicz, 2012). A *NY Post* article states that, "Freewheeling food deliverymen are giving Upper West Siders indigestion, riding their bikes illegally on sidewalks and mowing down pedestrians who get in their way" (Sutherland, 2010). Delivery cyclists tend to be depicted as predatory, reckless, poor, and immigrant in the media's public transcript. In the wake of Stuart Gruskin's tragic death after being hit by a delivery cyclist in 2009, there has been a deluge of anti-delivery cyclist rhetoric and policy in NYC with few efforts to understand the food delivery experience (Aaron, 2012; Block, 2009). In our analysis, media stories about food delivery cyclists often entirely excluded the voices of food delivery cyclists. Only 27 percent (20 of 74) of the media stories that talked about food delivery cyclists included at least one quote from a food delivery cyclist. Denying these workers the opportunity to voice their perspectives, the public discourse instills fear in the general public by depicting food delivery cyclists as aggressive outsiders. Effectively, the mostly white and affluent customers in NYC are crafting a colonizing narrative about the immigrant cyclists who deliver their food (Kennedy, 2012; Smith, 1999). Compounding this power imbalance within media depictions is the reality that immigrant delivery cyclists "have difficulty standing up for themselves because of language issues" (Fernandes and Wu, 2013).

Even fellow cyclists perceive delivery cyclists as outsiders, labeling them "busboys of the road" (BikeSnobNYC, 2012, p. 50), which positions delivery cyclists as an underclass among cyclists. The low status of food delivery cyclists is strongly affected by the intersectionality of their perceived identities as low-income, undocumented immigrants, male, and Chinese or Latino (Crenshaw, 1991). Asians and Latinos are often positioned as subordinated, disposable workers within the white–black racial binary (Lee, 1999; Pulido, 2006). Essential to racial hierarchies are labor markets, which often scapegoat undocumented immigrants for unfair labor practices that primarily benefit private interests while also preventing conditions of racial and economic solidarity (Kwong, 2009; Pulido, 2006). Thus Ancheta (1998) finds that Asians and Latinos undergo a distinct "outsider" racialization that falls along an American–foreigner binary. Effectively, food delivery cyclists often encounter systematic discriminations such as unjust working and street conditions based on their skin color *and* perceived foreignness.

Although food delivery cyclists account for large numbers of NYC's cyclist population, bike planners and advocates often do not include delivery cyclists in discussions about street design. The NYC Department of Transportation (DOT) proudly asserts an increase of 109 percent in cycling from 2006–2011, a figure that excludes most commercial cyclists (Delivery City, 2011). "Invisible" cyclists are not invisible because of their absence but because of systems designed to exclude them. "Invisibility" appears to maintain a false divide between working cyclists and more privileged cyclists, residents, and customers, and it negates and invalidates the lived knowledge that informs food delivery cyclists as they navigate city streets. "Invisibility" subtly absolves planners and advocates of the responsibility to include marginalized cyclists in bike planning. The invisibility discourse confirms that our society privileges the mobility of "ideal types – autonomous individualized agents who through their motion helped to produce the nation itself. But the unspoken Others here are the differently mobile – the undocumented immigrant for instance – who make citizen mobility special" (Cresswell, 2006, p. 752).

To deal with food delivery cyclists, the NYC Council passed ordinances that require delivery cyclists to wear bright reflective vests with restaurant IDs, helmets, and bike lights as well as attending mandatory traffic safety classes (Durkin, 2012). As a result, the brightly vested delivery cyclists give a visible impression that they need enhanced surveillance and policing. These specific rules only apply to delivery cyclists, which creates a visible stigmatization of food delivery cyclists and increased visibility for potential ticketing by the police. This practice corresponds to increasing evidence of racial profiling of cyclists by the police (Levine and Siegel, 2014; Swenson, 2013; Zayas and Stanley, 2015). Marginalized cycling populations are thus very visible, but in a way that perpetuates their criminalization.

Beyond mainstream media, food delivery cyclists are depicted as visibly "bad" cyclists within bike advocacy as well. In one example, Transportation Alternatives (2003) states that, "In neighborhoods like the Upper East and West Sides, persistent problems with pedestrian-unfriendly cyclists, many of them in a rush to deliver food, has created considerable enmity towards all cyclists." This shows how bike advocates contribute to creating a good–bad cyclist binary with the logic being that if only cyclists behaved, then people would accept their mobility practice. Bike advocacy has struggled and succeeded to build bike infrastructure in the face of fierce opposition in a car-dominant society, but these advances have come at a cost of privileging affluent, desirable cyclists (Stehlin, 2015). While the intention is to improve bikeability, this approach marginalizes undesirable users such as food delivery cyclists. Furthermore, this logic places the primary blame of bicycling hatred upon "bad" immigrant delivery cyclists while giving greater legitimacy to "desirable" cyclists and undermining solidarity between different groups of bicycle users. Despite food delivery cyclists being simultaneously visible as bad cyclists while invisible within bicycling advocacy, they have informed opinions when it comes to regulations and street safety (Tu, 2013). Instead of acknowledging that immigrant delivery cyclists who cycle for up to 12 hours a day have expert, intimate knowledge of unjust streets, the public discourse casts delivery cyclists as ignorant disruptors of order on the street.

Crossing borders illegally

> I was riding my bike to the Graduate Center in midtown Manhattan when I reached a car-snarled intersection. I had the green light and was squeezing by the cars just as two cyclists tried to get across the intersection against their red light. I squeaked by them causing the other cyclists to stop and yell at me, "Hey Chinaman, watch out!"
>
> —Do

Visible or invisible borders are created to delineate us from others so that a border demarcates a binary of "good" and "evil" where the powerful define their side of the boundary as "good" and the other less powerful side of the border as "evil"; those who have less power are subject to severe reprisals when trespassing across borders (Anzaldúa, 1987). Similarly, the movement of food delivery cyclists into mostly white, affluent neighborhoods is a kind of border crossing. Border crossings by the undocumented present a threat to American whiteness, resulting in consequences for those who cross illegally (Mize, 2008). The Chinese Exclusion Act of 1882 was based upon the conception that Chinese immigrant mobility threatened "good order" and thus it was "necessary to disconnect citizenship from the mobility of the immigrants" (Cresswell, 2006, p. 751). Similarly, the media commonly depicts food delivery cyclists as bringing chaos, danger, and threats to the established status quo to the affluent neighborhoods they deliver in:

> Good luck to Community Board 7, which has the audacity to want bicycle deliverymen to wear proper ID and, God forbid, obey traffic laws. Upper West Side residents tired of the terror will likely have to live with it, even if it means limping from injuries caused by careless, sociopathic cyclists.
>
> (Cuozzo, 2010)

To re-establish control, NYC has passed ordinances to surveil, regulate, and punish delivery cyclists alongside efforts to educate them on safety (Durkin, 2012). Pedestrian deaths caused by food delivery cyclists are exceedingly rare events, with the last occurrence being Stuart Gruskin's death in 2009. When we analyzed the difference in themes presented in the media *with* and *without* food

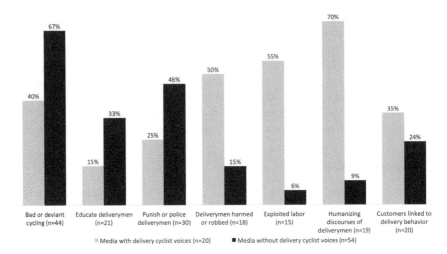

Figure 8.1 Media portrayal with and without food delivery cyclist voices (n=74)

Source: Do J. Lee, Helen Ho, Melyssa Banks, Mario Giampieri, Xiaodeng Chen and Dorothy Le.

delivery cyclist voices (see Figure 8.1), the media depictions *without* food delivery cyclist representation are 68 percent more likely to depict food delivery cyclists as bad or deviant cyclists. Furthermore, the media *without* food delivery cyclist voices is about twice as likely to talk about or recommend educating, punishing, or policing food delivery cyclists in the name of "public safety" than media *with* food delivery cyclist voices. Typically, bike or public safety is described in the public transcript as being safe *from* food delivery cyclists rather than having safety *for* food delivery cyclists. Safety discourses have often been used to hide racial discrimination such as the fear that bike lanes will bring criminal elements (Farr et al., 2015).

The public spaces of many U.S. urban cities have been subtly militarized in order to sequester the poor and undesirable, which results in cities that are highly segregated by race and class and maintained in part by unjust policing (Davis, 1992; Squires, 2001; Zamani, 2012). Residents often associate the movements of low-income immigrant delivery cyclists with transgression and criminality, even as they expect these feared bodies to serve them food as quickly as possible. Furthermore, this discourse ignores how the streets privilege car traffic (Norton, 2008). Car-based street spaces are not conducive, efficient, or safe for food delivery cycling and thus help to produce "irresponsible" behaviors, such as riding the wrong way or riding on sidewalks in order to deliver food quickly. This creates a dangerous street environment for delivery cyclists, which is exacerbated by increased demand for food delivery under bad weather conditions of rain, snow, and ice (Brustein, 2015). By ignoring these external pressures, the focus on educating and policing food delivery cyclists feeds into stereotypes of uneducated immigrants and resonates with how Hudson (2006, p. 31) suggests "in order to gain rights and remedies [ethnic minorities] have to demonstrate that they are 'the same' as white men."

Borders are heavily policed and similarly, broken windows or quality of life policing in cities has helped disproportionately incarcerate minorities (Alexander, 2012; Mize, 2008). Bicycling in car-based streets is seen as transgressive by NYC police officers, who often crack down on bicyclists for minor or even nonexistent infractions to defend car culture (Blickstein, 2010). That bicycling is seen as baseline transgressive is heightened by the perceived trespass of immigrant delivery cyclists and a public desire to police their mobility: "Get ready for slice and frisk. Reckless bike-riding pizza delivery guys and their traffic-swerving fast food cohorts are the target of a new crackdown" (Underwood and McShane, 2012). Since borders are constructed to mark those who are legal and those who are criminal, the movement of immigrant workers into white neighborhoods becomes especially criminalized with broken windows policing (Mize, 2008). This perceived criminality may be potentially exacerbated by the predominantly male gender of food delivery cyclists. In addition to being required to wear reflective vests, helmets, and bike lights, the NYC Council has banned electric bikes, which are most commonly used by Chinese food delivery workers (Mierjeski, 2014). These ordinances create a class, nativity, and racial divide in the rules being applied to NYC cyclists. Not only do delivery cyclists become more visible for policing, this creates a positive feedback loop in which delivery cyclists are cast as criminals while the evidence of their criminality is created through increased ticketing of people who often cannot effectively contest ticketing because they lack English fluency (Fernandes and Wu, 2013; Penhirin, 2015). Ticketing for NYC food delivery cyclists averaged about $44,000 collected per month in 2013 and 2014 (Penhirin, 2015) and for low-wage workers, fines can be a devastating form of financial dispossession: "he only made $200 or $300 a week, meaning the $175 fine he had received for riding an e-bike was crippling" (Mierjeski, 2014). For those individuals living undocumented, unjust policing may open up grave consequences: "many riders who are not [documented immigrants] worry that a police stop will put them at risk of being turned over to federal immigration officials" (Kilgannon and Singer, 2011). The criminalization of delivery cyclists takes on a character of public performance that resembles how segregated public buses in the Jim Crow era functioned as "moving theaters" of conflict, repression, and resistance (Kelley, 1994).

Crossing the border as undocumented immigrant workers also leads to exploitative and hazardous working conditions (Kwong, 2009; Mize, 2008; Pulido, 2006). Likewise, Kennedy (2012) finds that food delivery cycling is primarily characterized as "disposable employment" throughout its entire work process, which includes wage theft, risks of injury or death in a car-filled street without worker's compensation or health care, and the dangers of being robbed, physically assaulted, and even killed while delivering food. One example is the well-publicized lawsuit in which 36 Chinese food delivery cyclists successfully sued the Saigon Grill for extreme labor exploitation where their pay averaged

$2 an hour (Greenhouse, 2008). As we see in Figure 8.1, media accounts *with* food delivery cyclist voices are far more likely to craft humanizing and contextualizing narratives that speak to their concerns, such as labor exploitation, robbery, assault, murder, and dangerous streets (Albrecht, 2010; Gonnerman, 2007; Horan, 2005). In essence, safety and justice for food delivery cyclists is far different from what is done in the name of bike safety in NYC.

Through this interface of borders and policing, we contend that food delivery cycling is a sort of performative re-enactment in NYC of border crossings by the undocumented.

Mutual implication with food delivery cyclists

> My neighborhood has many restaurants and food deliverymen, but without any bike lanes. There is heavy traffic and it is extremely dangerous to ride my bike in my neighborhood, so I have given up riding. Only now, when my neighborhood has been targeted for gentrification and economic development are bike lanes being addressed. These bike lanes are not for the current residents or deliverymen, they are intended for the affluent. Food delivery cyclists are above all, human beings who deserve inclusion and respect.
>
> —Melyssa

Food delivery cyclists are singled out as individually irresponsible while ignoring the structures and systems that produce their irresponsible behavior (Lee, 2014). Demands from customers, restaurants, and tip-based livelihoods, in conjunction with streets designed for cars, create strong incentives for food delivery cyclists to bike the wrong way on a street, run red lights, or ride on sidewalks as coping mechanisms to do their work (Delivery City, 2011). Furthermore, crossing borders is not limited to the undocumented. By creating financial levers that create debt in the Global South, western countries and institutions facilitate the flow of transnational capital into the developing countries that displace and dispossess many people of their lands and resources, thereby accelerating mass migrations around the world (Harvey, 2005; Sassen, 2014). Thus people who are displaced and forced to migrate by these financial systems sometimes end up in cities where they work low-income service jobs like food delivery where they may serve food to the same people who are responsible for or benefit from transnational dispossession.

Stehlin (2015) finds that the bicycling movement has been complicit with the injustices of capital accumulation via gentrification and displacement in order to convince cities to rapidly change the shape of streets in the pursuit of bikeability and livability. By doing so, the bicycling movement works with cities to produce and recruit "ideal" cycling bodies—typically, white and affluent. Simultaneously, capital accumulation also works through the dispossessing effects of exploitative informal economies and flows of transnational capital, which has resulted in the expansion of "undesirable" bodies of cyclists such as immigrant food delivery cyclists within the very same spaces as "ideal" cyclists. Simply put, "good" cyclists cannot exist without "bad" cyclists when access to bike infrastructure is an amenity like access to food delivery.

Torre (2009, p. 119) proposes an approach of mutual implication that allows "individuals to remain complicated—that is allow them to be nos-otras—to hold multiple, even opposing, identities" whereby we are simultaneously colonizer and colonized, or likewise, simultaneously "good" and "bad" cyclists. Mutual implication asks us all to better understand how we are all implicated in each other's lives. In our media analysis, 27 percent (20 of 74) of media sources suggested that customer demand for fast delivery plays a role in "bad" food delivery cyclist behavior: "don't promise New Yorkers they'll get their [food] quickly because it may pressure delivery cyclists to ride the wrong way or on the sidewalk" (Siff, 2013). This form of mutual implication remains at an individual level of justice whereby each individual person must choose to tip better and accept food delivered more slowly in order to improve conditions for delivery cyclists and public safety. In contrast, the media rarely suggests mutual implication through systematic or structural solutions to improve food delivery safety. In terms of wage exploitation, a systematic solution might be laws requiring living wages not dependent on tips, accompanied by effective enforcement. Only 5 percent (four of 74) of the media sources spoke about inadequate street infrastructure as related to delivery cyclist behavior. In one such example, The Invisible Visible Man (2013) blog pointed out the disconnect between one-way streets and food delivery: "Would I follow all the street direction rules if the restaurant where I worked were on a one-way street and it would add five minutes to every trip to go the right way round the block to reach it?"

When heard, food delivery voices often provide counter-narratives and challenge the point and effectiveness of bike safety regulations:

> Many delivery workers in Chinatown are saying, "The legislators have never ridden a bike before and they don't know anything about food delivery." As a hot and humid summer approaches, wearing a vest and helmet will be a physical challenge to the workers ... All these various regulations were intended to protect the safety of the delivery workers. However, those on the front line of food delivery feel that the regulations are not necessary. "If the laws really want to protect the safety of deliverymen, then they should regulate the taxi cabs that cross into the bicycle lane."
>
> (Tu, 2013)

Thus bike safety programs that include the experiences of food delivery cyclists would look quite different than the educate-and-punish model. This means valuing the embodied knowledge and the hidden transcript of food delivery cyclists as integral to improving streets (Lee, 2015). Doing so might recast the "irresponsible" behavior of food delivery cyclists as indicating desire paths. Desire paths are the dirt trails created by human foot traffic as convenient paths between two points and thus desire paths have often been used to inform planning of street and sidewalk infrastructure. Since desire paths do not show up on asphalt streets, the "bad" behavior of food delivery cyclists signifies desire paths of where the bicycle infrastructure is lacking. As former NYC Councilwoman Jessica Lappin comments, "If we're going to remake the way city streets function, we need input from the people who use them [including delivery workers]" (Delivery City, 2011).

The transgressive mobility of food delivery cyclists points to avenues for disrupting structures of inequalities. By reconsidering transgressive border crossings as potentially productive, the bike movement can instead seek justice in the "space of radical openness," which is "a margin – a profound edge. Locating oneself there is difficult yet necessary. It is not a 'safe' place. One is always at risk. One needs a community of resistance" (hooks, 1990, p. 24). Validating the experiences of those on the margins allows for unjust street conditions to be revealed as hostile not only to food delivery cyclists, but to many others in the city. If we changed the street infrastructure to meet the needs of delivery cyclists who ride everywhere and in every direction, bicycling would be significantly safer and more accessible for many vulnerable and underrepresented cyclists such as the elderly, women, people of color, and children.

This potential of mutual implication with immigrant food delivery cyclists underscores the need to democratize the right to research and produce knowledge because "the capacity to produce globally useful knowledge is not evenly distributed" (Appadurai, 2006, p. 173). This requires actively seeking out the voices and embodied knowledge of the marginalized such as immigrant delivery cyclists. One approach might be community-based participatory research or participatory action research (Torre, 2009). This is less of a critique of bike planning and advocacy than a call for our missed opportunity of politically empowering marginalized cyclists to produce knowledge that strives to undo the unjust conditions in our streets and cities that affect us all.

Conclusion

> It's 2011. Entering the national bike conference for the first time with two high school interns, we three seem to be the only people of color in the room. I look around and on the opposite end of the room I see a brown-skinned man and I ran over to meet him. "Hi, I'm Helen. I'm from New York. Where are the rest of our people?" He laughed and replied, "I have two friends coming tomorrow." On the bus ride home afterwards, my interns questioned everything that happened: "The conference was cool, but it would have been easier to meet people if they were younger and looked like me." We went on to create the Youth Bike Summit the following year, an affordable, diverse bike conference for young people who love bikes from all over the U.S. and beyond. If what you want isn't there, sometimes you have to be your own role model.
>
> —Helen

This chapter explored how the pursuit of bike justice needs to account for how our public streets are often differently felt, used, experienced, and enacted by people based upon their social positioning, including that of race, class, and perceived foreignness. Immigrant food delivery cyclists are positioned as simultaneously invisible in bike advocacy and planning while visible as "bad" cyclists who trespass into white, affluent neighborhoods and thus threaten social order. Bike safety is therefore perversely transformed into safety *from* immigrant food delivery cyclists. This bike safety discourse ignores how "bad" food delivery cycling is produced by the time pressures of tip-based delivery livelihoods, unwelcoming car-based streets, and unjust policing. This takes on pressing meaning not only with rapid expansion of bike infrastructure but also as cities implement policies such as Vision Zero to reduce fatalities from car traffic (New York City, 2014). How we construct and enact public spaces is an expression of power and namely, who has it. Therefore, bike justice and equity is less an outcome than an ongoing reflexive process for critically examining and acting upon our mutual implication with dispossessed cyclists. In essence, bike movements that privilege justice for "ideal" cyclists cannot but be complicit in the injustices visited upon "undesirable" cyclists, resulting in a segregated bike justice. By valuing the everyday knowledge and experiences of marginalized cyclists as essential to the bike movement, we can better address bike justice in our here and now.

References

Aaron, B. (2012) Vacca Lectures DOT on NYPD Delivery Cyclist Enforcement. *Streetsblog.* September 7. Available from: www.streetsblog.org/2012/09/07/vacca-lectures-dot-on-nypd-delivery-cyclist-enforcement/ [Accessed September 5, 2015].

Albrecht, L. (2010) Saigon Grill Workers Call for Boycott Over Alleged Age Discrimination. *DNAinfo.* December 6. Available from: www.dnainfo.com/new-york/20101206/upper-west-side/saigon-grill-workers-call-for-boycott-over-alleged-age-discrimination [Accessed September 7, 2015].

Alexander, M. (2012) *The New Jim Crow: Mass Incarceration In The Age Of Colorblindness.* New York: The New Press.

Altheide, D. (1996) *Qualitative Media Analysis.* Thousand Oaks, CA: Sage Publications.

Ancheta, A. (1998) *Race, Rights, And The Asian American Experience.* New Brunswick, NJ: Rutgers University Press.

Anzaldúa, G. (1987) *Borderlands: The New Mestiza = La Frontera.* San Francisco, CA: Spinsters/Aunt Lute.

Appadurai, A. (2006) The Right To Research. *Globalisation, Societies and Education,* 4 (2), 167–177.

Applebaum, M., et al. (2011) *Beyond the Backlash: Equity and Participation in Bicycle Planning.* Urban Affairs and Planning Program at Hunter College. Available from: www.hunter.cuny.edu/ccpd/repository/files/es_beyond-the-backlash-2011.pdf [Accessed May 3, 2015].

BikeSnobNYC, (2012) *The Enlightened Cyclist.* San Francisco, CA: Chronicle Books LLC.

Blickstein, S. (2010) Automobility and the Politics of Bicycling in New York City. *International Journal of Urban and Regional Research,* 34 (4), 886–905.

Block, D. (2009) Family of Businessman Struck, Killed By Bicycle Hope $20M Lawsuit Will Create Tougher Safety Laws. *NY Daily News.* June 15. Available from: www.

nydailynews.com/new-york/bronx/family-businessman-struck-killed-bicycle-hope-20m-lawsuit-create-tougher-safety-laws-article-1.427803 [Accessed September 16, 2015].

Blue, E. (2013) *Bikenomics: How Bicycling Can Save The Economy.* Portland, OR: Microcosm Publishing.

Braun, V., & Clarke, V. (2006) Using Thematic Analysis In Psychology. *Qualitative Research in Psychology,* 3 (2), 77–101.

Brustein, J. (2015) Hope for Humankind: Delivery Guys Got Bigger Tips in the Blizzard. *Bloomberg Business.* January 28. Available from: www.bloomberg.com/news/articles/2015-01-28/hope-for-humankind-delivery-guys-got-bigger-tips-in-the-blizzard [Accessed September 7, 2015].

Crenshaw, K. (1991) Mapping the Margins: Intersectionality, Identity Politics, and Violence against Women of Color. *Stanford Law Review,* 43 (6), 1241–1299.

Cresswell, T. (2006) The Right to Mobility: The Production of Mobility in the Courtroom. *Antipode,* 38 (4), 735–754.

Cuozzo, S. (2010) Blame the City for 'Cycles' of Violence. *NY Post.* July 30. Available from: http://nypost.com/2010/07/30/blame-the-city-for-cycles-of-violence/ [Accessed September 19, 2015].

Davis, M. (1992) Fortress Los Angeles: The Militarization of Urban Space. In: M. Sorkin, ed. *Variations on a Theme Park: The New American City and the End of Public Space.* New York: Hill and Wang, 155–180.

Delivery City (2011) *Swept Up in the Debate on Bike Safety.* Available from: www.deliverycitynyc.com/page1.html [Accessed September 18, 2015].

Durkin, E. (2012) City Council Approves Mandatory Safety Classes For Commercial Cyclists. *NY Daily News.* October 11. Available from: www.nydailynews.com/new-york/driver-ed-bike-delivery-guys-article-1.1181448 [Accessed September 5, 2015].

Farr, M., Brondo, K., & Anglin, S. (2015) Shifting Gears: The Intersections of Race and Sustainability in Memphis. In: C. Isenhour, G. McDonogh & M. Checker, eds. *Sustainability in the Global City: Myth and Practice.* New York: Cambridge University Press, 285–305.

Fernandes, S. & Wu, T. (2013) The Motorbike Diaries. *The American Prospect.* Available from: http://prospect.org/article/motorbike-diaries [Accessed September 7, 2015].

Flegenheiner, M. (2013) Turning the City's Wheels in a New Direction. *The New York Times.* December 29. Available from: www.nytimes.com/2013/12/30/nyregion/turning-the-citys-wheels-in-a-new-direction.html [Accessed September 16, 2015].

Fuller, O. & Beltran, E. (2010) The Invisible Cyclists of Los Angeles. *Progressive Planning Magazine.* July 14. Available from: www.plannersnetwork.org/2010/07/the-invisible-cyclists-of-los-angeles/ [Accessed April 28, 2015].

Gonnerman, J. (2007) The Deliverymen's Uprising. *New York Magazine.* August 6. Available from: http://nymag.com/news/features/35540/ [Accessed September 7, 2015].

Greenhouse, S. (2008) For $2-An-Hour Restaurant Deliverymen, A $4.6 Million Judgment. *The New York Times.* October 21. Available from: www.nytimes.com/2008/10/22/nyregion/22saigon.html [Accessed September 6, 2015].

Grynbaum, M. (2011) For City's Transportation Chief, Kudos and Criticism. *The New York Times.* March 4. Available from: www.nytimes.com/2011/03/06/nyregion/06sadik-khan.html?_r=0 [Accessed September 18, 2015].

Harvey, D. (2005) *The New Imperialism.* Oxford: Oxford University Press.

hooks, b. (1990) *Yearning: Race, Gender, And Cultural Politics.* Boston, MA: South End Press.

Horan, K. (2005) For New York's Delivery Guys, Dangerous Work and Low Pay. WNYC. November 10. Available from: www.wnyc.org/story/83662-for-new-yorks-delivery-guys-dangerous-work-and-low-pay/ [Accessed September 7, 2015].

Hudson, B. (2006) Beyond White Man's Justice: Race, Gender and Justice in Late Modernity. *Theoretical Criminology*, 10 (1), 29–47.

Kelley, R. (1994) *Race Rebels: Culture, Politics, and the Black Working Class*. New York: Free Press.

Kennedy, P. (2012) Invisible Cyclists: The Role of Deliverymen in the New York City Restaurant Industry. Unpublished thesis. Pratt Institute.

Kilgannon, C. & Singer, J. (2011) Battery Power Gives Deliverymen a Boost, at a Cost. *The New York Times*. June 12. Available from: http://cityroom.blogs.nytimes.com/2011/06/12/battery-power-gives-deliverymen-a-boost-at-a-cost/ [Accessed September 7, 2015].

Kwong, P. (2009) What's Wrong with the US Immigration Debate? In: J. Maskovsky and I. Susser, eds., *Rethinking America: The Imperial Homeland in the 21st Century*. Boulder, CO: Paradigm Publishers, 300–312.

Lee, D. (2014) The Unbearable Weight of Irresponsibility and the Lightness of Tumbleweeds: Cumulative Irresponsibility in Neoliberal Streetscapes. In: J. Agyeman and S. Zavestoski, eds., *Incomplete Streets: Processes, Practices and Possibilities*. New York: Routledge, 77–93.

Lee, D. (2015) Embodied Bicycle Commuters in a Car World. *Social & Cultural Geography*, 1–22. doi:10.1080/14649365.2015.1077265

Lee, R. (1999) *Orientals: Asian Americans in Popular Culture*. Philadelphia, PA: Temple University Press.

Levine, H. & Siegel, L. (2014) Proceedings from *Summons: The Next Stop and Frisk*. Long Island City, NY: CUNY School of Law. Available from: http://marijuana-arrests.com/docs/Criminal-Court-Summonses-in-NYC--CUNY-Law-School-April-24-2014.pdf [Accessed April 21, 2015].

Marritz, I. (2015) Squeezed By Seamless, Restaurants Look for Other Paths Online. WNYC. April, 2. Available from: www.wnyc.org/story/squeezed-seamless-restaurants-look-other-paths-online/ [Accessed September 6, 2015].

Mierjeski, A. (2014) First They Came for the Electric Bikes . . . *Vice*. January 20. Available from: www.vice.com/read/first-they-came-for-the-electric-bikes-0000195-v21n1 [Accessed September 7, 2015].

Mize, R. (2008) Interrogating Race, Class, Gender and Capitalism Along the U.S.-Mexico Border: Neoliberal Nativism and Maquila Modes of Production. *Race, Gender & Class*, 15, 134–155.

Newman, K., & Wyly, E. (2006) The Right to Stay Put, Revisited: Gentrification and Resistance to Displacement in New York City. *Urban Studies*, 43, (1), 23–57.

New York City (2014) *Vision Zero Action Plan*. Available from: www.nyc.gov/html/visionzero/pages/the-plan/the-plan.shtml [Accessed September 18, 2015].

Norton, P. (2008) *Fighting Traffic: The Dawn of The Motor Age in the American City*. Cambridge, MA: MIT Press.

Penhirin, S., (2015) MAP: See Which Restaurants Got the Most Delivery Bike Violations. *DNAinfo*. May 5. Available from: www.dnainfo.com/new-york/20150505/lower-east-side/map-see-which-restaurants-got-most-delivery-bike-violations [Accessed September 4, 2015].

People for Bikes and Alliance for Biking & Walking (2015) *Race, Ethnicity, Class and Protected Bike Lanes: An Idea Book for Fairer Cities*. Available from: www.peopleforbikes.

128   *Lee et al.*

org/blog/entry/race-ethnicity-class-and-protected-bike-lanes-an-idea-book-for-fairer-citie [Accessed September 1, 2015].

Pucher, J., Thorwaldson, L., Buehler, R., & Klein, N. (2010. Cycling in New York: Innovative Policies at the Urban Frontier. *World Transport Policy and Practice*, 16, 7–50.

Pulido, L. (2006) *Black, Brown, Yellow, and Left: Radical Activism in Los Angeles*. Berkeley, CA: University of California Press.

Rakowicz, E. (2012) Uptown Food Delivery Workers Bone Up on Bike Safety. *City Spoonful*. Available from: www.cityspoonful.com/uws/ [Accessed September 5, 2015].

Sassen, S. (2014) *Expulsions*. Cambridge, MA: Harvard University Press.

Scott, J. (1990) *Domination and the Arts Of Resistance: Hidden Transcripts*. New Haven, CT: Yale University Press.

Siff, A. (2013) NYC to Crack Down on Food Delivery Cyclists. *NBC 4 New York*. February 22. Available from: www.nbcnewyork.com/news/local/Food-Delivery-Worker-Bicyclist-Reflective-Vest-Rules-Restaurant-Fines-Violations-NYC-192413661.html [Accessed September 2, 2015].

Smart, M. (2010) US Immigrants and Bicycling: Two-Wheeled in Autopia. *Transport Policy*, 17 (3), 153–159.

Smith, K. (2009) Dangerous Bike Riders Run Wild With Impunity in NYC. *NY Post*. May 23. Available from: http://nypost.com/2009/05/23/dangerous-bike-riders-run-wild-with-impunity-in-nyc/ [Accessed September 2, 2015].

Smith, L. (1999) *Decolonizing Methodologies: Research and Indigenous Peoples*. London: Zed Books.

Squires, G. (2001) The Indelible Color Line. *The American Prospect*. December 10. Available from: http://prospect.org/article/indelible-color-line [Accessed April 10, 2015].

Stehlin, J. (2014) Regulating Inclusion: Spatial Form, Social Process, and the Normalization of Cycling Practice in the USA. *Mobilities*, 9 (1), 21–41.

Stehlin, J. (2015) Cycles of Investment: Bicycle Infrastructure, Gentrification, and the Restructuring of the San Francisco Bay Area. *Environment and Planning A*, 47 (1), 121–137.

Sutherland, A. (2010) Upper West Siders Take on Out-of-Control Delivery Men. *New York Post*. July 30. Available from: http://nypost.com/2010/07/30/upper-west-siders-take-on-out-of-control-delivery-men/ [Accessed September 4, 2015].

Swenson, K. (2013) Biking While Black is a Crime. *Miami New Times*. October 31. Available from: www.miaminewtimes.com/news/biking-while-black-is-a-crime-6393767 [Accessed September 2, 2015].

The Invisible Visible Man (2013) *The Delivery Cyclist: An Appreciation of the Under-Appreciated*. May 26. Available from: http://invisiblevisibleman.blogspot.com/2013/05/the-delivery-cyclist-appreciation-of.html [Accessed September 2, 2015].

Torre, M. (2009) Participatory Action Research and Critical Race Theory: Fueling Spaces for Nos-otras to Research. *Urban Review*, 41 (1), 106–120.

Transportation Alternatives (2003) T.A. Launches "Working Cyclists" Program. Available from: www.transalt.org/sites/default/files/news/magazine/034Fall/06working.html [Accessed September 7, 2015].

Transportation Alternatives (2015) *Bicycling in New York City: Know the Facts*. Available from: www.transalt.org/issues/bike/bikefaq [Accessed September 18, 2015].

Tu, Y. (2013) Delivery Workers Question New Bike Regulations. *Voices of NY*. December 8. Available from: www.voicesofny.org/2013/04/delivery-workers-question-new-bike-regulations/ [Accessed September 7, 2015].

Tuckel, P. & Milczarski, W. (2009) Biking Behavior in Mid-Manhattan. New York, Hunter College. Available from: http://graphics8.nytimes.com/packages/pdf/nyregion/city_room/spring_2009_bikestudy_2.pdf [Accessed September 22, 2015].

Underwood, K. & McShane, L. (2012) NYC Targets Reckless Bike-Riding Delivery Guys – And Their Employers Will Face Fines if They Break Laws! *NY Daily News*. July 13. Available from: www.nydailynews.com/new-york/nyc-targets-reckless-bike-riding-delivery-guys-employers-face-fines-break-laws-article-1.1114315 [Accessed September 5, 2015].

Zamani, N. (2012) *Stop and Frisk – The Human Impact: The Stories Behind the Numbers, the Effects on our Communities*. New York: Center for Constitutional Rights.

Zayas, A. & Stanley, K. (2015) How Riding Your Bike Can Land You in Trouble with the Cops – If You're Black. *Tampa Bay Times*. April 17. Available from: www.tampabay.com/news/publicsafety/how-riding-your-bike-can-land-you-in-trouble-with-the-cops—-if-youre-black/2225966 [Accessed May 5, 2015].

9   Rascuache cycling justice

Alfredo Mirandé and Raymond L. Williams

In *The Buried Mirror* (1992), Carlos Fuentes points out that the most modern of all vehicles, the bicycle, was omnipresent in Mexico City in the late nineteenth and early twentieth centuries, so that in 1890 the bicycle was in great fashion in the Mexican capital. Fuentes evokes the figure of the cyclist as follows: "In a bold stroke of genius, Posada[1] resolved and united these contradictions in the figure of Death riding a bicycle, meshing the old and the new in the inevitability of death" (Fuentes, 1992, p. 295). Fuentes had several literary predecessors, for writers such as Mark Twain and H. G. Wells also wrote of their interest in the new fashion in the West that cycling was at the end of the nineteenth century.[2] Indeed, the image of death that marked late nineteenth-century Mexican art is still highly appropriate today, as hundreds of cyclists die in accidents with cars annually during the process of their commuter, recreational, or competitive cycling. The history of the bicycle and the auto-mobile are inextricably bound since their respective rise and, as we will discuss, issues related to bicycle justice, are still tied to the intimate connection between the bicycle and the automobile. In addition to death in accidents with cars that are sometimes homicides, unarmed Mexican cyclists have been shot and killed by police in southern California (Valles and Kandel, 2013). These issues, as well as the matter of parking space for automobiles versus parking security for bicycles, are the main bicycle justice concerns addressed in this chapter.

The advent of the automobile, cycling, and bicycle security

In the late nineteenth century, as Posada was doing his drawings of cyclists and the Mexican elite were showing off their two-wheeled objects of modernity, the American industries of cycling and of automobiles were engaged in parallel technological development that actively fed off each other. With both the United States and northern Europe at the height of the Industrial Revolution in the 1880s, the cycling industry was the driving force for several of the key technological innovations and inventions related to speeding up the production of much needed bicycles and making them lighter and more efficient. Two important technological innovations originally driven by the bicycle industry that became critical for the emergent car industry and other industries in the twentieth century were the pneumatic tire and metal tubing.

In the late 1940s, with the ascent of the car as a predominant form of transportation far outnumbering the bicycle, city planners began to create a new commodity related to automobile transportation—parking. In the city of Los Angeles, for example, the first parking meters were installed on city streets in 1949, and American cities in the western United States followed suit quickly. Given the smaller number of cyclists, and the impracticality of using bicycles as a primary vehicle for shopping, there was never an economic incentive to provide a parallel service making bicycle parking/security a commodity in the same way. Thus, the amount of resources dedicated to parking cars has totally outnumbered the resources for bicycle security.

With no market value established for bicycle parking/security, the installation of a few bike racks has become a minimal compensatory, after-the-fact solution to requests by cyclists, and these racks provide no bicycle security at all. To the contrary, they often serve as a focal point for bike theft. In our South–North perspective, we note that in the relatively new and progressive metro system in the city of Medellín, Colombia, there are some secure bike cages for bike commuters and there are similarly secure although limited numbers of boxes for commuting cyclists for Metrolink commuters at several southern California stations. These systematic approaches are to bike security as the twenty-first-century response to those 1940s inventions of car parking as a commodity.

Bicycle justice: a bottom up, rascuache perspective

In this chapter[3] we argue that attempts to regulate cycling by state and law enforcement are extensions of a general movement in society to regulate space by law and to marginalize the poor, students, and racial minorities from the urban landscape (see Duneier, 1999; Mitchell, 1997). The social-economic strata of cyclists in southern California begins with what we identify as rascuache[4] (Mesa-Bains, 2003), the typically unhelmeted and uniformless cyclists who most urgently rely on the bicycle for transportation. The experiences of these bikers are compared with the Catrín, or respectable, professional and elite cyclists who use bicycles for sport or recreation.

We begin by discussing the Mexican concept of rascuachismo and its application to the cycling scene. We then discuss the idea of the bicycle as an object that enables rascuache, youth, the poor, and subordinated persons to transcend geographical, psychological, social, economic, cultural, and spiritual borders. This is followed by an overview of the extant literature on legal attempts to regulate the urban landscape.

We contend that the experience of undocumented immigrants and unlicensed commuter cyclists in urban environments in southern California can be understood as an example of what in Mexico and among Chicanos[5] has been identified as rascuachismo, a vernacular term with uniquely Mexican origins and connotations. According to Ilan Stavans, rascuache is a Mexican colloquialism used "to describe a cultural item of inferior quality and proletarian origin" (Stavans, 2000, p. 193) such as the 1940s Los Angeles Pachuco fashion style and Cantinflas' uniquely Mexican working-class humor, style, and dress. However, like other terms, which traditionally had negative connotations such as the word Chicano itself, rascuache has been turned on its head. For example "Chicano art that is rasquache usually expresses an underdog, have-not sensibility that is also resource-ful and adaptable and makes use of simple materials . . ." (Ybarra-Frausto, 1991, p. 155, cited in Hispanic Research Center, 2001).

Rascuachismo is linked to Chicano structures of thinking, feeling, and aesthetic choices, as a sensibility that is not serious and elitist but playful and basic and projects an alternative aesthetic, what some would consider as "a sort of good taste of bad taste" (Ybarra-Frausto, 1991, p. 155). A listing of Rascuachismos would include the Mexican comedian Cantinflas, Chicano poet and artist José Montoya's fictional Royal Chicano Air Force with its adobe planes, velvet paintings, the early actors of El Teatro Campesino (Diaz, 2013; Roybal, 2013), comedians Cheech and Chong, and most relevant here, the calavera (skull) images of José Guadalupe Posada (Ybarra-Frausto, 1991, p. 155). It could also include recent immigrants riding low-end Costco bikes on paved bike paths in Orange County.

Rascuachismo is an underdog aesthetic that presupposes the perspective and world view of the have-nots but it is also a quality found in objects and places such as a rasquache car, bicycle or restaurant, and in social comportment, as in a person who acts rasquache (Ybarra-Frausto, 1991, p. 156). Responding to a material level of subsistence and existence instills an attitude of survival and inventiveness. But rascuachismo also intensely embodies the bicultural political subjectivity of Chicanas/os as border subjects and the "queer space of the border" (Roybal, 2013, p. 75). Thus, to be rasquache is to be witty, irreverent, and to subvert and turn ruling paradigms upside down (Ybarra-Frausto, 1991, p. 155).

"Sal si puedes": the bike as a vehicle for transcending borders

The recently deceased writer from Tijuana, Federico Campbell (1941–2014), portrays a classic rasquache character who describes his losses as an adolescent growing up on the border in the 1950s and early 1960s (Campbell, 1995, p. 7). From the dominant U.S. perspective, Tijuana, with its velvet paintings, oversized Mexican sombreros, striped ceramic donkeys, cheap curios, and bawdy bars represents the ultimate Mexican rasquache (Castillo, 1995, p. 7).

Throughout the novella "Everything About Seals" (Campbell, 1995), which appears in English in the volume *Tijuana: Stories from the Border*, the narrator-protagonist vacillates between being "down and out" and what Ybarra-Frausto calls "down but not out," and the latter is the character's condition in the end. Of particular interest for this chapter is the presence of the all-important bicycle belonging to the narrator-protagonist.

At the outset of the story, the bicycle provides the only means in the entire story for the protagonist's "happiness." His bicycle trip near the airport is described as "a fascinating spectacle that took me outside myself and made me forget the passage of time" (Campbell, 1995, pp. 29–30). In another key passage, at age 14, he writes that ". . . the bicycle was the only means I had to defend myself against the homey world of women and the gangs that terrorized the neighborhood" (ibid., pp. 58–59). At this point in the text, the narrator-protagonist has established the seminal importance of the bicycle not only as a means of transportation, but as something central to his very existence and identity: it is his happiness, his refuge from his dysfunctional family and from the gangs in his tough Tijuana neighborhood.

This story underlines not only the special kind of importance bicycles have for marginalized owners, but the bicycle as an extension of the self. In the end, unlike most other objects we possess, the bicycle, for many riders, becomes an extension of the rider's body and, consequently, an intimate part of oneself. Just as a cane or a wheelchair provides assistance for the elderly and disabled, the bicycle is a form of assistance to movement for humans in a variety of less advantaged economic and physical states.

Riding bicycles is, in effect, assisted walking.[6] Consequently, when owners lose their bicycles to theft, especially rascuache cyclists, they sometimes perceive it not simply as the economic loss of a neutral object but as the loss of a physical self. For the student commuter or working-class cycling commuter, for example, the loss of a bicycle can mean that, the next day, one cannot attend class or get to work.

Campbell uses objects such as bicycles and cameras to write about the period of the protagonist's biggest loss—his girlfriend, who dies. Thus, this is a story of loss that connects this chapter to how deeply significant bike security can be for many of the working-class and rascuache individuals who depend on their bicycles not only for transportation but for survival. In the world of trauma, all loss is repeated loss.

Bicycles are also an important object in several works of acclaimed Chicano poets, as well as writer Gary Soto's short stories about the lives of Chicana working-class children growing up in California. In "The Bike," Soto describes his experiences with his first bicycle as a five-year-old who defies his mother's orders not to leave the confines of his yard and stay off the forbidden Sarah Street (Soto, 1995, p. 234). As in Campbell's story, the bicycle provides a tool for rebellion and liberation. Although Soto felt pretty cool riding down the block in his brother's hand-me-down shirt, he was scared of taking the first curve out of sight of his mom onto the forbidden street (ibid., p. 234). "Mom said hungry dogs lived on that street, and red anger lived in their eyes. Their throats were hard with extra bones from biting kids on bikes" (ibid., p. 235). As he defiantly took the corner and turned onto Sarah Street, he returned immediately, but incredibly nothing happened. In fact, the foreboding street looked just like his street with parked cars, tall trees, a sprinkler hissing, and an old woman in her yard but no mad dogs (ibid., p. 235).

In another of Soto's short stories, "Broken Chain," the protagonist is convinced that looking grown-up or more handsome than average is not as important—or as attractive to a seventh-grade girl—as behaving in a grown-up way (Soto, 1990, pp. 1–12). As the plot unfolds, Alfonso rescues a little boy caught on the barbed-wire fence at his old elementary school. He is delighted when the boy's sister, Sandra, agrees to go biking with him. He asks to borrow his brother's bike but is refused. After school on Monday, as Alfonso is cleaning his bike, the chain breaks, and he now needs two bikes to go riding with Sandra. Ernie again refuses to lend his bike, then agrees, but the bike is dirty. At the climax of the story, Alfonso, riding with Sandra perched on the handlebars, comes to the realization that outward appearances are not that important after all and that Sandra likes him just as he is. Clearly, this experience of growing up is closely associated with a bicycle.

For Chicano youth, victimized by segregation, the bicycle often offers a modicum of escape from one's immediate surroundings. In *Summer on Wheels*, Soto (1995) describes the wacky adventure of Hector and Mando, ten-year-old best friends, in an action-filled tale of a six-day bike trip from East Los Angeles to Santa Monica.

Hector and Mando's adventures include starring in a commercial and being in a paintball battle (ibid., p. 88). Among the places Hector and Mando visit is a wax museum, a ramshackle studio with mattresses against the wall where one uncle works as a recording engineer, and a palatial mansion where another uncle works as a chauffeur. On the trip, they also learn important lessons about the importance of family. Some intense scenes are included when their bikes are almost stolen (ibid., p. 110) but even that incident works out and they end up winners at a local bingo night. In summary, an understanding of bicycle justice can begin with an appreciation of the idea that bicycles, unlike many other transportation vehicles, are often very personalized extensions of the human body, memory, and access to work of education and freedom. Bicycle policy, as many writers often suggest, is about more than urban commuting.

Rascuache bike users and cycling justice and security

The bicycles that Campbell's and Soto's characters rode offered them priceless experiences of freedom and exploration beyond their immediate environs. Like many other rascuache bike owners, they typically purchase heavy steel two-wheelers ranging in value from $50 to $300 and these owners fall into three groups: undocumented, working immigrants, and economically marginal college-level students. What these groups have in common is their economic exclusion from owning automobiles, although additional factors besides the strictly economic sometimes intervene. Among the most frequent is the inability to secure a driver's license because of age, undocumented status, and cost, lack of insurance, or legal constraints.

Many rascuache bicycle owners are commuters who travel in the most direct line they know to work and school, sometimes ignoring or simply unaware of bicycle routes. For example, some undocumented or unlicensed commuters in Riverside, California, ride on the dirt Gage Canal, safe from car traffic but on a route not used by other cyclists or necessarily intended by city planners to be a bicycle route. These commuters can be seen on similarly unorthodox but safe routes in Orange, San Diego, and Los Angeles counties.

Homeless camping cyclists similarly construct makeshift, rascuache "bike shops" with haphazard sets of extra wheels, parts, and tools for maintaining their bikes. Maintenance of these vehicles at regular bike shops is, for the most part, economically infeasible for rascuache cyclists. In the case of the low-income student commuters, many college students deal with the high cost of maintenance by creating de facto student cooperative bike shops; UC-Davis and UC-Santa Barbara are both pioneers and models in this area.

Both the criminal justice and transportation systems in many urban areas, particularly in automobile-dominated southern California, are not highly receptive to rascuache cyclists. This fact is underscored by the massive infrastructural investment in elaborate systems for parking for cars, a pioneer of which was the shopping mall, which allowed white middle-class suburbanites to avoid driving to the inner cities populated largely by communities of Color and vying for limited parking space on urban streets.

The construction of shopping centers highlighted the issue of parking space for cars by providing abundant parking for these motorized vehicles at the same time that the typical shopping center does not provide a secure place for cyclists to actually use these shopping centers and malls. In competing with downtown shoppers, shopping mall developers do offer a free commodity to car drivers— parking—in order to compete for the same basic group of potential shoppers, rather than expanding their markets for potential bicycling shoppers.

University campuses and athletic facilities designed and/or expanded since the 1950s have often followed the development model of the shopping mall. Nevertheless, the shopping-mall design of these three campuses makes current efforts to create bicycle-friendly campuses a challenge in terms of bicycle security, access to campus in and around it, and a bike-friendly climate. On these campuses, cars rule, bicyclists face challenges typical of other kinds of minority groups, and there is little practice of bicycle justice. The loss of bicycles by theft is treated by university officials as insignificant, even though many cyclists—and writers such as Federico Campbell—attempt to argue that bicycle theft can be hugely significant in their lives.[7]

The quasi criminalization of rascuache bicycle commuters

The quasi criminalization of rascuache commuters is often related to their wearing helmets. Rather than dealing efficiently with bike loss with improved security, policies are passed in promoting items such as bike helmets. On the state level, a proposed bicycle helmet law, SB192, was presented to the California State Legislature in 2015 by state Senator Carol Liu, D-La Cañada Flintridge (Los Angeles County). It would require adult cyclists to wear helmets or pay a $25 fine. Although the proposed legislation is facially neutral, it would have an adverse impact on rascuache cyclists. California would become the first state to require helmets for riders over the age of 18. The bill also requires cyclists riding at night to wear reflective clothing for greater visibility, although they are already mandated to have front and rear lights on their bicycles. A number of cycling advocates argue that counter to its avowed purpose, such a mandatory helmet law will discourage people from abandoning their cars and becoming regular bikers. The California Bicycle Coalition, the state's largest bicycle lobbying group, maintains that a mandatory helmet statute would lead to fewer bikers and make roads less safe by discouraging bicycling. In a press release, the group said, "we know that having more bicyclists and pedestrians on the streets makes them safer for everyone" (O'Connor, 2015).

We argue that the proposed mandatory helmet law was directed specifically at rascuache cyclists, as this is the only group that typically does not wear helmets, primarily for economic reasons. A high quality helmet might cost as much, or more, than their inexpensive bikes. Moreover, by creating this law, the California legislature set up a scenario to further criminalize, harass, and control economically disadvantaged cyclists.

California's "Three Foot" law went into effect in September 2014, requiring drivers to stay at least three feet away from cyclists while passing (Nelson and Stevens, 2014). If driving conditions make a three-foot buffer impossible, drivers must slow to a "reasonable and prudent speed and wait to pass until the cyclist is safe. A driver who gets too close to a bike would be fined $35, or $220 if there is a crash that injures a cyclist" (ibid.). Although the proposed law is ostensibly intended to protect all cyclists, it is unlikely that the law will do much to protect cyclists, especially rascuache types who do not typically travel major highways or thoroughfares.

A number of observers have commented on the prevalence of racial profiling by law enforcement and the problem of driving, walking, or riding while Black or Brown. One of the most notorious cases related to the criminalization of the rascuache cyclist took place in Gardena, California, on June 2, 2013. A Mexican cyclist rode a bike to a CVS store in Gardena in search of a stolen bike that a family member had just lost. A video showed the police shooting and killing the unarmed cyclist who raised and lowered his arms several times before he was shot. Because the loss of the bicycle had the potential of becoming a major loss for the family, it made sense for a member of the family to attempt to recover the stolen bike.

The case came to light and gained national attention recently when a Federal District Judge rejected the Gardena and police department's privacy claims in seeking to block release of the taped shooting (Winton and Smith, 2015). While police did not say what caused officers to fire their weapons, the incident apparently stemmed from a report of a bike theft at a CVS pharmacy (Valles and Kandel, 2013).

There is a third hybrid group, lowrider cyclists, who neither use cycling as a form of transportation nor for sport and leisure but as an alternative rascuache aesthetic or art form that is a reflection of their ethnic and political identity (McQuilkin, 2009; Miller, 2014). Lowrider bicycles first made their appearance in the 1960s with the introduction of the 1963 Schwinn Sting-Ray bicycle, which continues to be extremely popular among Chicano urban youth but the low-slung Latino lowrider bicycle was the antithesis of the Sting-Ray's chopper design (Penland, 2003). Like lowrider car enthusiasts, lowbikes were embraced by younger members of car clubs. "Mirroring their motorized counterparts, lowbike artists lowered, elongated, and customized the Schwinn frame to the degree that many of their creations can no longer be ridden, and they exist wholly as aesthetics objects" (McQulkin, 2009, p. 1).

Catrín cyclists

Having discussed the rascuache cyclists who use bikes as a mode of transportation, rather than for sport, leisure, or pleasure, we now turn to a discussion of Catrín cyclists. The image of the Catrín cyclist is drawn from Posada's famous painting of La Catrina or "La Catrina Calavera," which shows an image of a female skeleton dressed in a hat characteristic of the upper class outfit of a European of the early twentieth century. She is presented as a satirical portrait of those Mexican natives who, Posada felt, were aspiring to adopt European aristocratic traditions in the pre-revolutionary era. La Catrina has become an icon of the Mexican Día de los Muertos, or Day of the Dead.

We use "catrín/catrina" to characterize "respectable," rich, upper-middle class recreational and commuting cyclists. Their bicycles and clothing vary, but many used by fully employed commuters range from $400 to $4,000. For the most part, they wear helmets, most do not wear clothes made by the cycling industry, but they often wear reflective material to improve their visibility and efficiency, in addition to distinguishing themselves from rascuache cyclists, who are the most frequently harassed by police and motorists. The helmet law and the new three-foot law in California invite police agencies to focus not on the cyclist as criminal but on the illegal aggression of the dominant car citizenry against rascuache and, to a lesser extent, Catrín cyclists.

Rascuache and most Catrín commuters have the economic ability to use Metrolink trains and other public transportation systems, and a relatively small but regular group of cycling commuters use their bicycles to connect between Metrolink stations and their homes and places of employment. But space is limited and sometimes cyclists perceived as rascuache are asked to de-board if any given car exceeds the limit of four bicycles.[8] Since 2012, a small number of rush hour Metrolink trains have designated bike-specific cars for bike commuters, and these cars increase the probability that all cyclists will be able to board. In a system truly committed to bicycle justice, this token insertion of bicycle-specific cars would become the norm on all Metrolink trains. Up to this point we have contrasted both groups of cyclists, noting that while the rascuache are often subjected to police harassment and abuse, the latter, commuter, recreational, or sporting cyclists are viewed as respectable and are generally afforded the equal protection of the law. Rascuache cyclists generally turn to cycling out of economic necessity and use cycling as a way to commute from one place to another because they cannot afford an automobile or otherwise lack access to public transportation. Catrín cyclists, on the other hand, use cycling for recreation and/or sport. For Catrín cyclists, the bicycle is not always an alternative mode of transportation.

Sustainable biking justice

While economic, legal, and aesthetic concerns govern the use and modification of bicycles for transportation or exhibition, a larger concern is their use for environmental purposes and sustainability. Numerous sources confirm that the major source of carbon emissions created by humans is by driving cars (gasoline use). The average American household carbon footprint is 50 tons CO_2 per year (Jones and Kammen, 2013). Nevertheless, bike-commuters are sometimes treated as less desirable passengers on Metrolink, particularly on weekends when lower rates allow cyclists with lower socioeconomic levels, the rascuache, to use them.[9] Bike security is a critical issue throughout southern California, where bike theft is a major challenge for cyclists in both groups. Cyclists simply are not accorded the same kind of security accorded to cars. Parking services typically use the word "parking" for spaces assigned to bicycles, as if they were cars, and thus avoids the real issue, which is not "parking" but bike security.

Biking for all? Not really. The cyclists of privilege in southern California are generally white and middle-to-upper-middle class, consisting mostly of professional commuters on the Metrolink and members of recreational cycling clubs. An exception is Adobo Vélo, a relatively large (over 300) Filipino cycling club and a few other ethnic minority clubs. Upper-middle-class professionals on the Metrolink, easily identifiable by their distinctive cycling clothes and expensive ($2,000–$12,000) bicycles, are a small group of commuting cyclists. They are typically well treated by Metrolink employees, who are often aggressive with rascuache weekend riders. In public domain streets, Catrín riders increase their safety through their numbers, sometimes taking over entire lanes of streets by riding en masse, and in doing so, reaffirm their right to public space in ways that rascuache cyclists cannot.

Many of southern California's transportation systems built since WWII were constructed with the unsustainable assumption that the automobile would be the primary and permanent mode of transportation for commuting and recreation. As city managers and urban planners radically change this assumption in cities such as Portland, Minneapolis, Long Beach, and Claremont, where sustainable means of transportation have official priority over cars on many streets, urban spaces in Latin America are also beginning to provide a planning and policy model for the mostly non-sustainable urban space of southern California. In Guadalajara, Mexico, for example, the installation of Vía RecreACtiva Metropolitans (walking, cycling, community building) on Sundays has connected two formerly disjointed neighborhoods, transforming the urban space in positive ways. In Bogotá and Medellín, Colombia, long sections of the most trafficked streets are closed to bicycle and pedestrian traffic. This Ciclovía has become the role model for several cities, including Los Angeles, California, which has celebrated several CicLAvia Sundays in the downtown area. Appropriately enough, in recent years, Bogotá has also been ranked highly among the most sustainable cities in the world, and Medellín has received international recognition for its progressive transportation and ecological policy. In the latter, bicycle paths and routes are available to all the major college campuses in the city, as well as to many of the metro stations. Cities such as Guadalajara, Bogotá, Medellín, Mexico City, and Curitiba, Brazil, all offer worthwhile models from the South for our cities in the North.

One of the noteworthy features of the Colombian concept of ciclovía is its democratization effects in the central sections of cities such as Los Angeles, Medellín, and Bogotá.[10] To a large degree, pedestrians, commuter cyclists, and recreational cyclists from all three socioeconomic groups can be found in the ciclovía. In opposition to freeway and suburban space, which isolates humans from contact with others of different socioeconomic status, the ciclovía provides a space for equal access to all who chose not to use motorized vehicles, safe from car traffic. Ciclovía is a temporary and specific space not only for biking justice, but also a space in which bicycles are ridden as pieces of art, such as the rascuache art of the specially constructed lowrider bicycle.

Regardless of the lofty goals of ciclovía and other reform efforts, social class and socioeconomic disparities remain significant impediments to the implementation of a just and sustainable cycling policy on both sides of the border. Cycling policy in the United States clearly favors Catrín, middle and upper-class recreational cyclists over the rascuache riders who use bicycles not for speed, sport, or recreation but out of economic necessity. Despite the liberatory potential of ciclovía to provide a space for equal access to all who chose not to use motorized vehicles, safe from car traffic, on a recent trip to Colombia one of the authors was dismayed to learn from first-hand experience that there is much red-tape and bureaucratic paperwork associated with registering for ciclovía. The result, unfortunately, is that it is an option available largely only to upper middle-class, relatively affluent persons.

In a recent ethnographic study of the implementation of cycling policy in Mexico City, Rodrigo Meneses-Reyes (2015) similarly found that despite the City's avowed commitment to an alternative and more sustainable biking policy, the everyday implementation of these policies by police practices "intersect in a variety of ways to reinforce the use of automobiles at the expense of other forms of mobility, such as cycling."

The City of Los Angeles is an exceptionally interesting case in the context of this entire discussion, for few other U.S. cities have been as impacted by the growing Latino population or as extensively planned by car-oriented planners and policy makers. As Gerardo Sandoval has discussed in his study of Latino immigration and the growth of MacArthur Park, the Mexican population in Los Angeles has had a significant impact in changes in Los Angeles (Sandoval, 2010). As follow-up to the Colombian invention of ciclovía imported into Los Angeles, in August of 2015 the City of Los Angeles launched a major policy shift in urban transportation by announcing plans to make the entire city more bicycle friendly. Using European and Latin American models,

Los Angeles is slowing down car traffic and providing more space on the streets for cyclists.

In conclusion, today's urban planners, legislators, and policy makers at state and city levels, as well as at numerous private and public institutions, struggle to deal with the contradictions and conflicts that arise when car-planned urban spaces attempt to adapt to a post-car twenty-first-century world. Today's car commuters have grown up in a world of commoditized and comfortable use of space for cars, from driving with comfortable space at high speeds to parking them. As Federico Campbell's story reminds us, however, cyclists known to be committed to sustainability are also often intimately connected to their bicycles as extensions of themselves. Sustainable forms of transportation, such as bicycles, invariably come into conflict with both car users and car-oriented planners and policy makers.

As these issues are negotiated, the Posada image of death and lack of bicycle justice hovers over the diverse southern California cycling communities even more often than it did in the Mexican artist's nineteenth century Mexico City. Seen from South–North and from the bottom-up, the greening of U.S. urban space in its cities as well as on its college campuses will find natural allies with both the growing Latino population as well as its growing cycling communities, that include rascuache, lowriders, and the entire gamut of two-wheeled California commuters.

Notes

1 José Guadalupe Posada (1852–1913) was a late nineteenth century Mexican artist, printmaker, and political cartoonist, renowned for his satirical depictions of death.

2 Mark Twain has written: "Get a bicycle . . . You will not regret it, if you live." (Angier, 2015). H. G. Wells is widely known for his statement "When I see an adult on a bicycle, I have hope for the human race" (Bravo, 2014, p. 21).

3 The methodology used in this chapter is an eclectic combination of standard practices in the humanities and social sciences. We employ mixed methods from our respective disciplines to compensate for the lack of available data in some spheres of this chapter. One author, Raymond L. Williams, is a humanist in Hispanic literary studies with 22 years of experience as a cycling commuter, published cycling activist, and bicycle club member of over a dozen clubs. Alfredo Mirandé, is sociologist and lawyer with published identities as an observer of urban issues and "Rascuache" scholar. In this chapter, both authors cite from literary texts, urban transportation studies, urban sociology, and notes and observations recorded in field journals.

4 Also spelled *rasquache*.

5 The term Chicano (Xicano) refers to persons of Mexican origin residing in the United States on a relatively permanent basis, regardless of one's place of birth or immigration status. It is also used as a nickname for mexicano.

6 There is a rich and emergent literature on prosthetic embodiment. Drawing on Pierre Bourdieu's work on habitus, Mauss (2006) focused on how everyday uses of the body shape our world views. Bicycle scholars like Vivanco (2013), in turn, have extended the concept of "sociotectnical assemblage" to explain how bicycling can become an integral part of the rider's experience of a particular street or place, as was the case for

Campbell and his magic realists bike rides on the outskirts of the Tijuana Airport. See, also Langan, (2001), Nelson (2001), and Patton (2005).

7 At UC-Riverside, for example, thefts are reported by e-mail to the campus community, but bicycle theft is systematically minimized or ignored.

8 Williams' field journal notes.

9 Williams' field journal notes.

10 Observations about the city of Medellín are thanks to the good will of Chancellor Juan Luis Mejía of the Universidad EAFIT and Professor Leonardo García Jaramillo, who invited Raymond L. Williams to Medellín in July, 2015. Williams became familiar with the ciclovía in Medellín. Also thanks to BoConcepts, that lent him a bicycle to ride in the El Poblado neighborhood for a democratizing cycling event on Sundays. BoConcepts does not sell or rent them but, rather, lends them to non-bicycle owners.

References

Angier, N. (2015). The Bicycle and the Ride to Modern America, *New York Times*, Times, July 14, 2015, D1. www.nytimes.com/2015/07/14/science/the-bicycle-and-the-ride-to-modern-america.html

Bravo, P. (2014) *Biciosis*. Mexico City, D.F.: Debate Editorial.

Campbell, F. (1995) *Tijuana: Stories on the Border*. Translated and Introduced by Debra A. Castillo. Berkeley, CA: University of California Press.

Castillo, D. A. (1995) Borderlining: An Introduction. Pp. 1–26 in Campbell, Federico. *Tijuana: Stories on the Border*. Translated and Introduced by Debra A. Castillo. Berkeley, CA: University of California Press.

Diaz, E. M. (2013) The Necessary Theater of the Royal Chicano Air Force. *Aztlán: A Journal of Chicano Studies*, 38.2, 41–70.

Duneier, M. (1999) *Sidewalk*. New York: Farrar, Straus and Giroux.

Fuentes, C. (1992) *The Buried Mirror: Reflections on Spain and the New World*. London: André Deutsch. www.huffingtonpost.com/2015/02/19/california-helmet-law_n_6716100.html.

Hispanic Research Center. (2001) Rasquache. Arizona State University. http://mati.eas.asu.edu/ChicanArte/unit2/rasquache.html (accessed February 2, 2016).

Jones, C. M. & Kammen, D. M. (2013) Spatial Distribution of U.S. Household Carbon Footprints Reveals Suburbanization Undermines Greenhouse Gas Benefits of Urban Population Density. *Environ. Sci. Technol.* http://pubs.acs.org/doi/abs/10.1021/es4034364 [accessed August 15, 2015].

Langan, C. (2001) Mobility Disability. *Public Culture*, 13.3, 459–484.

Mauss, M. (2006) *Techniques, Technology and Civilization*, Schlanger, N. (Ed.). New York: Berghahn Books.

McQuilkin, K. S. (2009) *Primer on the Aesthetics, Fabrication, and Culture of Lowrider Bicycles in West Texas: Participant Observation through the Lens of a White, Middle-Class Male, Artist/Educator*. (Ph.D. diss., Texas Tech University).

Meneses-Reyes, R. (2015) Law and Mobility: Ethnographical Accounts of the Regulation of the Segregated Cycle Facilities in Mexico City, *Mobilities*, 10.2, 230–248, DOI: 10.1080/17450101.2013.853388.

Mesa-Bains, A. (2003) Domesticana: The Sensibility of Chicana Rasquachismo. Pp. 298–315 in Arredondo, G. F., Hurtado, A., Klahn, N., Nájera-Ramírez, O. & Zavella, P. (Eds.), *Chicana Feminisms: A Critical Reader*. Durham, NC: Duke University Press.

Miller, D. (2014) *Creating Aztlán: Chicano Art, Indigenous Sovereignty, and Lowriding Across Turtle Island*. Tucson, AZ: University of Arizona Press.

Mitchell, D. (1997) The Annihilation of Space by Law: The Roots and Implications of Anti-Homeless Laws in the United States, *Antipode*, 3, 303–335.

Nelson, D. M. (2001) Stumped Identities: Body Image, Bodies Politic, and the Mujer Maya as Prosthetic. *Cultural Anthropology*, 16.3, 314–353.

Nelson, L. & Stevens, M. (2014) 3-Foot Buffer Zones for Cyclists to Take Effect Across California. September 14. www.latimes.com/local/la-me-bike-clearance-20140917-story.html [accessed September 14, 2015].

O'Connor, L. (2015) California Mandatory Bicycle Helmet Law Would Make Riding Less Safe, Advocates Say. February 19. www.huffingtonpost.com/2015/02/19/california-helmet-law_n_6716100.html [accessed February 2, 2016.]

Patton, J. (2005) Multiple Worlds on Oakland's Streets: Social Practice and the Built Environment. *Visual Anthropology Review*, 20.2, 36–56.

Penland, P. R. (2003). *Lowrider History, Pride, Culture*. St. Paul: Motorbooks International.

Roybal, K. R. (2013) Pushing the Boundaries of Border Subjectivity, Autobiography, and Camp Rasquachismo. *Aztlán: A Journal of Chicano Studies*. 38.2, 71–93.

Sandoval, G. (2010) *Immigrants and the Revitalization of Los Angeles: Development and Change in MacArthur Park*. Amherst, NY: Cambria Press.

Soto, G. (1990) *Baseball in April and Other Stories*. Orlando, FL: Harcourt.

––––––––. (1995) *Summer on Wheels*. New York: Scholastic. Reprinted in *Growing Up Chicana/o*, ed. Tiffany Ana López, pp. 234–236. New York: Avon Books.

Stavans, I. (2000) *The Essential Ilan Stavans*. New York: Routledge.

Valles, M. & Kandel, J. (2013) 1 Killed, 1 Wounded in Gardena Shooting. *NBCLA News*. Published at 2:18 PM PDT on June 2, 2013.

Vivanco, L. (2013) *Reconsidering the Bicycle: An Anthropological Perspective on a New (Old) Thing*. New York: Routledge.

Winton, R. & Smith, D. (2015) A Rare View of Police Tactics Under Stress. *Los Angeles Times*, July 16.

Ybarra-Frausto, T. (1991) Rasquachismo: A Chicano Sensibility. Pp. 155–162 in Del Castillo, Richard Griswold, McKenna, Teresa & Yarbro-Bejarano, Yvonne *Chicano Art: Resistance and Affirmation, 1965–1985*. Berkeley, CA: University of California Press.

10 No choice but to bike

Undocumented and bike-dependent in rust belt America

Joanna Bernstein

Introduction

Diego wakes up early in the morning while it's still dark in a dingy but well-kept apartment to go to work cleaning hotel rooms in the university area. He rides his bike through the darkness to the hotel, which is luckily only a few miles from his house. Diego is grateful for the relatively short ride to work. He has had to take much further trips in the past. He mounts his two wheels helmet-less, status-less, unaware of what the traffic laws actually are, but he manages to follow them well enough, and makes his way to the hotel. When Diego arrives at the hotel, which sits on top of a major chain restaurant and hardly pays him minimum wage, he finds himself at ease, even if just for a brief moment, before he enters work. While inside the hotel, he is less visible, more protected. Once he steps back outside nine hours later to again mount his bicycle and return home, he re-enters a more dangerous realm that he will not leave until he finds his two wheels back home, and dismounts from his bike to his front porch.

The notion, or perhaps the assumption, that biking is fun, free, and liberating for everyone is overwhelmingly pervasive and seldom questioned or discussed among mainstream bike advocates and enthusiasts. Regardless of more privileged cyclists' reasons for biking, they all have one thing in common: they are choosing to bike, they don't have to bike. Not all cyclists have the luxury of choice. Three undocumented Guatemalans living in Pittsburgh, PA—Diego, Jeremias, and Jose—fall into the less luxurious category. Biking is their best option, but it is not what they would choose. Their livelihood in this country depends on it. At the same time, biking exposes these three to more risk than they would otherwise encounter if they were to walk or take public transportation to their destination. For a citizen or an immigrant with legal status, mounting and riding a bike inherently carries less risk in myriad ways. Most significantly, for cyclists with legal status, biking cannot be the catalyst for their removal from the United States.

Undocumented immigrants like Diego, Jeremias, and Jose (not their real names; all subject names are pseudonyms to help protect their identities), by contrast, can face consequences as far reaching as eventual deportation from the United States back to their home countries—just for biking. This potentially life-changing risk causes fear and paranoia on the part of many undocumented cyclists. Every single time these three men mount their bicycles to take a trip across the city, they risk sacrificing their invisibility for criminality. A protected bike lane may shield undocumented immigrants from the risk of being hit by a car or truck, but it fails to ease their legal and social vulnerability, and it can't change anyone's immigration status. The undocumented cyclist's experience riding in a 'protected' bike lane is a metaphor for the "simultaneous processes of inclusion and exclusion which underscore the schizophrenic context within which illegality exists and which undermines imagining undocumented immigrants as part of the larger society" (Chavez, 1991, p.257).

This chapter shares the story of Diego, Jeremias, and Jose and how biking plays a poignantly oppressive, as opposed to liberating, role in their daily lives. As undocumented immigrants, they struggle to navigate the system and make ends meet while doing their best to stay under the radar at the same time. To be clear, the fear that is felt by undocumented cyclists exists in a spectrum. There are significant contextual factors that shape the extent to which fear underlines an undocumented cyclist's overall experience. These include the length of time spent living in the United States, the ability to communicate in English, literacy levels, and geographic location, amongst others. All undocumented immigrants that use bicycles as their primary form of transportation are therefore not necessarily experiencing fear and paranoia at the same levels or in the same way as Diego, Jeremias, and Jose.

In addition to being undocumented and speaking very little (if any) English, Diego, Jeremias, and Jose are all illiterate in Spanish. In fact, Spanish isn't even their first language. Their native language is a Mayan dialect called Ixil (pronounced ee-sheel). Ixil is also the name of the indigenous group to which Diego, Jeremias, and Jose belong. Neither Diego, Jeremias, nor Jose ever went to school. Their families, or at least the remaining living members, couldn't afford it. Much of Santa Maria Nebaj, the municipality where the three men are from, was virtually destroyed and burned to the ground by the Guatemalan Army during the country's Civil War, which resulted in the systematic killing of an estimated 200,000 Mayans (Wilkinson, 2004). Diego, Jeremias, and Jose recall riding bikes every now and again to run small errands in Guatemala. Now, they bike every day through crowded streets, weaving between traffic and humans, hoping to make it to work and then back home safely.

Sharing the poignantly intimate stories of Diego, Jeremias, and Jose should help start a much needed dialogue within the bike community, as well as between bike- and immigration-oriented agencies and organizations, surrounding the differential experiences of undocumented cyclists and the social, legal, and physical risks that they disproportionately face as a result of having no choice but to bike. Bike advocate planners and policy makers also need to understand that migration and settlement are complex and social processes that are ongoing and non-random (Browning and Rodriguez, 1985, p.277). Bicycle organizations need to advocate for immigration reform and integration at the local (and national) levels by working alongside undocumented Latino cyclists in order to better understand the issues that these cyclists face, while attempting to change the risk context that fervently shapes the undocumented cyclist's experience. Bicycle and active transportation organizations can begin to reach undocumented Latino immigrant cyclists by connecting with community-based organizations that work with Latino immigrants, many of whom tend to be undocumented.

Collaborating with community-based organizations that already have developed trusting relationships with undocumented Latino immigrants can create avenues for meaningful civic engagement to take place that bike organizations may not be able to create on their own. While genuine in their intentions, many organizations, bike and non-bike alike, that seek to connect with undocumented Latino immigrants like Diego, Jeremias, and Jose, often find their efforts to engage members of this community unsuccessful. In this chapter, I share my personal experiences as a planner and organizer while working in the undocumented Latino immigrant community, both formally and informally, in order to help bicycle advocacy organizations better understand how to work successfully to engage undocumented cyclists, and advocate for immigration reform and immigrant integration as it pertains to biking and public safety.

The place

Having grown up in the city of Pittsburgh, spending substantial amounts of time in many of its various neighborhoods and quadrants, I can't recall ever having heard much (if any) Spanish on the street. There were few of the taquerias, bodegas, or other more traditional Latino-owned small businesses that I was used to seeing in certain neighborhoods in Philadelphia or New York—two cities with sizable, Latino immigrant populations that have put down roots on various street corners by building small businesses. Kids kick soccer balls outside while their parents shop a bodega's narrow aisles for everything from tortillas to beans, from cilantro to a particular type of Bimbo brand snack that most closely resembles a Hostess cupcake. I felt very little Latino cultural presence in my childhood Pittsburgh, especially in comparison to larger, more prominent immigrant groups in the area who had established cultural footprints in the area, from, say, India or China.

I first left Pittsburgh for college in North Carolina in 2006, and then again in 2010 for graduate school in Eugene, Oregon. When I returned to Pittsburgh in the fall of 2013, following my departure from Oregon and a brief three-month stint in Nicaragua, I realized that things had changed. A population that was, for all intents and purposes, invisible seven and a half years ago, now appeared to have a small yet undeniable presence. There were a handful of small businesses that acted as much as community gathering spaces and cultural institutions as they did grocery stores and taquerias. It was no longer uncommon to pass groups of immigrant day laborers washing down street tacos with Mexican Cokes or Jarritos fruit-flavored sodas for lunch outside markets with Spanish names.

According to United States Census figures, the Latino population in the City of Pittsburgh grew 72 percent between 2000 and 2010. This statistic represents an increase from 4,400 people in the year 2000 to 6,964 residents in 2010. Despite the demographic growth within the Latino community documented in both the U.S. Census and American Community Survey, these numbers are lower than the actual size of the Latino community in Pittsburgh. Undercounting takes place in virtually all immigrant communities, particularly those communities whose members may be undocumented (Bernstein, 2012). The Latino community in Pittsburgh is therefore larger than the Census portrays. The actual size of the population, however, remains unclear.

Another aspect of civic life that appeared to have drastically changed over the seven and half years I spent away from Pittsburgh was the number of people riding bikes and the presence of new cycling infrastructure. Despite the city's challenging, hilly topography and the intimidating lack of bike infrastructure in many neighborhoods (granted, the situation is improving in some of these areas at the moment) more people are making bicycles their primary form of transportation. Pittsburgh's Mayor, Bill Peduto, has been a long time bike advocate. His administration maintains a strong and intimate working relation-ship with Bike Pittsburgh, the city's largest and most prominent bike advocacy organization. At the same time, the city of Pittsburgh has witnessed an unexpect-edly "dramatic increase" in its bike commuter population over the past several years (Streets Blog USA, 2014). The League of American Bicyclists conducted an analysis of the bicycle commuter data released by the 2013 American Community Survey. Incredibly, these numbers show a "'meteoric' 408% increase in Pittsburgh bike commuting since 2000, the largest jump of any city in the nation" (Bike Pittsburgh, 2014).

The unprecedented skyrocketing of the city's bike commuter population, and the strong, collaborative relationship that the mayor's administration maintains with Bike Pittsburgh, helped Pittsburgh get selected by PeopleForBikes for their 2014–2016 funding cycle of the Green Lane Project. PeopleForBikes includes both an industry coalition of bicycling suppliers and retailers and a charitable foundation. The organization has invested more than $2.1 million in com-munity bicycling projects, including the Green Lane Project, which helps U.S. cities build protected bike lanes. The program selects leading cities around the country and connects them with the skills and support they need to plan and rapidly install connected, low-stress bike networks on their existing streets. The Pittsburgh program is currently in its second year and two brand new protected bike lanes in high traffic areas have already been built.

Indigenous, undocumented, and on bicycles: experiences, fears, and contradictions

Diego Brito Corio is originally from Santa Maria Nebaj, Guatemala, a municipality in the northern department of El Quiche. Diego speaks fluent Spanish despite the fact that it is not his first language, Ixil. The Ixil people are an indigenous Mayan group native to Guatemala. The majority of the Ixil people live in and around three municipalities in the Cuchumatanes mountains: Santa Maria Nebaj, San

Gaspar Chajul, and San Juan Cotzal. The shape and proximity of these three municipalities to one another earned the area the name 'the Ixil Triangle.' During the long, arduous, and excruciatingly violent Guatemalan Civil War, certain indigenous groups and their respective regions and municipalities were targeted more heavily by the Guatemalan army than others because of their villages' proximity to suspected rebel and counter-insurgent groups that hid in the mountains plotting their takeover of the Guatemalan government and military (Grant, 2013). The Ixil people were one of those targeted groups. According to Guatemalan judge Jazmin Barrios, "the Ixils were considered public enemies of the state and were also victims of racism, considered an inferior race" (ibid.). Furthermore, "the violent acts against the Ixils were not spontaneous, they were planned beforehand" (ibid.).

The most violent years of the Civil War in Diego, Jeremias, and Jose's hometown were symbolized by smoke. The municipalities and mountain towns throughout the Ixil Triangle were literally burned to the ground, and many of their residents were "disappeared, or code for killed" (Wilkinson, 2004, p.85). Without any warning, soldiers from the Guatemalan army locked women and children inside their homes before setting them on fire and watching them burn to the ground. The Ixil peoples who were not killed during the horrific invasions that took place during the war (the indigenous casualties that took place during the war were officially recognized as genocide by many international courts when the war ended in 1996) had no choice but to flee into the dense Cuchumatanes mountains and go into hiding—some for more than a decade—in order to survive and dodge soldiers wanting to execute them (Nelson, 2015).

Diego, Jeremias, and Jose, along with other members of the Ixil community from Santa Maria Nebaj that also reside in Pittsburgh, said that today the Ixil Triangle, in addition to being extremely poor, has now essentially been taken over by 'Las Maras,' or members of the violent Central American street gang La Marasalvatrucha. "There is very little work," said Diego. "And if you do work and make money, Las Maras will find you and take it from you and then try to make you join their gang." He continued to explain that everyone in the community understands that declining an invitation to join La Marasalvatrucha means putting both your life, and all of your family's lives, in grave danger. It's join or die. One of Diego's main reasons for leaving Guatemala for the United States was to avoid the constant looming threat of being targeted and recruited by La Marasalvatrucha.

Diego has been in the United States since 2008. "I've known I was going to (live and work) in the United States since I was little boy," Diego told me on one occasion. He spent five years in Miami, an area with a historically large and diverse Latino population, before moving to Pittsburgh in early 2012. While living in Miami, Diego found himself commuting almost exclusively by bicycle for the first time. He recalls having been in several accidents while biking as a novice in a big city with intimidatingly bustling streets. "I didn't know what I was doing [on my bike] and I was hit by a motorcycle." Now, several years later, Diego feels more comfortable on his bike, at least in terms of his ability to navigate traffic and avoid accidents. These days, he proudly refers to his cycling abilities as 'avanzado,' or advanced. No one taught Diego how to ride his bike and develop the skills that give him the confidence to label his riding ability as 'avanzado.' On the contrary, he had to learn on his own.

In the article "Bike to Death" (Gerda and Santana, 2013), another undocumented Latino immigrant cyclist named Mario expressed a sentiment similar to Diego's when discussing how he transformed from a timid novice to a confident and proficient cyclist on his own: "I used to be afraid of bikes," he said. "I started riding when my car broke down. I used to walk, it took me two hours on bus and then I started riding bikes." One day, a friend came by and offered to sell Mario his bike. He bought it for $9. "I walked it home because I didn't know how to ride it. I started practicing at home," said Mario. "Today, I'm an expert" (ibid.).

But he, too, had to become an expert on his own.

Both Diego and Mario, compared to some of their counterparts, appear to have had certain knacks for teaching themselves to bike on busy streets in densely populated cities without incurring any major injuries. This, however, is not the case for all undocumented immigrants. Some learn more slowly. According to a 2005 Federal Highway Administration study, Latinos are especially threatened by cycling accidents (Gerda and Santana, 2013). The study is mostly quantitative and as a result does not offer much in the way of explanations regarding why Latino cyclists disproportionately suffer from more bike accidents and fatalities than all other ethnic groups, excluding whites. Bike organizations and advocates need to communicate and engage effectively with Latino cyclists, particularly the undocumented, in order to fill in these information gaps and develop a more comprehensive understanding of the factors and circumstances that contribute to their higher injury and fatality rates.

I first encountered Diego Brito Corio during the fall of 2013 while volunteering at Casa San Jose, then a newly established resource center for Latino immigrants. The organization is located in South Pittsburgh, one of the most isolated parts of the city from a transportation perspective, but a central location for many members of the city's newer and growing Latino population. Diego arrived at Casa San Jose with his 'nephew' Jeremias Perez, a timid 16-year-old Ixil boy also from Santa Maria Nebaj (or just 'Nebaj,' according to the locals) who spoke very limited Spanish. After Diego and I had known each other for about a year, he revealed to me that Jeremias was not really his nephew. This did not come as much of a surprise to me as I had suspected that Diego wasn't really Jeremias' uncle as he seemed entirely too young.

Jeremias' parents had called Diego from Guatemala when they heard that Jeremias had been picked up by immigration and asked Diego if he could take in Jeremias and become his legal guardian. Needless to say, Diego agreed. Jeremias was picked up by ICE (Immigration and Customs Enforcement) at the U.S.–Mexico border while trying to enter the United States in August 2013. Adult immigrants who are apprehended at the border trying to cross without documents are automatically deported. But since Jeremias was an unaccompanied minor when caught, he was sent to a shelter for child migrants where caseworkers labor tirelessly to locate and identify family members who live in the United States. In Jeremias' case, social workers were fortunate enough to locate Diego, his 'uncle' in Pittsburgh, and make him Jeremias' guardian.

Once settled and situated in the tiny Casa San Jose basement, Diego pulled a manila envelope out of his backpack and handed it to me. The envelope contained guardianship paperwork from the Office of Refugee Resettlement (ORR). Diego and Jeremias are both illiterate and never went to school to learn Spanish and they needed assistance filling out the paperwork. All designated guardians have to be fingerprinted and submit notarized paperwork that gives detailed personal information to the federal government. While the paperwork is sent to ORR and not ICE (the two federal agencies are separate and don't traditionally work together), any undocumented individual who becomes a guardian to an unaccompanied minor is essentially confirming their undocumented immigration status by merely filling out and sending in the paperwork. This means Diego took a risk to protect Jeremias.

Over time I learned from Diego that Jeremias had an older brother named Jose who had already been living with him for a couple of years. They had grown up together and been friends in Nebaj. Their families were close, too. Despite the fact that Jose is actually Jeremias' older brother, he was not able to petition to be Jeremias' guardian because Jose has already been deported once and therefore could be flagged by ICE for admitting his current presence in the United States. Diego has never been apprehended by ICE, so it was slightly safer for him to apply to be Jeremias' guardian. I met Jose not long after meeting Diego and Jeremias. Jose's first language was of course Ixil, but more like Diego and less like Jeremias, he spoke Spanish fairly well, which enabled our conversations to flow more freely. I learned that Jose originally attempted to enter the United States when he was 19 but was apprehended by ICE at the border. He spent two months in an ICE prison in Texas before being deported back to Guatemala. The following year he attempted to cross the border again, this time successfully.

Jose, like Diego, had a timid, humble, and calming aura about him that drew me to him instantly. When I went to the apartment where the three men were living at the time, Jose had what appeared to be fresh cuts and bruises on his legs. Jose and Diego explained that when Jeremias didn't make it home the night before, Jose went out on his bike to look for Jeremias. During his search, a group of young men started to harass and chase Jose on his bike. Jose feared the men wanted to rob him and take his bike, so he tried to speed away. While Jose did eventually escape the men, he took a bad spill in the process and sustained minor injuries. He was not wearing a helmet and had not called the police to report the incident.

Jose did not call the police because he feared the possibility of being turned back over to ICE. Jose made himself vulnerable the night that he went out on his bike searching for his younger brother, but he was too fearful to advocate for himself and file a police report. This incident exemplifies how bike safety and immigration status intertwine, impacting undocumented individuals' ability to advocate for themselves if they face injustice or are victims of crimes while on their bikes. Bike advocates and organizations should recognize the barriers that the undocumented face to reporting incidents and should work directly with the undocumented cyclists in order to come up with strategies. These cyclists should have the freedom to contact the appropriate authorities if someone is threatened or injured. Today they do not have this freedom.

In the summer of 2015, about a year and a half after I initially met Diego and Jeremias, I began to conduct open-ended, informal interviews with the family members about their experiences as undocumented cyclists. I spoke with them on several occasions, both together and individually. The larger themes that I sought to explore through their experience with bicycling included choice, fear, and opportunities for civic engagement. I first interviewed Diego and Jeremias together. It was a breezy afternoon that followed a muggy morning, so I suggested that we sit outside. I could tell that they were apprehensive about sitting outside, but I knew them well enough at that point to know that it is okay for me to push them to be less shadowed sometimes. We situated ourselves on a sidewalk table outside a coffee shop that sat on the busy, commercial street where both men worked. They both sported silly, nervous smirks as we talked about biking and they watched the world go by, for a change.

I began our first conversation by simply asking what tasks they used their bikes for. They both explained that they relied exclusively on their bikes to get to and from work, and to run any other errands as needed. "I bike to get to work because it's more direct and faster than the bus," said Diego. Both men stated that they only ride the bus if there is heavy rain or snow. Weather permitting, they ride everywhere.

Mid-conversation, after a series of questions surrounding the struggles and fears that come with being an undocumented cyclist, I asked Diego and Jeremias a more 'positive' question, or so I thought. "Okay," I started, "what do you guys like about biking?" Neither of them said a word. They just looked at me with blank stares as if they hadn't understood the question, but I knew that they had. "*El ejercicio . . .?* [The exercise?]" I timidly suggested. "*Sí,*" they both said in unison. "*Pero eso es la unica cosa* [But that's the only thing]," added Diego. When I asked Jose the same question a couple of weeks later at their home, he answered "*nada* [nothing]," without a moment of hesitation. When speaking with Diego, Jeremias, and Jose about their feelings and experiences relying on bicycles for transportation, I asked if any of them had ever heard of someone getting deported for biking. They all said that they hadn't. Despite the fact that none of them had ever heard of biking resulting in deportation, each one of them individually conveyed that fear was always flowing through them during their journeys on two wheels, in different forms and ways.

I first heard of an undocumented person getting deported for biking while working on my graduate thesis in Oregon. "You know you can be deported for biking, right?" Israel told me. An undocumented Mexican man who spoke perfect English, he had been living in the United States for over half of his life, and he continued to tell me that failing to signal when turning or not having both front and back lights on your bike after dark is enough to get pulled over and asked for identifying documents by law enforcement. Israel continued to explain that it isn't exactly breaking a traffic law on a bike in and of itself that's a deportable offense. More so, it's that biking, under the worst of circumstances, can be a mechanism for being turned over from local law enforcement to ICE, which means entering the federal immigration court system, which can then lead to deportation depending on the details of each individual's case and any past history that that person may have with either local law enforcement or ICE. There are no statistics about how many deportees entered or re-entered the federal judicial system via apprehension on a bicycle, which makes it difficult to quantify this issue. Qualitatively, this no doubt has effects on the lives of undocumented cyclists.

At this point in time, driver's licenses, or 'driver cards' as they are called in some places, are available to undocumented immigrants in only 11 states. Pennsylvania is not one of those states. Undocumented individuals who choose to drive without licenses run a major risk of being turned over to ICE if they are pulled over for any reason (or lack of a reason). A more hostile or less welcoming local police officer can elect to notify ICE that they have a suspected undocumented immigrant in their custody. When I asked Diego, Jeremias, and Jose if they felt safer riding a bicycle as opposed to operating a motor vehicle without a license, they all ultimately expressed the same sentiment. They never really feel 'safe' at all, but they view biking as the less risky of the two options because driving without a license means inherently breaking the law, while riding a bicycle does not because it does not require government documentation. This is not to imply that riding a bicycle without a legitimate government-issued ID (even if it was issued by a foreign country's consulate within the United States) is risk-free for undocumented cyclists. Still, Diego, Jeremias, and Jose would rather bike than run the risk of being pulled over in a car without a driver's license.

Out of the three men, Jose appeared the most fearful when it came to his physical safety while riding his bicycle. Despite the fact that he never said anything radically different than Diego or Jeremias during our various informal interviews, the stoic expression on his face that radiated most powerfully from his eyes rang with pure terror. When I asked Jose if he had any knowledge at all of traffic laws, he said that he didn't. Diego, despite identifying as an advanced cyclist, also said that he did not know what the traffic laws were, or what most of the signs mean, with the single exception being the stop sign, which made everyone in the room laugh. All three men said that they would like to learn the traffic laws so that they can better protect themselves on their bikes and also avoid accidentally breaking the law and gaining the attention of the wrong police officer.

Developing an effective and fun engagement strategy for teaching traffic laws to illiterate immigrant cyclists who speak very little English, while tapping into their personal experiences surrounding cycling and their identities as immigrants in the United States, takes creative methods. To this end, artist and urban planner James Rojas has developed an interactive planning model called Place It, a participatory model building workshop that helps engage the public in planning and design processes. Participants are able to learn about planning while having their individual identities validated during the design process (Rojas, 2010). In September 2014, Diego, Jeremias, and Jose all participated in Place It workshops in Pittsburgh that asked them to create a model of their ideal city. When I asked them if they thought doing a Place It workshop surrounding biking and safe streets would be a good way to go about learning more about traffic laws and how to bike safely, they all immediately said yes.

Civic engagement tactics for reaching undocumented Latino cyclists

In order for biking to truly be more equitable, bike-oriented community advocates will have to invest serious time and energy on strategies for reaching and engaging undocumented Latino cyclists. For cyclists like Diego, Jeremias, and Jose, immigration issues should be a central action item under the bike equity umbrella. The bike advocates that wish to represent their needs to policy makers will have to fight for structural changes and immigration reform(s) pertaining to undocumented cyclists, as opposed to just focusing on getting more Latino immigrants on bikes. These new bike advocates for undocumented Latino cyclists will need to get to know these cyclists on a personal level in order to understand where biking and immigration overlap. Advocating both for and alongside undocumented cyclists will make their experience on two wheels more positive and less risk-filled.

When it comes to working with undocumented Latino immigrant cyclists, bike organizations cannot rely on employing the same methods for civic engagement that have been used successfully with other seemingly similar marginalized populations in the past (Bernstein, 2012, p.45). In order to even get undocumented cyclists to show up to bicycle-oriented events or community workshops, bike organizations lacking relationships with these groups need to identify the organizations and individuals that work with the Latino immigrant community and attempt to connect with them. The individuals and organizations that have established trusting relationships with this target group have access to the social capital that exists within the Latino immigrant community.

If it were not for the personal relationships and the trust that I have managed to develop with many undocumented Latino immigrants over time, writing this chapter and obtaining specific, personal information about biking and deep-seated fears would not have been possible. I never viewed Diego and Jeremias as mere clients when I was working with them at Casa San Jose. I viewed (and still do view) them as resilient human beings. Yes, they needed a great deal of help, and they will continue to need a great deal of help as long as they continue to reside in this country. But while an incredibly shy Diego and equally intimidated Jeremias and I sat in the tiny Casa San Jose office together for the first time filling out immigration paperwork, I didn't just ask them the questions on the papers. I slipped in more personal questions, too. Where exactly in Guatemala were they from? How long had they been in Pittsburgh? Did they speak a dialect? What did they think of things here? This is part of a community ally's skill set: making people feel at home, when they are so far away.

In my case, I was always interested in getting to know the personal stories of the clients that walked through Casa San Jose and Huerto de la Familia's doors beyond helping them with their immediate needs. Now I understand that if I had not made an effort to neutralize the inherent service-provider-receiver power imbalance between us, then I'm not sure I would have been able to call up immigrants like Diego, Jeremias, and Jose and invite them to participate when meaningful opportunities for civic engagement did arise.

While working at nonprofits that served undocumented Latino immigrants and their families in both Pittsburgh and Eugene, Oregon, my colleagues and I were approached by government agencies, educational institutions, social service agencies, and other nonprofits and community groups seeking to connect and engage with this population. Neither of these organizations worked exclusively with undocumented Latino cyclists or facilitated major communication between bike advocates and Latino immigrant cyclists, but the examples discussed below have value as methods for reaching and engaging undocumented cyclists. More often than not, the agencies and individuals that approached our organizations did not offer to pay or compensate us for acting as a major cultural and linguistic liaison between the outside organization and undocumented Latino immigrants. Both of the organizations that I worked with strongly supported bolstering opportunities for civic engagement with Latino immigrants, but they do not exist to act as token liaisons or 'connectors,' as often referred, between undocumented immigrants and outside organizations looking to engage them.

While working at Huerto de La Familia and Casa San Jose and living in their respective locations, I came to grow and solidify trusting personal relationships with both my immediate clients as well as other members of the larger Latino immigrant community. Through the invaluable interactions and conversations that my colleagues and I had with community members from this population, which took place both formally and informally, we developed specific cultural knowledge about undocumented Latino immigrants and the many unique dynamics that existed within their communities. Casa San Jose (Pennsylvania) was primarily a social service organization while Huerto de la Familia's (Oregon) main programs surrounded organic gardening and the development of food and agricultural based micro-enterprises for Latino immigrant and mixed status families. Both of these organizations took on a great deal of extra time and labor by planning and facilitating the outreach strategies and implementation processes necessary to reach and engage undocumented Latino immigrants and their families.

Essentially all of the civic engagement work that my colleagues and I undertook, such as encouraging our clients to attend an event or gathering that aimed to put them in touch with another agency's resources, was extra work. Substantial amounts of time and energy are consumed by the outreach process, as individuals working with undocumented Latino immigrants on a day-to-day basis understand. Due to education and comprehension issues, some immigrants—like Diego, Jeremias, and Jose—lack context or information about what issues a seemingly self-explanatory event cover. Even if a municipality or organization posts flyers in Spanish at a Latino grocery store where dozens, if not hundreds, of local immigrants shop every day, words on a piece of paper do not get the job done. Even for immigrant individuals with more formal education and perfect literacy skills, a generic flyer won't be enough to pull them away from their busy schedules to a new or special event. In my experience as a community liaison, Latino immigrant culture, particularly among undocumented Mexicans and Central Americans, is both very personal and informal. Every single time that one of the agencies I worked for was tasked with getting undocumented immigrants to events, we would have to make individual phone calls and send out multiple batches of detailed text messages informing people about an event or workshop. We would go around the community talking to Latino business owners about what they could do in order to promote an event. This work is time consuming, but in my experience it is absolutely essential that the personal outreach takes place. If it doesn't, an event may completely fail—meaning that nobody shows up. I have seen this happen on more than one occasion.

Conclusions and recommendations for bike advocates and organizations

As bike organizations and advocates consider the broader risks that underlie undocumented Latino cyclists' experiences, they should visualize themselves as the next major proponents of both local and national immigration reform. When bike advocates approach organizations that work with undocumented cyclists in an effort to better understand their needs so that they can more successfully work together and advocate for these immigrants, the immigrant-serving organization should be compensated. The specific methods and engagement tools that bike planners use to engage undocumented cyclists must be culturally appropriate and interactive. Sit-down, 'town hall'-style meetings won't always do the trick. Instead, bike advocates and planners should consider using models like James Rojas' Place It in order to tap into the internal dynamics of the undocumented cycling community. Most importantly, bike advocates need to remember that their task is not to put more undocumented Latino immigrants on bikes. First, let's attend to the current undocumented cyclists, welcoming them into our communities, making them more comfortable, and reducing the fear they feel on two wheels.

References

Bernstein, J. (2012) *Maneuvering the System: How Undocumented Latino/a Immigrant Survive in Lane County*, Oregon. Master's Thesis. University of Oregon. p.45.

Bike Pittsburgh. (2014) New census numbers show Pittsburgh has the nation's largest bike commuter jump since Y2K. Available from: http://bikepgh.org/2014/09/23/

new-census-numbers-show-pittsburgh-has-the-nations-largest-bike-commuter-jump-since-y2k/ [Accessed August 8, 2015].

Browning, H. & Rodriguez, N. (1985) The Migration of Mexican Indocumentados as a Settlement Process: Implications for Work. *Hispanics in the U.S. Economy.* George J. Borjas and Marta Tienda (eds.). Orlando, FL: Academic Press, 26–40.

Chavez, L.R. (1991) Outside the Imagined Community: Undocumented Settlers and Experiences of Incorporation. *American Ethnologist* 18 (2), pp.257–278.

Gerda, N. & Santana, N. (2013) Bike to death. *Voice of OC.* Available from: http://voiceofoc.org/2013/05/bike-to-death/ [Accessed August 10, 2015].

Grant, W. (2013) Guatemala's Rios Mott found guilty of genocide. *BBC.* Available from: www.bbc.com/news/world-latin-america-22490408 [Accessed August 10, 2014].

Nelson, J. (2015) Odysseys: Pittsburgh offers refuge from atrocities in Guatemala. *Pittsburgh Post Gazette.* Available from: www.post-gazette.com/newimmigrants/2015/01/12/Odysseys-Pittsburgh-offers-refuge-from-atrocities-in-Guatemala/stories/201411280090 [Accessed March 3, 2015].

Rojas, J. (2010) An explanation of Place It. Available from: www.placeit.org/about.html [Accessed August 1, 2015].

Streets Blog USA (2014) How Pittsburgh builds bike lanes without sacrificing public consultation. Available from: http://usa.streetsblog.org/2014/11/19/how-pittsburgh-builds-bike-lanes-fast-without-sacrificing-public-consultation/ [Accessed September 5, 2015].

Wilkinson, D. (2004) *Silence on the Mountain: Stories of Terror, Betrayal, and Forgetting in Guatemala.* Durham and London: Duke University Press. U.S. CENSUS www.census.gov

11 Aburrido!

Cycling on the U.S./Mexican border with Doble Rueda bicycle collective in Matamoros, Tamaulipas

Daryl Meador

Introduction: Doble Rueda in Matamoros, Mexico

The Mexican city of Matamoros, Tamaulipas lies 30 km west of the Gulf of Mexico and directly underneath la frontera (the border) of the United States, sharing three international bridges with Brownsville, Texas. Once a spring break destination for vacationers from the United States, Matamoros is now described in news headlines as "ground zero" for Mexico's Drug War (Burnett, 2015). It is the base city of the Gulf Cartel, and infamously faces sporadic shootings and kidnappings stemming from cartel rivalry and infighting. The two main forces of power meant to control the cartel—the Policía Federal and the United States Border Patrol (CBP)—have both fallen into overwhelming corruption. In this embroiled context, residents of Matamoros live normal day-to-day lives but after dark many retreat to their homes and hesitate to leave until the morning.

On Thursday nights, residents of some of the outer barrios (neighborhoods) —ostensibly the more dangerous areas of the city—wait on their porches and rooftops to watch their streets briefly transform. Families cheer and dogs bark from rooftops when as many as 250 bicyclists flood their streets. Many riders are fitted with colorful lights and several tow trailers with loud speakers or sleeping children inside. The ride is remarkably inclusive and familial; it is diverse in age and cheerfully noisy. The group doesn't move fast, which gives them the time to greet the members of the community with cheers and waves. Organizers of the cycling collective Doble Rueda (Double Wheel) rotate through in reflective vests, graciously "plugging" intersections against passing cars to keep the group flowing through potholed city streets with no cycling infrastructure.

This tight knit group of riders started cycling together on one Thursday evening in June of 2013. On one of their early small group rides, a friend quipped "Aburrido!" (boring!) in response to a lull in conversation. "Aburrido" has now become Doble Rueda's unofficial slogan as they ride in their festive transportation celebrations. Two years later, in the strenuously restrictive context of Matamoros, their rides typically number over 200. They have built a vibrant and burgeoning weekly community event for all types of cyclists that is feeding into a larger growing cycling community in the city.

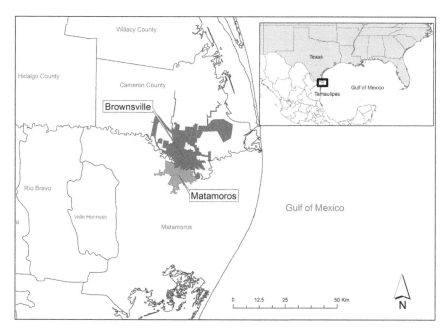

Figure 11.1 Map of the urban sprawl of Brownsville and Matamoros

The extreme situation has in many ways dictated the group's methodologies—with little support from the political and social context, they have worked from the ground up, striving to organize a truly inclusive community. Within the vacuum of corruption and violence there has been space to build a cycling community that relies on culturally specific grassroots power. In a space that is so defined by its demarcations and boundaries—whether territorial, political and social—the sizable bicycling group rides that traverse the troubled city once a week are truly unprecedented. On Doble Rueda's group rides, bicyclists yell and cheer nearly continuously, referencing inside jokes or quoting popular song lyrics. Amongst this, the most frequent word heard is an exuberant "Aburrido!", ironically calling attention to their lively rides.

What is the significance of this word that's become a slogan for the group, printed on their handmade patches next to an image of a bicycle? In the unpredictable and troubled city, declaring any activity a banality is a subversion—it's a reclamation of activity and space from the politics, corruption and tragic myths that hold the city hostage. This chapter will explore how Doble Rueda uses the bicycle as a means to free space and activities from the many delimitations within the troubled city. Their story demonstrates how bicycle dependent riders are creating spaces of freedom and empowerment within a difficult social and political context. The content is based on firsthand interviews with Doble Rueda members, collaboratively undertaken with the help of Doble Rueda organizer Andrés Cárdenas in the summer of 2015.

Geographic and historic context

Urban context

Because Matamoros lies in such direct proximity to the border, it is impossible to discuss it in detail without considering its transborder neighbor, Brownsville, Texas. The downtown areas of both cities lay within walking distance of the Gateway border crossing, one of three bridges crossing the Rio Bravo Del Norte (the Rio Grande River). People often speak of the two cities as "divided" by the river, which demarcates the physical border. It's perhaps more productive and accurate to consider them as "brought together" by it, a natural source of sustenance, trade and cultural identity.

The urban and spatial designs of the two cities make for an interesting comparison, especially as they pertain to cycling infrastructure and cycling communities. While Matamoros contains roughly twice the population of Brownsville, Brownsville's urban sprawl is considerably larger. Brownsville constantly expands north, covering land with large tracts of parking lots and four lane roads, making it less habitable for cycling. In recent years the local government in Brownsville has undertaken multiple efforts to create a more bike-friendly city; miles of paths have been built, bike lanes installed on streets and a Cyclovia occurs monthly in the summertime. Despite these efforts to encourage cycling, the infrastructure is mostly used recreationally, typically by cyclists training on high-end road bikes.

In 2013, Brownsville was registered as the poorest metroplex in the United States (Clark, 2013). Many of its low-income residents live in colonias—densely populated neighborhoods formed by developers in the 1950s to fulfill housing needs in the region. Colonias often lay in floodplains and have existed for decades with various levels of built infrastructure, some with no basic drainage or paved roads. Here, many residents live below the poverty line and have very few choices for mobility, relying heavily on public transportation. Cycling remains a low-priority item in the midst of the multiplicity of infrastructural issues faced by the communities.

Matamoros' urban design, in contrast to Brownsville, is compact. Visiting the mall does not require crossing a large parking lot, as it does in Brownsville, but merely walking across the sidewalk. In this way, the urban design encourages cycling and many residents use a bicycle for their daily means of mobility, either to commute or as a job itself. It's common to see delivery riders on sturdy BMX bikes with large makeshift baskets or vendors pedaling three-wheel bikes with large carts full of ice cream or tacos for sale. These riders—typically low-income workers who consider the bicycle a means of transportation and sustenance rather than a recreational tool—are usually from the outer barrios.

In Matamoros, government funding for cycling infrastructure is scarce. If any funding is allocated, projects suffer from poor planning and implementation. A bike path was built outside downtown Matamoros, expected to extend to some maquiladoras—free-trade factories where a large portion of Matamoros residents are employed. What could have been a productive tool for working class commuters was never finished due to political turnover and corruption. It currently ends at a high-traffic street outside the city and is hardly used for cycling—it has instead been taken over by street vendors.

Both cities share a culture of car-centricity. In Brownsville, large roads and urban sprawl encourage it. In Matamoros, local stereotypes and standards glorify cars as status symbols. Many residents drive large American pickup trucks that overwhelm the small streets. Used cars are abundant and cheap in Matamoros, so even low-income families will often own more than one. Many residents endure long toilsome work days, perhaps on a delivery bike or in a factory, only to spend huge portions of their wages on gas and car upkeep. In the city in general, the bicycle is still considered an inferior form of mobility to the automobile. One member of Doble Rueda describes a past job on the delivery bicycle in Matamoros as particularly grueling:

> I had a job in which I had to pedal all day long and that meant to be under all kind of weather, sun and rain. Some shifts were very long and I just started hating the bike. I was doing it for the job. I was under pressure and had to be really fast on the bike thus I was overwhelmed and I just quit.

He didn't begin riding again until he joined the collective.

One member of Doble Rueda, Moises (known to everyone as Moi), has been riding his bicycle in Matamoros for 40 years and currently commutes 33 km every day on his bicycle to his job in a maquiladora. He knows that many residents of Matamoros avoid everyday cycling because they feel unsafe amongst the road traffic and the public transportation. Public transportation in Matamoros takes the form of refurbished school buses from the United States that are driven aggressively and are effectively too big for Matamoros' streets. In Moi's opinion, the bus drivers "only care about their business and they see bikes as something that's in their way," a dynamic that inhibits many citizens from using their bicycle daily as he does.

Matamoros' political and social context

Mexico's ongoing Drug War and its relationship with the border strains and inhibits growth in all facets of urban life in Matamoros. While U.S. policing and securitization of the border has a long and violent history, the attitudes of U.S. policy as well as the general context of drug-trafficking-related violence in the Borderlands has shifted dramatically since former Mexican president Felipe de Jesús Calderón declared his war on drugs in 2006 (Correa-Cabrera et al., 2014). Many have noted that the most tangible response to Calderón's offensives were sharp increases in violence as cartels found an opportunity to weaken rival groups and seize territory, eventually leading Mexico down a path that many consider to be towards a "failed state" (Correa-Cabrera et al., 2014, 44; Tuckman, 2012). In a vicious cycle, these upticks in violence sparked further border militarization from the United States for fear of "spill-over violence" into the United States, a phenomenon that Correa-Cabrera et al. have argued is virtually nonexistent despite the ongoing political discourse emphasizing it (2014, 44).

Intermingled in the border imbroglio is the issue of immigration, a dire and complex dynamic of the border and especially the Rio Grande Valley of Texas surrounding Brownsville. The long stretches of desolate and hot ranch lands north of Brownsville are notoriously dangerous areas to cross, compounded by reports of United States Border Patrol's neglect of immigrants needing medical aid (Democracy Now!, 2015). While Matamoros is certainly impacted by its relationship with immigration, its most acute internal issues are related to the narco (cartel) presence. Matamoros is the base city of the Gulf Cartel and the city and the surrounding state Tamaulipas have witnessed violence from rival faction battles and cartel infighting. The Gulf Cartel's influence in the city is pervasive—everyone knows someone who is connected to it, be it a friend or family member. The Gulf Cartel is infamous for its recruitment of the city's youth.

While threats of violence in the region remain sporadic yet acute, one of the most damaging aspects of the ongoing conflict is the culture of fear engendered in large part by foreign media coverage. Corporate-owned news media outlets profit from the sensationalization of the violence on the border. This prevailing culture of fear is one of the biggest propagators of violence in the border regions as "government actors and non-governmental personnel [utilize] the spectacle for material gain at the expense of civil society" (Correa-Cabrera et al. 2014, 48).

In Matamoros, this profiteering is evident in the corruption that runs deep through the powers meant to dispel drug trafficking and cartel violence. Matamoros' civil police force was disbanded in 2011 due to corruption and replaced by the Policía Federal. Many residents of Matamoros now believe that the Policía Federal, with boundless resources and facing little accountability, are just as co-opted by cartels as the civil police once was. The soldiers' silent and ominous patrolling in the city instills an ethos of fear in itself.

The United States Border Patrol, increasingly militarized, is a similarly severely compromised form of law enforcement. Corruption and rampant abuses of power within the U.S. Bureau of Customs and Border Protection (CBP) at large are well documented. In Brownsville and the surrounding Rio Grande Valley, corruption creeps from the Border Patrol to local politicians. As reported by NPR, there is no denying that the local economy in Brownsville benefits from the existence of the Gulf Cartel across the border and the high volume of drug smuggling it brings to the region (Burnett and Penaloza, 2015). Residents of Matamoros recount stories told by local drug dealers who will bring bribes to CBP agents at border sites just outside of Matamoros to allow safe crossing of contraband. Sometimes the bribes consist of women, who the CBP agents take to a local motel while the cartel conducts its business at the border.

Doble Rueda's stories

Embodied experiences

Riding a bicycle in this context, Doble Rueda members have many stories to tell. While riding along the dirt paths atop the levee of the river on the outskirts of the city, they've seen groups crossing the Rio Grande in unsanctioned areas to reach the United States. A Doble Rueda member remembered, "The people making them cross looked at us and said, 'You can't come through this trail, we're working here.' They were super polite. We just turned around and rode back along the levee." In Matamoros, the cyclists witnessed a drug dealer take up arms to defend one of their weekly group rides against an aggressive driver. After the driver repeatedly honked and endangered the group of cyclists, attempting to pass in a narrow lane, a man with a gun emerged from another car, approached the driver and forbade him to pass. He then turned and cheered as the bicyclists continued to proceed unimpeded.

Residents describe the bicycle to be the safest form of mobility in Matamoros. At night, many refrain from walking or driving in cars for fear of kidnappings, but on a bicycle, you're less likely to be stopped or spoken to. One cyclist in the city described it as such:

> I personally feel safer riding a bike than driving a car. In a car I feel I have a lot more to lose, it's more risky to get caught in an episode of violence from the federal authorities, local authorities or the organized crime. In the bike, even though I'm more frail, I feel safer, protected, free.

One of the biggest benefits afforded by the bicycle on the border is the speed it offers when crossing between the two countries. Oftentimes the lines to cross, both pedestrian and automobile, are so extensive that the process can take hours. But with no infrastructure specific to bicycles in the physical crossing, cyclists bypass the lines of automobiles and wait at the front for a CBP officer to call them forward. Once in the front of the line, groups of bicyclists usually take turns with cars out of courtesy, but there are no official rules for the process. Doble Rueda organizer Elida, a citizen of Mexico and the United States, crosses three or four times a week on her bicycle, which can be a process a quick as five minutes. She stated that:

> Sometimes they can be mean to the cyclists . . . they say 'You need to wait for 3 cars to cross before you pass', and I just go along with it because if I ask them where that rule is written they will just make the situation worse. But sometimes they're nice, they say, 'I wish I rode my bicycle more!'

As a border city, mobility in Matamoros is contentious and controlled; it is a dichotomous space with physical, political and social boundaries. The space is largely defined between the United States and Mexico, the cartel and the government, violence and peace, immigrant and Border Patrol. As the anecdotes about cycling through the border checkpoints illustrate, cycling as a means of mobility doesn't seem to be formally considered by these powers, and this gives it a special significance. It seems to slip through loopholes, not just through the border checkpoint but through many of the other restrictions within Matamoros. Somehow, the lack of infrastructure, and the fact that bikes simply don't fit the existing channels and protocols, proves beneficially exploitable. Mobility is full of meaning and is the product of various forms of power and so cycling in this context allows a type of freedom (Cresswell, 2006).

Despite the tangled situation in Matamoros, the city's growing cycling community is large and diverse. Besides those previously mentioned residents who use a bicycle for daily means of mobility or as a means of livelihood, there are many who use the bicycle for commuting and for recreational purposes.

Other than Doble Rueda's Thursday night rides, multiple weekly social rides occur in the city. Experienced road riders form small groups on the weekends to make the 76-km (47-mile) round trip ride to Playa Bagdad, the coastal beach east of the city. On Tuesday evenings a group of cyclists ride under the name Insolente, a traditionally women-only ride that occurs in multiple cities around Mexico. Group rides occur throughout the week made up of mostly recreational riders. On Wednesday, a sizable group on mountain bikes races along the make-shift paths on the levee of the Rio Bravo. They call themselves Night Riders Matamoros.

Methodologies

Of all these groups, Doble Rueda is the only one that defines itself as a collective, describing themselves as, "*sin fines de lucro, apartidista, laico, plural e incluyente*" (without profit, non-partisan, secular, plural and inclusive) (Doble Rueda Matamoros Facebook, 2013). The group operates based on a horizontal structure and holds open, monthly roundtable meetings to plan and organize upcoming rides and events.

These organizational factors are typical for groups inside the BiciRed web of bicycle collectives in Mexico. BiciRed exists to connect bicycle collectives across the country and encourage communication and support between them. The collective has three forms of membership based on involvement in the network's activities, and Doble Rueda is the lowest level, Miembro Simpatizante. Their status requires Doble Rueda to participate in two of BiciRed's activities per year. In the summer of 2015, one such activity asked collectives to hold Lucha Libre themed rides to symbolically "fight" for the rights of bicycles in city streets. On one hot summer evening in Matamoros, the better part of Doble Rueda's weekly ride wore colorful Lucha Libre masks (or even full, tight fitting outfits) on the 15 km ride.

Most collectives in BiciRed, including Doble Rueda, require that no members of the collective are members of the local government. This is meant to keep the interests of the collective based on the needs of the people rather than political agendas. As cycling has grown in popularity in Matamoros, local politicians have attempted to harness it for their own campaigns. Some hold bike rides in support of their candidacies, or invite Doble Rueda to rallies by offering a new bicycle as a raffle prize. Doble Rueda denies these requests; while they believe a relationship with local government is imperative to fostering more cycling support in the city, they refrain from endorsing any specific political party or candidate. They also remain realistic about what the intentions of the local politicians really are. Doble Rueda organizer Leslie described:

> There have always been cyclists in Matamoros. Not for the sport but out of necessity . . . and I've never seen any adaptations made to the city to support it. Recently I think [local politicians] have seen that urban cycling has been growing, that it's like a fashion, so they see it as an opportunity for them. So it's not really support . . . it's all politics. They don't ask us what we need and then work with us to improve our situation. They see us as a mass of people and take advantage of that for their own benefit. That's how I see it.

Doble Rueda's horizontalism is reflected in the unique breadth and makeup of their weekly rides. They encompass bicycles of all types—children's bikes, cruisers, three-wheel bikes, road bikes, and working bikes with years of wear on them. The group places the newest riders in the front of the group to set the pace and they don't leave anyone behind. If anyone needs maintenance along the way, the organizers ask everyone to stop and wait until the problem is remedied. The organizers take the front of the group and alternate plugging intersections from cars passing through. When the last rider has passed they cycle quickly back to the front and repeat the process again. Sometimes two or three organizers will dismount their bicycles to physically lie in a corner parking lot to prevent cars from passing through it, striking dramatic poses as they do so. The organizers are consistently emphatically gracious to the waiting automobile drivers, striving to maintain a respect for all road travelers.

Not all rides in Matamoros are as inclusive. Many of the recreational rides will drop participants in the occurrence of a flat tire and will maintain higher speeds so they can make it through traffic lights without plugging. Doble Rueda's inclusiveness is appreciated. Moi described, "[People] see that in Doble Rueda there are no politics, no discrimination or anything. So people feel comfortable." Doble Rueda organizer Chava remarked, "People ask me sometimes what they need to do to join us, if they need to sign some papers or something. You don't need anything to join—just a bike, yourself and bienvenidos."

Sustainability

The collective's main objective is to promote cycling in the city as a means of transportation that promotes, "*prácticas de convivencia y movilidad urbana asustentable en la ciudad*" (coexistence and a sustainable urban mobility in the city) (Doble Rueda Matamoros Facebook, 2013). Many of the organizers and weekly Doble Rueda riders commute daily by bicycle and find it not just sustainable but liberating. Leslie describes that cycling allows her to, feel like I own my time . . . I know how long it'll take me to get to the places I'm going to. I don't depend on someone else or on public transportation . . . that makes me feel free, in a way. Like some kind of independence.

Moi used to commute to the factory by public transportation but since switching to cycling, he's noticed improvements in his health as well as his financial situation: "It's not that we want to be different, or prove to society that we are different. It's about using what my financial possibilities allow me to." Besides these benefits, Moi feels he experiences a different city by bicycle:

When you ride you learn. I learned for example to look up at the sky . . . you can notice if it'll rain, you learn how to observe the clouds, to feel the direction of the wind . . . or if the rain will catch you on your way. You get extraordinary abilities.

Doble Rueda organizer Joel finds cycling to be a much more convenient and effective mode of transportation than local public transportation:

Unfortunately here in Matamoros there are the same buses as when I was a kid: obsolete, not functional. Now we have a new thing, the 'unofficial' taxis, that are expensive and sketchy, maybe they offer a good service but I don't trust them. In Matamoros, the public transportation is very deficient, purposely deficient, so yes, here I rather bike than use any other local public transportation method.

These unofficial taxis don't pay any civil fees but are taxed by the cartels instead.
While many who join the weekly rides are recreational cyclists, Doble Rueda promotes cycling as a viable and liberating mode of everyday transportation in Matamoros. This means challenging the local stereotypes that signify cars as a status of wealth and bicycles as signifying the opposite. This has in many ways informed the collectively designed rutas (routes) of the weekly rides.

Routes

The group has mapped four pre-determined routes so far, each around 15 km and extending in different directions of the city. The chosen route for each week is listed in the Facebook event page for every ride so that riders can join along the way. The collective hopes to reach all directions of the city have so far included the Eastern and Southern barrios. Cyclists in these largely low-income and ostensibly dangerous areas typically view the bicycle as the habituation of an exhausting work day, not as a viable form of mobility and community. This is an understandable view considering that their status as workers on the bicycle places them in situations of extreme vulnerability, pedaling long hours through narrow, poorly maintained and crowded streets. An important contradiction is raised about the danger of this experience compared to many of Doble Rueda

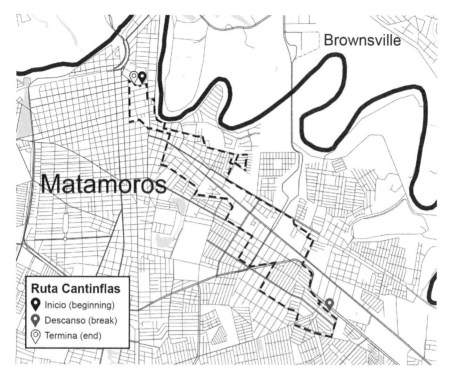

Figure 11.2 One of Doble Rueda's pre-planned group ride routes

members' descriptions of the bicycle as the "safest" form of mobility. But Doble Rueda maintains an awareness of these differences in experience and build them into the ways they organize.

Many citizens from the central areas of the city believe these outer neighborhoods are too dangerous to visit. Doble Rueda purposefully rides through these barrios to challenge and overcome these stereotypes. The hope is twofold: first, to have low-income cyclists see the bicycle as a meaningful transportation option and hence reconsider spending so much of their household budgets on cars; and second, to encourage recreational riders from the center of the city to reconsider their fearful opinions of the outer barrios after spending time in them.

Each route makes one stop at roughly halfway at a small local bodega. For 10–15 minutes, bicycles file in and fill a short block. A line forms out of the door of the bodega and hundreds of people briefly congregate with drinks and snacks. With these stops, the rides encourage integration into local businesses of the less visited and under-serviced neighborhoods of the city. In each store the rides visit, as well as in other local businesses the cyclists frequent, Doble Rueda leaves flyers that read, "Toma Uno" (take one), a strategy for reaching community members who may not have access to the internet.

Figure 11.3 Flyers advertising Doble Rueda's weekly group rides

Doble Rueda's community impact

Doble Rueda's mission statement not only considers cycling to be a sustainable mobility but one that promotes prácticas de convivencia (coexistence). Within the city's large culture of fear, local businesses struggle and cultural events are few and far between. Most urban development projects are left permanently unfinished after political turnover. Those projects that do get pushed through are usually poorly planned, ineffective and even damaging to local environment. Corrupt local politics and a lack of adequate law enforcement create an environment many consider unsafe. On Doble Rueda's group rides, however, newer members often mention the security they feel in the large group. They also often join without knowing anyone but meet other cyclists from their neighborhoods who they begin to commute with. Community is built through the rides, extending even outside of the context of cycling because it gives residents a much needed opportunity to simply meet each other. Doble Rueda organizer Joel described:

I see [cycling] as a way of relaxing and to go to the city without fear or stress, without thinking that something bad will happen to me. I think it works the same way for other people too. Maybe they don't realize that because they see the bike as a simple object, but because the fact that we are a group of people, somehow a manifestation, people are actually participating in a movement. By forming part of that movement, they are also forming part of a protest . . . part of a social unconformity. So it is a form of being against violence, because even though it is a place where a lot of violent events occur, people won't stop biking and they won't stop going on the collective bike rides. Moreover, people start losing their fear once they've been with the group, they feel comfortable going on their own too. That danger, which is a real one, is also magnified. People break away from those ideas, they take their own bike and see they can safely go 20 or 30 kilometers.

In Matamoros, a city in the midst of an ongoing war with no end in sight, hope for governmental support of cycling seems bleak. But the silver lining of this context is that with no support from official institutions, the fervent cycling community blossoming there is instead advocating from a grassroots level and thus creating a more equitable environment for cycling.

Some cyclists in Matamoros have dreams of it becoming a cycling metropolis like Amsterdam with bike lanes throughout the downtown area. Doble Rueda remains skeptical of these ideas, which they feel will result in a situation similar to that in Brownsville—infrastructure that doesn't service the majority of the city, but is populated by recreational riders on high-end bikes. In the narrow streets of crowded downtown, there is little room to add bike lanes and little patience from car drivers either. As Moi described:

A lot of times we want to imitate other countries, like our neighbor here, the U.S., and their designated bike lanes. But sometimes it's not as easy as painting the line, people have to get used to the idea that bicycles are also vehicles and they have needs.

Bicycle lanes in downtown streets with little room would likely aggravate the situation between cyclists and car drivers.

Recently, some federal money was offered to the city to improve its bicycle infrastructure. Some local cyclists lobbied to spend the money on paving a path along the levee of the Rio Grande. Here, an upper dirt trail offers miles of uninterrupted riding. Smaller off-road trails breakaway down the banks of the levee, providing significantly difficult mountain bike routes. The upper path, now made of compacted dirt, is already enjoyable by any type of bike. It's often used recreationally, and a Doble Rueda organizer critically posited that because many of the cyclists who use this path bring their bicycles there by car, the next step in the paving of it will be paving a parking lot nearby.

The focus on downtown and recreational parks doesn't consider the majority of the people in Matamoros. The majority of the city works in factories outside of downtown and would benefit from bicycle paths facilitating a commute to work or bicycle lanes on the larger streets in the outer barrios. These are the types of cycling infrastructure Doble Rueda would likely support, given the opportunity.

But before lobbying for cycling infrastructure, the collective first considers an even more basic form of mobility: walking. Infrastructure for pedestrians is also severely lacking in Matamoros. The city streets were historically traversed by carriages which were slow enough that many pedestrians shared the streets with them. Because of this, sidewalks are narrow and remain that way today. Many show years of wear with no upkeep and contain obstacles such as light posts or large trash cans. Today, many pedestrians continue to walk in the streets that are overcrowded with cars, trucks, huge public buses and bicycles. The city often discusses widening sidewalks, but similar to other infrastructural projects, the discussion never formalizes into action.

Doble Rueda is hesitant to lobby for complex cycling infrastructure without first laying the basis of adequate pedestrian infrastructure. And with no money flowing in for this, they look to simpler forms of organizing around a safer city for cyclists and pedestrians alike. The group advocates for lowering the speed limit in the city and promotes education through signage and community events. Once a year the collective hosts a bicycle summit in Matamoros called Encuentro Ciclista. The organizers host workshops on basic bicycle maintenance, urban riding, relationships with pedestrians and pedestrian areas, amongst other subjects. They also host guest speakers, both local, regional and from other countries, as well as open, round table discussions.

Every few months the organizers will approach a local business that they have previous connections with—oftentimes a bodega or a cantina that they frequently visit—and ask permission to paint a mural on a blank wall of their building. Each mural features an image that is bicycle related but culturally specific. One features an image of the Argentine writer and bicycle enthusiast Julio Cortázar riding a bicycle with books flying behind him. Another mural features modified lyrics of a popular song, replacing the word "mar" with "bici": "*En el mar la vida es mas sabrosa*" (In the sea, life is tastier). The mural depicts an octopus whose tentacles form bicycle wheels.

The group also facilitates cultural events surrounding bicycling such as the monthly Bicine film screening. The last Thursday of each month the collective chooses a cycling related film and hosts its screening at a local bar after the ride. The group facilitates community rides to la playa (the beach) and hosts community campouts for special occasions, such as Doble Rueda's birthdays, in the local Parque Calmecac.

Conclusion

Matamoros, Tamaulipas, as a case study offers several profound insights, especially when comparing the city and its cycling community to its transborder neighbor. Brownsville, Texas, exhibits many of the common trends in cycling development in the United States. As the white, upwardly mobile cyclist moves outwards away

Figure 11.4 A mural painted by Doble Rueda depicting Argentine writer Julio Cortázar

from the downtown area near the border, so do the bicycle paths. On a day-to-day basis, most of the cycling infrastructure is used by recreational riders on high-end bicycles.

Matamoros represents somewhat of an inverse situation; as a compact urban design, the city is much more spatially conducive to cycling. But the city offers little valuable support to cyclists and very few infrastructural plans have been designed, much less finished. In this context, cycling falls within a spectrum of empowerment and disempowerment, depending on the context. Recreational riders often stick to the areas they know, ostensibly the "safe" areas of the city that are physically better developed. Many low-income residents cycle in more vulnerable positions. Cycling based occupations require tiresome work on narrow, busy streets in an unsafe city.

While remaining aware of these differences, Doble Rueda utilizes cycling's empowering capacities within the city. Many describe riding with Doble Rueda to be an incredibly safe experience. Doble Rueda utilizes cycling as a safer form of mobility that bypasses many of the city's restrictions. Cycling allows access to neighborhoods many feel unsafe driving or walking in after dark but will visit by bicycle. The bicycle also allows unique exploration of the physical border area along the levee of the Rio Bravo, a landscape dotted by subtle traces of immigration and cartel presence. It allows for swift passing through the arduous border checkpoints where residents often stand in line or idle in their cars for hours.

Perhaps most importantly, cycling offers a uniquely communal mode of traversing the many boundaries in the city, both visible and invisible. Doble Rueda doesn't shy away from the countless spaces of the city that are hard to cross. The organizers safely lead hundreds of riders through heavily potholed streets, abrupt speed bumps, narrow alleys and high traffic four-lane streets. Indeed, these streets are rough because they are in the neglected parts of the city that many will refuse to visit for fear of violence. In these neighborhoods, the cyclists pause to greet businesses, build relationships and grow their community even beyond cycling. Then they continue on their route, travelling at a slow but steady pace and verbally alerting each other of upcoming obstructions with cries of "*pozo!*" (pothole) or "*tope!*" (bump).

Cycling in the United States is often based on reaching higher speeds and efficiency, usually for the benefit of the middle-class commuter or lycra-clad road racer. Indeed, cyclists from the United States who join Doble Rueda's rides find the pace to be painfully boring. The slow pace is integral to the ethos of the collective, however, which prioritizes new riders and vigilantly leaves no rider behind. The rides travel slowly because their objective is not to get anywhere fast, but to get somewhere together. And the gringos' boredom only further elaborates the rich humor and irony of the most often heard exclamation on the Doble Rueda rides: "Aburrido!" There seem to be many significances to this cheer. In the midst of Matamoros' many complexities, this small act of declaring a communal space banal has an intensely empowering effect, illustrated in the ironic excitement of its cheers.

Despite Matamoros' lack of physical cycling infrastructure, Doble Rueda is building an extraordinarily rich human and social infrastructure. This is found in the participants providing bicycle maintenance for one another, in their economic support of local businesses along bicycle rides, and in their collective practice of plugging intersections. This practice of rotating from front to back of the large group works in a similar form to paceline rotation in professional road bicycle racing. Pacelining entails the practices of "pulling or leading a pack of riders into the headwind, or "drafting," taking position behind other riders in zones of reduced wind resistance to conserve energy. These politics of rotation in road racing are often based around protecting and conserving the energy of the favorite rider for a final sprint. How can we compare this to Doble Rueda's politics of rotation? Remaining in an ethos of solidarity rather than speed, they are protecting the entire group rather than an individual.

Doble Rueda's outwardly simple methodologies stem from ideological choices, the effects of which are most acutely seen in the rapid growth of the collective and their group rides. Within Matamoros' strenuous and divided social and political climate—a climate of war—the collective has found fertile ground to build a cycling community in the interests of a diverse community. With no foreseeable end to the city's entangled situation, it seems the potential for growth will only increase. While Matamoros represents an extreme situation, many cities around the world can draw comparisons to the power structures that exist there and the social boundaries they create. Doble Rueda is using the bicycle to draw attention to these social boundaries and convince more people to cross them on two wheels.

Acknowledgments

Thank you to Andrés Cárdenas, whose first-hand information and generosity made this project possible. Additional thanks to the rest of the members of Doble Rueda who took the time to tell their stories, to Leslie Azkary Bazaldúa Zamora and Andrea Avidad for their help with translation, and to Liam Quigley for help with research.

References

Burnett, J. (2015) Matamoros Becomes Ground Zero as Drug War Shifts on Mexican Border. *NPR*. [Online] April 1. Available from: http://npr.org. [Accessed: August 18, 2015].

Burnett, J., & Penaloza, M. (2015) Corruption on the Border: Dismantling Misconduct in the Rio Grande Valley. *NPR*. [Online] July 6. Available from: http://npr.org. [Accessed: September 14, 2015].

Clark, S. (2013) Census Bureau: Brownsville Poorest City in U.S. *Brownsville Herald*. [Online] November 7. Available from: www.brownsvilleherald.com [Accessed: September 20, 2015].

Correa-Cabrera, G., Garrett, T., & Keck, M. (2014) Administrative Surveillance and Fear: Implications for U.S.-Mexico Border Relations and Governance. ERLACS European Review of Latin American and Caribbean Studies   Revista Europea De Estudios Latinoamericanos Y Del Caribe, [Online] 96: 35–53. Available through: www.jstor.org/. [Accessed: September 10, 2015].

Cresswell, T. (2006) *On the Move: Mobility in the Modern Western World*. New York: Routledge.

Democracy Now! (2015) Mass Graves of Immigrants Found in Texas, But State Says No Laws Were Broken. *Democracy Now!* [Online] July 16. Available from: www.democracynow.org/ [Accessed: September 21, 2015].

Doble Rueda Matamoros Facebook. (2013) ¿Qué Es Doble Rueda Matamoros? [Online] Available from: www.facebook.com/DobleRuedaMatamoros [Accessed: September 12, 2015].

Tuckman, J. (2012) Mexico Drug War Continues to Rage in Region Where President Fired First Salvo. [Online] *The Guardian*, November 30. Available from: http://guardian.co.uk [Accessed: September 12, 2015].

12 Civil Bikes

Embracing Atlanta's racialized history through bicycle tours

Nedra Deadwyler

Introduction

Civil Bikes, a bicycle tour company based in Atlanta, is not just about giving rides in the park. Civil Bikes works to challenge peoples' perceptions of bicycling in the City of Atlanta, all the while preserving the city's unique history and also contributing to the city's transformation by building community through dialogue. As Atlanta develops and places emphasis on new modes of transportation by building infrastructure, Civil Bikes is committed to elevating the voices of and providing historical context of marginalized communities in its presentation of Atlanta. Civil Bikes offers bicycle tours that highlight the shifting demographics of Atlanta's neighborhoods, programs that are woman-centered and empowering, and serves as an advocate for active transportation and design incorporating the needs of citizens across a range of neighborhoods. This chapter will explore Civil Bikes' programs using first-hand accounts of the owner, literature on neighborhood history, bicycling trends in Atlanta, and reflections on the process of contemporary urban social change, especially how the urbanizing creative class is shaping these changes in Atlanta. The chapter will explore the ways in which Civil Bikes uses a racial, income, gender, and age inclusive outlook to shape the future of bicycling, transportation and development in Atlanta.

Atlanta history and neighborhood change

Atlanta is a city that has gone through many different historical periods, which were shaped by official and social norms that segregated Atlanta. During the 1960s, a significant time in the formation of the city's identity, Atlanta was a key stronghold of the Civil Rights movement and is the burial place for Civil Rights leader Dr. Martin Luther King Jr.

Atlanta, like many US cities, is shaped by the processes of racial segregation, white flight, and the effort by whites to contain minorities in certain neighborhoods (Henderson, 2004). Atlanta's segregation was caused by actions of both the private and public sectors which resulted in the lack of access to adequate employment, transportation, and housing for black residents. These policies have historically shaped the geographic development of the city, with the Northern region of the city being more affluent and white, and the Southern and Eastern regions being more black and lower-income (Keating, 2001; Henderson, 2004).

Racialized attitudes have also historically shaped the development of mass transportation infrastructure. As whites began moving from the inner core of Atlanta to the outer suburban areas, discussions over investments in regional public transportation began. The Metropolitan Atlanta Rapid Transit Authority (MARTA) was established in the 1960s to develop regional rail throughout the Atlanta metropolitan area. Planners made several attempts to expand MARTA service into the North but failed mostly due to continued segregationist attitudes (Henderson, 2006).

As Atlanta depended on cars more than the national average, air quality became a threat to the city's economic health and the health of its residents. Air quality concerns dissuaded some businesses from operating in Atlanta, which prompted the business community to form a coalition headed by the Metropolitan Atlanta Chamber of Commerce. Part of the mission of the coalition was to advocate and invest in policies that favored alternative transportation systems. The coalition invested in what are called "edge cities" and created "community improvement zones" where neighborhoods were to be walkable, bike friendly, and have mixed-use developments. A majority of these types of investments have been in the Northern areas (Henderson, 2004).

The current investments in walkable and bicycle friendly cities are known to cater to the "creative class" (Florida, 2014), and have been shown to contribute to gentrification and displacement of existing communities (Zavestoski & Agyeman, 2014; Maciag, 2015). These investments include public transportation systems, improved infrastructure for walking and bicycling, and development based on local businesses. Appealing to the creative class, however, fails to take into account the multiple identities that make up the complete fabric of a community, and effort must be made to support those voices and cultures that have been marginalized. The experience of marginalized groups must be understood in the variety of experiences based on the intersecting identities of race, class, gender, and age (Reddick et al., 2014).

One neighborhood that is currently undergoing massive amounts of creative class-driven redevelopment is Sweet Auburn Historic District (Lynch, 2013). Georgia State University has purchased blocks of buildings in order to expand its classrooms and administrative buildings. Central Atlanta Progress (CAP) granted money to businesses in 2014 for façade improvement. Although preservationists encouraged adaptive reuse of old building stock such as The Bell Building, Atlanta Daily World, and the Trio Laundry building, the university has not recognized the historic value of the buildings it acquired unless there is previously awarded historic designation. In the Sweet Auburn district many people have been displaced from the neighborhood as apartment buildings, public housing and section 8 homes have been bulldozed. Mixed-income and multi-use buildings, empty lots, and parking lots have replaced the buildings. The neighborhood of Dr. Martin Luther King, Jr. is only remembered for his contribution and the full scope of history has been under-interpreted and forgotten as buildings there are underutilized, crumble and fall down. In both 1992 and 2012, Sweet Auburn was placed on the "Most Endangered" historic place list, and actively recalling the individuals, civic groups and organizations, law firms, professional offices, social clubs, performance halls, churches, and educational sites becomes imperative for preservationists (Burns, 2012). Wheat Street Garden Apartments, subsidized housing developed by Wheat Street Baptist Church, is now the site of Atlanta's first urban garden, Truly Living Well. Wheat Street Baptist Church is planning to develop a grocery store and other commercial buildings (TSW, 2015), as this area sits in a food desert. The removal of buildings displaced many individuals and families, which made up a larger community that supported the local economy, and is now a center for new businesses and informal economies.

The shifting investments in the creative class in Atlanta have impacted the conversation on placement of bike infrastructure and the perception of who bikes in the city. The mainstream US cycling industry highlights the ideals of youth, whiteness, and athletic ability. However, the goal of advocates should be to encourage active transportation and active lifestyles. Additionally, newly developed infrastructure should be inclusive of all individuals who bike, walk, or take public transportation and equitably spread out across the city. Atlanta bicyclists have historically been diverse in terms of race, income, and gender identity. The *Atlanta Daily World*, the first daily black newspaper in Atlanta, has documented blacks using bicycles in Atlanta from the early 1930s through the 1990s. Blacks opened bicycle shops in both the Auburn Avenue district and on Hunter Street (now Dr. Martin Luther King, Jr. Drive), formed bike clubs and hosted a variety of bike related events and competitions. Children participated in competitions across the Southern region in black and white communities and won bikes for academic achievements. Other *Atlanta Daily World* stories tell of long-distance travel of adults and youth on bicycles, with special attention given to Bill T. Wright. Wright rode across the country to push the federal government for a nationally connected bicycle trail network. Another notable black bicyclist, George A. Towns Sr., was an educator at Atlanta University and Civil Rights leader with NAACP, who used a bicycle as an alternative to public transportation in resistance against Jim Crow segregation in public transportation (Towns Hamilton, 1974). Today the tradition continues in Atlanta with non-profits such as "WeCycle" and bicycle clubs like "Black Girls Do Bikes" and MACC (Metro Atlanta Cycling Club), black-owned home-based bike shops, storefronts such as Aztec Cycles, and other minority-run bike businesses including Civil Bikes.

In regards to age and race, bicycling trends reported by the Atlanta Regional Commission (ARC), a regional planning organization, show the breakdown of bicyclists in Atlanta as 62 percent male and 38 percent female. The age group with the highest population of cyclists in Atlanta is 25–34-year-olds, closely followed by 35–44-year-olds and 45–54-year-olds (ARC, 2014). According to League of American Bicyclists (2013), a national bike safety and advocacy organization, the largest increase in bike ridership between 2000 and 2009 is among black, Asian, and Latino riders. Black and Latino riders are more likely to be involved in a fatal bike accident because these communities lack bikeways and other mechanisms for safe riding practices (League of American Bicyclists, 2013). It is important for bicycle advocates and transportation planners to embrace this picture of people on bicycles and create an environment and infrastructure to facilitate the transportation needs of these groups.

Civil Bikes

As the creative class relocates to Atlanta, Civil Bikes believes that an understanding of the area's historical context and the culture of its people is key to understanding and contributing to the community. Civil Bikes is poised to sustain the stories that are often forgotten once the buildings come down or are slated for adaptive reuse, by working with minority communities to keep both culture and stories available in the social discourse.

Civil Bikes' programs are developed to follow in the footsteps of the likes of Dr. Martin Luther King, Jr., John Wesley Dobbs, and Ruby Parks Blackburn to call the populace to be present for civic engagement. Civil Bikes' programming takes shape around discussions about vibrant communities such as Sweet Auburn and the Old Fourth Ward and links their histories to the larger context of Atlanta's history coming out of slavery, the Civil War, and present day. Topics covered in Civil Bikes tours include economy and employment, Southern politics and segregation, the formation of Black Atlanta and citizenship, the Civil Rights movement, and contemporary community activism.

Figure 12.1 Civil Bikes visits the birthplace of Dr. Martin Luther King, Jr.

Photo: Cameron Adams.

Civil Bikes diverges from other bike tour and advocacy companies by using the city's history and landscape to entertain, educate, and advocate. Civil Bikes' tours aim to address the complex historical narratives of Atlanta. The tour guides engage in conversations with participants around the history of the pre- and post-antebellum periods and racial hostility under Jim Crow including the formation of the Ku Klux Klan, the 1906 race riot, the Great Fire of 1917, and urban renewal as it shaped the Atlanta landscape, both social and physical. The main point of these historical narratives is to convey that all communities are impacted by the complex racial past of Atlanta, no matter the person's racial or ethnic heritage. Civil Bikes believes that dialogue, sharing experience, and engaging history will create empathy and build positive relationships and interactions between communities.

Tours are designed to help visitors and residents (new and long-time) understand local history and culture, and to create a positive connection with places such as Sweet Auburn and other communities that have lost their economic viability. During tours, participants transverse multiple decades as they explore buildings, empty lots, murals, and expressways. Sounds of people's voices, horns blowing, and music intertwine with the tour guides' well-researched narratives and reflective commentary on the landscape. Participants visit the places of Civil Rights events and activities of daily living; in doing so they connect to people of the past and present.

Civil Bikes' tours point out the many leaders, reformers, and philanthropically minded men and women who built Atlanta's Sweet Auburn neighborhood, making it the nation's "richest Negro street" as proclaimed by *Forbes* magazine in 1956 (Hatfield, 2006). Using the bicycle, in a rapidly gentrifying city, to educate, inspire, and build connections across perceived barriers, Civil Bikes becomes both a participant in and preserver of history. When sharing little-known stories, the tours illuminate communities that experience oppression because of their race, gender, sexual orientation, national identity, language, or disability. Through the use of the bicycle and historical narratives, Civil Bikes shares a contemporary perspective on Civil Rights issues. The American Civil Rights movement is shown to be alive as new faces of civil and human rights struggles are brought into the conversation, such as housing, education, employment, and immigration, which becomes an evolutionary part of the landscape. Tours integrate sight, sound, and touch to create an immediate multi-sensory connection to Civil Rights events. Tour guides report that participants are thoughtful and politically progressive with a working understanding of institutional racism. Participants express a desire to create positive environments and communities that serve everyone regardless of race, class, gender, age, or citizenship status. The power of Civil Bikes is that it uses history to bring a range of people together.

Another major program undertaken by Civil Bikes is bicycling education classes. Many of those who attend a class discuss their fear of riding on Atlanta roads because of distracted or discourteous drivers, the amount of traffic and the high speeds of cars. The need for safe places to ride is consistent across communities and demographics. Civil Bikes also takes into consideration that people of color are more likely to have unsafe biking conditions. On a recent tour, an Asian immigrant woman from Gwinnett County, a white mother from Alpharetta (an affluent Northern suburban community), and a black man from a South Atlanta neighborhood all expressed the same need for developing defensive biking skills in order to navigate traffic safely. Participants have shared their frustrations with the dominance of cars on Atlanta streets. Local bicycling advocacy groups are developing ways that they could help residents be more comfortable riding bikes but experience great opposition as Atlanta continues to be a car-centric city. During the education class, participants learn the best biking practices and ways to get involved in advocacy efforts to make riding a bicycle safer.

Due to women's lower rate of cycling, there is a special need for cycling education among women and this is a need that Civil Bikes aspires to fill. Women can often be intimidated by typical bicycling groups where men dominate, so Civil Bikes hosts bicycle education classes for people who identify as women, transgender, or femme (WTF). WTF-identifying individuals are targeted with specific programming to increase health and wellness and bicycling proficiency. Civil Bikes attempts to create a space where women can find classes conducted by an understanding and patient instructor. Classes aim to increase knowledge and confidence by covering issues with bicycle parts and repairs and knowing what to expect when receiving service from a bicycle shop. Bicycle education classes are held in conjunction with Atlanta Bicycle Coalition (ABC), and private lessons are available as well.

To increase its reach, Civil Bikes has formed partnerships with several local bicycle and community groups. Through a partnership with ABC and an ARC advisory group, Civil Bikes participates in transportation planning processes as they impact bicycling in the region, including bicycle lanes and trails. Civil Bikes recently participated in a bike equity meeting hosted by ARC, in which Civil Bikes recounted the experiences of those who would benefit from improved bikeways and sidewalks. ARC and ABC are consciously seeking ways to expand active transportation without further exacerbating issues around displacement and gentrification. The goal of these advocacy groups is to create healthy and livable communities across the region. These organizations are also concerned with equity and seek out leaders from diverse communities to provide insight into the distinct needs of each community. For example, when creating the vision for the improvement of Lee Street in the West End, a historically black neighborhood within a thriving black business district, they looked for solutions for how to serve automobiles, pedestrians, bicycles, and mass transit. ABC worked with Livable Lee Street, a community advocacy group, to host a listening session to discover the needs of those living in the area. The discussion focused less on bike lanes and more on investments to support those who are on foot and use public transportation.

Conclusion

A diverse group of people participates in Civil Bikes programs: men and women, cash-strapped and cash abundant, young and old, straight and queer, and those educated in institutions and those educated by experience. The diversity of the participants reflects the diversity and inclusion that Civil Bikes wants to see as Atlanta continues to develop. Civil Bikes advocates for increasing active transportation infrastructure equitably while continuing to maintain the vast and rich cultural heritages that reflect the city's history. Civil Bikes takes the idea of inclusion seriously and fights against lopsided development. Placing tour participants in the context of geography not only provides valuable historical context of how Atlanta came to be but also exposes people to exclusionary policies that in many ways hampered healthy development across the city. Educational classes geared toward those who identify as WTF increase the likelihood that more people will partake and receive the benefits of cycling. Advocating for inclusive policy changes is Civil Bikes' way of being activist-oriented and vociferate that development does not have to mean displacement.

This chapter has shown that development and bike infrastructure in Atlanta has typically favored white Northern areas of the city, often at the expense of the black residents even while bicycling has been a tool that black residents have historically used as a way to fight for civil rights. Time will reveal how Civil Bikes' work in education and tours impact how Atlanta continues to develop and if small businesses such as Civil Bikes are able to change the discourse of bike advocacy and policy.

References

Atlanta Regional Commission (ARC) (2014). Regional Bicyclist Survey [Online]. Available from: http://documents.atlantaregional.com/bikeped/research/TAMD_ARC_ Regional_Bicyclist_Survey_data_overview_040214.pdf [Accessed November 23, 2015].

Burns, R. (2012). Commentary: Atlanta's Neglect of the Sweet Auburn District is a Civic Shame. *Atlanta Maganize* [Online]. Available from: www.atlantamagazine.com/civil rights/commentary-atlantas-neglect-of-the-sweet-aubu/ [Accessed November 23, 2015].

Florida, R. (2014). The Creative Class and Economic Development. *Economic Development Quarterly* 28 pp.196–205.

Hatfield, E. A. (2006). Auburn Avenue (Sweet Auburn), *New Georgia Encyclopedia* [Online]. Available from: www.georgiaencyclopedia.org/articles/history-archaeology/ auburn-avenue-sweet-auburn [Accessed November 23, 2015].

Henderson, J. (2004). The Politics of Mobility and Business Elites in Atlanta, Georgia. *Urban Geography* 25 pp.193–216.

Henderson, J. (2006). Secessionist Automobility: Racism, Anti-Urbanism, and the Politics of Automobility in Atlanta, Georgia. *International Journal of Urban and Regional Research* 30 pp. 293–307.

Keating, L. (2001). *Atlanta: Race, Class and Urban Expansion*. Philadelphia, PA: Temple University Press.

League of American Bicyclists (2013) About the League [Online]. Available from: http:// bikeleague.org/content/about-league [Accessed November 23, 2015].

Lynch, T. (2013) From Vision to Reality: Reviving Two African-American Main Streets [Online]. Available from: www.preservationnation.org/main-street/main-street-news/

story-of-the-week/2013/130225sweetauburn/from-vision-to-reality.html [Accessed November 23, 2015].

Maciag, M. (2015). Gentrification in America Report [Online]. Available from: www. governing.com/gov-data/census/gentrification-in-cities-governing-report.html [Accessed November 23, 2015].

Reddick, R.J., Bukoski, B.E., Smith, S.L., Valdez, P.L., & Wasielewski, M.V. (2014). A Hole in the Soul of Austin: Black Faculty Community Engagement Experiences in a Creative Class City. *Journal of Negro Education* 83 pp.61–76.

Towns Hamilton, G (1974). Oral History Interview, July 19, 1974. Interview G-0026. Southern Oral History Program Collection (#4007) in the Southern Oral History Program Collection, Southern Historical Collection, Wilson Library, University of North Carolina at Chapel Hill [Online]. Available from: http://docsouth.unc.edu/sohp/ playback.html?base_file=G-0026&duration=01:34:37. [Accessed November 23, 2015].

TSW (2015) TSW – Wheat Street Master Plan. TSW.

Zavestoski, S., & Agyeman, J. (Eds.) (2014). *Incomplete Streets: Processes, Practices, and Possibilities*. New York: Routledge.

13 Decentering whiteness in organized bicycling

Notes from inside

Adonia E. Lugo

Introduction

"I'm so tired of hearing about environmental justice," said the white woman, a former federal employee and the head of a professional association related to bicycle planning. We were standing in the hallway of an office in Washington, D.C., and I had just introduced her to a colleague, another white woman. I was taken aback by this statement, not only because my own job for the last year had focused on bringing the principles of environmental justice into the work of a bicycle advocacy organization, but also because we had just spent an hour discussing the challenges of working in a male-dominated field. What did she mean by "environmental justice"? I smiled politely and went back to my office.

A few months later, on the other side of the United States, I had another awkward moment. A member of the board for the organization where I worked had stopped me to introduce someone, and as the three of us stood outside a conference that was wrapping for the day, a white woman passed us. "See you at the other, whiter summit," she quipped to my two white companions without stopping. I had never met this woman, but the bike advocacy world is small enough that I knew who she was. This remark seemed intended to indicate that the speaker was "in the know" regarding the critique of whiteness in bicycle advocacy, but as the lone person of color in the interaction, I felt like the butt of the joke.

The challenge of transforming bicycle advocacy, planning, and policy, what the Introduction to this volume terms "organized bicycling," is in many ways a personnel question. Whose racialized cultural norms dominate by default in these professional spaces, and whose are othered? What is the "human infrastructure" of these fields? As I have chronicled elsewhere (Lugo, 2013; Lugo, 2015), promoting bicycling should entail identifying and expanding the social networks and cultural attitudes that support the practice. This human infrastructure is similar to what Batterbury and Vandermeersch (Chapter 14, this volume) refer to as the "demand side" of bicycling. Through participant-observation in national bicycle advocacy and planning networks between March 2013 and March 2015, I found that bicycle professionals tended to understand inequity as something they could fix through learning to speak in the name of historically marginalized groups. Less common, and less supported, were efforts to change the field's own composition, changing who these expert speakers could be. In this chapter, I trace the othering of people of color activists' concerns in organized bicycling. These findings came from my own firsthand experience working as a woman of color in the field and from my role as a collaborator with many other people of color working on bicycle projects.

Environmental justice and transportation

Why is environmental justice (EJ) relevant to bicycle advocacy, policy, and planning? Bicycling takes place in racialized landscapes and its advocates see it as best supported through environmental design interventions such as cycle tracks and off-street paths (see Goddard, Chapter 7, this volume). Julian Agyeman began his 2005 book on "just sustainabilities" by making a distinction between EJ *concerns* and the EJ *movement*. The former have been around for much longer than the latter, and Agyeman pointed to 1492 in particular as an origin point for EJ concerns. This is because people of color's struggle to control land use and property has been historically tied up with the global power dynamics of colonial domination. Racism is not separate from land use, but rather something that has structured what are considered appropriate decision-making processes about it for hundreds of years. This is why EJ activists and scholars support viewing "environment" as an intersectional concept (Pulido, 1996). Activists have expanded the definition of environment from wilderness conservation to protecting where we live, where we work, and where we play. This is why practices and policies relating to street design, transportation modes, and other claims on public space merit an EJ analysis.

The executive branch of the federal government supported this view in 1994, when President Clinton signed Executive Order 12898, "Federal Actions To Address Environmental Justice in Minority Populations and Low-Income Populations." The order required all federal agencies to define how their work would be attentive to EJ. The U.S. Department of Transportation (USDOT) has since defined its EJ principles through three commitments that emphasize minimizing the unequal distribution of adverse "human health and environmental effects," ensuring "full and fair participation by all potentially affected communities in the transportation decision making process," and ensuring that some groups do not have a long wait before receiving the benefits of public transportation investments (USDOT, n.d.).

Like the principles of EJ first drafted at the National People of Color Environmental Leadership Summit in 1991, this USDOT commitment goes beyond questioning the distribution of environmental bads and goods and points to the personnel side of the equation: who is participating in transportation decisions? In organized bicycling, this participation has become increasingly professionalized, and this raises questions about inclusion similar to those brought up around the professionalization of the environmental movement (see discussion in Pulido, 1996, p.23). Because there was an organized environmental movement,

EJ leaders had to challenge that establishment's erasure or othering of people of color and their concerns. I have observed a similar dynamic in bicycling, and I now turn to a historical analysis of how the bike community came to be one where race and racism were seen as irrelevant.

The production of whiteness in bicycling

How does a practice like bicycling become racialized? That is, how do we trace "the process of grafting a racial meaning onto various phenomena within the context of unequal social relations" (Pulido et al., 1996, p.420) in bicycling? Geographers Pulido, Sidawi, and Vos recommended identifying racializing processes using historical analysis, and there is well-documented bicycle advocacy history to draw on in this case. I am particularly interested in the assumption that it is most common for bicycling to be taken up enthusiastically as a choice practice, as it was by its original advocates in the late nineteenth century. Though these white elites lobbied to access public resources to build roads that would allow them to travel farther on their new machines, they did not develop a consensus that bicycling should be for everyone.

In early 2014, I worked with urban planner and active transportation advocate Naomi Doerner to develop a historical exhibit that would be on display for attendees at the National Bike Summit, an annual conference and lobbying event organized by the League of American Bicyclists. The League had hired me in November 2013 to develop an "equity initiative" tasked with transforming both its organizational culture and the bike movement more broadly through resources and reports such as this historical exhibit. Today's League traces its origins to the League of American Wheelmen (LAW) founded in 1880 when bicycle clubs around the eastern United States decided to join forces. Their causes were "good roads," access to parks (where cyclists' speed was seen as a threat to public safety), and bicycle race administration. We called the exhibit "United Spokes: Together in American Streets," and attempted to document moments when bicycle advocates set limits on what forms of bicycling would be part of their movement. Our intention was to show that bicycling has never taken place in a vacuum, but rather has been a part of broader trends.

The conference organizers placed the exhibit in an out of the way room at the back of the conference facility, but made no protest when an attendee asked me to help him move the exhibit to the heavily trafficked registration area because he thought it should be more visible. Here the exhibit stood for the remaining two days of the conference.

The posters provided information about the "color bar" passed by LAW members in 1894 that banned non-whites from membership in the organization (see Introduction, this volume). We put it in the context of the broader trend toward legal segregation in that era, as illustrated by the 1896 "separate but equal" decision from the Supreme Court in the case of *Plessy v. Ferguson*. The exhibit also told conference attendees about Marshall "Major" Taylor. Taylor, the best bicycle racer in the world in the 1890s and a black man, has become an important symbol for African-American and multiracial recreational cycling clubs. Because of his racing abilities, the LAW and other racing organizations bent their segregation rules in order to make him their champion. Major Taylor was at his prime during an era when the American masses looked to bicycles for entertainment and when bike races filled Madison Square Garden. But it was also a time when white competitors threatened his life, as happened several times during the racing season of 1897, according to Taylor biographer Andrew Ritchie (2009).

Taylor is often invoked as evidence that not all early bicycle enthusiasts were white. There can be no doubt, though, that plenty of participants in early organized bicycling wished it were so. Our exhibit showed an 1897 Currier & Ives caricature that mocked black people having the audacity to ride bicycles as though they were fancy white people. And when bicycles became more affordable, bicycle industry historian Bruce Epperson found, "working-class white Southerners were so bigoted that they wouldn't even ride in the same roadways as their black counterparts" (Epperson, 2010, p.97). These were not fringe views, as attested by a cycling trade journal's commentary on the LAW color line:

> In the south, where he is better understood, the people who do not want him in the League or any other white man's organization put up with his indolence, his lack-brain carelessness and his thievish and other uncomfortable proclivities, and when he is hungry feed him and let him go the even tenor of his care-free ways. The negro, outside of a few lemon-hued and saddle-colored specimens with enough white blood to make them cheeky, have no wish to belong to the LAW, and mighty few of them have the necessary $2 to spare.
>
> (*The Referee*, March 30, 1894, quoted in Ritchie, 2009)

It is well known that Major Taylor encountered vicious racism as a bicycle racer, but his professional career was not the first time Taylor had crossed the boundaries of race. In researching his life, I learned that a very young Taylor had become the companion of a white child of the same age. Unlike his parents, who worked for this white family, and his brothers and sisters, Taylor became something like a member of the household. Ritchie points out that this created a rift between Taylor and his birth family, and perhaps it set him up to have unusual expectations that white people would see him as an individual rather than as a member of a demonized race.

Let us advance for a moment to the present, when I am teaching at a minority-serving university. In a course on race and gender, I asked my students to reflect on how they learned to define themselves as belonging to particular racialized and gendered groups. Many of them shared moments when they were called bananas, oreos, or coconuts. These terms each refer to somebody who looks Asian (banana), black (oreo), or brown (coconut), but actually thinks like a white person on the inside. I have also heard these terms among fellow bike advocates who are people of color. In our own communities, we may have struggled to fit in. We know all too well that as individuals we cannot speak for a collective. And yet this is what we are sometimes asked to do as community advisers around bicycling. My students grasped that racialized identity emerges through a complex set of practices; it is not as simple as being born in the know because of one's skin color. Many of us learn how to navigate the expectations of multiple racialized groups. In organized bicycling, I have found that accommodating whiteness is a skill set people of color know from experience and deploy as needed.

Back to the history lesson. Due to the increasing supply of bicycles and the public's turn to automobile ownership, bicycling gained a new utilitarian status in the twentieth century, though the elite pastime of leisure cycling continued. Over the decades, utilitarian bicycling became the purview of the poor and the juvenile, except for a patriotic burst of bicycle usage during World War II as part of the domestic conservation effort. The postwar era made car ownership more symbolic of American progress than ever, and though in the realm of public transportation activists began to question segregation with bus boycotts, the bicycle did not have a champion. This changed in the 1970s, when some activists turned 1960s protest energy toward a dawning awareness of ecological crisis, both in nature and in city streets.

Unlike the civil rights movement's focus on institutional change, this new bike movement promoted "do it yourself" values tied to individual power. Perhaps most clearly in the new pastime of mountain biking, untrained mechanics started perfecting their machines' performance and teaching others how to make old bikes good again (McCullough, 2013). Riding together, wrenching together, and protesting together led to the organic flourishing of bicycle subcultures around the United States. What was not questioned was how racial segregation impacted who became a part of these subcultures and who did not. The little research available on the topic suggests that interest in socializing around bicycles extended into other racialized communities as well (Zack Furness, personal communication). This inattention to segregation's effects allowed whiteness to become re-entrenched in organized bicycling, even at a time when bicycle enthusiasts were starting to become aware of how marginalized they were as road users. For many years, "bike equity" would refer to the need to make space for bicycling on public roads. The most important distinctions were not race or class, but whether you were a driver or a cyclist.

The early 1990s offered another potential moment to decenter whiteness in bicycling, when the autonomous event Critical Mass began self-organizing in San Francisco and spread to cities around the world (Carlsson, 2002). This direct action statement of what streets could be like with fewer cars brought attention back to urban streets and connected bicycling with alterglobal power movements. However, at the same time, organized bicycling was moving toward a new strategy of promoting bicycling through land use and transportation investment. This created a new need to protect the respectability of bicycle politics, and by the 2000s many advocacy groups were distancing themselves from local Critical Mass movements. They seem to have lost interest in the grassroots collective just as the populist ethos of Critical Mass opened the door for more people to develop a personal relationship with bicycling in city streets.

The history exhibit's final commentary encouraged advocates to embrace the diversity that was already present in bicycling, breaking down the divide between organized bicycling and the everyday life of the practice. Very few people commented to me about the exhibit, and its presence was not incorporated into the conference in any formal way. Because there has been little attention to integrating professional bicycle advocacy, policy, and planning, even as bike insiders access more public resources than ever, we can be in the room and invisible at the same time. At a formal dinner at that year's National Bike Summit, I was seated next to a white man and key figure in organized bicycling who played an influential role in choosing new leaders. He told me that all the women-oriented and people-of-color-oriented biking projects he'd seen seemed merely "hipster." It was the strongest statement I had yet encountered that people like me were not worth being taken seriously. Bike equity was a growing trend, but its success would be decided by the people in charge, not the barely tolerated others.

Decentering whiteness

Still, othered individuals continue to try and participate in bicycle advocacy, despite the numerous signals that our concerns are still seen the same way that people outside of bike advocacy see bicycling: as a nice but frivolous thing, the icing on the cake. What it means for bike advocacy to be white-centered is that the burden is on us to be bananas, oreos, and coconuts, rather than individual selves formed through racialized experiences. We're not experts on some foreign race; we're fellow activists with complex perspectives. Allowing these perspectives to become influential would decenter whiteness in organized bicycling and would be a big step toward full and fair participation in planning a less car-dependent future. Decentering whiteness in organized bicycling will mean welcoming diverse perspectives and strategies so that accommodating other racialized norms is not a burden that falls on the shoulders of people of color participants.

In the summer of 2015, I attended a very different kind of summit held in Minneapolis. It was the biannual gathering of the National Brotherhood of Cyclists, a network of black and multiracial cycling clubs. People attended from Major Taylor clubs from around the country and the friendly crowd shifted seamlessly between organized panels and social events. At one panel, I heard Zahra Alabanza, co-founder of community ride Red, Bike and Green Atlanta, giving advice about how to support efforts like hers. "Look at who is in power," she said; "who are you writing checks to, how is that power distributed among folks who want to do the work?" Decentering whiteness in organized bicycling will mean redefining what constitutes "work" in the field, and how it is valued. In a "state of the movement" report released in November 2015, the Alliance for Biking & Walking found that most resources at their member organizations go toward influencing policy and infrastructure development. The community rides that have evolved since Critical Mass struggle to find legitimacy among an advocacy community focused on infrastructure "wins."

Red, Bike and Green (RBG) emerged in Oakland, California, in 2007, the brainchild of Jenna Burton, who saw potential in organizing a group bike ride centered in and showcasing the black community (Red, Bike and Green, n.d.). The ride's name and principles honor pan-African solidarity and the black diaspora. In a moment when more attention is going to diversity in bicycling than ever before, groups like RBG have become a media spectacle more than they have been seen as worthy investments. They simply do not fit the "supply side" model (see Batterbury and Vandermeersch, Chapter 14, this volume) that has become dominant in organized bicycling.

Organized bicycling should take the opportunity offered by the enthusiasm of the women of RBG and many other rides and collectives now existing across the country. These individuals demonstrate dogged tenacity; as one of them, I know that few resources have gone toward supporting us as we do the emotional work of fitting into spaces where colleagues or collaborators let us know through microaggressive ignorance that we should be careful not to be too different. How are we supposed to guide change when we are warned, as I was in December 2014, that to remain employed with bicycle organizations we must remain loyal to bosses who are still mostly white men? Even people hired to lead change are pressured to fit into the existing culture, especially when they themselves visibly represent that change.

Conclusion

If they want to further EJ in bicycling, bicycle advocacy, policy, and planning professionals can decenter whiteness in two major areas: hiring and spending and education about the role of race and racism in urban design.

Hiring and spending

Examining who qualifies for leadership in organized bicycling is an important way to open the field. It says something that in the recent Alliance report, ten executive directors chose not to list their race (Alliance for Biking & Walking, 2015). Were they people of color fatigued with being reduced to a racialized status, or were they white individuals who believe themselves to be living in a "post-racial" world? While it may continue to be a challenge to find accurate information about the human infrastructure of organized bicycling, the Alliance report moved in the direction of what environmental leaders have been doing with the Green 2.0 Project since 2013 (Green 2.0, n.d.). There are also informal networks such as the Bike Equity Network, an email list that connects hundreds of bike grassroots organizers and advocacy professionals. The more that job postings circulate in spaces like that, the more we will diversify our human infrastructure for bicycling. Internally, organizations can also move toward more transparent agenda-setting processes that empower a broader group of people to innovate advocacy strategies.

Education about race/racism in urban design

Urban planners are just beginning to scratch the surface on the eurocentric values embedded in urban design and the other colonial legacies affecting their work (Mock, 2015), a limitation identified by people of color planning scholars (Thomas, 1994; Diaz, 2005). I was reminded of this in September 2015, when I spoke about eurocentric tendencies in bike planning on my blog and a professional advocate emailed me to ask where he could learn more. This was a white man employed by a policy organization that provides technical assistance to community groups interested in safer streets. Individuals like him are exactly who needs to learn more about colonialism, racism, and its effects on our land use history, present, and future. The Association of Collegiate Schools of Planning (ACSP, n.d.) is leading in the move to develop more balanced planning education through the work of their Committee on Diversity, and bicycle planning educators could push their pedagogical activities in this direction as well.

Dancing between our in-group understandings of race and white expectations, the oreos, coconuts, and bananas know that getting a place at the table is just a starting point. Over time, though, getting us incorporated into the human infrastructure of bicycle advocacy, policy, and planning will bring justice into public spending on streets.

References

Agyeman, J. (2005) *Sustainable Communities and the Challenge of Environmental Justice.* New York: NYU Press.

Alliance for Biking & Walking (2015) The State of the Movement: Benchmarking Biking and Walking Advocacy. [Online] Available from: www.bikewalkalliance.org/storage/documents/State_of_the_Movement_final.pdf. [Accessed December 6, 2015].

Association of Collegiate Schools of Planning. (n.d.) *Committees.* [Online] Available from: www.acsp.org/about/committees. [Accessed November 30, 2015].

Carlsson, C. (Ed.) (2002) *Critical Mass: Bicycling's Defiant Celebration.* Oakland, CA: AK Press.

Diaz, D.R. (2005) *Barrio Urbanism: Chicanos, Planning, and American Cities.* New York: Routledge.

Epperson, B.D. (2010) *Peddling Bicycles to America: The Rise of an Industry.* Jefferson, NC: McFarland & Co.

Green 2.0 (n.d.) *About Us.* [Online] Available from: www.diversegreen.org/about-us/. [Accessed December 6, 2015].

League of American Bicyclists (2014) United Spokes: Together in American Streets. [Online] Available from: http://bikeleague.org/sites/default/files/Equity_exhibit_report.pdf. [Accessed November 30, 2015].

Lugo, A.E. (2013) CicLAvia and Human Infrastructure in Los Angeles: Ethnographic Experiments in Equitable Bike Planning. *Journal of Transport Geography.* 30 pp.202–207.

Lugo, A.E. (2015) Can Human Infrastructure Combat Green Gentrification? Ethnographic Research on Bicycling in Los Angeles and Seattle. In Isenhour, C., McDonogh, G. and Checker, M. (Eds.) *Sustainability in the Global City: Myth and Practice.* New York: Cambridge University Press, 306–328.

McCullough, S. (2013) *Mechanical Intuitions: The Origins and Growth of Mountain Biking.* Ph.D. dissertation, University of California, Davis.

Mock, B. (2015) There Are No Urban Design Courses on Race and Justice, So We Made Our Own Syllabus. *CityLab*, May 14. [Online] Available from: www.citylab.com/design/2015/05/there-are-no-urban-design-courses-on-race-and-justice-so-we-made-our-own-syllabus/393335/. [Accessed November 30, 2015].

Office of the President. (1994) Executive Order No. 12898. *Federal Register.* 59(32). [Online] Available from: www.archives.gov/federal-register/executive-orders/pdf/12898.pdf. [Accessed November 30, 2015].

Pulido, L. (1996) *Environmentalism and Economic Justice: Two Chicano Struggles in the Southwest.* Tucson, AZ: University of Arizona Press.

Pulido, L., Sidawi, S., & Vos, R.O. (1996). An Archaeology of Environmental Racism in Los Angeles. *Urban Geography.* 17 pp.419–439.

Red, Bike and Green. (n.d.) *About.* [Online] Available from: www.redbikeandgreen.com/about-3/. [Accessed November 30, 2015].

Ritchie, A. (2009) *Major Taylor: The Fastest Bicycle Rider in the World.* San Francisco, CA: Van der Plas/Cycle Publishing.

Thomas, J.M. (1994). Planning History and the Black Urban Experience: Linkages and Contemporary Implications. *Journal of Planning Education and Research.* 14 pp.1–11.

U.S. Department of Transportation. (n.d.) EJ at DOT. [Online] Available from: www.fhwa.dot.gov/environment/environmental_justice/ej_at_dot/dot_ej_strategy/index.cfm. [Accessed November 9, 2015].

14 Community bicycle workshops and "invisible cyclists" in Brussels

Simon Batterbury and Inès Vandermeersch

Introduction: rights and justice

The appreciation and full recognition of the "right to mobility" of urban residents to transport is an important aspect of social justice (Cresswell, 2010). Some residents are unable to access mainstream transport systems for reasons of cost and geographical proximity. In many cases access to other urban services and opportunities depend on mobility. Several attributes of urban residents – their residential location as well as their social status and income – affect their basic rights to access convenient and affordable transportation, in the same way that social, economic, spatial, and environmental injustices play out in many other aspects of urban life (Lefebvre, 1968). For example, housing costs and low incomes can diminish access to public transport for inner city residents that would appear to be surrounded by it.

Non-active travel, particularly private vehicle use, is prevalent among those with more discretionary income (Tuong, 2014). "Sustainable mobility" policies in contemporary cities try to provide moral or material incentives to reduce vehicle congestion and pollution by using active transport modes in preference to private vehicles (Affolderbach and Schulz, 2015; Banister, 2008). Sustainable mobility planning also provides better infrastructure for pedestrians, bikes, and public transport, as a form of supply-side urban investment. But it overlooks the politics of persistent injustices in the urban transportation system. Not everybody can take the bus, train, or tram to work, or cycle or walk. What if there is still no accessible public transport? No money for fares? Street dangers to women and children, or racially motivated violence on the streets and at train stations? Simply "supplying" public transport and cycle routes through public and private investment does not address all of these problems effectively.

To go further, we need to consider more radical mobility policies that acknowledge the lived experiences of transport users, who could help to determine the barriers to improved mobility they face in disadvantaged communities or sectors of society, and then "co-produce" workable solutions with transport and infrastructure experts. Demand-side factors like reducing personal risks and enhancing transport capabilities and expertise among commuters and travellers are vital for encouraging urban residents to consider more sustainable modes of transport. Increasing bike ownership across race, class, and gender is an important contribution to "material equity" (see Introduction, this volume). Supply-side investments, by contrast, facilitate mobility but cannot actually force residents to use them. In Europe's top "cycling cities" in the Netherlands and Denmark, for example, demand for cycling as a quotidian transport mode is high, and it exists in a dialectical relationship with a cyclist-friendly built environment constructed to facilitate it (Gössling, 2013). While these countries are not universal templates given their specificities, planners elsewhere ignore at their peril the elements of demand-side bike culture, and the knowledge of routes, infrastructure, and urban place and space that individuals have (Batterbury, 2003). In other words, sustainable mobility cannot be left to the official "experts" alone. Community participation in bike planning, then, is part of bicycle justice.

Our aim in this chapter is to expose a hitherto understudied aspect of bicycle justice, namely efforts to establish and run "community bike workshops" or "*ateliers vélo collectif*" using one European city, Brussels, as an example. These are autonomous and self-help initiatives that are largely "invisible" to main-stream engineers and planners because they are bottom-up, rarely sanctioned by governments, occasionally edgy and anarchic, traverse gender and racial identity, and they are part of an ever-shifting not-for-profit transport sector.

Brussels illustrates demand-side sustainable transport very well, because a number of initiatives fight against pervasive automobility, reclaiming "rights" to mobility and public space. We asked how its many workshops operate, what contribution do they make to bike culture and to rights to the city – and for whom? Interviews were conducted in community bike workshops and among transport organisations in 2014–2015. We posed questions about their mission, participation, premises, and links to mainstream organisations (Batterbury, 2015; Vandermeersch, 2015). We did not survey their clientele in any depth. Vandermeersch is a mechanic and workshop organiser as well as a researcher; Batterbury researched for ten weeks, as an outsider to Brussels but as part of the first academic exploration of the operation and socioeconomic contributions of community bike workshops worldwide (Bike Workshops Research, 2015).

Community bicycle workshops

Bicycles make a contribution to tackling, or partially reversing, the growth of automobility, the ubiquitous and unpleasant tendency of those with sufficient assets to favour cars over other transport modes for reasons of prestige, convenience, and habitual inactivity (Urry, 2004). Bicycles are quite capable of tackling many transport injustices, as they fill in gaps in networks and provide transport for almost anybody, including disadvantaged social groups. They do this quietly, without pollution, and at low cost (Horton, 2006). They remain marginal in terms of their traffic volumes, but they are illustrative of community efforts to roll out sometimes radical mobility actions and policies, as we will show.

"Community bike workshops" offer alternatives to bike shops, and are less commercial in their aims. They have been around for over 30 years in western nations, and their numbers are on the rise, sometimes as part of community ventures that have a strong social outreach mission or an activist basis (Carlsson, 2007; von Schönfeld, 2015). They are "do it yourself" responses to mobility problems that aim to increase community cohesion. They are small "urban commons" where people come to repair their bikes, source second-hand and scavenged parts, and learn maintenance skills. As Donald Strauss (2015) says, 'Wrenching co-ops are self-sustaining, socially, economically, and environmentally just institutions open to all who want to learn, volunteer, and participate' (p. 108). Almost all are not-for-profits, they usually rely on volunteers to assist the clientele although a few have paid staff, and they are based in cheap or free premises. The clientele make voluntary or fixed-rate financial contributions to use the workshop, or in some cases they donate their own labour instead. Some are decidedly anti-capitalist or anti-car; but all try to contribute to sustainable transport through the transmission of bike repair skills, regardless of their political leanings. In France, this is termed *vélonomie*, or the creation of a self-sufficient or autonomous bicycle citizen capable of riding safely and keeping their own bike maintained. Parts and bikes are salvaged; cheap and low carbon transportation is constantly created regardless of the participants' social status or identity.

Europe and the Americas have many such workshops in towns and cities. Some are networked. In France, they are linked in a federated "movement" of sorts called Heureux Cyclage (www.heureux-cyclage.org). There is an international email list for bike workshops called The Think Tank, and its network organises the annual Bike!Bike! conference in North America and Mexico (https://en.bikebike.org). Whether or not their organisers participate in wider networks, most workshops concentrate on serving just one city neighbourhood, although people coming from further afield are not refused help. Research on the culture of cycling generally, of which they form a part, is an emerging field (Aldred and Jungnickel, 2014; Carlsson, 2007; Bicicultures, 2015; Horton et al., 2007; Strauss, 2015), but discussions of bike workshops are still very sparse. For example, key researchers John Pucher and Ralph Buehler (2008, 2012), who strongly support mainstream adoption of cycling in cities and better planning, do not discuss them.

Workshops in Brussels

Brussels, Belgium, is a multilingual and multicultural "small world city" (Corijn and van der Ven, 2013). There are about 1.2 million people in what is known as the Brussels-Capital Region, which is made up of 19 communes, or local government entities. Its governance structure is complex, because of historical differences between Flemish- and French-speaking communities since the formation of Belgium in 1830. On first appearance it seems a rich city, with prestigious buildings and cultural institutions, and most of the political and administrative functions of the European Union are based there. Nonetheless, it has a high unemployment rate (20.4 per cent in 2013, www.statistics.irisnet.be). About half of the highly skilled workforce commutes from outside the Capital Region, and the city itself has a persistent underclass of long-term unemployed. The "Brussels Paradox" describes this coexistence of economic success and social polarisation (Oosterlynck, 2012). There is a considerable level of disadvantage within parts of the city, and a racial and linguistic diversity. Aside from skilled and often temporary expat workers, the city has substantial populations of Italians, Spanish, Turkish, Moroccans, and Congolese, some being descendants of guest workers in manufacturing who came to Belgium in earlier decades. The city is also a refuge for many asylum seekers and immigrants without legal status.

Bike use in the city transcends class, race, and social status. The numbers of cyclists are slowly rising, aided by a city bike share scheme that has seen moderate success (the *Villo*). Cycling mode share is embarrassingly low, compared to Flemish cities outside Brussels and against Belgium's Dutch neighbour, at only 2.5–4 per cent of all trips (Bruges, Belgium is 25 per cent; Antwerp, Belgium is 16–23 per cent; Ghent, Belgium is 14–20 per cent; Amsterdam, Netherlands is 22–40 per cent, see www.cityclock.org/urban-cycling-mode-share). There are important structural reasons for this. Unlike some of its neighbours, the city is hilly, and for decades it had strong support for automobility, particularly post World War II. Even today, a quirk in fiscal policy means it is easier for employers to give free use of a company car to employees than a higher salary. In Brussels, recent government statistics show 36.7 per cent of cars registered in the city are company owned, mostly diesel powered, and these encourage employees to drive for personal and work related trips (Beckx and Michiels, 2014). Driving 2–5km in the city is quite common, even though the public transport system of trams, buses, trains, and métro (subway) is quite extensive. Driving behaviour is generally thought to be poor – for example, advanced cycle boxes at stop lights often have a car in them and parking restrictions are widely ignored. There are, however, many one-way streets in the centre where only bikes are allowed to travel against traffic, seemingly without major incidents so far!

In Brussels, community bike workshops have grown rapidly over the last five years, and they are well attended by *Bruxellois*. A strong desire to remain "DIY" and independent exists in several workshops (Vandermeersch, 2015; Carlsson, 2007), while others are in the non-profit social enterprise economy, hiring paid workers, and working in partnership with government. Some are supported by larger cultural or cycling organisations. Aside from their transportation objective, workshops are meeting-places for cross-cultural interaction, new ventures, and building the "social economy". Brussels' cycle spaces are 'significant sites of social encounters' (Jensen, 2013, p. 225). The spatial distribution of workshops is shown in Figure 14.1, against a welfare indicator for the 19 communes.

Eight of 14 workshops shown are in communes with above average government welfare payments to citizens, indicating a level of economic disadvantage. Most are in the inner city or fringes, with a small number in outer suburban locations, particularly close to a university campus (the two Ateliers Voot and Vélo Pital).

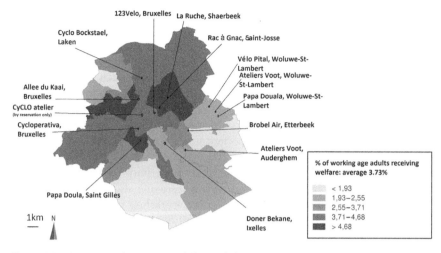

123Velo, Bruxelles   La Ruche, Shaerbeek

Cyclo Bockstael,
Laken

Rac à Gnac, Saint-Josse

Vélo Pital, Woluwe-St-
Lambert
Ateliers Voot, Woluwe-
St-Lambert

Allee du Kaai,
Bruxelles

Papa Douala, Woluwe-St-
Lambert

CyCLO atelier
(by reservation only)

Cycloperativa,
Bruxelles

Brobel Air, Etterbeek

Ateliers Voot,
Auderghem

% of working age adults receiving
welfare: average 3.73%

< 1,93
1,93–2,55
2,55–3,71
3,71–4,68
> 4,68

Papa Doula, Saint Gilles

1km   N

Doner Bekane,
Ixelles

Figure 14.1 Location of community bike workshops in Brussels, against percentage of
working age adults receiving state welfare payments

Note: Data from Observatoire de la santé et du sociale Bruxelles Capitale and IBSA, SPF Economie
– Statistics Belgium.

Source: Simon Batterbury.

Three domains of the Brussels workshops illustrate their strengths and
weaknesses: people, premises, and networking beyond the workshop. Workshops
appear to be fertile ground for bicycle justice, but they currently struggle with
limited capacity, staffing, or premises.

The people

The bike workshop is not a well-known feature of city life. Some members of the
public we talked with actually confused them with bike shops, and their locations
are often away from prominent retail strips. Many are relatively new, dating from
the late 2000s, with Atelier Kaai opening in 2004. For those that use them, they
learned of a workshop through word of mouth, social media, limited workshop
advertising, and through Brussels' cycling subcultures.

Each workshop functions slightly differently. Workshops are staffed by people
who are – largely – cycling enthusiasts and community development practitioners. They, and the workshop clientele and their bikes, are all "participants" in
the unique social field of the workshop, which combines camaraderie with
practical actions and pedagogy. As one organiser says, "it's a tiny village in the
middle of the city" (*c'est un tout petit village au milieu d'une ville*) (Vandermeersch,
2015, p. 31). Because most workshop volunteers also hold jobs or are students,
hours of operation can be limited. Evening and weekend opening hours are most
common.

The volunteers and workshop organisers play slightly different roles, as in any volunteer organisation. The workshop organisers (*les responsables d'ateliers*) need basic management skills to connect the workshop to utilities, manage keys, pay bills, order a few new spare parts at bulk prices, check that rosters are full with volunteers (without which the workshop cannot open), and complete annual accounts. Organisers innovate on the job, and rarely have much help in doing so or any training in non-profit management in the Belgian context, or in the legal requirements of running a workshop. Only one workshop had an organiser trained in non-profit administration, courtesy of a foundation training grant. The volunteer teams, meanwhile, are important for directing citizen and community engagement, and the division of essential tasks like stripping down bikes and sorting to create a stock of parts – a key workshop activity. There are difficulties in marrying a desire to tinker around with bikes while also maintaining some forward planning and strategising to keep the workshop functioning. Even in the world of volunteer-run community enterprises, a modicum of efficiently is required. Brussels also has some paid mechanics, for example in the Rue Voot workshops, who operate in more established organisational structures and with slightly larger budgets (Vandermeersch, 2015).

Workshops are variations on a theme; each functions slightly differently. Only four workshops have written rules to which volunteers must adhere when on the premises, concerning the handling of tools and relationships with clientele. These internal policies are more common in American workshops (Batterbury, 2015). All agreed, without much enthusiasm, that accounts have to be drawn up and receipts kept. For example, as one organiser commented

> yeah I keep my receipts, I am useless at accounting, I've just got an envelope for them . . . I really need an accountant and I would pay them to sort it all out. (*Beh je garde mes tickets, je suis nulle en compta, j'ai juste une enveloppe à tickets . . . je cherche absolument un comptable, j'ai envie de le payer pour qu'il me mette en ordre.*)
>
> (Vandermeersch, 2015, p. 38)

Among the 44 mechanics known to be volunteering in 13 workshops in mid-2015, only one was a paid bike shop mechanic beyond his workshop participation, and five in total had full training in bike repair. Some learned their mechanical skills in *Points Vélos* (repair stations in the major train stations, most run by the Belgian NGO CyCLO). The majority of organisers do not have formal qualifications, although technical colleges in Brussels offer relevant courses where they can learn basic skills. Some volunteers work across more than one workshop, viewing their contributions and friendships to exceed a single shop. Even when they are worn thin, interviewees expressed a passion for being a part of the workshop project; "I love working here: I'm in love with this workshop", one said (*j'adore faire ça ici, cet atelier, je suis amoureux de cet atelier*) (Vandermeersch, 2015, p. 36).

Those mechanics who regard the bike as an education tool operate rather like teachers. They are patient with the customers, showing them how to do mechanical tasks, but they also expect punctuality and confidence from other volunteers. As workshops become more popular, it is not always possible to attract skilled volunteers – levels of mechanical abilities differ, and professionalism varies; advice to customers on how to stick with a tricky repair (like removing a rusted bottom bracket) or to complete a repair task can be haphazard. After all, this is the community sector and so it is dependent on the skills and knowledge of those moved to participate.

Some participants are activists who identify as profoundly anti-car, but it is difficult to generalise. We noted that some volunteers are certainly urban radicals; Brussels has a long tradition of countercultural protest and alternative politics. All volunteers see bike use as essential for the city and for tackling its appalling traffic congestion and pollution, and they support it strongly in their volunteering and other actions. But for some, it is also a "war" or a source of resistance identity. Workshops are an element in this struggle, against cars or against the conformity of the state. Because of this image, and despite the diversity of reasons why workshop users visit them, members of the public may consider some workshops unwelcoming to non-radicals.

Workshops replicate the skewed gender relations found among bike riders. Most volunteers and visitors are men. Very few women in Belgium are trained bike mechanics and Brussels is no exception. The general view is that it is a man's job, although women are of course found in bike shops and cycle teams in positions of responsibility as managers, in charge of logistics or particular non-mechanical tasks. Brussels workshops, despite their sometimes militant politics, are hardly more egalitarian; there were three women mechanics among 44 surveyed. Vandermeersch is one of them, and all three felt welcomed in their workshops. It is likely that her mechanical skills have legitimated her presence among a male-dominated fraternity. Among the workshop clients, women are again in the minority. This simply reflects the reality on the streets, in professional cycling, and among daily cyclists, at least in Brussels. There are some statistics in French-speaking Belgium outside Brussels, where there are around 25 workshops. Some 32 per cent of workshop visitors were women in a recent survey (www.lheureuxcy clage.be/les-ateliers). The situation may be less skewed in Flemish-speaking Belgium, where so many people cycle for everyday transport.

In general, the clientele are diverse in their origins. The racial composition of the clientele has never been surveyed and it would be hard to do so but, we suspect, reflects neighbourhood demographics. One North African said:

> I was not paid to say this, but I promise you, this is the only place where I talk with whites and Flemish. Yeah, I see them at the supermarket, but we do not talk. Here we are together, we work together. It's funny, but the team are the only whites that I really know. (*On ne m'a pas payé pour dire ça, mais je vous promets, c'est le seul endroit où je parle avec des blancs et des flamands. Bah, je les croise au supermarché, mais on ne se parle pas. Là, on est ensemble, on travaille ensemble. Elle est marrante cette équipe, mais c'est les seuls blancs que je connais vraiment.*)
>
> (Vandermeersch, 2015, p. 32)

The struggle for operating space (premises)

As community-based non-profits, bike workshops are not equipped to pay for market-rate commercial real estate. A few workshops, such as Working Bikes in Chicago and the Bicycle Kitchen/Bicicocina in Los Angeles, own their premises, but this is rare. Across Europe, workshops find space in squatted or borrowed premises, in buildings awaiting planning permits for redevelopment, or in premises offered or subsidised by local or regional government. If there are genuine commercial rents to meet, this means earning enough revenue to cover these costs, and the only place to do this is through bike sales or charging for services. This can conflict with the mission of serving the local population in a particular neighbourhood, if that population is very low income.

Our interviews reported major difficulties in securing premises on anything other than precarious terms in Brussels. Several, like Cycloperativa in the Annessens neighbourhood (with a high population of recent immigrant residents, particularly from North Africa), have an attachment to that place and its people and want to remain in the local area (the *quartier*). In 2015, Cycloperativa lost their rented premises, and moved to a storefront a few blocks away that is awaiting planning permission for redevelopment. Finding this space required using the organisers' social capital and networks in the neighbourhood. The stock of tools, bikes, and work benches and stands were moved with cargo bikes by several volunteers in one day, and the shop, which was in rough but serviceable condition, was made functional and connected to power and utilities within two weeks.

Such relocations are common and while requiring effort, they are seen as part of the life of a workshop that serves a community while keeping costs very low. One mechanic said that:

> to begin, and to maintain continuity, you must have a workshop, a place to work, in the neighbourhood. Without that it just isn't possible. (*Pour commencer, la continuité, faut qu'on continue à avoir un local, un endroit pour le faire, dans le quartier. Euh, sans ça, c'est juste pas possible.*)
>
> (Vandermeersch, 2015, p. 40)

Technically, workshops can operate as mobile entities, using cargo bikes and setting up almost anywhere, but some stands and tools are too big or heavy, and spare parts and junk bikes need to be stored. Some do operate in this way occasionally, but still have a home base. One of the most spacious workshops in Brussels is 123Vélo, which is situated on the ground floor of a squatted former government building with an intentional community above it that supports and uses the workshop (Figure 14.2).

It began as the effort of one individual but has grown significantly over the last five years. Its customers come from many countries, with different racial backgrounds, and speak many languages. Vélo Pital, by contrast, is on the medical campus of the Université Catholique de Louvain in the eastern suburbs and has a more stable ground-floor space and a less diverse clientele.

Figure 14.2 123Vélo workshop and its founder

Source: Simon Batterbury.

A respondent whose workshop had been forced to move two times listed the negative repercussions of working in temporary spaces: the chaos of moving, the loss of some local supporters and visitors from the immediate locality and even some volunteers. The volunteer mechanics we interviewed made it clear that to contribute to community development and social cohesion, "you must stay there, in the neighbourhood, or you lose support". (*Il faut rester à la, à la mesure du quartier, aussi non on le perd*) (Vandermeersch, 2015, p. 40). None of the workshops sought better premises just to expand; the quest was for stability, not profile or position. Managers were most concerned about optimising their operations and placing them on a more sustainable footing over time. That said, a few wanted to expand their reach, and Papa Doula workshop has done so by setting up a second shop in a suburban location, Woluwe. The Rue Voot workshop, which employs salaried mechanics and has the support of local universities, making it more "professionalised", has evolved into a paying non-profit with usage fees. It occupies two commercial spaces, one of which is subsidised by VUB (a university) because of the high numbers of students that use it. Above all, workshops want to remain accessible to the general public and in a building that makes this possible. Workshops operate very differently from bike shops in this regard; they can get by with back street and out-of-the-way locations, and unattractive premises, as long as there is sufficient room to stage repair sessions and store a stock of bikes and parts.

Each workshop has its own feel, though there are common spatial elements across them. Aside from stacks of junk bikes (mostly solid commuter bikes) and some restored machines for sale, there are working spaces and collections of stripped down parts in tins, drawers, and diverse receptacles. Tools are accessible and usually available to visitors rather than jealously managed. The more established workshops have sofas, a fridge, and a place to make hot drinks. Electricity is necessary for evening activities. Running water and some heating is desirable, but a full set of utilities is not required for the limited opening hours that some workshops maintain. Several are wired for sound and internet. The workshops certainly nurture a bike culture; we have attended sessions with few or no clientele, where instead volunteers interact, tidy the workshop, and discuss other projects over a drink; and others so full that people spill out onto the street.

Networks and linkages

One might expect that bike organisations would work together as a broader coalition, since they are institutions within a shared culture with similar aims to get more people mechanically competent and on bikes, reducing automobility. But within the workshop movement, views differ on this point, and commitment to networking is variable. There are two elements to consider: the extent to which workshops themselves work together, and their links to other types of organisations.

Progressive bike networking (*réseaulution*) was talked about in all the workshops. As stated above, networks of workshops do exist in other countries and internationally. *Bruxellois* organisers are particularly familiar with the French network Heureux Cyclage. Networking was seen as positive, although the autonomous nature of each collective can create clashes in approach and values between workshops. For example, researcher Del Real identified problems between the two major workshops in Strasbourg, France, where one was more "conventional" than the other, and in Paris the two workshops she interviewed had split over whether to remain distanced from government support (Del Real, 2015). In Brussels, some workshop organisers expressed a need to strategise together, while others desired only informal contact (for example, rebalancing stocks of recovered bikes and parts across multiple workshops, an activity common in US workshops). Ideas for cooperation across workshops in Brussels include co-ownership of a small truck to transport used bikes; bulk discount buying of bike parts like cables and inner tubes; a joint website and media presence; and above all, redressing the lack of formal training for many of the volunteers. This would contribute to "opening" the workshop movement more widely.

Workshop organisers are already active in broader pro-cycling initiatives. These include the monthly Critical Mass (*Masse Critique* or *Vélorution*) rides, a large *Vélorution Universelle Bruxelles 2015* event that included a critical mass ride of 1,000 people and a conference, a car-free day in central Brussels, the *Clean Air BXL* anti-air pollution campaign, and *Cyclehack BXL* which is part of a global movement to enable citizen and grassroots design solutions for problems facing urban cyclists (http://CyclehackBXL.be). All of these adhere to a broadly Lefebvrian ethos of support for social justice and citizens' rights and define air pollution, traffic collisions involving cyclists, and a lack of cycling knowledge among the general public as infringing on these rights. Bike workshops are seen as practical spaces for addressing these problems.

The number of cyclist advocacy groups in the city is impressive, but incongruous since the modal share for bikes remains very low. Cyclists are all but "invisible" in the transport statistics, yet they are well represented and supported. Workshops in Brussels have an ambivalent relationship with mainstream "sustainable" planning and mobility organisations. The main bike organisations working in the city are membership organisations, Fietsersbond (the Flemish national bike organisation) and GRACQ (*Groupe de Recherche et d'Action des Cyclistes Quotidiens*), the francophone equivalent which operates in Brussels and Wallonia. Many workshop managers and volunteers are members of one of these two, which fight for infrastructure improvements and safety, something workshops are not equipped to do. CyCLO, which began by running community workshops decades ago, has "mainstreamed" its activity successfully. These organisations are interested in cultural change favouring active travel by bike, but their modes of operation are very different. In addition, there have been instances of tension with bike shops that have been around much longer and whose owners have felt their customer base is being eroded by teaching people to fix their own bikes. When Rue Voot was first established, bike shops organised a short protest strike, but this did not persist.

Beyond their own potential network, bike workshops partner with outside community-minded individuals and organisations. Nurturing key local contacts strengthens the capacity of each workshop to temper disagreements stemming from sociocultural and age differences among participants and users. In terms of wider links, Cycloperativa best illustrates the importance of developing and maintaining good links to the neighbourhood and its own social organisations. While the mechanics enjoy their participation in the workshop, it has a particular aim to act "for and with" (*pour et avec*) local people. There are a number of directions in which these partnerships could expand; for example, cognate non-profits like Tournevie86 (which loans out tools) and Repair Café87 (workshops to fix household items) are poorly connected with bike workshops today, despite their obvious synergies.

Conclusion

We have highlighted the considerable differences between community bike workshops in just one city, where cyclists are less visible than motorists and public transport users. Workshops are individualistic, local, gendered spaces, and most are only sporadically part of a wider bike justice "movement", though they may be active in other bike initiatives and events. They capture and enhance citizens' intention to cycle, regardless of whether good infrastructure and state support exists. Despite their edginess and sometimes transitory nature, they increase demand for cycling, and they maintain it.

Bicycle justice includes the actions of community bicycle workshops. They are part of a global movement, particularly strong in Europe, which includes radical citizen-led and more mainstream sustainable transportation solutions. Most of the participants we interviewed emphasised that they were grassroots in their orientation. There is a definite transition, best represented in Brussels by CyCLO and its numerous pro-cycling efforts, towards professionalisation and mainstreaming their actions. This is commonly the next step that workshops follow across Europe, and tends to diminish some of their conviviality, anti-establishment sentiment, and it increases workshop fees. To date, though, only a few workshops have transitioned to having secure workshop space and paid staff, similar to trends elsewhere (Strauss, 2015).

It is unlikely that all workshops will professionalise, or even that the distribution of city workshops shown in Figure 14.1 will remain the same in a few years, as actors and premises come and go. The workshops are not just about bicycles, anyway; they also promote community strengthening and act as social hubs for individuals who are drawn together by a desire to improve the urban commons. The participation and socialisation of local North African youth in workshops like Cycloperativa is a sign that some workshops are as much about offering a space for socialisation and activities as they are about promoting bicycling itself.

The Brussels case offers parallels with North American cities. It is a city with a small but growing number of cyclists and with a very dense population of immigrant communities in the inner city, some of whom cycle and use workshops. Its automobility problems are severe, and generated by previous rounds of car-dominated transport investment and current tax laws that favour company cars. "Sustainable mobility" planning is now tackling the problem, but we have argued that generating a "bike culture" (to create *demand* for cycling) is just as vital as fixing dangerous intersections, laying new bike paths, and installing parking. There are urban processes that may be seen through a bike workshop lens: how, in such an environment that is hostile to most forms of bicycle justice, do alternative and grassroots initiatives like these pursue a social and a mobility agenda? In Brussels, workshops have succeeded in supporting *vélonomie*, and at the same time creating new spaces of socialisation and cultural exchange in the city. The "invisibility" of these movements and their participants to mainstream policymakers and the general public is unjustified. Meanwhile, and despite this, they are slowly contributing to a new social production of space, and to vibrant two-wheel communities. *Vive l'atelier!*

Acknowledgements

Simon would like to thank the Brussels Centre for Urban Studies at Vrije Universiteit Brussel (VUB) for a visiting fellowship in 2015, and the editors for their forbearance after a major bike accident. We thank all our interviewees for their time and dedication, and Bas de Geus, Bas van Heur, Nicola Dotti, and Adonia Lugo for comments.

References

Affolderbach, J., & Schulz, C. (2015) Mobile Transitions: Exploring Synergies for Urban Sustainability Research. *Urban Studies*. [Online] Available from: http://usj.sagepub. com/content/early/2015/05/12/0042098015583784.full. [Accessed 29 November 2015].

Aldred, R. & Jungnickel, K. (2014) Why Culture Matters for Transport Policy: The Case of Cycling in the UK. *Journal of Transport Geography*. 34 pp.78–87.

Banister, D. (2008) The Sustainable Mobility Paradigm. *Transport Policy*. 15 pp.73–80.

Batterbury, S.P.J. (2003) Environmental Activism and Social Networks: Campaigning for Bicycles and Alternative Transport in West London. *Annals of the American Academy of Political and Social Science*. 590 pp.150–169.

Batterbury, S.P.J. (2015) Oily Handshakes: Bicycle Workshops; Sustainable Urban Transport and the Community Economy. Stadssalonsurbains series, Brussels Academy, Brussels. June 12.

Beckx, C. & Michiels, H. (2014) *Analysis of the Belgian Car Fleet 2013*. Mol: Vito NV.

Bicicultures. (2015) *Resources*. [Online] Available from: http://bicicultures.org/resources/. [Accessed: 29 November 2015].

Bike Workshops Research. (2015) [Online] Available from: www.bikeworkshopsresearch. wordpress.com. [Accessed: 29 November 2015].

Carlsson, C. (2007) "Outlaw" Bicycling. *Affinities: A Journal of Radical Theory, Culture, and Action*. [Online] 1(1). Available from: http://journals.sfu.ca/affinities/index.php/ affinities/article/view/9/37%26lt%3B. [Accessed: 29 November 2015].

Corijn, E. & van der Ven, J. (2013) Brussels, A Small World City. In Corijn, E. & van der Ven, J. (eds.). *The Brussels Reader: A Small World City To Become the Capital of Europe*. Brussels: VUB Press, 13–27.

Cresswell, T. (2010) Towards a Politics of Mobility. *Environment and Planning D: Society and Space*. 28 pp.17–31.

Del Real, B. (2015) *Community Bicycle Workshops as Community-Driven Urban Planning in France*. M.A. thesis, University of Melbourne.

Gössling, S. (2013) Urban Transport Transitions: Copenhagen, City of Cyclists. *Journal of Transport Geography*. 33 pp.196–206.

Horton, D. (2006). Environmentalism and the Bicycle. *Environmental Politics*. 15(1) pp.41–58.

Horton, D., Cox, P. & Rosen, P. (2007) *Cycling and Society*. London: Ashgate.

Jensen, A. (2013) Controlling Mobility, Performing Borderwork: Cycle Mobility in Copenhagen and the Multiplication of Boundaries. *Journal of Transport Geography*. 30 pp.220–226.

Lefebvre, H. (1968) *Le Droit à la Ville*. Paris: Anthropos.

Oosterlynck, S. (2012) From National Capital to Dismal Political World City: The Politics of Scalar Disarticulation in Brussels. In Derudder, B., Hoyler, M., Taylor, P.J. & Witlox, F. (eds.). *International Handbook of Globalization and World Cities*. Northampton, MA: Edward Elgar Publishing, pp.487–496.

Pucher, J. & Buehler, R. (2008) Making Cycling Irresistible: Lessons from the Netherlands, Denmark and Germany. *Transport Reviews*. 28(4) pp.495–528.

Pucher, J. & Buehler, R. (eds.) (2012) *City Cycling*. Boston, MA: MIT Press.

Strauss, D. (2015) *Ridazz, Wrenches, and Wonks: A Revolution on Two Wheels Rolls into Los Angeles*. Ph.D. thesis, Antioch University.

Tuong, N.T.C. (2014) Determinants of Private Mode Choice in Ho Chi Minh City, Vietnam: From the Individual Perspective. *World Transport Policy and Practice*. 18(1) pp.56–69.

Urry, J. (2004) The System of Automobility. *Theory, Culture and Society*. 21(4–5) pp.25–39.

Vandermeersch, I. (2015) *Évaluation de l'impact social d'une initiative citoyenne: le cas des ateliers collectifs de vélos à Bruxelles*. M.A. thesis, Haute École de Namur-Liège-Luxembourg/Haute École Louvain en Hainaut, l'Institut Cardijn, Belgium.

von Schönfeld, K.C. (2015) How Bottom-Up Cycling Initiatives Make Cities Sustainable. [Online] Available from: www.theprotocity.com/bottom-up-cycling-initiatives-making-cities-sustainable/. [Accessed 29 November 2015].

15 Community disengagement

The greatest barrier to equitable bike share

James Hannig

The bike share frenzy is sweeping the world, and it seems that every city, large and small, wants this trendy new mode of transportation. Despite becoming increasingly more popular, many bike share systems across North America have received criticism for not reaching minority and low-income populations. In response, several bike share operators have taken measures to reach these underserved communities by removing financial barriers, placing stations in underserved neighborhoods, and partnering with various community organizations (Buck, 2012; Kodransky and Lewenstein, 2014; League of American Bicyclists, 2014). While these efforts have been largely conducted in good faith, data indicate they have had little effect in raising membership in low-income and minority populations (LDA Consulting, 2014).

To date, most efforts to reach underserved communities have focused on mitigating the physical, financial, and cultural barriers to bike share. While these barriers present real challenges for bike share operators and users alike, focusing on addressing barriers can lead bike share operators and planners to make assumptions on the perceptions of bicycling and bike sharing in underserved communities. Without input from members of underserved communities, decision makers may fail to understand the significance these barriers may play in an individual's life. Recent research in places such as Philadelphia, Minneapolis/ St. Paul, and Milwaukee support this claim, suggesting that community engagement rather than simply removing barriers may be more effective in providing equitable access to bike share (Hoe and Kaloustian, 2014; Martin and Haynes, 2014; Hannig and Schneider, 2015).

Furthermore, recent federal guidance on equity practices in transportation planning urges practitioners to use engagement and outreach strategies to ensure "full and fair participation" and to prevent the "denial of, reduction in, or significant delay in the receipt of benefits by minority and low-income populations" (Federal Transit Administration, 2012, p. 2). While these environmental justice guidelines specifically apply to projects receiving federal funding—and not all bike share systems do—it should stand to reason that if public funding is used for implementing bike share, investments should be distributed equitably throughout a community.

This chapter provides an overview of how equitable bike share has been approached, briefly explores the environmental justice framework that applies to bike share, and presents a few lessons that have been learned by engaging underserved communities. Many of the claims presented in this chapter originate from the author's research conducted between May 2014 and May 2015. The study aimed to understand how those in underserved communities perceive biking and bike sharing and whether other models existed that could better address their specific transportation needs. The research approach involved interviewing 14 community partners from Milwaukee, Wisconsin, and 12 from Minneapolis and St. Paul (the Twin Cities), Minnesota. These community partners represented organizations such as social service providers, housing authorities, bicycle advocates, transit advocates, institutions of higher education, and other nonprofit organizations, many of whom had a relationship with the local bike share operator.

Bike share and barriers

To better understand what equitable bike share might look like, we first must explore what bike share is at its core, how it has evolved over the years, and what has been done to increase access to this new transportation infrastructure. In its most basic form, bicycle sharing or bike share is a form of transportation in which users temporarily access a bicycle, often for short trips. In most cases, bike sharing allows a user to access a bicycle from a starting point (a station established by the system's operator), use the bicycle, and later deposit the bicycle at another (or the original) station within the bike share network (Toole Design Group, 2012; Gauthier et al., 2013). With origins dating back to the 1960s in The Netherlands, bike sharing is not a new concept (Gauthier et al., 2013). In the mid-2000s, technological advances (e.g. radio frequency identification (RFID), credit card readers, and real-time GPS) led to the resurgence of bike sharing schemes around the world. Many systems now utilize automated self-serve kiosks at each bike share station (Toole Design Group, 2012; Gauthier et al., 2013; Buck, 2012). As of 2013, over 600 bike share systems were in operation around the world and the list continues to grow (Gauthier et al., 2013). Yet, despite being a relatively new and affordable means of transportation, concerns of inequity have been raised as many low-income and minority communities have not been served by or included in a number of bike share service areas.

It should be noted that not all bike share systems make use of this technology. A few operators, including ValloCycle in Birmingham, Alabama; River Riders in Wisconsin Rapids, Wisconsin; and Ecobici in Buenos Aires, Argentina, have embraced low-tech approaches that are discussed later in this chapter (Wisconsin Department of Health Services, 2014; Gartner and Ochoa, 2013; Ecobici, 2015; Wright, 2012; ITDP, 2015). Other organizations, such as Cycles for Change in Minnesota, operate bicycle libraries which offer long-term bicycle loans for participants (Stoscheck and Baum, 2013). While some may argue these libraries are not true bike share systems, the author insists that they be at least considered related in that they provide a user with temporary access to a bike.

Several planning documents have been circulated to describe the modern bike sharing phenomenon and to assess the broad implementation and impact of bike sharing (Toole Design Group, 2012; Shaheen et al., 2012; Gauthier et al., 2013). Bike share operators have faced several challenges in successfully implementing bike share programs including sustained operational funding, establishing partnerships with public transit agencies and institutions, ensuring equity and service access (Shaheen et al., 2012), and rebalancing the bicycle inventory (Gauthier et al., 2013).

Most guidance documents note the complexity associated with establishing a bike sharing network that reaches an optimal number of riders within a sustainable operating budget (Toole Design Group, 2012; Shaheen et al., 2012; Gauthier et al., 2013). The resulting network is often "small, only covering downtown areas and immediately adjacent residential neighborhoods" (NYCDOT, 2013, p. 14), where stations are often located accordingly "because the high density and number of visitors were expected to produce strong ridership [i.e. revenue]" (Glazier, 2014). Furthermore, this network configuration is often at the expense of no stations serving low-income neighborhoods (NYCDOT, 2013, p. 14) or in communities of people of color (which tend to be associated with poverty) (Hoffmann, 2013).

As a result, few low-income or minority individuals use bike share systems. The demographics of surveyed bike share users in four North American locations (Montreal, Toronto, Washington D.C., and the Twin Cities [Minneapolis and St. Paul]) were telling of the apparent inequity of many bike share systems. Respondents were under the age of 34 (80 percent), college-educated (85 percent), and white (near 80 percent), with incomes of $35,000 and above (85 percent) (Shaheen et al., 2012). While the study did not note how these values compared to the respective data for the overall population, its authors observed that "more than 85% of the sample [had] a Bachelor's degree or higher—far exceeding the level of the general population" (Shaheen et al., 2012, p. 65). Additional studies have also explored demographic data of bike share systems and concluded that the memberships of most systems remain predominantly white, affluent, and male (Buck et al., 2013; LDA Consulting, 2014).

Much of the discussion and guidance for equitable bike share practices has focused on measures operators can take to mitigate barriers such as the difficulty some low-income and minority communities have in securing credit cards (Toole Design Group, 2012). While the number of possible barriers to low-income and minority individuals is manifold, and mirror those to bicycling in general, most fall into one of three categories: structural issues (e.g. physical access or logistical access), financial issues (e.g. user costs, lack of access to bank accounts), and informational and cultural issues (e.g. informational barriers, cultural barriers) (Glazier, 2014; Kodransky and Lewenstein, 2014; League of American Bicyclists, 2014).

Physical barriers, such as the lack of stations in low-income communities, appear to be conceptually easier to mitigate; however, these barriers include "procedural and operational barriers" such as access to the Internet or driver's licenses, which are often required for account set-up and maintenance (Kodransky and Lewenstein, 2014, p. 14). Financial barriers include the user costs, which are often too high for low-income users. As Kodransky and Lewenstein (2014) noted, "the pricing structure of many systems can also exacerbate the financial burdens of participation. Most systems require an initial lump sum membership payment, which is unlikely to be a priority for cash-strapped households" (p. 15). Furthermore, many low-income households do not have access to credit cards or bank accounts. "This 'unbanked' population accounts for roughly 17 million people across the US – or 1 in every 12 households and largely consists of low-income individuals" (Kodransky and Lewenstein, 2014, p. 16).

Informational and cultural barriers reported by Kodransky and Lewenstein (2014) cover a number of factors closely related to the question of how bike sharing is perceived by underserved communities. Informational barriers (e.g. lack of information, understanding, and language translation) prevent potential low-income users from understanding the benefits of bike share or even how to use it. Cultural barriers include "distrust of authority, discomfort with shared mobility systems," or preference for more culturally acceptable modes of transportation such as cars (Kodransky and Lewenstein, 2014, p. 18). These cultural factors indicate that the general receptiveness or level of trust in bike share may be largely dependent on how its use could impact one's status among peers and the community at large.

Not all barriers are limited to the user's perspective. Whether it is perceived lack of demand or increased liability (e.g. risk of vandalism, theft, or injury), Kodransky and Lewenstein (2014) suggest that many bike share operators have an aversion to risk that deters many from serving low-income communities. As has been common to most bike share systems, stations are often placed in areas with high activity and population density, sometimes with the intent that stations will be placed in less dense areas once the financial risk has decreased. This trend illustrates the blurred interpretation of whether bike share is intended to be a public resource or a business.

While operators are undertaking a variety of efforts (Toole Design Group, 2012; Glazier, 2014; NYCDOT, 2013) to reach underserved populations, a few notable case studies emerged in a study of equity programs in 20 North American cities (Buck, 2012). Nice Ride Minnesota (Twin Cities' bike share operator) located 30 stations (20 percent of their system) in areas in need and offered installment payment plans. Arlington County in Virginia offered financial assistance, subsidized memberships, and provided tailored outreach to its non-English-speaking Latino community. Boston's Hubway provided subsidized annual memberships of five dollars and free helmets to qualified low-income individuals. Montgomery County in Maryland offered financial assistance, subsidized entire memberships for qualified low-income individuals, and offered "subcontracting procurement preferences for minority-owned small businesses." Similarly, Denver

B-Cycle and Montreal BIXI recruited riders by partnering with a local Goodwill Industries and youth-service program, respectively (Buck, 2012).

In 2014, Nice Ride Minnesota launched a pilot project called the Nice Ride Neighborhood (NRN) program. Nice Ride Minnesota partnered with various community organizations in an effort to reach underserved communities. The program has been viewed as largely successful in changing the perceptions of biking and creating "communities that bike" in the Twin Cities (Martin and Haynes, 2014). The program used "specially designed orange bicycles" that were distributed to participants via community partner organizations or "liaisons". The bicycles differed from Nice Ride's "kiosk-based" bike share bikes (i.e. "green bikes") in many ways, most importantly in that they did not need to be returned to a dock and there was no payment mechanism. For all intents and purposes, the bikes were the personal responsibility of the user. Each participant was offered training and upon completion of the program requirements would receive a $200 voucher at bicycle shops located in their community (Martin and Haynes, 2014).

Perception check: debunking assumptions and including communities

Why then, with all of these efforts to remove barriers, does bike share continue to fall flat in low-income and minority communities? Some believe providing street infrastructure and access to be the solution. According to this view, what underserved communities need are bike lanes, bike share stations, and subsidized memberships, and bike share will eventually take hold in time with the right marketing campaigns. Others suggest that the key to unlocking equitable bike share lies in designing the right balance between cost and convenience (NACTO, 2015). While they have merit, the danger in both of these approaches is that they are often formed in a vacuum without input from community members. Bicycle advocates and planners have made assumptions of how biking and bike sharing are perceived in underserved communities based on limited or broad data without actually engaging the community. These assumptions may lead to the personal values of advocates and planners prevailing over the needs and desires of the communities. As one community partner from Milwaukee said, "you're cutting people out by making assumptions" (Hannig and Schneider, 2015, p. 32).

Between November 2014 and February 2015, I interviewed several representatives of underserved communities, or community partners, who were willing to share their thoughts on assumptions they felt were being made without consulting members of these communities. When asked whether people in underserved communities will use bike share, one Milwaukee interviewee responded, "[saying] 'nobody is going to use it' is wrong! There are a lot of people that want to be healthy and do things with their family." One respondent from Milwaukee compared bike share to an unexpected successful mobile library as an example of a resource not assumed to be of interest in their community. The mobile library, or MPLX, is "the Midwest's first fully automated 24-hour library," offering the surrounding neighborhoods without access to a nearby staffed branch library a location to check out and drop off library books, CDs, and DVDs (Milwaukee Public Library, 2015). The respondent said:

> I think people would [have an interest in bike share]. The people in this community never cease to amaze me. When I first heard about the mobile library [MPLX], I thought, 'people don't go to the library and don't read books.' But I am amazed by how many people and kids I see using it . . . When people are exposed to new opportunities, they will take advantage of those resources.

A number of participants in my research expressed concern that some bike share operators seem hesitant to place stations in underserved communities because they believe that people will not use them. One participant in Milwaukee compared such sentiments to the stereotypes that "black people do not drink coffee" or "use libraries." He and others suggested that prejudices like these are born out of ignorance and the assumptions often made by those in decision making roles. Community partners offered that when engaged openly, communities will take ownership of resources available.

When asked if people in underserved communities want bike share, one interviewee from the Twin Cities responded that "we might not want this." Another interviewee from the Twin Cities questioned, "would these orange bikes [NRN program] have been here otherwise? [. . .] It's not just about 'giving' us this wonderful creation." Responses such as these challenged the notion that gentrification is a major concern when assuming how bike share may be perceived in underserved communities. One Milwaukee interviewee expressed frustration with decision makers being disconnected from underserved communities, saying, "consultants tell us what we can or can't do. When you're gone, we're still here. People aren't invested; not there to see it through. You gotta believe in it." Similarly, a participant from the Twin Cities described gentrification as being a lack of community engagement, observing, "no focus groups, no studies . . . that's where it gets dangerous. No one's asked what they want their neighborhood to look like . . . There comes a point when people aren't asked what their opinion is, that's when it's considered gentrifying." Many bicycle advocates and planners struggle with whether their actions gentrify the very communities they are trying to reach. While some interviewees agreed that bicycle infrastructure and bike share risk gentrifying neighborhoods, most also saw value in getting more community members on bikes. At its core, biking has real benefits to individuals regardless of income level, race, or status. As one Twin Cities interviewee put it:

> [the conversation] is dominated by white people and by white language and that culture that already exists . . . trying to implant that culture instead of build a culture in and of itself . . . We need to create access . . . It can be whatever you want it to be. Don't impose your culture; just create access. That's the idea. And just put people in charge that are passionate about it.

A number of community partners noted that regardless of whether bike share may have some "built-in" inequity or risks of gentrification, underserved communities deserve equal access to it. One participant observed that even if the personal or cultural value of bike share is unknown or slow to grow at first, youth in underserved communities will grow up with it in the community and may very well use it. She noted:

> I don't think they will be used as much as in other neighborhoods and I don't care. We need to have the opportunity. The access needs to be here. It will take a while for people to get used to them, but people will use them . . . If anything, we're training the next generation.

Contrary to what some bike share planners may think, people in underserved communities have opinions on bike share and many are even receptive to it. They have locally informed ideas about how bike share could be better tailored to the specific needs of their communities. Asking community members is the key to discovering what needs could be met by bike share.

Moving forward: community-driven solutions

While some evidence indicates that mitigating barriers, such as Boston's Hubway subsidy program for low-income individuals, can increase bike share use in underserved communities, experts agree that the most successful programs invest an incredible amount of time and effort into building partnerships and engaging underserved communities (NACTO, 2015, p. 3). The importance of engaging and including underserved communities in the decision making process cannot be stressed enough. Not only is doing so in the spirit of environmental justice guidance on "full and fair participation," but involving the community in a meaningful way can have far-reaching and long-lasting effects on how biking and bike sharing are perceived by underserved communities. Furthermore, including these communities in decision making can help in addressing barriers and more importantly can help identify what equitable bike share may actually look like.

When communities are included in the decision making process, the possible ideas and solutions are virtually limitless. Many practitioners may feel that opening the decision making process to the public would result in infeasible, unusable feedback that would interfere with developing consensus. However, progressive guidance and case studies indicate that fostering meaningful involvement with communities "as a partner in developing solutions" can impart a sense of ownership and "overcome potential cynicism or mistrust" (FHWA, 2015, p. 35; Aimen and Morris, 2012). Below are just a few examples of the feedback bike share operators and planners could expect to receive by engaging underserved communities that I heard in my research. It is important to note that while many of these examples may be applicable to other cities, they should not necessarily be viewed as prescriptive solutions that ensure equitable bike share practices anywhere. The inherent value of community-driven solutions is reflective of the process used and relationships forged to develop them.

Almost every person I interviewed stressed that the key to realizing equitable bike share systems is to develop a relationship with the communities in question. As one Milwaukee interviewee put it, "we continue to underutilize, underappreciate the importance of relationships with the community." Any meaningful relationship begins with developing trust through honest dialogue, transparency, and invested time. Trust can only be achieved by including the community in the decision making. Underserved communities must be engaged early in the process of planning bike share systems. Trust, or distrust, starts on day one. If decisions are made prior to initiating dialogue with the communities, partners noted that perceptions of distrust and gentrification will have already been established.

In addition to coordinating with underserved communities early in the process, community partners and members must be included in the decision making process in a meaningful way. Community partners suggested that residents would be invaluable in identifying key locations in which to place bike share stations. One interviewee from Milwaukee noted that, "if it's worth doing, you need to spend the time upfront socializing with the community. You need the community's help in interpreting the data and making decisions." Feedback from members of the community would also be crucial for effectively identifying and mitigating barriers to bike sharing. Interviewed community partners suggested that community members would provide creative solutions that may be overlooked or dismissed by someone without an intimate understanding of the community's needs.

In many underserved communities, access to biking and bike sharing is the least of some residents' concerns. Many communities have been plagued with decades of neglect, which in many cases has perpetuated racial tensions, poverty, unemployment, and widespread inequity. In order to engage communities on a meaningful level, planners and decision makers need to understand the underlying context and challenges facing underserved communities. Bike sharing will not likely have a wide-reaching impact in alleviating these challenges; however, providing a platform for community members to participate in the decision making process may build trust and help to develop creative solutions. Furthermore, community members may help in redefining how biking and bike sharing fit into the overall transportation needs of underserved communities.

Possibly the most radical theme to emerge, more noticeably during interviews in Milwaukee, was an interest in bike sharing as a primarily recreational activity instead of as a means to commute or run errands. This sharply contrasts with previous assumptions of how bike share systems should be used. A palpable excitement arose during interviews when participants imagined how—and where—members from their community could use bike share. Few discussed it in terms of utility, but instead many imagined ways to connect and experience their neighborhoods in a different way—and as a group. Several Milwaukee interviewees suggested that they could envision a few bike share stations located in or around parks with wayfinding signs or maps available to explore features of the parks and surrounding neighborhood amenities. One participant described it as "being a tourist in your own neighborhood."

Recent studies suggest that this sentiment may not be unique to Milwaukeeans. More than 65 percent of participants in Citi Bike's NYCHA program used bike sharing for recreation (fun or exercise) with only 7 percent using it for running errands, 7 percent for commuting to work, and 11 percent for other activities (Stead, 2015). As noted by Stead (2015), "it fascinatingly goes against the findings of previous studies, which show bicycle usage amongst low-income populations to be utility driven as opposed to recreational" (p. 58). Feedback from focus groups in Philadelphia may also support this observation; as summarized by Hoe and Kaloustian (2014):

> the focus group revealed that while many low-income people think about biking as a form of recreation, they do not use, or even think about, biking as a means of transportation. In order for bike share to be successful in these communities, there will need to be a fundamental shift in attitudes surrounding bikes in general, biking as an activity, and commuting on bikes.
>
> (p. 41)

Researchers in the U.K. suggested that biking recreationally (e.g. in parks and the local neighborhood) may provide "an environment for acquiring [bicycling] skills [. . . where] potential risk [can] be managed" (Nettleton and Green, 2014, p. 245). In effect, biking for recreation in parks and neighborhoods is a proving ground where residents can practice and develop their biking skills and eventually become comfortable (and interested) in biking for transportation. Once people get used to biking and using bike sharing, the system can be expanded to serve more utilitarian activities. This is also the theory behind open street events modeled after the Colombian ciclovía.

In tandem with promoting bike share as a recreational activity, bike share planners and decision makers should strategically partner with and place stations near parks, public housing, and transit. While it is important to include community members in identifying the best locations for bike share in their neighborhoods, feedback from community partner interviews indicated that parks, public housing units, and transit transfer points are key locations for underserved community members. If bike share stations were located at these important interfaces to the community, residents will find a use for it as a resource. However, stations cannot simply be placed at these locations without some sort of training or orientation. Bike share planners and operators should seek partnerships with the stewards of these parks, public housing locations, and transit stops.

Long-term bicycle loan programs appear to be an effective entry point to bike sharing. Among many benefits, programs such as the NRN program changed the perception of biking for many participants by increasing their level of personal comfort; utilizing valuable relationships between community partners and the community; including orientation and training; incentivizing the biking experience in a monetized way; and most importantly, building a community that bikes.

In many ways, these programs address barriers to bike share by empowering participants to take ownership of the bicycle both figuratively and literally. Testimonials of such experiences indicate that programs such as these have the ability to transform individual's perceptions of biking. As one NRN participant reflected, "You know, I hadn't been on a bicycle for years and years, so I was afraid of falling and hurting myself. I was afraid of getting run over by other vehicles and that kind of thing" (Martin and Haynes, 2014, p. 20). In some cases, they appear to have led individuals to realize transportation options they never thought they had, including bike sharing. Another NRN participant commented:

> [bicycling] It became a lifestyle. I used it all the time to run errands, I used it to go to work, to go to the bank and to the post office. I just used it, I started using it you know, in terms of a lifestyle.
>
> (Martin and Haynes, 2014, p. 17)

As noted throughout this chapter, building relationships among decision makers, community partners, and the community are crucial in developing equitable bike share practices. While the NRN evaluation notes that there was some miscommunication and confusion as to the community liaisons' role, it acknowledged that the program's success was largely due to the "proactive engagement" and "great deal of behind the scenes work" from these partners (Martin and Haynes, 2014, p. 18).

The NRN evaluation also drew attention to the importance of community building among participants. The visibility of the orange bikes caused participants to feel connected to one another. Many also noted that the supportive nature of the group rides added to this sense of creating a biking community (Martin and Haynes, 2014). Feedback from participants indicated that some of these relationships may have existed prior to the NRN program; however, the camaraderie and connections experienced in the program were no less real.

Bike share planners and decision makers need to better accommodate women, families, and groups. Feedback from community partner interviews and recent studies overwhelmingly indicates that underserved communities desire more opportunities to ride as families or groups. Providing these opportunities would reduce some barriers including the complexity of trips for individuals responsible for children; personal safety and comfort; and "sticking out in a bad way." One Milwaukee interviewee described this as, "there needs to be a coolness factor. Kind of like when you see a guy in a nice suit." Research indicates that women in underserved communities may be particularly disenfranchised by bike share for a number of reasons including, but not limited to, risk of harassment or assault; inequitable societal beauty standards; and the complexity of family responsibilities (Hannig and Schneider, 2015). Opportunities to include families, women, and community groups could be accommodated by programs or group rides sponsored and organized by bike share operators. These events should be mindful of accommodating all levels of ability by bringing a variety of bicycle types, including children's bikes and trailers.

Equity at the forefront

The community-driven recommendations above indicate that solutions to providing equitable bike share go beyond simply accessing these new systems. It takes building relationships with underserved communities and redefining how and where bike share can be used. It means reconsidering what challenges (transportation or otherwise) people in underserved communities face every day and how bike share could address those needs, if it even can. It also means looking at the planning process in terms of how environmental justice is achieved. Are public dollars being equitably invested? Are members of underserved communities being included in the spirit of "full and fair participation" and receiving the benefits of bike share? What would bike share look like if it embraced environmental justice guidance?

Though largely undocumented in English, an alternative low-tech approach to bike sharing has been widely successful in Buenos Aires, Argentina. Possibly one of the most equitable bike share systems in the world, Ecobici's bike share system is free (for up to one hour) to any resident with a proof of address. Not only does this subsidized system universally allow for all residents to equally benefit, but its mix of automated and manual stations provides alternatives to access (Gartner and Ochoa, 2013; Ecobici, 2015). In addition to its recently installed automated kiosks, Ecobici employs manual stations where "an attendant records the user's information and helps with checking in or out the bike" (Wright, 2012; ITDP, 2015).

Buenos Aires' treatment of bike share as a form of public transportation poses interesting policy questions for cities and operators in North America: how effective are subsidies in lowering the risk to operators when investing in underserved communities? How much of a system could or should be subsidized? What sources of subsidies are or could be available? Would a subsidized bike share be used differently (i.e. would underserved communities be more receptive)? It is likely no coincidence that after five years, "biking now represents 3.5% of all trips in [Buenos Aires]" (ITDP, 2015).

In the U.S., Philadelphia's bike share system, Indego, launched in April 2015 with the notion that bike share is a legitimate mode of public transportation that should be "inclusive and accessible" (Indego, 2015, p. 5). From the onset, the planners and operators of Indego did not stray away from the word equity, but instead declared that it would be the first truly equitable bike share system in the U.S. To this end, Indego designed an "Intensive Intervention" approach which included research, marketing, infrastructure, and pricing considerations geared toward including low-income communities (Indego, 2015, p. 9). Based on input from strategic partners, such as the Bicycle Coalition of Greater Philadelphia, Temple University, and underserved communities, Indego committed to initially installing 20 stations in low-income neighborhoods, providing cash memberships for individuals without credit cards, offering a variety of memberships that are competitive with transit fares, and using culturally competent marketing techniques (Hoe and Kaloustian, 2014; Indego, 2015).

It is too early to tell whether the efforts undertaken by Indego and its partners have resulted in ridership unseen in underserved communities across North America. However, putting equity at the forefront of bike share planning and design begs the question: what does equitable bike share really look like? In the case of the River Riders Bike Share in Wisconsin Rapids, Wisconsin, it can look very different. Launched in June 2015, this community-based bike share system consists of 65 donated bicycles and four stations: a YMCA, a hospital, a hotel, and a grocery store (Wisconsin Department of Health Services, 2014). While tiny in comparison to most modern bike share systems, River Riders prides itself on being a low-cost (i.e. free), grassroots way "to increase bicycle use in the community" (Wisconsin Department of Health Services, 2014). Its operators believe that this community-driven model is replicable anywhere, and that the key to increasing investment and use in the program is through involving "as many community members and organizations as possible" (Wisconsin Department of Health Services, 2014). They also urge practitioners to "be creative when identifying potential partners," noting that youth organizations can play an important role in planning a system (Wisconsin Department of Health Services, 2014).

These examples demonstrate that a conversation—a dialogue—has emerged between operators and community members, between academics and practitioners, and among communities themselves. This dialogue may prove to be the key to maintaining a sustainable bike share system that uses public funding to address public transportation needs. Equity and justice in bike share must be defined by the communities that experience inequity and injustice. Representatives of people living in underserved communities can attest to the importance of building meaningful relationships with communities. Doing so builds trust and empowers communities to participate in activities such as biking and bike sharing.

It is the obligation of practitioners, advocates, and researchers to make sure that all people have equitable access to all modes of transportation, especially if any public funding is used. However, equity needs to be defined better in terms of what it means to communities with specific—often unmet—needs. In some cases, the definition may be different than is assumed, and that is okay. It is practitioners' obligation and challenge to address the needs of different communities equitably. Considerable work and research is still necessary to truly realize equitable bike share in North America. In the spirit of environmental justice, bike share planners and operators must go beyond mitigating known barriers to bike share and instead should include underserved communities in decision making process, especially when systems are publicly funded. Furthermore, practitioners must to a better job of defining the purpose of and need for bike share in terms of how communities benefit from or are affected by it. Only then will we have a real understanding of what equitable bike share looks like in underserved communities.

References

Aimen, D. & Morris, A. (2012) *Practical Approaches for Involving Traditionally Underserved Populations in Transportation Decisionmaking*. National Cooperative Highway Research

Program (NCHRP) Report No. 710. http://onlinepubs.trb.org/onlinepubs/nchrp/nchrp_rpt_710.pdf [Accessed September 18, 2015].

Buck, D. (2012) *Encouraging Equitable Access to Public Bikesharing Systems*. Thesis. Virginia Tech Alexandria Center School of Public and International Affairs.

Buck, D., Beuhler, R., Happ, P., Rawls, B., Chung, P., & Borecki, N. (2013) Are Bikeshare Users Different from Regular Cyclists? A First Look at Short-Term Users, Annual Members, and Area Cyclists in the Washington, D.C., Region. *Transportation Research Record: Journal of the Transportation Research Board*, no. No. 2387 (2013), pp. 112–19.

Ecobici (2015) Buenos Aires Ciudad. Ecobici. http://ecobici.buenosaires.gob.ar/ [Accessed March 4, 2015].

Federal Transit Administration (2012) Environmental Justice Policy Guidance For Federal Transit Administration Recipients. *Federal Register Volume 77, Issue 137*. C 4703.1. www.fta.dot.gov/documents/FTA_EJ_Circular_7.14-12_FINAL.pdf [Accessed May 10, 2015].

FHWA (Federal Highway Administration) (2015) *Environmental Justice Reference Guide*. www.fhwa.dot.gov/environment/environmental_justice/resources/reference_guide_2015/fhwahep15035.pdf [Accessed August 10, 2015].

Gartner, A. & Ochoa, M. C. (2013) The Most "Human" Bike-sharing System in the World Lives in Buenos Aires. *The World Bank: Latin America & Caribbean: Opportunities for All*. http://blogs.worldbank.org/latinamerica/most-human-bike-sharing-system-world-lives-buenos-aires [Accessed November 7, 2014].

Gauthier, A., Hughes, C., Kost, C., Li, S., Linke, C., Lotshaw, S., Mason, J., Pardo, C., Rasore, C., Schroeder, B., & Treviño, X. (2013) *The Bike-share Planning Guide*. Institute for Transportation and Development Policy. www.itdp.org/wpcontent/uploads/2014/07/ITDP_Bike_Share_Planning_Guide.pdf [Accessed November 7, 2014].

Glazier, E. (2014) "Bikesharing's Two Environmental Justice Hangups." *Rebuilding Troy*. http://rebuildingtroy.com/2014/10/14/bikesharings-two-environmental-justice-hangups/ [Accessed February 7, 2015].

Hannig, J. & Schneider, R. J. (2015) "Perceptions of Bike Sharing in Underserved Communities within Milwaukee and the Twin Cities." Thesis. University of Wisconsin-Milwaukee.

Hoe, N., & Kaloustian, T. (2014) *Bike Sharing in Low-Income Communities: An Analysis of Focus Groups Findings*. Temple University. Institute of Survey Research. http://b.3cdn.net/bikes/fc16c31cbff25139a1_3cm6bfs04.pdf [Accessed April 23, 2015].

Hoffmann, M. L. (2013) *Our Bikes in the Middle of the Street: Community-building, Racism and Gentrification in Urban Bicycle Advocacy*. PhD diss. University of Minnesota.

Indego (2015) *Meet Indego: Philadelphia's Bike Share Spring 2015*. Online presentation. www.dvrpc.org/breakingground/2015/pdf/Stober.pdf [Accessed September 18, 2015].

ITDP (2015) *Buenos Aires Launches Automated Bike Share*. www.itdp.org/buenos-aires-launches-automated-bike-share/ [Accessed March 5, 2015].

Kodransky, M., & Lewenstein, G. (2014) *Connecting Low-Income People to Opportunity with Shared Mobility*. Institute for Transportation & Development Policy. Living Cities. [Accessed January 10, 2015].

League of American Bicyclists (2014) *Strategies for Equitable Bike Share*. Equitable Bike Share. http://bikeleague.org/content/equitable-bike-share [Accessed November 7, 2014].

LDA Consulting (2014) *2013 Capital Bikeshare Member Survey Report*. Capital Bikeshare. www.capitalbikeshare.com/assets/pdf/CABI-2014SurveyReport.pdf [Accessed October 12, 2015].

Martin, L. & Haynes, M. (2014) *Nice Ride Neighborhood Program: Final Evaluation Report*. University of Minnesota. Urban Research Outreach-Engagement Center & Minnesota Evaluation Studies Institute.

Milwaukee Public Library (2015) *Milwaukee Public Library Express at Silver Spring*. www.mpl.org/hours_locations/mpl_express.php [Accessed April 19, 2015].

NACTO (National Association of City Transportation Officials) (2015) "Can Monthly Passes Improve Bike Share Equity?" NACTO *Bike Share Equity Practitioner's Paper #2*. http://nacto.org/wp-content/uploads/2015/09/NACTO_Can-Monthly-Passes-Improve-Bike-Share-Equity.pdf [Accessed September 17, 2015].

NYCDOT (New York City Department of Transportation) (2013) *NYC Bike Share: Designed by New Yorkers*. www.nyc.gov/html/dot/downloads/pdf/bike-share-outreach-report.pdf [Accessed November 7, 2014].

Nettleton, S. & Green, J. (2014) Thinking About Changing Mobility Practices: How a Social Practice Approach Can Help. *Sociology of Health & Illness*, 36, pp. 239–51.

Shaheen, S., Martin, E., Cohen, A., & Finson, R. (2012) Public Bikesharing in North America: Early Operator and User Understanding. *Mineta Transportation Institute*, No. 11–26. http://transweb.sjsu.edu/PDFs/research/1029-public-bikesharing-understanding-early-operators-users.pdf [Accessed November 7, 2014].

Stead, T. (2015) *Sharing is Caring: An Analysis of Citi Bike's Discounted Program for NYCHA Residents*. Thesis. Pratt Institute.

Stoscheck, C. & Baum, M. (2013) Best Practices for Bike Libraries. *Cycles for Change*. http://cyclesforchange.org/sites/cyclesforchange.org/files/pdf/bike_library_best_practices_web_0.pdf [Accessed November 7, 2014].

Toole Design Group (2012) *Bike Sharing in the United States: State of the Practice and Guide to Implementation*. www.pedbikeinfo.org/pdf/Programs_Promote_bikeshareintheus.pdf [Accessed November 7, 2014].

Wisconsin Department of Health Services (2014) *Wood County: Rural Bike Share*. P-00780F. www.dhs.wisconsin.gov/publications/p0/p00780f.pdf [Accessed October 15, 2015].

Wright, C. (2012) "Mejor en Bici—Buenos Aires Bike Lending Program." http://wander-argentina.org/2012/03/mejor-en-bici-buenos-aires-bike-lending-program/ [Accessed March 4, 2015].

16 No hay peor lucha que la que no se hace

Re-negotiating cycling in a Latino community

*Martha Moore-Monroy, Ada M. Wilkinson-Lee,
Donna Lewandowski and Alexandra M. Armenta*

Pima County, Arizona, is known as one of the cycling meccas in the United States. The county bicycling program has received recognition for being a cycling-friendly community. Tucson and East Pima County Region have held a Gold award recognition as a bicycle-friendly community from the League of American Cyclists since 2006 (League of American Bicyclists, 2015) and was ranked 12th among the 50 top bike-friendly cities in the nation in 2012 by Bicycling Magazine (Huffington Post, 2012). The county is the home of El Tour de Tucson, a premiere bicycling event drawing national and international professional riders. The cycling infrastructure and support from the Pima County Department of Transportation (PCDOT) is exceptional. PCDOT hosts an extensive bicycle education program providing free bicycle skills and repair classes, and are nearing completion of The Loop—131 miles of interconnected shared-use pathways. The cycling assets successfully reach the predominantly white and affluent areas. From 2001 to 2009, cycling rates rose fastest among African Americans, Hispanics, and Asian Americans (Pucher, Buehler & Seinen, 2011). As mentioned in the Introduction to this book, despite these strong cycling assets the Latino community remained disconnected from local bicycling resources. For many Latinos, cycling is a primary means of transportation. The disconnection with cycling resources among Latino communities is not due to a lack of interest or cultural barriers. Thirty-six percent of Pima County residents are Latino (U.S. Census Bureau, 2014). The bike center described in this chapter serves a community that is 88 percent Latino.

The Pima County REACH Coalition formed ten years ago as a community partnership to address health disparities related to substance abuse and diabetes in two underserved neighborhoods. Coalition membership was open to area residents, members of two neighborhood associations, the University of Arizona, and any individuals and institutions interested in collaborating. The coalition has grown over the years and expanded its focus to address additional community concerns. The Pima County REACH Coalition increased access to physical activity opportunities through the creation of a self-sustaining community bicycling center built upon community assets and also by addressing barriers to physical activity in the communities located within the Sunnyside Unified School District (SUSD) boundaries. The primary barriers to cycling included concerns about safety, lack of bicycles, and bicycles in disrepair (REACH Nutri-Bike Coalition, 2013).

Evolution of our community-based coalition

Initial activities included several neighborhood strategic planning sessions held to identify the primary problems shared by these neighborhoods and to prioritize solutions. During this assessment, members focused on policy issues related to physical activity and nutrition, and the development of an educational outreach model for diabetes prevention and control. Specifically, community members addressed these issues through the development and dissemination of culturally relevant health information, leadership, advocacy, outreach, and prevention activities. The coalition developed an asset-based approach focusing on community leadership. The coalition builds on significant community assets including grassroots leadership and committed community-based organizations (CBOs). Part of the success can be attributed to the established roles of coalition members, a history of transparency, trust and commitment in that community fostered over more than ten years. The University of Arizona (UA) and other local governmental institutions and representatives play a back-seat role in the coalition; they are there to provide resources and technical assistance as required. The community residents and CBOs lead the coalition. The leadership has grown from a need to organize in response to issues that include environmental racism, health disparities, and unequal distribution of resources.

The communities represented have historically experienced systematic discrimination demonstrated in part by the infamous Arizona SB1070 law, an oversaturation of liquor licenses, and limited access to opportunities for physical activity due to environmental pollutants such as Trichlorethylene (TCE). Additionally, neighborhoods lack parks and other recreational facilities. Some open spaces have not been developed by the school district or parks department because they are located over the TCE plume. As a result of these issues, time to develop trusting relationships was necessary. This put the Pima County REACH Coalition in a prime position to address this project since the coalition has implemented successful projects in the area for more than ten years.

Partner contributions resulted in the creation of a culturally relevant community led bicycling center. These community partnerships enabled each of the organizations to accomplish their own objectives in addition to the center. The coalition partners most instrumental in the development included: two predominantly Latino communities located on the Southside of Tucson, the UA, Pima County Department of Transportation Bicycle and Pedestrian Program, Wheels for Kids, the Roy Drachman Boys and Girls Club, and Perimeter Bicycling Association of America. The coalition focused on bringing cycling resources to the Latino community to address the high incidence of diabetes and other chronic diseases and the limited access to safe, community relevant physical activity resources and opportunities.

The Pima County REACH Coalition developed a successful, sustainable community led approach to improve the access to cycling resources and infrastructural improvement for Latinos addressing key challenges to build on community assets. The success of this project was primarily due to the coalitions' strong commitment to community led participatory action, and attention to making the program and approach replicable. What was key to the efficacy of the project was utilizing an asset-based approach. Rather than an approach where the university comes in to fix the community's problems, the cycling project was driven by strong community leadership and built on community assets and pooled resources which resulted in a strong, relevant, sustainable project (Israel et al., 2001). The community provided the leadership for the coalition which resulted in relevant projects and helped when the inevitable disagreement occurred between members. It is important for practitioners to remember social structures creating and supporting inequality evolved over time; an effective approach to eliminating inequality takes a long-term investment of time, resources, and commitment of partners. This bicycle program developed over a ten-year period and continues to evolve.

Challenges and assets

This community bicycling project responded to the recurrent need of a sector of Pima County largely comprised of Latino households. The focus area is the SUSD, which includes the Sunnyside, Barrio Nopal, and Elvira neighborhoods. The work has been an ongoing partnership with these neighborhoods and our coalition's mission is developed and reevaluated to continually meet the needs of the changing environment. An overview of community challenges is warranted to provide the historical context for addressing the cycling needs of the Latino community and provide insight into the social and structural environment that impedes access to physical activity opportunities and provides unique resources often overlooked by mainstream cycling programs. The three neighborhoods share a history of strong leadership, community-based initiatives, and health disparities. The percentage of children in the three communities is 3 percent higher than in Pima County and the U.S. Eighty-nine percent of residents are Latino in the communities compared to 33 percent in Pima County and 15 percent in the U.S. Approximately 80 percent of residents in the communities speak a language other than English at home compared to 28 percent in Pima County and 20 percent in the U.S. (REACH Nutri-Bike Coalition, 2013). There are limited resources for physical activity because of environmental pollutants, TCE, and the continual residual effects of this contamination; neighborhoods lack parks and other recreational facilities. Some open spaces have not been developed because they are located over the TCE plume. This is a strong example of a community that might be viewed as complacent or not interested in cycling—they are the "invisible or overlooked riders." In reality, their lived struggles connect bicycling to larger issues of inequality of health, wealth, and security.

Despite these challenges, the neighborhoods are rich in assets. Local leaders, businesses, and organizations are active. The Sunnyside, Elvira, and Barrio Nopal Neighborhood Associations—created in 1988, 1990, and 2012 respectively—have been effective community advocates and change agents. Their success is demonstrated by the creation of a community park, garden, street improvements, and environmental advocacy, among others. These neighborhoods have a history of effective coalitions focusing on specific social problems such as substance abuse, teenage pregnancy, senior health, and environmental contamination.

Community leadership keys to success

According to Norris and Pittman (2000), effective local and regional collaborations bridge sector, race, and class divisions. These researchers add that broad-based coalitions make it possible to develop innovative strategies to address complex issues because they can tackle the vexing issues no single institution, sector, program, or grant can handle alone. They improve the health status of a community as a byproduct of institutions, individuals, and communities working together. While health care providers play a key role in efforts to reduce health disparities, one implication is that by restricting membership to health care professionals, it limits a coalition's capacity to impact the root causes of health disparities. A number of researchers have pointed out that diverse membership is essential to a coalition's success (Norris & Pittman, 2000; Quigley et al, 2001; Wolff & Maurana, 2001). These scholars define diverse membership as the inclusion of representatives outside of traditional health care settings, such as schools and policy makers. Over time, as the number, size, and scope of Pima County REACH Coalition activities grew, new coalition partners came into the group, bringing with them additional resources seen as necessary to accomplish new goals. For example, in response to community-based training to evaluate neighborhood infrastructure related to physical activity, local transportation staff, landscape architects, and planners were invited to join the coalition. The coalition currently includes: promotoras (Community Health Workers), residents, health organizations, grocery stores, county departments of transportation, safe routes to school, school districts, local grocers and businesses, neighborhood associations, government CBOs, local area health education centers (AHEC), the county health department, librarians, community health centers, churches, and the Arizona Association of Community Health Outreach Workers (AZCHOW). The breadth of the coalition membership allowed it to create projects focused on individual behavioral change, neighborhood change, and environmental policy issues (Israel et al., 2001). The promotoras played key roles in the success of the projects as they ensured community leadership and engagement (Hunter et al., 2004; Livaudais et al., 2010; Viswanathan et al., 2009).

The Pima County REACH Coalition builds upon the common goals and interests of community residents as well as the organizational partners. The diverse and broad-based membership allows each member to achieve their mission/goals and pool scarce resources. Since credit can be shared infinitely (not a finite resource), this provides an incentive and significant reward for participation. Each organization and community member can take credit for the success of the coalition which allows them to justify their participation. The initiatives were sustained through pooling resources, building on community strengths and assets, as well as planning as if the funding would end tomorrow.

Issues and approaches used to engage the community via the coalition

A major contribution of the Pima County REACH Coalition was conducting focus groups with community members through cultural humility and partnership synergy to identify the needs and perceptions of the Latino community (Minkler, 2005).

Focus groups were conducted in both English and Spanish with several themes emerging that were shared between both groups. First, that there is a need for physical activities that children can participate in, with one participant stating, "If you provide them with activities they will be happy, they will have better academic achievement and can concentrate more in order to be healthier." Second, a need for safe public spaces was identified, with one participant remarking, "There is a park near my home but the park is often empty because the people that do use it are strange and to tell you the truth, you are afraid to even go there."

Further, there were concerns about the safety of children if they decided to play on or near neighborhood streets. One participant stated, "In our neighborhood cars speed by and should be very careful because of the children especially if the kids are riding their bikes or playing." These concerns echoed the findings from the Safe Routes to School National Partnership (2012) which advocates for legislation that maintains speed limits in school zones, builds sidewalks and bike lanes, and educates on topics pertaining to pedestrian and bicycling safety. Finally, both the English and Spanish focus groups identified a need for community leaders as vehicles for the dissemination of information, as often neighborhood residents would find out about events only after they had already occurred.

Community led cycling assessment

In 2005, the Sunnyside and Elvira Advocates for Health partnered with the University of Arizona's College of Public Health and the Pima County Bicycle and Pedestrian Program to conduct a community cycling assessment. The initial results revealed children and families in the neighborhood were not cycling. The barriers included safety concerns due to poor infrastructure, concerns about crime, lack of access to bicycles, bicycles in disrepair, and a general lack of knowledge of bicycle maintenance and repair (Moore-Monroy, et al., 2008).

In 2013, the REACH Nutri-Bike Coalition conducted a second community bicycling assessment, including a bikeability assessment, of the Barrio Nopal, Elvira, and determined the expectations and needs of those neighborhoods as they related to a bicycling program. Local children and adults who completed surveys identified several barriers to bicycle riding in their respective communities. The respondents identified barriers impeding bike use including: fear of bike theft (55 percent) and inadequate facilities to secure bikes (55 percent). The most common barriers participants reported were perceptions of unsafe roads and traffic. Route assessments were performed and problems were identified in all four of the south/north thoroughfares in the Sunnyside neighborhood. Inconsistent bike lanes, inconsistent road markings, extensive road damage, hazardous conditions created by debris, high speed limits, and cracks and road articulations make biking on these roads unsafe. Similar problems were identified on every road heading north/south in the Elvira and Nopal neighborhoods and in every east/west thoroughfare. The safety concerns created by these hazardous conditions hindered bicycle access to community assets and adjacent neighborhoods. Our route assessment results provide additional evidence to the finding of Ahlport et al. (2008) regarding the need to change the physical environment such as adding bicycle lanes and using traffic calming measures to improve the active travel infrastructure and the need to address these issues among ethnic and economically diverse communities. Key informant interviews indicated that crossing at major intersections was unsafe and that crossing at designated crosswalks was not conducive of safe biking practices (REACH Nutri-Bike Coalition, 2013).

Failure of the traditional bicycle planning approach

In the mid-2000s, the Pima County Bicycle and Pedestrian Program began building a bicycle safety education program which has become one of the largest in the U.S. While quite successful in most neighborhoods, initial attempts to bring the classes to the underserved neighborhoods in the Sunnyside Unified School District fell flat. The program had approached the project in the same way it had implemented the education program in other more affluent areas. Thousands of dollars were spent to translate the curriculum and program workbooks into Spanish, hire and certify Spanish-speaking instructors, identify locations in the target area to hold the classes, schedule a full slate of Spanish-language classes in these new locations, and advertise these classes in the local Spanish-language media outlets. The staff of the Bicycle and Pedestrian Program then waited for students to sign up for the classes. No one did. After approximately three months and a dozen cancelled classes, the Spanish-language classes were removed from the public schedule (although Spanish-language classes could still be scheduled when specifically requested).

It was not until joining the coalition and applying an asset-based community led action approach that bicycle education began to flourish in the area. The cycling center is just one of many projects developed by the leadership of the continually evolving community coalition. The unique barriers to cycling had to be understood and met in a way that was culturally relevant for an education program to be successful. It is unlikely that the community cycling center would have been conceived of through the traditional planning approach.

Although the early efforts of the Pima County Bicycle and Pedestrian Program targeted and addressed some very important factors such as translating materials into Spanish and hiring and certifying Spanish-speaking instructors, the program overlooked two critical components necessary to the success of any program: community buy-in and community driven (Minkler, 2005). It was not until the Pima County Bicycle and Pedestrian Program became a partner with the Pima County REACH Coalition that they tapped into a multilevel approach to reaching the Latino community. First, the coalition included the key stakeholders from the community who could promote and give their seal of approval of the program being offered to the community. Second, the coalition also had a cadre of promotoras who are trusted sources of information in the Latino community. The promotoras not only referred Latino families to the program but also went through the bike safety classes to demonstrate to the Latino community that anyone regardless of gender, age, or physical ability could attend the program and do well. This last point should not be overlooked because this action by the promotoras addressed some of the cultural challenges often mentioned by mainstream researchers stating in a very simplistic manner that Latinos and specifically older Latinos and Latinas may not engage in a new physical activity due to cultural or generational norms. There was a large age range among our promotoras yet they all chose to fully participate in the classes so they could provide the most comprehensive information to the community. By seeing people of all ages and body types participating in the program, many of the apprehensions community members had were lessened.

Early bike project

Based upon the assessment conducted in 2005, the coalition developed a long-term strategic cycling plan providing the base for the current center. The coalition addressed the barriers to cycling with small projects that did not require large amounts of cash or resources. A group of high school students partnered with the Pima County Department of Transportation (PCDOT) to identify safe routes to popular destinations and developed a map tailored for the community. This was key because although the PCDOT publishes a regional cycling map, it is primarily intended for commuting cyclists, and thus identifies mostly through-routes and major streets with bike lanes. Such a map is not particularly suitable for casual neighborhood cycling nor for child cyclists, and is an example of how the current cycling maps further alienated the socially marginal bicycle users as described in the Introduction to this book. Furthermore, the county map does not include routes to destinations of specific importance to the neighborhoods. Two small grants were secured from a community foundation and the mayor's office to buy two bike trailers full of tools to repair bikes and covered the cost of training community members in bicycle maintenance and repair. A student from the college of public health developed a repair manual in conjunction with PCDOT staff which was translated into Spanish and published by the county. The bike repair manual has been updated and expanded several times, and is not only used by the two neighborhoods, but distributed and utilized in free bicycle repair classes throughout the county. The bike repair trailer became so popular in one of the neighborhoods that it resulted in donations of used bikes to the neighborhood to be fixed and distributed.

These early successful activities provided the basis for the development of the cycling center given the name "Cycling Cyclones" by the children attending the cycling classes.

Cycling Cyclones

Building upon a strong history of effective community led social action, the Pima County REACH Coalition pooled resources from key partners to develop a successful self-sustaining community cycling center in the Southside of Tucson. The members of the coalition identified the Roy Drachman Boys and Girls Clubhouse as an ideal location to house the community cycling center. The willingness of the Boys and Girls Club to act as the organizational home for the community cycling center played a key role in the success of the project. It provided the foundation of this project by supplying staff as well as office and activity space for bicycle safety instruction, bicycle repair programs, and helmet distribution in the targeted area. Establishing the clubhouse as the cycling center was just the first step in this multilayered process.

Along with the help of the coalition and the newly established cycling center, Pima County had a new avenue for introducing their programs and services to the communities within the Sunnyside Unified School District. The Bicycle and Pedestrian Program would become an essential partner in providing the necessary resources and guidance to help with the development of the cycling center. They were able to contribute bicycle safety classes, trainings on bicycle repair, staffing for classes and community events, helmet fitting and distribution.

With funds provided through the Pima County REACH Coalition, bilingual community members were trained and certified as cycling instructors through the League of American Bicyclists. After completing their required training hours, these community members were placed on the Pima County Bicycle and Pedestrian Program's schedule to teach bike safety classes out of the Roy Drachman Boys and Girls Clubhouse. The classes offered included Traffic Skills 101 for both youths and adults, mechanics classes, and Get Back on Your Bike classes.

To promote and bring awareness of the cycling center, various community events were held at the Boys and Girls Clubhouse. The first bicycle event was a kickoff to promote the opening of the neighborhood cycling center. There were various stations set up for families to learn about bike safety and nutrition. Free youth-sized helmets were fit and distributed. The Pima County Bicycle and Pedestrian Program provided a fleet of bicycles and set up a skills course to promote safe and proper riding techniques. One of the bigger events was a community "Bike-In-Baile."

Figure 16.1 Flier depicting the "Bike-In-Baile" event sponsored by the REACH Coalition members

Source: Olivia Ruiz, Youth Program Director at the Roy Drachman Clubhouse, Boys and Girls Clubs of Tucson.

Adults, youths, and families were invited to come and learn about bike safety and enjoy a community bike ride around the neighborhood. Following the community bike ride, there was a live performance by a local Latin rock band. Free lunch was provided to all those in attendance.

Due to the success of the bicycle classes, the Boys and Girls Clubhouse decided to implement a youth bicycle program into their curriculum. Club members are divided into three groups based upon their age. Each group meets once a week and is taught proper bike safety and goes on group rides. With help from the Perimeter Bicycling Association of America, bicycle ambassadors assist with bike safety classes and rides on a weekly basis. This club has seen tremendous success, so far having held a total of 67 club sessions, with an unduplicated membership of 258 members, and an average attendance of 19 people per session. It is noteworthy that only 3 percent of the membership identifies as white or Caucasian. Additionally, 293 helmets have been fitted and distributed since the beginning of the program.

Barriers and issues encountered

The partners encountered some challenges in the planning and implementation of the first activities at the cycling center. Initially, there was lower than anticipated participation in the adult safety classes, and coalition members discussed what strategies might be successful to increase participation levels. Several possible reasons for the lack of participation in bike safety classes were identified. First, individuals within the community are interested in cycling but do not have easy access to bicycles. Second, many of the bicycles are in disrepair. Finally, individuals had difficulty signing up for bike safety classes through Pima County due to a lack of Spanish-speaking staff.

The REACH Community Health Workers and other members of the coalition developed strategies to ensure the bicycle safety classes and activities were effectively marketed to the community and an alternative sign up method was developed. Potential participants are now able to register directly through the Boys and Girls Clubhouse, which ensures that the county receives all the required information regarding registration. They also worked with the Pima County Bicycle and Pedestrian Program to create a bilingual message on their answering machine to help people feel comfortable signing up for classes.

As for the issue of individuals' lack of access to a proper working bicycle, the coalition turned once again to their key partners. Wheels for Kids is a nonprofit organization that takes used bicycles, refurbishes them, and donates them to community members who otherwise would not be able to afford a bicycle of their own. After meeting with members from the organization, Wheels for Kids donated a fleet of bicycles to the cycling center that are lent out to community members so they can participate in community events and classes. The clubhouse was also designated as a drop off location for bike donations. The organization will continue to search for youth-sized bicycles so more children can participate in the bicycle club. Members have also volunteered their time at events to repair bikes for community members.

One unforeseen barrier had to do with nutrition and the children participating in the bicycle events or classes. The majority of the children attending the Roy Drachman Boys and Girls Clubhouse are on free or reduced lunch. As a result, on the weekend when community events were held, it became necessary to provide food. Children were unable to participate in the physical activities because they had not eaten a proper meal. Working with community partners to identify resources to provide snacks at the events became essential. The identification of the need to provide comprehensive tools for the success of the Latino community is evident in this example. Bicycling advocates can no longer approach lack of access to cycling resources from a narrow viewpoint. As researchers and community advocates, we must identify the systemic and structural barriers that often impede the Latino community from being active cyclists. We must acknowledge and identify the environmental and structural barriers within the Latino community including access to nutritious meals, safe green spaces, and access to cycling resources, and ensure that culturally responsive infrastructure will be available when an individual seeks out these resources.

How the bike program relates to biking justice issues

Long-term approach

The most important factors to the success of the bike program include the following factors:

1. It is community led (Israel et al., 2001; Minkler, 2005);
2. There is a long-term commitment of stakeholders and partners (Moore-Monroy et al., 2013);
3. The stakeholders and partners pool their resources (Moore-Monroy et al., 2008);
4. There is an established level of trust and social capital (Leban, 2011);
5. Planning is approached as if funding could end at any time (Wolff & Maurana, 2001);
6. The program builds upon existing community assets (Roosa et al. 2002);
7. The center and programs are culturally and community-relevant (Roosa et al., 2002); and
8. Small successes and accomplishments celebrated by the coalition as partners work toward long-term goals as a means to keep people engaged and able to justify their investment of time and resources.

This approach developed over years of work with coalitions is a new finding not specifically addressed in discussions related to the sustainability of coalitions. It may be that researchers make assumptions and while this is well known, often the rush and time pressures associated with projects can distract from the human side of community programs. This is a good example of what Minkler (2005) referred to as attending to cultural humility and partnership synergy in order to ensure sustainability of a coalition and project.

As discussed above, the current cycling center is built upon ten years of partnership, and on long-term relationships. Partners participated in community events beyond the cycling project including community clean-ups at 6 a.m. on weekends, community festivals, and assisting with information and resources when necessary. The projects were led by the residents of the community ensuring they met the interests and culture of the community and were accessible. This project has moved forward as a result of this commitment as well as closely aligning it with community interests and the mission of organizational partners. The long-term commitment and investment helps to build the trusting relationships and social capital needed to engender community engagement to be successful and sustainable. Aligning the program goals with organizational missions and community interests encourages the different stakeholders to pool resources and allows for the project to move forward despite fluctuations in funding streams and grant cycles. The group abides by the tenet: plan as if the money might disappear tomorrow because it often does. Federal and foundation grants are often for very short time periods as they neglect to understand that long-term investment is necessary to create long-term, effective sustained change.

The fluctuations in funding often make communities feel as if there is only interest in the community as long as there is some type of financial gain. This working principle was put to the test in the last grant the coalition received. What was supposed to be a five-year contract was reduced to one year as a result of a cut in federal funds. Due to their significant social capital and strong community assets and partner resources, the coalition was able to develop a sustainable bike center while increasing the capacity of the staff at the Boys and Girls Clubhouse and PCDOT to provide relevant services to the community. What was hoped to be accomplished in five years was actually completed in a year and a half and continues to thrive to the present day.

The coalition recently received funding to replicate this model in Ajo, Arizona, a remote rural community in Pima County. The coalition will utilize the same framework to adapt a model successful in an urban environment to meet the needs of a small, very remote multicultural community (Native American, Latino, and Anglo) located three hours from Tucson on the border of the Tohono O'odham Nation.

This project provides a transformative example for researchers, advocates, and organizations interested in understanding the complexities of collaborating in a community led project that addresses the idea of emancipatory bicycle justice. It includes addressing the relevant social determinants of health such as socioeconomic conditions, exposure to crime and violence, and availability to community-based resources for recreational activities, contributing to health disparities in the community related to chronic disease, overweight and obesity. Community leadership, engagement, and capacity building are crucial to the success of any project created to improve conditions for a specific population.

We challenge the reader to move beyond tried and true approaches including one-size-fits-all and traditional methods used by city planners and government agencies where planners first develop the ideas and then consult residents for input and feedback in order to refine them. The authors respectfully ask planners, community health professionals, government, and nonprofit organizations to consider including the priority community in every aspect of the community assessment, program development, implementation, and evaluation processes. By doing so, the partners will gain invaluable information and insight about the community and will avoid the common mistakes often made when researchers, nonprofit organizations, or government agencies rush in with an a priori approach not vetted by the community. This process is not easy and requires a significant investment of time and resources. If cycling advocates, government agencies, nonprofit organizations, universities, and communities are truly interested in gaining insight and shifting the current paradigm of cycling to make cycling more accessible and relevant to underserved communities, utilizing this framework will push the mainstream dialogue and include leadership and participation from groups historically excluded from the conversation.

References

Ahlport, K.N., Linnan, L., Vaughn, A., Evenson, K.R. & Ward, D.S. (2008) Barriers to and Facilitators of Walking and Bicycling to School: Formative Results from the Non-Motorized Travel Study. *Health Education & Behavior*, 35(2), pp.221–244.

Huffington Post. (2012) *Best Bike Cities in the U.S.: Bicycling Magazine's Top-Rated Regions*. [Online] Huff Post Green. Available at: www.huffingtonpost.com/2012/05/23/best-cities-biking-cycling-bicycle_n_1536262.html [Accessed October 28, 2015].

Hunter, J.B., De Zapien, J.G., Papenfuss, M., Fernandez, M.L., Meister, J. & Giuliano, A.R. (2004) The Impact of a Promotora on Increasing Routine Chronic Disease Prevention Among Women Aged 40 and Older at the U.S.-Mexico Border. *Health Education & Behavior*, 31(4 suppl), pp.18S–28S.

Israel, B.A., Schulz A.J., Parker, E.A. & Becker, A.B., (2001) Community-based Participatory Research: Policy Recommendations for Promoting a Partnership Approach in Health Research. *Education for Health: Change in Learning & Practice*, 14(2), pp.182–197.

League of American Bicyclists (2015) *Bicycle Friendly America*. [Online] Available at: www.bikeleague.org/bfa [Accessed October 28, 2015].

Leban, K., (2011) *How Social Capital in Community Systems Strengthens Health Systems: People, Structures, Processes*. [Online] Available at: www.coregroup.org/storage/Program_Learning/Community_Health_Workers/Components_of_a_Community_Health_System_final10-12-2011.pdf [Accessed October 28, 2015].

Livaudais, J.C., Coronado, G.D., Espinoza, N., Islas, I., Ibarra, G. & Thompson, B. (2010) Educating Hispanic Women About Breast Cancer Prevention: Evaluation of a Home-Based Promotora-Led Intervention. *Journal of Women's Health*, 19(11), pp.2049–2056.

Minkler, M. (2005) Community-Based Research Partnerships: Challenges and Opportunities. *Journal of Urban Health: Bulletin of the New York Academy of Medicine*, 82(2 suppl ii), pp.ii3–ii12.

Moore-Monroy, M., Rosales, C.B., Coe, M.K., De Zapien, J.G., Meister, J., Barajas, S. & Swanson, G.M. (2008) Innovative Solutions: Engaging Non-Traditional Partners to Reduce Health Disparities. *Manifestation: Journal of Community Engaged Research and Learning Partnerships*, 1(1), pp.24–32.

Moore-Monroy, M., Wilkinson-Lee, A.M., Verdugo, L., Lopez, E., Paez, L., Rodriguez, D., Wilhelm, M.S. & Garcia, F. (2013) Addressing the Information Gap: Developing and Implementing a Cervical Cancer Prevention Education Campaign Grounded in Principles of Community-Based Participatory Action. *Journal of Health Promotion and Practice*, 14(2), pp.274–283.

Norris, T. & Pittman, M., (2000) History/Background. The Healthy Communities Movement and the Coalition for Healthier Cities and Communities. *Public Health Reports*, 115(2–3), pp.118–124.

Pucher, J., Buehler, R. & Seinen, M. (2011) Bicycling Renaissance in North America? An Update and Re-Appraisal of Cycling Trends and Policies. *Transportation Research Part A: Policy and Practice*, 45(6), pp.451–475.

Quigley, H.A., West, S.K., Rodriguez, J., Munoz, B., Klein, R. & Zinder, R. (2001) The Prevalence of Glaucoma in a Population-Based Study of Hispanic Subjects. *Archives of Ophthalmology*, 119(12), pp.1819–1826.

REACH Nutri-Bike Coalition. (2013) *Needs Assessment of Biking in South Side Tucson Neighborhoods: Barrio Nopal, Elvira and Sunnyside*. *Internal Report for the NRC-REACH*

Pima County Coalition. Tucson, AZ: The University of Arizona, Center of Excellence in Women's Health.

Roosa, M.W., Dumka, L.E., Gonzales, N.A. & Knight, G.P. (2002) Cultural/Ethnic Issues and the Prevention Scientist in the 21st Century. *Prevention & Treatment,* 5(1).

Safe Routes to School National Partnership (2012) *About Us Safe Routes to School National Partnership.* [Online] Available at: www.saferoutespartnership.org/about [Accessed February 26, 2013].

U.S. Census Bureau (2014) *State & County Quick Facts.* [Online]. Available at: http://quickfacts.census.gov/qfd/states/04/04019.html [Accessed November 17, 2015].

Viswanathan, M., Krashnewski, J., Nishikawa, B., Morgan, L.C., Thieda, P., Honeycutt, A., Lohr, K.N. & Jonas, D. (2009) *Outcomes of Community Health Worker Interventions. Evidence Report/Technology Assessment No. 181.* Rockville, MD: Agency for Healthcare Research and Quality.

Wolff, M. & Maurana, C.A. (2001) Building Effective Community—Academic Partnerships to Improve Health. *Academic Medicine,* 76(2), pp.166–172.

17 Collectively subverting the status quo at the Youth Bike Summit

Pasqualina Azzarello, Jane Pirone and Allison Mattheis

Introduction

> I have come to believe that bicycling is like the hub of a wheel; it's the central point to which all the spokes connect. By insisting on an intergenerational effort within bike advocacy, we secure the longevity and broader community investment in our growing movement.
>
> – Kimberly White (Youth Bike Summit Co-founder, Youth Keynote Speaker 2011, Baruch College '14)

The Youth Bike Summit (YBS) is an annual event that brings together educators, activists, students, teenagers, practitioners, researchers, policy makers, and community leaders to engage around youth, bicycles, education, and advocacy. The mission of the Youth Bike organization is to "transform our local communities and strengthen our national movement by empowering bicycle leaders" and since 2011 it has served as a space for spontaneous involvement and long-term investments in youth and communities (youthbikesummit.org). In this chapter, a former K-12 teacher and critical educational researcher, Allison Mattheis, helps document the story of the YBS and the efforts and insights of two of its adult leaders, Jane Pirone and Pasqualina Azzarello. Youth participant insights are also highlighted throughout in order to emphasize how this work is youth-led, not just youth-focused.

This chapter begins with introductions to Azzarello and Pirone, explains their involvement, and gives an overview of what the YBS is and how it came to exist. The following section lays out a theoretical framework informed by transdisciplinary design concepts and community-focused youth empowerment goals that is then used to frame three themes drawn from analysis of a series of interviews with these two key YBS figures. Finally, we conclude with insights relevant to other bicycle advocacy efforts and implications for work with youth and communities. By exploring the challenges inherent in creating youth-led spaces, this description of YBS' work to disrupt traditional organizational processes provides a perspective that is relevant beyond bicycle advocacy.

Background and context

Introductions

Pasqualina Azzarello was director of Recycle-A-Bicycle (RAB), a non-profit based in Brooklyn, when she helped organize the first YBS in 2011. She came to this position from a background in painting and public murals and over 20 years of work as an artist and arts educator. While working on an MFA thesis that applied ancient healing rituals to areas of her own neighborhood undergoing drastic changes due to a boom in high rise building construction, she deepened her interest in how people experience their transforming urban environments culturally, politically, and economically. She first became involved with RAB when she was commissioned to work with children at their school-based bike shop in Washington Heights to paint a mural in the neighborhood. Over the next few years, Azzarello maintained her connection to the organization as a volunteer while working full-time as an artist. After successfully writing a grant to the New York City Department of Transportation Urban Art Program she set up an internship program for schools around the city and started to deepen her involvement with RAB as an administrator. As Azzarello describes it, her assumption of the role of director happened gradually:

> I had been volunteering for Recycle-A-Bicycle during a particular period of its growth and transition and at that time, I began to take on more adminis-trative responsibilities. Before then, the idea and practice of nonprofit management had really not been a part of my identity. Little by little I got to know what was entailed, and I began to really love and believe in the work. In time, I was offered the position of executive director and it was once I really stepped into that role that I understood just how much my background and experience as a public artist had absolutely prepared me for the job.
>
> (6–22–15)

Jane Pirone is an Associate Professor at Parsons School of Design who joined the steering committee of the YBS and became its official institutional liaison and academic partner in 2012. She describes bike trips she took as a teenager as formative experiences and has long been involved in activism around bike commuting. Through her role as a member of a New School task force to explore and promote bikes on campus, and consideration of her research interests, she noted a lack of focus on "using the bicycle as more than a technology or tool of transportation, but as a social and cultural system and mechanism to under-standing, creating and being in our urban environment." Pirone came to see bicycles as "a catalyst to actually engage in our urban experience" (2012) and founded a curricular and research initiative called urbanBIKE to engage students at The New School in exploring the bicycle as more than just an object to be designed; it was also a pedagogical tool for experiential learning. Through this work, she developed connections with like-minded activists and educators across New York City. Pirone explained that urbanBIKE stemmed from:

> Our belief . . . that a city that fully supports and embraces cycling elevates the quality of life tremendously by allowing one to engage an urban space on a more human level and increase exchanges—both with the environment and between people—which the isolation of the car prevents.
>
> (2012)

Pirone invited the founder of RAB, Karen Overton, to be a guest speaker in her urbanBIKE studio at Parsons, and through this connection was eventually introduced to Azzarello. Both describe the unique strengths and support provided by their other organizational affiliations as key to the success of establishing the YBS as a robust entity of its own, and point to their own shared interests in public art and community activism. As Pirone put it "we're very compatible collaborators and what we could do together versus what our capacity is as individuals on our own is incredible!" They describe their work in terms of Community of Practice theory, and participate in larger dialogues around engaged learning as part of organizational visioning, assessment, and evaluation.

Overview of YBS

The first YBS was held in January 2011 on the campus of The New School in Manhattan. Serendipity is evident in the timeline of events that led up to the original summit (see Figure 17.1) and in subsequent organizing. The energetic response to the initial event convinced Azzarello of the need to continue it as an annual convening, and her connection to Pirone allowed for Youth Bike to establish a formal relationship with The New School as an academic partner. As Pirone described it, "the stars aligned"; she, Azzarello, and the youth organizers were able to draw upon their ingenuity and take advantage of existing networks in order for the 2012 event to come together. In 2013, Pirone joined the steering committee as an official organizer of YBS, and in 2015 the summit took place in Seattle, the first time it was held off The New School campus. The Twin Cities of Minneapolis/St. Paul will host the 2016 meeting, with hopes that the event will subsequently travel to different communities across the country. Traveling allows YBS to highlight the work of a range of organizations, encourage involvement of new institutional partners, and increase youth participation beyond New York City.

The guiding principles of the YBS are that:

- we believe in the capacity of youths to lead;
- we believe in the power of the bicycle as a catalyst for positive social change;
- we believe in the importance of a diverse, multicultural, and equitable movement;

- we believe when youths ride bikes, our communities are healthier and more sustainable;
- we believe that sharing and learning together will make each of us stronger. At the YBS, each and every person has something to teach, to share, and to learn.

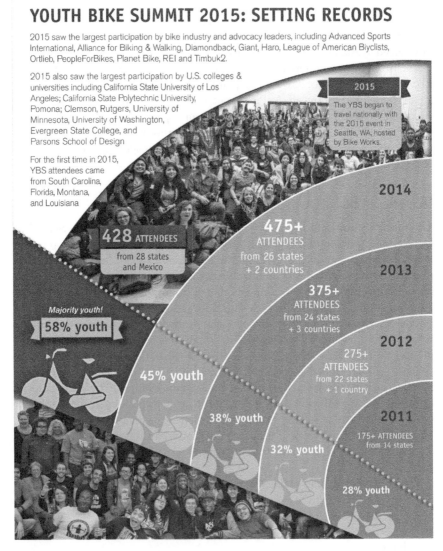

YOUTH BIKE SUMMIT 2015: SETTING RECORDS

2015 saw the largest participation by bike industry and advocacy leaders, including Advanced Sports International, Alliance for Biking & Walking, Diamondback, Giant, Haro, League of American Bicyclists, Ortlieb, PeopleForBikes, Planet Bike, REI and Timbuk2.

2015 also saw the largest participation by U.S. colleges & universities including California State University of Los Angeles; California State Polytechnic University, Pomona; Clemson, Rutgers, University of Minnesota, University of Washington, Evergreen State College, and Parsons School of Design

For the first time in 2015, YBS attendees came from South Carolina, Florida, Montana, and Louisiana

2015

The YBS began to travel nationally with the 2015 event in Seattle, WA, hosted by Bike Works.

2014

475+ ATTENDEES
from 26 states + 2 countries

428 ATTENDEES
from 28 states and Mexico

2013

375+ ATTENDEES
from 24 states + 3 countries

Majority youth!

58% youth

2012

275+ ATTENDEES
from 22 states + 1 country

45% youth

2011

175+ ATTENDEES
from 14 states

38% youth

32% youth

28% youth

Figure 17.1 Participation in YBS 2011–2015

Source: YBS 2015 Impact Report.

While the YBS was born of a local grassroots initiative and has developed through the collaborative efforts of a community bike organization leader and official connections with The New School, it is also an indication and demonstration of the simultaneous, collective efforts of youth bike education organizations across the US. The YBS is a living, dynamic, exploratory space where the ideas, vision, and practices of individuals and organizations can synthesize and generate the next steps of the movement itself.

Theoretical frameworks

Conceptually, both Pirone and Azzarello bring art and design perspectives to their work with the YBS that heavily influence how they view communities and urban planning. In describing her attitude toward existing transportation and cities, Azzarello noted that "we live in a postmodern world with a modernist infrastructure" and that understanding this contradiction is key to changing it. Pirone similarly believes that the world is constantly being "built and rebuilt" and that active, experiential engagement is necessary to rebuild it in ways that meet human needs. The organization of the summit and the consideration of the role of bicycles in larger systems reflect their understanding of "design" as both a noun and a verb. Their professional expertise and social commitments have been translated into philosophy that sees "the world as a creation" and emphasizes connections between public art, public transportation, and public engagement in the practice of the YBS.

Transdisciplinary design perspectives

In describing the design philosophy behind her urbanBIKE initiative in a 2012 article, Pirone quotes inspiration from the words of anthropologist Tim Ingold: "the world of our experience is a world suspended in movement, that is continually coming into being as we – through our own movement – contribute to its formation." Rather than focusing just on the development of objects or examining problems of material use in isolation, transdisciplinary design perspectives emphasize the interconnectedness of the built environment and social processes. This approach recognizes that how people move through shared urban spaces has a direct relationship with the emerging forms of these urban spaces, acknowledges that urban lives are in constant flux, and conceives of design as a continuous process rather than a finished state. Transdisciplinary design efforts view and position contributors as not simply solving problems of form and function, but as engaged followers of a process integrating a larger matrix of social, cultural, material, economic, political, and ecological concerns through participatory strategies. In relating this perspective specifically to a goal of increasing the practice of cycling in cities as a healthy and viable option for individuals, planners and designers must think about the bike not just as an artifact, but as a system to be analyzed on three simultaneous levels: the individual, organizational/institutional, and governmental/municipal. Through such a lens, these community-engaged practices are also viewed as inherently ideological and cultural, and ultimately embodied as narrative.

Translating this theoretical approach into practice means emphasizing collaboration over competition by creating room for multiple perspectives. Through interviews with Azzarello and Pirone, it became clear that both are very aware of how their individual work in a particular place and time relates to collective goals. Pirone describes her background and development as a designer, and her role as a researcher and educator at Parsons, in a way that reflects an awareness of larger systems. She came to see bicycles as a point of intervention through a more universal examination of transportation infrastructure failure and community needs. In contrast, Azzarello came to her work in bike advocacy from a very deliberate, arts-focused interaction with her neighborhood. Her involvement grew from working with a small group of youth to express themselves and their interest in bicycles through art, and gradually she became connected to the larger world of transportation advocacy. Informed by these different starting points and conclusions, the adult organizers of YBS understand the need for new, shared models of operation that are structurally sound yet flexible enough to allow for growth and sustainability. They have put this into practice by utilizing new technologies, opening up access to new participants, and empowering new leaders.

Youth empowerment and engagement

Youth development involves a "focus on the whole person within his or her context and not simply on one issue or problem or one set of skills" (Kress, 2006, p. 48). Despite its name, YBS is not (only) a space for teenage bike mechanics and BMXers to meet, or for adults to use a captive audience to promote a particular perspective on transportation design and planning. Rather, it engages youth in experiences and discussions that blend recreational interests and activist goals and invites those with more experience to support new directions suggested by younger participants.

Academic research relevant to the efforts of the YBS can be found in the public health literature, but with a noticeable gap. There are several studies that highlight youth empowerment and advocacy for policy change relative to tobacco and other substance use prevention programming, sexual health outreach and other social issues (see e.g. Nutbeam, 1997; Holden et al., 2005; Wang, 2006; Strater et al., 2011), but these often involve the implementation of adult-planned efforts through the education of young people. When looking for work specific to the promotion of bicycles and the role of youths in influencing transportation policy, physical activity is addressed as a community-based public health intervention to reduce obesity rates (e.g. Gustat et al., 2015) or bicycle-focused programming is described as outreach to "at-risk" youths (e.g. Kinnevy et al., 1999). Bicycles are rarely referenced or conceptualized as a tool for engaging youths with urban access issues.

From its origins as a spontaneously developed grassroots event, the YBS has grown into a space for coordination and collaboration among those involved in existing efforts across the country. This has given Azzarello and Pirone a unique vantage point for witnessing the emergence of trends in grassroots youth empowerment programs that use bikes as an engagement tool. Some of these organizations are involved in formal Community-Based Participatory Action Research and Youth Participatory Action Research projects, with deliberate modes of data collection and dissemination of findings. As praxis-oriented approaches to community engagement, projects based on this framework "provide young people with opportunities to study social problems affecting their lives and then determine actions to rectify these problems" (Cammarotta and Fine, 2008, p. 2). Other organizations involved are focused primarily on the hands-on practice of teaching bike repair and empowering youth to safely engage with streets and other public spaces in their communities. As Pirone explained, YBS is "a very bottom up thing where part of the success is the fact that all of this exists and has been [happening out in local communities], it's just not been acknowledged" (6–1–15).

As described by Checkoway and Gutierrez (2008, p. 2), empowered youth participation "is about the real influence of young people in institutions and decisions, not about their passive presence as human subjects or service recipients" and focuses on outcomes related to community change. This is the perspective embodied by the YBS. In the next section of this chapter we present three main themes that help tell the story of YBS in the words of those involved and illustrate the important role this event plays in adding youth voices to conversations about bicycle use and transportation policy. By connecting these stories to the framework of community-engaged design and research practices we also offer examples of how such work can benefit from the input of diverse constituencies and honor the important everyday efforts of the individuals and organizations involved in this work. The theme of scale is explored in each story by identifying connections between the global and the local in the incidents described.

From silenced to centered: youth voice and urban planning

The first YBS developed in direct response to the experiences of two youth who traveled with Azzarello to the League of American Bicyclists' annual National Bike Summit in Washington D.C. in 2010. While debriefing on the bus on the way home, they discussed noticing that in a conference meeting of almost 700 people from across the country, they could count the number of people of color in the room and encountered hardly any other young people. This posed a direct contrast with their lived experiences in New York City, as Azzarello described:

> Kim and Kristi were from Flatbush, Brooklyn, and it was also their first time in DC so right off the bat there was a sense and experience of being outside of the familiar. They described that when we all first walked

into the National Bike Summit that year, they knew right away that something was really different, but they couldn't exactly put their finger on it. And then . . . within moments it was like, "wait a minute," "whoa," . . . and a lot has changed in the National Bike Summit over the last five years in terms of diversity of all kinds. But it really was a profound and overwhelming sense and understanding that there were no youth in the room, that there were very few people of color in the room, and there weren't nearly as many women in the room as there were men. I think that year there may have even been just a handful of people younger than 35.

(6–1–15)

The two 17-year-old participants explored the nation's capital by bike, attended conference sessions, and lobbied elected officials on Capitol Hill. Although the chance to talk to their representatives was empowering, it was eye-opening for them and Azzarello to feel like there was not much other conversation around issues specific to youth and marginalized communities in many of the white male-dominated planning discussions. In some sessions it seemed as if the planners and transportation advocates were much more concerned about constructing protected bike lanes than they were focused on protecting people in cities from violence. Many of the other attendees of the conference embraced the presence of the youth, however, and their reactions led Azzarello to reconsider her own role as an advocate and educator:

The instant we got there it was so clear that everyone in that room wanted to talk to Kim and Kristi, because they were young. Right away there was an energy—people asked, "wait, how did you get here? What are you doing here?" and "why are these issues important to you?" And of course they had so much to say. And that became an impactful moment for me in my life as an educator where I understood that opportunities like these do not only mean making sure my students have a positive experience and feel comfortable and able to be themselves [in a] new environment. This is actually of tremendous value for everyone in this room and for transportation advocacy as a whole. Everyone in this room will be better off when listening to and learning from people with different perspectives and experiences with biking. People ride bikes for different reasons and bringing these reasons and the politics behind these reasons into the decision-making arena felt necessary and overdue.

(6–1–15)

In contrast to the National Bike Summit, the YBS centers youth voice and perspectives. Youth speakers and presenters are present throughout 85 percent of the program, including the keynote address, 40 workshops and hands-on maker spaces, and a four-hour intensive visioning session that focuses on identifying goals and steps individuals can each take to achieve them. In 2012, for example, youth leader Alpha Barry was listed alongside Congresswoman Nydia Velazquez as keynote speaker, and in 2013 Local Spokes Youth Ambassador Devlynn Chen appeared on the program with Enrique Peñalosa, the former mayor of Bogotá, Colombia. Beyond the keynote addresses, programs from the past five summits show how youth accomplishments and promise are highlighted in many different ways, and how many teenagers who become involved in local organizations are given leadership roles that they are able to enhance through the national meeting. YBS is also focused on bridging high school students with college students to build programming that will provide support for these young leaders through post-high school and college experiences.

Workshops are led or co-led by youth around a range of activities, from arts and crafts to organizing advocacy efforts. A procession is also held to mark the beginning of each summit—an important symbolic event that unifies the participants and also provides a powerful visible manifestation of youth presence in the urban spaces where the summit is held. These organizational features demonstrate how YBS avoids the trap of falling into deficit thinking or "poverty discourses" described by Gordon (2013) in her examination of the role of youth empowerment development efforts in an urban gardening program; research supports the need to focus on the youth as leaders, rather than in need of leadership. YBS intentionally cultivates a supportive, creative, and inclusive space where every voice, every vision, and every story is welcomed and encouraged to be shared.

Sharing bikes, sharing knowledge: building networks of community bike shops

Contextualizing the work of the YBS at a more micro-level of organization, the creative collaborative culture fosters a space for sharing specific site-based practices. Rather than seeking to translate these experiences directly into large-scale replicable models, this sharing often serves to bring resources back to specific efforts. Azzarello describes many of the groups that have attended the YBS as "intensely local" community bike shops and youth organizations that are intentionally *not* big and don't necessarily have a desire to expand in a traditional sense. These organizations exist to serve a particular local need and niche and often don't have opportunities to connect with similarly focused groups in other places. The success of the organizers in drawing so many participants from around the country in a short period of time signaled that they had tapped into an important and unmet need. The excerpts below capture details Azzarello shared in recounting her expectations when organizing the first YBS:

> That first year, I wasn't able to send an announcement until five weeks before the event. Once I had the green light, I literally sent an email to 40 colleagues in New York and New Jersey and I just hoped that they would come. And the next thing I knew . . . the New York City Department of Health and Mental

Hygiene got wind of it, all these people were calling, and that first year the first person to walk in—he was a young man, a college student, and he came up from a small school in North Carolina, just got off the bus—first trip to New York City—and he had seen it on a listserv and he came to the YBS. So we had 175 people from 14 states in five weeks of the word getting around.

And I remember having a conversation with my staff an hour before it started, something along the lines of, "all we know is that something is going to happen—we don't know what will happen, but something will happen— maybe no one will come, whatever it is, it's okay—we're here to see what happens." And the fact that this many people wanted to be here (and I know what it takes to fundraise and get a bunch of kids from Tucson to New York on four weeks' notice), and all these people showed up and it just—that was the big lesson. That the success of the YBS had more to do with the creating of a space that was meaningful to people—where people felt they belonged— than anything else.

And wow! . . . it really exposed the work that's being done, the work that's been done for so long, and the hunger to connect. Traditionally, there aren't a lot of opportunities for these grassroots groups to connect, and people who work with youth to connect, and certainly for youth to connect. And so the feeling was strong after the first YBS was that we needed to do it again. Just so there's a place to go and to connect each year. So that was a huge takeaway, and really a huge motivator to continue to build this.

(6–1–15)

The "Sunday Visioning" session, which brings together all participants on the final day of the summit to provide a space for creative brainstorming that can apply ideas to action, is a particular way that these unique and hyper-local initiatives can come together on a national scale to strengthen the local, rather than the other way around. The YBS Steering Committee includes eight different youth-based community bike shops across the US: Bikes Not Bombs (Boston, MA), Bike Works (Seattle, WA), Community Cycling Center (Portland, OR), Cycles for Change (St. Paul, MN), Neighborhood Bike Works (Philadelphia, PA), Phoenix Bikes (Arlington, VA), Recycle-A-Bicycle (New York, NY), and West Town Bikes (Chicago, IL). These organizations engage youth ages 8–18 through intensive cycling, earn-a-bike, and job training programs. The growing involvement of college and university students also extends YBS participation to match the United Nations' definition of youths as including people up to the age of 24. What's more, the organizations on the steering committee are engaging youth who can be considered "invisible" or "unreachable" cyclists, particularly in traditional urban planning and bicycle advocacy methods which often leave aside issues of classism and racism. These are youth who live in low-income, underserved communities, in urban and rural environments throughout the US.

"Alchemy and transformation": practices of listening and remaking

As particular goals have solidified into signature elements of the YBS, the event strives to remain open to developing new practices. One of the goals of the organizers is, in fact, to focus on (as Pirone put it) "how to keep this thing alive and dynamic so it doesn't become what it's not supposed to be." In this way, the scale of influence and engagement of the YBS is constantly shifting, based on changes in local and global contexts. Pirone emphasizes the flexibility and openness of the event as key to its uniqueness:

> It's very much a space that's not about imposing things and unifying things and kind of getting everybody in lockstep, it's actually really the other way around . . . It's not that we're not helping to influence and shape and all of those things, but it's done in this manner where the primary method is listening and being very, very sensitive to . . . inclusion.
>
> (6–1–15)

Although donations from sponsors are key to being able to fulfill YBS' commitment to keeping the meeting affordable and accessible for attendees, especially youth attendees, it has been successful in maintaining the agenda-setting and goal-authorizing power of the steering committee. A Youth Advisory Committee is a key part of the decision-making process; the nature of youth leadership leads to high turnover of participants which also maintains dynamism and brings new energy to the organization with each new cycle of involvement. Embracing change and committing to constant reinvention, YBS makes what other advocacy groups treat as challenges into fundamental elements. Pirone notes that:

> I feel like we have a very strong belief around this—which is very antithetical to the way most of these national organizations operate—[they demonstrate] a distinct discomfort in many, many things coexisting in the same space. And we actually are not only supportive of that but feel that diversity and the multiplicity of perspectives, the multiplicity of approaches, the multiplicity of voices, is actually part of the value in the intersectionality of discovering when these things are able to be put side by side, or cross over, overlap, or even create tensions with each other. Because that's how we really learn and grow, not when everything is really clean and neat and binary.
>
> (6–1–15)

One such tension that youth advocacy and urban cycling efforts share is defining the appropriate use of technology and the role of electronic communication in organizing. The YBS certainly takes advantage of social media to connect like-minded people and groups and to promote its efforts, but remains committed to the value of physical connection and attends to the human aspect of cycling and collective sharing. Pirone contrasts this with traditional design and urban planning approaches:

> the world is more and more going into the "we really want this computerized, quantifiable, binary, because it's clean and easy, and we can automate that." And what I think we try to do is say "well, no, for this to really work and it to be really about community and be really about real people on the ground every day, it can't be – it's not that." In fact, what it is is embracing this incredible heterogeneity.
>
> (6–1–15)

The YBS sees maintaining nimbleness at the edges as essential to movement building, and sees attending to the "things at the fringes, the things at the intersections" as key to success. Rather than identifying one programming objective or community design element to apply everywhere, a multiplicity and hybridity of approaches and ideas are embraced. Including—and embracing—uniqueness on a small scale and using that to recognize variation in broader goals is the YBS approach, in contrast to other efforts that (often unintentionally) end up smoothing out differences into homogenized objectives.

Insights and implications for practice

Youth leadership development programs that focus on social injustices or inequitable access face the challenge of avoiding deficit-thinking perspectives that can result in disempowering attitudes on the part of adult organizers. Many otherwise progressive initiatives that provide opportunities for youth to develop strong feelings of self-efficacy through skills development can fall into a focus on individual capacity and success that (often unintentionally) dismiss the very real impact of structural and institutional barriers on youth lives (Gordon, 2013). Rather than approach young people's involvement with these structures in a decontextualized manner, the YBS provides a space where urban planning topics are discussed alongside opportunities to enjoy the physicality of bicycling. Becoming an expert youth bike mechanic is not seen as disconnected from issues of who can safely navigate streets without being racially profiled or sexually harassed. Lobbying legislators to demand improved public transportation infrastructure and access to recreational spaces in low-income communities is seen as similarly important to developing programs to allow young people to bike to high school.

Individual impacts

During our conversations, Pirone and Azzarello shared many anecdotes about individual young people whose lives were deeply impacted by their involvement

Figure 17.2 Photograph of Alpha Barry

Source: YBS 2015 Impact Report.

with empowering local bike organizations, many of whom have been highlighted at YBSs. Azzarello shared the story of Carlos Suero, a former middle school participant in RAB in Washington Heights, who is now a New York City high school teacher who is involved in bike-to-school organizing efforts. In her keynote address at the World Bike Summit in 2015, Pirone shared the stories of three other youth participants:

Alpha Barry is a young man from Guinea and was a keynote speaker at the YBS in 2012. He's lobbied Congress on Capitol Hill, has advocated for more bike infrastructure and connectivity in his neighborhood of Jamaica, Queens, and as a sophomore in high school, he helped lead technical advisory committee meetings about the planning and development of the Brooklyn Waterfront Greenway. Last year, US Congresswoman Nydia Velazquez personally invited Alpha to introduce her at her swearing in ceremony. Alpha is now a sophomore at the State University of New York and wants to be a Congressman someday.

Kimberly White is a co-founder of the YBS and was a keynote speaker at the 2011 Safe Routes to School National Conference. By sharing her story of how wrenching and pedaling, and the mentors she encountered along the way, led her to a new world of opportunity, she brought 600 people to their feet. Kimberly has since become a US citizen and graduated from Baruch College, where she studied environmental law.

Figure 17.3 Photograph of Kimberly White
Source: YBS 2015 Impact Report.

Figure 17.4 Photograph of Devlynn Chen
Source: YBS 2013.

In 2013, after **Devlynn Chen** presented the keynote address at the YBS, alongside Enrique Peñalosa, she went on to intern at the League of American Bicyclists. She worked with League of American Bicyclists staff to create a comprehensive report on engaging youth in bike advocacy. Devlynn is a junior at Dickinson College in Pennsylvania, where she is studying to become a biologist and volunteers at the school bike coop. Devlynn also serves on the League's Equity Advisory Council.

Collective influence

As Azzarello noted in one of our conversations, rather than thinking about youth-engaged community work as "investing in the future," we must recognize that "youth are leaders *now*." The Political Action Center, a yearly feature of the YBS, is one way the event strives to provide opportunities for youths to coordinate their efforts. The demand for increased programming at the local and national level comes from both youth advocates and the youth themselves who are actively seeking ways to learn new skills, organize for change, and be involved in decision-making processes that impact their communities. The fact that this demand cannot be met by the current capacity of small local bike shops and organizations highlights the need for greater involvement and support from public and industry sources:

> on a local level [having] these small community bike shops—and certainly the ones that work with youth—makes so much sense. There's such a huge impact that these shops have for these kids and for their communities. Once the resources exist and you put them together in such a way and make some adjustments here and there, there exists this remarkable potential for it to work. You're getting bikes back on the street, you're able to make a living, you're creating opportunities for job training for teenagers and providing new options in low-income communities . . . Bikes are affordable, bikes are accessible, etcetera, etcetera, etcetera. And so on the local level they make sense. That's why there are so many shops and why they're growing and growing by their numbers.
>
> And one of the things that we found at the Youth Bike Summit is that by doing it over the last five years, by coming together nationally, by creating the space where everyone is welcome and this tremendous idea exchange can happen, and by sharing challenges and best practices, and really building that into our model, what happens as a result is that the local efforts are [able to be sustained]. People learn how to fundraise, groups learn from each other doing staff exchanges and . . . there's so many examples, but it's really—at the end of the day it's this coming together nationally that serves to strengthen these local efforts.

(Azzarello, 6–1–15)

The YBS also provides useful insight into the challenges of other grassroots community efforts as they grow. Pirone and Azzarello are both concerned with the tensions of maintaining spontaneity and flexibility while also establishing a certain degree of organization that allows for sustainability. They both focus on maintaining it as a space where there is "freedom to create and recreate" in order to "keep the operation vital."

Conclusion

As an event, the YBS represents a successful convening of like-minded community groups from across the country engaging in forward-thinking and collaborative organized sharing of ideas and experiences. As a phenomenon, it is an example of the generative space that can be opened up to voices that are often denied access to institutional authority, and the empowerment that can come with deliberate dismantling of hierarchies.

Eclectic activism and organizational goals are built in to the mission of the YBS in recognition that developmentally, youth are supposed to be exploring new ideas and learning new things and trying them out. In order to meet the needs of youth, the YBS should be a space of experimentation and of sharing. As Christens and Peterson (2012) identify in their conceptual reframing of youth empowerment in the face of sociopolitical control, "despite being prevented from some forms of civic participation (e.g. voting), many young people are highly cognizant of social and political issues, and many are developing participatory competence through direct involvement in efforts to change social and political systems" (p. 623).

This is also something that the broader community of bicycle and transportation advocacy would do well to learn from. Pirone emphasizes that she doesn't mean to criticize the positive efforts of many long-standing organizations and their goals of addressing infrastructure from highly technical perspectives; rather, she hopes that YBS can offer an alternative approach:

> I think that most people that get involved in advocacy, period, they are people that want to make their communities better. They often just are limited by like their own perspective and what they think is the solution. And I think that youth spaces are usually way more generative, and it's just sort of more natural to be like, "Okay, something weird just happened and we have to [deal with it] and have a teachable moment." And we don't expect that a bunch of people who are 15 are necessarily going to behave the way a bunch of people that are 50 are.

> Because that really is where the richness is and it's what wasn't being heard in that bigger space [of the National Bike Summit]. Given the right prompts and space, youth say amazing things because they're really smart and they're just looking at the world in a slightly different way. And sometimes it's a less inhibited way and sometimes it's a more real way.

(6–1–15)

Azzarello also reflected on how other bicycle initiatives sometimes claim a commitment to reaching diverse communities but have trouble putting this into action. She emphasizes the need to actually listen to these communities in order to include their voices and then meet their needs:

> In traditional advocacy planning . . . listening over time to what communities want and why, to where people are coming from, is just so rarely a part of that process. And I think that this listening, and listening over time, and allowing for what gets heard to help guide our decisions for what comes next, is central to the value that we bring to this work.
>
> (6–22–15)

By building trust with local organizations over time, YBS is a place where communities are willing to share their perspectives. The respect for the wide range of efforts happening around the country and the action-oriented feel of the YBS is a feature that both organizers emphasized as appealing and inspiring. As Azzarello described:

> I think that the Youth Bike Summit works because of the work that people are doing already. And the depth of the connections that are able to happen [at YBS], both for hardworking, dedicated community-leading adults and also for all these young people—who are mostly in high school and in college and can often feel incredibly alone in the universe, because of who they are, because of what they believe, because of what it feels like to be marginalized in an unjust world—this is the community we work with. These are the kids at the YBS. I think that the space of the YBS is an unusual one in that it's inclusive, it's welcoming, it's a space where people of all ages are reminded that there's room here to be exactly who you are, and where people are encouraged to share, to learn, and to be open to surprise. Being seen and being heard is a matter of being valued and I think that's a very real impact of the YBS.
>
> (6–22–15)

In Azzarello's phrasing, the essence of the YBS is its focus on "creating a meaningful moment" for all involved. As Pirone put it:

> You know, we realize that no one organization, no one anyone, no one at all can even come close to addressing any of these things because all of these things are so interconnected. They're so complex. They're so steeped in long histories so that the model really became about: How do we learn how to collaborate? How do we learn how to partner? How do we learn how to coexist together and find the strength that everybody can be bringing into the conversation? Because that's the only way these things can be addressed.
>
> (7–6–15)

Many more transportation advocacy-focused efforts would do well to consider how including youth voices, and those of other communities often not heard in planning spaces, can collectively enhance all efforts.

References

Cammarotta, J. & Fine, M. (2008) Youth Participatory Action Research: A Pedagogy for Transformational Resistance. In Cammarotta, J. & Fine, M. (eds.). *Revolutionizing Education: Youth Participatory Action Research in Motion.* New York: Routledge, pp. 1–11.

Checkoway, B.N. & Gutierrez, L.M. (2008) Youth Participation and Community Change. *Journal of Community Practice.* 14(1–2) pp.1–9.

Christens, B.D. & Peterson, N.A. (2012) The Role of Empowerment in Youth Development: A Study of Sociopolitical Control as Mediator of Ecological Systems' Influence on Development Outcomes. *Journal of Youth and Adolescence.* 41 pp.623–635.

Gordon, E. (2013) Under-Served and Un-Deserving: Youth Empowerment Programs, Poverty Discourses and Subject Formation. *Geoforum.* 50 pp.107–116.

Gustat, J., Richards, K., Rice, J., Andersen, L., Parker-Karst, K. & Cole, S. (2015) Youth Walking and Biking Rates Vary by Environments around 5 Louisiana Schools. *Journal of School Health.* 85(1) pp.36–42.

Holden, D.J., Evans, W.D., Hinnant, L.W. & Messeri, P. (2005) Modeling Psychological Empowerment among Youth Involved in Local Tobacco Control Efforts. *Health Education and Behavior.* 32(2) pp.264–278.

Kinnevy, S.C., Healey, B.P., Pollio, D.E. & North, C.S. (1999) BicycleWORKS: Task-Centered Group Work with High-Risk Youth. *Social Work with Groups.* 22(1) pp.33–48.

Kress, C.A. (2006) Youth Leadership and Youth Development: Connections and Questions. *New Directions for Youth Development.* 109 pp.45–56.

Nutbeam, D. (1997) Promoting Health and Preventing Disease: An International Perspective on Youth Health Promotion. *Journal of Adolescent Health.* 20 pp.396–402.

Strater, K.P., Strompolis, M., Kilmer, R.P. & Cook, J.R. (2011) Self-Reported Needs of Youth and Families: Informing System Change and Advocacy Efforts. *Global Journal of Community Psychology Practice.* 2(3) pp.1–12.

Wang, C.C. (2006) Youth Participation in Photovoice as a Strategy for Community Change. *Journal of Community Practice.* 14(1/2) pp.147–161.

18 Mediating the 'white lanes of gentrification' in Humboldt Park

Community-led economic development and the struggle over public space

Amy Lubitow

Introduction

In urban areas throughout the United States, bicycling is increasingly touted as an environmentally friendly way to enhance transportation choice. Discourse around the proliferation of bicycling infrastructure development in American cities often obscures complex aspects of community-level choice regarding transportation, including the placement and implementation of bike lanes. In this chapter, I explore the context behind community tensions surrounding bike lane development in Chicago along a stretch of Division Street in the Humboldt Park neighborhood. Known as *Paseo Boricua* ('Puerto Rican Promenade'), the area is the business district and cultural center of the United States' second largest Puerto Rican community (Wilson and Grammenos, 2005).[1] Adorned with a pair of 60-foot high Puerto Rican flags and large murals depicting Puerto Rican heritage, Paseo Boricua is embraced as a symbol for community self-determination and a home base for resistance against gentrification. Initial proposals beginning in 2003 to install a bike lane on this stretch of street were met with community resistance and a veto from then-Alderman Billy Ocasio, the preeminent political figure of Chicago's 26th Ward (which contains Humboldt Park).[2]

Given this neighborhood context, this chapter considers how community engagement with bicycling as a form of community-led economic development can mediate perceptions and experiences of gentrification in the Humboldt Park neighborhood. Seventeen interviews with community bicycle advocates, city officials, and transportation planners in Chicago are used to explore the tensions surrounding gentrification, neighborhood identity, and cycling facilities.[3] I suggest that, although community engagement around urban infrastructure decisions may have limited utility in stemming rapid gentrification, community-led economic development projects can dramatically alter the experiences and perceptions of local residents. Specifically, I suggest that a community-led bike shop in Humboldt Park has allowed local residents to become empowered both economically and politically in ways that impact broader decision-making processes in Chicago.

City context: bike lane expansion in Chicago, Illinois

In recent years Chicago, the nation's third largest city, has made significant investments in bike infrastructure and has seen corresponding increases in usage. Between 2000 and 2010 its bicycle commuter rate more than doubled from 0.5 percent to 1.3 percent and in 2012 *Bicycling Magazine* ranked it as the fifth most bicycle-friendly city in the United States (Chicago DOT, 2012, p.10). In keeping with these trends, in 2012 the city announced a plan to increase its network of on-street bikeways to 645 miles by 2020, nearly tripling its current network size. Mayor Rahm Emanuel introduced the plan with the claim that his vision "is to make Chicago the most bike-friendly city in the United States" (Chicago DOT, 2012, p.7). Emanuel has articulated that the cycling plan is motivated, in part, by the desire to attract technology companies and "entrepreneurs and start-up businesses" to Chicago while investing in progressive and sustainable forms of transportation (Davies, 2012; Rotenberk, 2012).

This framing of cycling infrastructure as a locally beneficial economic development tool to attract young, affluent residents to the city sheds light on why some residents of the Humboldt Park neighborhood made a connection between bike facility development and neighborhood displacement. The perception of bike lanes as 'white lanes of gentrification' speaks to broader concerns about how changes to the built environment may be a catalyst for undesirable neighborhood changes.[4]

Neighborhood context: Humboldt Park, Chicago

The Humboldt Park neighborhood in Chicago has long been home to one of the largest Puerto Rican populations in the United States. Despite the establishment of an economic and cultural center for Puerto Rican residents in Chicago, displacement has pervaded the Puerto Rican experience in America (Flores-Gonzalez, 2001; Rinaldo, 2002). Low-wage work brought waves of Puerto Ricans to settle in downtown Chicago in the 1940s. However, the construction of a number of universities, hospitals (and the related influx of white workers) in the inner city forced the community westward (Flores-Gonzalez, 2001). By the 1970s, West Town (which borders Humboldt Park to the East) became home to a large percentage of Chicago's Puerto Rican population, and organized resistance against further displacement coalesced (Betancur, 2002; Rinaldo, 2002).

Ongoing development that threatened to push residents out of West Town encouraged many Puerto Ricans to join a public struggle for self-determination as they protected their neighborhoods. As Betancur details, this effort "included confrontations with city hall and police over services and police brutality" and "development of a large network of local organizations and service agencies controlled by Latinos" (2002, p.797). Despite these and other efforts, West Town gentrified rapidly and the Puerto Rican population fell from 42 percent to 25 percent between 1970 and 1980 (ibid.). Nearby Humboldt Park quickly became the primary home of those displaced.

A stretch of Division Street in Humboldt Park known as *La Division* has, over the past 30 years, grown to embody the community's organized efforts to establish deep roots in Chicago. In fact, it has become more commonly known as *Paseo Boricua* ('Puerto Rican Promenade') distinguishing it in name from adjacent stretches of Division Street that expand into other Chicago neighborhoods. This renaming underscores the view of Humboldt Park as "a recognizable economic, political, and cultural space for Puerto Ricans" (Flores-Gonzalez, 2001, p.9). While family, community, and cultural offerings attract Puerto Ricans to live near Division Street, organizations like the Puerto Rican Cultural Center (PRCC) and the Division Street Business Development Association (DSBDA) work to make it affordable and viable to stay for the long term (Wilson and Grammenos, 2005). Puerto Rican community-building remains intimately linked to resistance against the gentrification that has advanced westward from the city center for decades, disproportionately displacing Puerto Ricans and other minority populations in its wake (Betancur, 2002).

This chapter is based upon 17 interviews conducted with cycling advocates, Chicago city officials or staff, and residents of Humboldt Park. Interviews were further supported by attendance at a two-hour meeting of the Mayor's Bicycle Advisory Council Meeting (overseen by CDOT staff and attended by more than a dozen Chicago-area organizational representatives). Additional observations were collected through four days of active participation at Humboldt Park's community bike shop and education center, West Town Bikes/Ciclo Urbano (WTB/CU).

Interview participants reflect a diverse range of ages, racial and ethnic groups, with a relative balance between genders. Participants were recruited either because they played a prominently public role in the neighborhood (e.g. local Alderman), were a visible public figure related to bicycling in Chicago (e.g. professional, paid, bicycling advocate or a city planner), or were active participants at WTB/CU. All interviews were inductively coded and analyzed for recurrent themes and concepts (Thomas, 2006). Observable patterns and themes across the data inform the findings presented below.

The 'white lanes of gentrification'?: race, class, and bike lanes

In 2012, a series of blog posts on *Grid Chicago* featured content about whether or not new bike lanes proposed for Division Street in Humboldt Park could be considered the "white lanes of gentrification" (Greenfield, 2012a). The blog posts started an online debate in which community members and officials weighed in on the meaning and purpose of bike infrastructure in the neighborhood. For some, there was a perception that expanding bike lanes into minority communities symbolically paved the way for gentrification by white outsiders.

One interviewee described the distinctions that many other interviewees made regarding the complex relationships between white cyclists and neighborhood change:

> People who are involved in bicycle advocacy [often] identify as a "cyclist", and . . . there's little interest in providing a facility in your neighborhood for those people . . . It's always been white guys who've come and like, invaded them and said, "We're here to save you, we're here to help you." And yes, Puerto Ricans in Humboldt Park have made a stance [against gentrification] . . . And certainly bicycle facilities, bikes for a very long time, have been seen as a recreational activity of privileged white people.

A Puerto Rican politician representing the neighborhood reflected upon these dynamics at length—extended portions of this interview are included to demonstrate his perceptions of the type of people moving into the neighborhood, coupled with his concerns about bike lanes utilizing public space in unsettling ways:

> A lot of these bikers that have come in to this neighborhood . . . they're hipsters by and large . . . the group that follows them . . . are the more affluent yuppies . . .
>
> And so I have resisted a lot of what they would wish to have . . . I did a study to calm down the traffic on Humboldt Boulevard . . . and the city department [said] "Why don't you consider also a bike lane?" I said I don't want that because . . . the bikers that will take the bike lane . . . they will continue . . . So I said "No I'm not gonna do that, for safety [reasons]". I always use the safety reason. Because then they will take over . . . You know, now it's this lane, then it's this other lane, they remove the cars from the streets, [then it's] "let's give up the whole street to walking" . . . And I think there is a lot of resent (sic) for it. I hear a lot from residents complaining about these people, they think that they own the streets, you know, they don't respect [us].

The excerpts above are illustrative of an ongoing perception of bike lanes as a significant mechanism of gentrification and a means by which public space is appropriated in service of neighborhood 'outsiders.' In the latter quote is also evidence of city-level requests for bike lane development and, implicitly, this respondent notes that 'safety' is leveraged as a rhetorical strategy to resist city-imposed infrastructure; the complex politics of gentrification are not brought into the official city-level conversations or contestations of the bike lanes.

According to Jose Lopez of the Puerto Rican Cultural Center, it is not so much the bike lanes themselves, but the *process* by which the lanes are implemented that is deemed problematic:

It was not that we and Alderman Ocasio opposed the lanes . . . but at the time it was viewed as a process that mostly involved white people . . . Our attitude was that we would support the lanes as long as there was community engagement . . . We never really got a response from the city and that was the problem.

(Greenfield, 2012b)

Interviewees who were residents of the Humboldt Park area underscored the perception that meetings regarding infrastructure decisions often failed to actively engage local Puerto Rican residents:

On big projects community input [can be] mandated as part of the plan. And how is that executed? The Department of Transportation sends out a notice to residents . . . and set up their own meeting, and who shows up to it? . . . outsiders who are bicycle advocates . . . who want to ride through those neighborhoods. They aren't necessarily residents of those neighborhoods, and I don't think are the best voice of those neighborhoods . . . I find that often planners and engineers make plans for pavement and not necessarily plans for people.

In part, the abbreviated decision-making processes preceding the development of the Division Street bike lanes can be connected to the nature of bicycling initiatives in Chicago. Mayor Rahm Emanuel's attempts to expand bike infrastructure in the city have been spurred on by the availability of federal funding and as a result bike facilities have often been installed quite quickly. While efforts may be made to conduct community outreach, rapid outreach may not adequately capture community desires. One minority community organizer summarized this dynamic:

In Chicago . . . there's no process . . . for public meetings . . . there's no mechanism by which community members . . . especially in underserved communities, where people can be asking for what they need in a proactive way. What often happens is either the Department of Transportation or the city department . . . they're pushing for a network of better streets for everybody, but . . . on the community level there may not be a mechanism that's proactively telling them where each of these resources should go and how they should be used.

This quote highlights the constraints that city bureaucracies face in attempting to utilize hard-won public funds for infrastructure development while also conducting appropriate and meaningful outreach to communities.

A failure to conduct adequate outreach when attempting to fast track a bicycling infrastructure project can have negative implications. Six interviewees cited the same story centered on the rapid implementation of a bike lane in an area close to Humboldt Park. In this situation, the city painted bike lanes that directly interfered with a space utilized for church parking on Sundays. Interviewees described how community members were angry about the intrusion into this space and suggested that a lack of input from clergy and local residents led to conflict over the newly striped roadway. One Puerto Rican participant summed up this dynamic: "[CDOT] didn't do enough research about where they were putting these things . . . they took a space that was a community space . . . and without talking to them, they plopped something down. And that was really bad for everybody."

This story highlights how the city's failure to adequately engage the community ultimately wasted resources that might have been used in other areas where the lanes would have been more appropriate. This created a situation in which bicyclists lost out; three participants reported that churchgoers now park illegally in the bike lanes on Sundays. It also created a dynamic in which some community members became resentful of bike lane development, both because of the lack of outreach and because of the rapid, hierarchical implementation of infrastructure.

In Humboldt Park, the establishment of bike facilities reveals the complex nature of public space; community concerns regarding development and ongoing gentrification are mediated by a broader lack of transparent mechanisms to determine how to use and augment the street. Although Puerto Ricans in the area have a dynamic history of bike ridership, broader economic trends and a complex political environment have contributed to a perception that bicycle facilities are, symbolically and perhaps literally, a means of elite outsiders colonizing the public space that Puerto Rican residents have consistently fought to maintain.

Mediating gentrification? Community engagement and community-led economic development

West Town Bikes/Ciclo Urbano (WTB/CU), a community-led bicycle training center and repair shop, evolved out of the nonprofit Bickerdike Redevelopment Corporation's 'BickerBikes' program that began in 2004. Although the program has served Humboldt Park and adjacent neighborhoods since its inception, it didn't open a storefront on the Paseo Boricua until 2009. As a community organization, WTB/CU prioritizes education and outreach to community members, while also running an apprenticeship program and bike shop staffed by local residents. Many interviewees suggested that the Puerto Rican community sometimes felt that biking was for white outsiders; thus, WTB/CU engaged in significant outreach to both minority adults and youths.

When asked how to start to transform the centralized planning structures in Chicago, interviewees consistently called for a grassroots, community-led rather than city-imposed approach. They maintained that leveraging the connections, expertise, and trust of established individuals and organizations in a neighborhood can generate more appropriate and open planning processes. As one white organizer put it:

I think the role of outreach and being part of the community and finding ways to do that in a sustainable way really helps the work a lot. It helps us find those champions, it helps us find the strategies that work.

This interviewee suggests that community members are in touch with the 'strategies that work' in their neighborhood and are more sustainable in the long term. In addition to the general belief that grassroots advocates are more in touch with how to encourage the mass of appeal of bikes to a diverse group of residents, interviewees routinely highlighted the economic opportunities provided by bicycles. A white male organizer/advocate commented:

my intuition is that the notion of sustainability for communities of color, where it's going to be most appealing is where we can connect it to economics and jobs. Because that is something that is much more relevant and much more current, really.

Considering the socioeconomic constraints that many of Chicago's non-white communities face, development that provides economic opportunity will be well-received by at least some community members. In their experience, multiple organizer/advocates found success by framing language related to bikes in this manner. One interviewee, a white male from Humboldt Park, described the economic frame as a means to connect bikes to much larger issues in his community:

Bikes fit into community building far better than just pursuing bicycle advocacy and activism . . . there are much bigger issues that the community was dealing with, such as housing and education, healthcare, jobs, that bikes could be a part of, and that there was much larger, much greater interest from the community in addressing those issues.

Similarly, a CDOT staff member who oversees bicycle initiatives in Chicago noted the city's broader interest in developing job-training programs like WTB/CU's:

The ultimate goal of the mayor was to create this bike apprentice program . . . we wanted youth in these at risk communities to actually have the skills and opportunities and recognize that . . . bike related fields are actually open to them as a potential career.

However, a white male organizer/advocate spoke to the idea that bikes are understandably not always the main priority of residents of these neighborhoods:

there are larger concerns in these communities that don't have bicycle facilities, and so how can they even be concerned about whether or not they have facilities . . . I am really concerned about the health and wellness of my community in a much different way. Not whether or not it's safe to jog with my dog, but whether or not it's safe for my children to walk to school without being ran down by out of control traffic or being shot at.

Interviewees suggested that so long as its value is not overstated and the magnitude of more basic local safety concerns is acknowledged, bike infrastructure may be embraced as a viable community improvement. In particular, advocates in Humboldt Park focused their discussions on economic opportunity and safer streets, while still emphasizing the importance of respecting the neighborhood's cultural identity. One leader at WTB/CU described how the organization has developed into a multifaceted resource for residents of Humboldt Park:

> As far as employment goes West Town has been able to offer lots and lots of opportunities. It's not just wrenching at a bike shop. There's all kinds of advocacy and outreach that can be done . . . and instruction, training our kids to go and teach the youth programs . . . it's not just about bikes but teaching all these soft skills of what it means to have a job, show up on time every time . . . be able to take initiative.

Due in part to the close relationship that WTB/CU has maintained with trusted organizations such as the Puerto Rican Cultural Center in Humboldt Park, many of the neighborhood's residents have embraced bikes and bike infrastructure. The early resistance to bike lane construction, which began in 2003, was due to it being perceived as yet another imposition by a largely white-led city government. Furthermore, this imposition was thought to be driven by developers seeking to expand the city center westward without regard for the history of Puerto Ricans in Chicago. In a drastic shift from this original stance, many interviewees described the burgeoning bike culture in Humboldt Park with a sense of ownership. One WTB/CU organizer who had grown up in Humboldt Park reflected on the way that the bike shop and its programs had generated alternatives:

> [WTB/CU is] this business that's gonna help un-gentrify . . . [and it is not] a boutique . . . or just a random juice bar . . . or something like a oxygen shop (he laughs) . . . this brought another world into this community . . . Bringing bikes . . . and explaining and teaching how to use a bicycle . . . and how much a bike can change your life . . . how you can use it as a tool to make your life better.

One Puerto Rican worker at WTB/CU who had completed the youth programs and was now a leader in the organization described how the economic development model had transformative potential:

I like to educate my younger generation on how much it's a choice to change their lives . . . There's a word, derived from gentrification, and I like to use it, it's (gente)rification . . . it comes from gente, which means people, and (gente)rification is when people from their own community open up businesses, change their community for their own people.

These examples are suggestive of a public space being reformulated in the service of economic needs and community interests. WTB/CU represents an innovative attempt to build community power, politically and economically, through education and employment opportunities.

Discussion

Top-down infrastructural decision-making mechanisms do little to offset anxieties and tensions about both the literal and symbolic means by which gentrification occurs. This study reveals that, whether or not bikes are catalysts for gentrification, for many people bikes do *symbolize* gentrification in meaningful ways.

The emergence of WTB/CU in this space represents an important mechanism through which local residents can, in some ways, offset the alienation of development. The bike center's appeals to local cultural identity, when merged with economic development strategies designed to directly serve the neighborhood, have generated new spaces for residents to politically and socially engage with the politics on their street. The space established by WTB/CU allows for minority youths to generate their own environmental, political, and social ethos. In turn, this regroupment has created the capacity for many WTB/CU participants to engage with broader efforts to challenge hegemonic decision-making processes in Chicago. Although WTB/CU may not be dramatically transforming the landscape of urban planning in Chicago, the organization represents a vital space for community identity and political voice to grow.

In closing, I would like to suggest that the top-down approach to decision-making present in Chicago is unlikely to adequately reflect the interests of all residents. If bicycling is to be the environmentally friendly, healthy, and sustainable transportation solution that it has the potential to be, decision-making processes at the city level must also consider how to enhance community engagement. Although WTB/CU represents a powerful effort to build engagement and voice, urban planners must take seriously community concerns by generating opportunities for a more participatory public sphere.

Planners must remain mindful that changes to street design, particularly the implementation of bike facilities, are often intimately tied to community concerns about ongoing neighborhood changes. Bicycles have great potential to revolutionize how people use and interact with public space, but a truly just and socially sustainable bike infrastructure must incorporate community concerns and avoid strictly technological, universalized assumptions about the use and value of bicycles.

Acknowledgments

This research was supported by Portland State University's Faculty Enhancement Grant. The author wishes to thank Bryan Zinschlag and Nathan Rochester for their contributions. This chapter has been adapted from an earlier work. The final, definitive version of this chapter was first published in *Urban Studies*, doi: 10.1177/0042098015592823 by Sage Publications Ltd, All rights reserved. © Urban Studies Journal Limited, 2015. It is available at: http://usj.sagepub.com/.

Notes

1 I use 'Division Street' and 'Paseo Boricua' interchangeably; both describe the segment of street between Western and California Avenues in Chicago.
2 Chicago's legislative branch consists of 50 'Aldermen,' each representing one of the city's 'wards.' Using the unwritten but historically entrenched rule of 'Aldermanic privilege,' these officials can veto any development project within their jurisdiction.
3 The full version of this article printed in *Urban Studies* expands on the methodology used in this research.
4 This term was first given voice in Portland, OR, in 2001 when a community leader referred to a proposed bicycle lane as the 'white lanes of gentrification' at a public meeting (Portland DOT, 2001, p.21). The referential quote has since been used to describe similar perceptions of the bike lane on the Paseo Boricua (Greenfield, 2012a).

References

Betancur, J.J. (2002) The politics of gentrification: The case of West Town in Chicago. *Urban Affairs Review*. 37. pp.780–814.

Chicago DOT (Department of Transportation) (2012) *Chicago Streets for Cycling Plan 2020*.

Davies, A. (2012) Rahm Emanuel thinks bike lanes will attract tech companies to Chicago. *Business Insider*. [Online] December 5. Available from: www.businessinsider.com/chicagos-bike-lanes-for-tech-companies-2012-12 [Accessed August 1, 2015].

Flores-Gonzalez, N. (2001) Paseo Boricua: Claiming a Puerto Rican space in Chicago. *Centro Journal*. 8 (2). pp.7–23.

Greenfield, J. (2012a) Bike facilities don't have to be the 'white lanes of gentrification'. *Chicago Grid*. [Online] May 10. Available from: http://gridchicago.com/2012/bike-facilities-dont-have-to-be-the-white-lanes-of-gentrification/ [Accessed September 1, 2015].

Greenfield, J. (2012b) Jose Lopez offers the PRCC's perspective on the Paseo bike lanes. *Chicago Grid*. [Online] May 11. Available from: http://gridchicago.com/2012/jose-lopez-offers-the-prccs-perspective-on-the-paseo-bike-lanes/ [Accessed September 1, 2015].

Portland DOT (Department of Transportation) (2001) *Interstate Corridor Community Involvement*.

Rinaldo, R. (2002) Space of resistance: The Puerto Rican Cultural Center and Humboldt Park. *Cultural Critique*. 50. pp.135–174.

Rotenberk, L. (2012). Chicago likes bikes and it's about to prove it-in a big way. *Grist* [Online] December 14. Available from: http://grist.org/cities/chicago-like-bikes-and-its-about-to-prove-it-in-a-big-way/ [Accessed November 24, 2015].

Thomas, D. (2006) A general inductive approach for analyzing qualitative evaluation data. *American Journal of Evaluation.* 27(2). pp.237–46.

Wilson, D. & Grammenos, D. (2005) Gentrification, discourse, and the body: Chicago's Humboldt Park. *Environment and Planning D: Society and Space* 23. pp.295–312.

Index

For Product Safety Concerns and Information please contact our EU
representative GPSR@taylorandfrancis.com Taylor & Francis Verlag GmbH,
Kaufingerstraße 24, 80331 München, Germany

Printed and bound by CPI Group (UK) Ltd, Croydon, CR0 4YY
08/05/2025
01864528-0003